PLURALISM AND IDENTITY

STUDIES
IN THE HISTORY OF RELIGIONS
(*NUMEN* BOOK SERIES)

EDITED BY

H.G. KIPPENBERG • E.T. LAWSON

VOLUME LXVII

TUTA SUB AEGIDE PALLAS · 1683 ·

PLURALISM AND IDENTITY

STUDIES IN RITUAL BEHAVIOUR

EDITED BY

JAN PLATVOET

AND

KAREL VAN DER TOORN

E.J. BRILL
LEIDEN · NEW YORK · KÖLN
1995

The paper in this book meets the guidelines for permanence and durability of the Committee on Production Guidelines for Book Longevity of the Council on Library Resources.

Library of Congress Cataloging-in-Publication Data

Pluralism and identity / edited by Jan Platvoet and Karel van der Toorn.
p. cm. — (Studies in the history of religions, ISSN 0169-8834 ; v. 67)
"Papers presented at an international conference in Leiden University on 14 and 15 January 1995"—P. 3.
Includes bibliographical references and index.
ISBN 9004103732 (hard : alk. paper)
1. Rites and ceremonies—Congresses. 2. Ritual—Congresses. 3. Religious pluralism—Congresses. 4. Identification (Religion)—Congresses. I. Platvoet, Jan. II. Toorn, K. van der. III. Series: Studies in the history of religions ; 67.
BL600.P58 1995
291.3'8—dc20 95-16624
CIP

Die Deutsche Bibliothek – CIP-Einheitsaufnahme

Pluralism and identity : studies in ritual behaviour / ed. by Jan Platvoet and Karel van der Toorn. – Leiden ; New York ; Köln : Brill, 1995
(Studies in the history of religions ; Vol. 67)
ISBN 90-04-10373-2
NE: Platvoet, Jan [Hrsg.]; GT

ISSN 0169-8834
ISBN 90 04 10373 2

PRINTED IN THE NETHERLANDS

TABLE OF CONTENTS

PART THREE
RESPONSES TO RELIGIOUS PLURALITY

EPILOGUE

INDICES

INTRODUCTION

RITUAL RESPONSES TO PLURALITY AND PLURALISM

Jan Platvoet & Karel van der Toorn
(Leiden University)

The origin of this book

The studies collected in this volume were presented as papers at an international conference in Leiden University on 14 and 15 January 1994. Except for Prof. Joseph Sadan, of Tel Aviv University, and Prof. André Droogers, of the Free University at Amsterdam, all the presenters were members of an inter-university research group, based in Leiden since 1992. It was established in order to study the role of religions in situations of religious pluralism. In what manner did religions respond to the presence of other religions in their societies, in ancient as well as in modern times? The need of a comparative study of the reactions of religious communities to religious plurality and pluralism[1] in diverse times and places, of their roles in these encounters, and of the changes these situations produced in them, had been brought home forcefully to this research group by the upsurge of religious movements which have pursued the reform of their societies as well as their religions with varying

[1] The research group only used the term 'pluralism' in its discussions before and during the conference, stipulating its meaning in its programmatic statement as: *the co-existence of two or more communities of believers with a different religion in a specific geo-historical setting.* That situation of co-existence of religions is found in many societies in the past as well as in the present. Platvoet, in his two essays in this volume, however, terms the *situation* of the co-existence of two or more religions within a society 'religious plurality'. He reserves the term 'religious pluralism' for that cultural and/or religious *ideology*, or attitude, which positively welcomes the encounter of religions. This mentality is typical of community religions, of the most recent religions, and of a recent transformation of the major religions of the doctrinal, missionary type. That receptive attitude is, however, traditionally utterly foreign to 'orthodox' religions of that expansive type. They fostered, and foster, in their believers an attitude of competitive, if not aggressively militant, combat of other religions and reform of 'deviant religiosity' in situations of religious plurality by their exclusive claims to doctrinal truth and their missionary nature. They do so also in order to strengthen the identities, group cohesion and boundaries of their religious and/or ethnic communities. That attitude of watching over boundaries by the strict regulation and severe limitation of interaction *ad extra* is also a marked cultural trait, and ideology, of many 'plural', vertically or horizontally segmented societies. A further distinction, between (situations of) internal and external religious plurality, will be made below when the essays collected in the third part of this volume are discussed.

degrees of militancy in the past two decades; not to mention the all too-recent 'ethnic cleansing' atrocities perpetrated in the name of religious differences.

One project in the programme of this research group was specifically designed to contribute to the development of theory in an area of common interest to all the members of this research group. It was meant to serve as *trait d'union* between the other research projects which the members pursued within the programme. The aim of this project was to study how ritual, ritual injunctions and ritual categories were used for demarcating a religious community's boundaries and identity *vis-à-vis* other religions in situations of (religious) plurality. The conference and this volume of essays are the outcome of this joint research project.

The studies presented deal with a subject that has been severely neglected in the study of religions. The course of mankind's history has mainly been one of steadily increasing communication between its societies, both in amicable and profitable ways by the exchange of goods and ideas, and in hostile and destructive ones by prejudice, discrimination, plunder and war. Yet students of religions[2] have for a long time tended to ignore the role of religion in the encounters between peoples, nations, and religious communities. The major reasons for this omission were, firstly, their legitimate but virtually exclusive, and therefore one-sided, concentration on the correct representation of the insider views of the believers expressed in particular in scriptures and other religiously inspired texts[3]; secondly, their preoccupation with religions as well-articulated, structured systems of belief representations (or 'doctrines'); and thirdly, an ideologically inspired aversion against, and fear of, social-scientific, 'reductionist' explanations.[4]

Due to these descriptivist and systematizing bends, and fear of explanation, these scholars of religions paid little attention to the study of the ecological, social and other 'contexts' of a religion. That research may take two forms: study of the ways in which a religion has been shaped by its contexts, and that of the manners in which a religion has moulded its contexts by its functions, 'religious'

---

[2] By which are meant here those in the historical and comparative disciplines of *Religionswissenschaft* as practised mainly in Faculties of the Theology in continental Europe and in Departments of Religious Studies in Faculties of Arts in the Anglo-Saxon world.

[3] And also in myths, liturgies, devotional acts, iconographic and other arts, architecture, the organisation of the communities of believers, interviews, etc.

[4] Cf. Platvoet 1994.

as well as 'secular'[5], in them. It follows that most of these scholars of religions have shown little interest in the study of the part a religion played in the shaping of identities in a person, group, people, or nation; in the functions of ritual behaviour in the social life of a group; in the rituals of boundary maintenance between ethnic groups, peoples, nations and societies with different identities, customs, cultures and religions which share a common public arena but are bent upon keeping their identities distinct and their communities separate; and in the processes of boundary dissolution and integration when there is no need or desire to keep groups apart or beliefs different.

It is only recently that this primarily notional approach to religions as systems of belief representations has begun to be complemented and corrected by ethological and contextual ones. The first takes religious behaviour as the central object of research; the second studies it as part of the believers' wider interests and goals, i.e. as not merely cult and devotion towards postulated beings, but as also part of social, political, economical, legal and other behaviours, including encounters, religious and secular, with outsiders and their communities and religions, and a religion's reactions to those encounters, and its reactions to internal religious diversity.

Its structure

Five of the papers presented at the Leiden conference describe responses of religions to situations of religious plurality. They deal with processes of change internal in religions in response to the situation of religious plurality, internal or external[6], in which they find themselves. These mainly descriptive papers by van der Toorn, Beck, Kaptein, van Koningsveld, and Wiegers, form the third part of this volume. Van der Toorn's article deals with a religious group in ancient Israelite religion; the other four are islamological papers.

Three other papers deal, wholly or in part, with the ritualization of the encounter between religions. They are the essays, also mainly

[5] The distinction between the 'religious' and the 'non-religious', or secular, functions of a religion may be made in modern western societies on the basis of the historical processes of institutional differentiation and separation which developed in the past few centuries and more recently in most other modern societies world-wide. That distinction can, however, be made only analytically, and not substantively, in many other societies and historical periods because religion is not found in them as a separate institution set apart from e.g. the prevailing ecology, economy, social structure, political order, etc.

[6] This distinction will be explained below.

descriptive, by Nugteren, Sadan, and Platvoet, and are presented in part two.

They are preceded, in part one, by five articles of a mainly theoretical nature. They are Platvoet's on ritual theory; Snoek's on the conditions under which a group may feel a strong, weak, or no need at all to demarcate itself from other groups; Belier's on the absence of that urge among Australian Aborigines; Drooger's on a model for the study of the interaction among religions in a plural society; and ter Haar's, on African Christian communities in the Netherlands which do not wish to demarcate themselves from Western Christian communities.

Part one: Ritual theory, identity, and religious plurality

Platvoet reviews ritual theory in anthropology of religion, in order to develop an operational definition of 'ritual' suitable for heuristic and analytical purposes in situations of religious plurality. His definition differs from the one the research group had adopted as its common instrument. That stipulated 'ritual' as any sequence of customary symbolic actions; a 'rite' as a customary symbolic action; 'customary' as referring to the standardization of symbolic actions through repetition in social interaction and their being learnt in the processes of socialisation; 'symbolic' as expressing and conveying meanings from a sender to a receiver, and therefore always entailing communication; and 'action' as comprising both verbal and non-verbal modes. In this inclusive definition 'ritual' was not, as scholars of religions usually do, restricted to religious rites, but expanded to include secular ceremonies as well.

On the basis of a critical study of the development of theories on ritual in anthropology of religion since Robertson Smith and Durkheim, Platvoet first develops a 'synthetic' operational definition of ritual by delineating thirteen analytical dimensions of ritual, and then constructs from some of them another operational definition for the analysis of rituals of confrontation between religions that meet in contests for political power. He defines 'ritual' provisionally as:

> an ordered sequence of stylized social behaviour that is different from ordinary interaction by its alerting qualities by means of which it focuses its audience's, and at times a wider public's, attention onto itself as a special event at a special place and/or time and with a special message. It does this by the use of appropriate consonant complexes of dense core symbols specific to each culture. It achieves by them not only the smooth transmission of a multitude of messages—some overt,

> many covert—, and stimuli through the redundant transformations of the symbols used in multi-media performance; but also, in often unnoticed ways, the usually latent, and occasionally manifest, political and other purposes of those who perform a ritual, *ad intra*—within corporate groups—, as well as *ad extra* and *ad intra* in situations of plurality and pluralism.

Contrary to recent trends in anthropology of ritual, Platvoet sees ritual not only as a hidden, and for that very reason, effective instrument of power, or, as was held in earlier theory, as the expression of social structure only, or again, as in earliest theory, as restricted to religious and 'magical' acts. He contends that apart from all these, ritual is also communication of both implicit and explicit messages, and may have overt in addition to its covert strategic goals. He also stresses that ritual is not necessarily customary: it may be a sequence of symbolic actions performed in a unique event designed and constructed for a particular purpose. He draws these 'anti-Durkheimian' conclusions from his analysis of the historical data which he presents in his contribution on the Ayodhya events.

Snoek's contribution does not, it is true, deal with encounters between different religions, but between Masonic Grand Lodges, and among Pentecostal churches, i.e. between modern Western religious groups which share many similarities. On the basis of findings of group dynamics research, Snoek formulates a general hypothesis which may prove valid for any process of shaping, marking, maintaining and increasing the distinctiveness of a particular group's identity, including that of religious communities in situations of religious plurality. It suggests that the need and urge to mark out a group as different and distinct, will vary in proportion to its degree of similarity to other religious communities or denominations of the same type around it. The greater the similarity, the more urgent the need for demarcation from competing groups by stressing a particular, and in itself often arbitrary and insignificant, difference. As in commercials, a religious group's confidence needs to be unshaken that it excels in at least one 'crucial' aspect, for it not to lose the members it has within its fold and to draw in others. Snoek states that conflicts between groups emerge because they are similar, and that they increase when they become more similar; conflicts rarely occur between groups that are utterly dissimilar. However, when groups become, or are perceived to become, so similar as to be almost identical, they merge because the conflict of interests between them has collapsed.

The chapter by Belier describes a case which may be interpreted as support for Snoek's hypothesis as well as seriously qualifying it. It is important also because it describes a negative case: that of groups which are, and see themselves, as socially and culturally distinct, and which regularly interact, also in religious rituals, but do not use religious ritual for expressing their distinctive identities nor for maintaining boundaries between them. The Australian aboriginal societies—the Murngin and Arunta—analyzed by Belier, were no strangers to war and violence, as is evidenced by the fierce Murngin fights on the 'matrimonial battle field' and the Arunta practice of ritualised revenge. Nor were they without some measure of group demarcation, particularly at the local level, through localized totemic clans with the Murngin which were grouped into two exogamic moieties at the supra-local level, and through localized, patrilineal totemistic groups with the Arunta, grouped at the supra-local level in two groups of each two moieties. However, whereas war and violence divided the clans, rituals, which were often in some manner inter-group in character, united them. Moreover, these communities struck a balance between division and union by allotting a particular period of the year to war and violence, and another to ritual. The general picture which emerges seems to show that rituals were, like articles of trade, in great demand and spread quickly among many local groups over a wide area.

If we confront the uniting effect of Australian Aboriginal rituals with Snoek's hypothesis, two opposite reasons, in terms of Snoek's graph, may be adduced to account for this odd state of affairs: the Aboriginal communities were either so similar or so dissimilar as to have no need for the use of religious ritual as separator and identity marker. These theoretical solutions would leave Snoek's hypothesis unassailed. In view of the weak boundaries of many local aboriginal communities and their integration into some sort of supra-local unity, e.g. among the Murngin that of belonging to one of two totemic moieties, the first argument, of extreme similarity undoing the need for demarcation, would seem to hold. However, other ethnographic data seem to suggest also that degrees of similarity existed between these societies which theoretically ought to provoke the need for demarcation in them, such as the differentiation of the exogamic moieties by (fictional) 'languages' which were used as emblems for marking groups as different. The crux, and solution, of this problem seems to lie in the fact that the varieties of Aboriginal religion, cults and rituals were not used, in pre- and early colonial times, as instruments of competition in a market for scarce goods, such as women, but were themselves a scarce good, and were, therefore, eagerly sought and bought. Their religions being neither orthodox nor even orthoprax but in constant change through eager adoption of, and adaptation to, new inventions, were not capable to serve separating goals. Nor was there any felt need to use them for boundary maintenance, as the need for unity was more pressing than the need for separation; besides, more effective means were available for that purpose whenever that need arose.

This ties in with remarks made by Belier in his conclusion about the developments of an Australian aboriginal religion—in the singular!—in recent decades by the Aboriginal liberation movement. In the colonial situation, the need for Aboriginal religion as demarcator was felt in particular by white anthropologists sympathetic with the cause of the Aboriginals, some of whom began to mix description with prescription. That call for the demarcation of a collective Aboriginal ethnic identity, as a minority which suffered a two century long history of oppression by the Christian white majority, has recently caused some Aboriginal leaders (in particular those trained in Western ways and thought and able to fight it with its own weapons) to move towards a unified Aboriginal religion to serve their cultural and political purpose of separating a collective Aboriginal ethnic identity from the white community. One may, however, argue that Belier's statement that 'the religious definition of social differences is a result of colonial processes' represents too narrow a view, although he is clearly correct in asserting that the religious definition of identity is 'not inherent in our humanity.' It is merely one of the cultural options available to humankind, albeit the one that has been used widely, in very different ways, by many societies during most periods of the history of mankind. Belier's contribution proves that the Western colonization of Australia is also one of them.

André Droogers' contribution to this volume is important for yet another reason. He presents a conceptual framework designed to serve as an heuristic and analytical instrument in the study of religious pluralism—or plurality, to use Platvoet's term. This model is meant to help us discover the different ways in which religions respond, and may be expected to respond, to the situations of religious plurality in which they exist. Their reactions are, Droogers proposes, the outcome of the interaction between the three dimensions of a religion in a situation of plurality: its external dimension, its internal one, and the 'supernatural' one. The external dimension pertains to the inclusive or exclusive positions which religions take *vis-à-vis* the religions they encounter in their society and the wider world: whether they see them as complementary, or adopt a polemical attitude towards them. The attitude a religious community takes to other religions is intrinsically related, Droogers contends, to its 'inner dimension': the relations prevailing among its members, including the religious specialists, if any; and to its 'supernatural' dimension: the relations which the believers assume to exist between them and the meta-empirical beings which they believe exist and affect their lives. The core relationships in each of these three groups: external, internal, and 'supernatural', are also determined by the religious group's conception of power and meaning. And these again are not unrelated, because power entails, in part, the control of meaning in a religious community.

Droogers specifies how power and interpretation are interdependent in each of the three dimensions of his model. In the external dimension, the definition who qualifies for membership of the community, and who does not, is not only a matter of the beliefs shared, but also of the relationships of sub- and superordination postulated, or not postulated, by their beliefs, and about who has the right to grant admission, which is an exercise of power. Moreover, even non-members may find themselves dominated by a religious majority which excludes minorities. In the internal dimension, power is at work when hierarchical offices are allocated; these appointments are legitimised by the beliefs shared and may be subverted from that same basis. If a strict hierarchy prevails internally, there is no room for pluralism, neither *ad intra* nor *ad extra*. Droogers suggests that when external pluralism is normal and not problematic, it is an extension of internal pluralism. In the 'supernatural' dimension, power is present in both the submission of believers to the unseen beings which they believe to exist, and in their attempts to 'use' them for pragmatic and strategic purposes. The intertwining of power and meaning is reflected in the shared doctrines which provide the basis for both the submissive and the utilitarian attitudes towards the postulated beings. Religions with a heavy emphasis on submissiveness, assume an exclusive position in situations of religious plurality, and it follows that utilitarian religions take tolerant, inclusive positions.

Droogers proves the utility of his complex instrument by providing us with finely textured analyses of the attitudes towards plurality of Umbanda and Pentecostalism, two religions which are very popular in Brazil, which is a society that may serve, as perhaps no other, as a laboratory for the study of plurality and pluralism. Droogers concludes with a plea, firstly to the social scientists to include the supernatural dimensions in their analyses, because it contains explanatory power for the 'terrestrial' processes of community building, identity-shaping, and power-playing; and secondly to scholars of religions to accept that the study of religions must include not only description but also explanation.

Gerrie ter Haar's contribution is based on insights culled from Van Gennep's description of the tripartite structure of rites of passage, which Turner terms 'life crisis rituals', and from the latter's expansion on it in his theory on liminality and ritual. She applies these ideas to the situation and aspirations of the communities of Ghanaian Christians in Amsterdam, many of whom are illegal immigrants. In their liminal state between their origins in West Africa and their incorporation into Dutch society, these Ghanaian-led churches have no desire or use for demarcation from other Dutch Christian communities. On the contrary, they have an urgent need for communion with the Dutch churches, although this is often refused them. The demarcation, in this case, is imposed from the outside. The Ghanaian communities stress their identity as Christians and—in terms of Snoek's graph—their 'collapsing' similarity and identity with the Dutch Christian churches. But the latter select Africanness as the hallmark of these immigrant churches, thereby stressing their dissimilarity from the Dutch churches. That enables the latter to impose upon the former the demarcator 'African' and legitimise their keeping these immigrant Christian communities at a distance. They are considered so dissimilar as not to qualify for communion with Dutch churches. The African-led churches are thus driven into a double exile: away from their roots in Ghana and unwelcome in the communion of the Christian churches in the Netherlands.

Ter Haar's analysis is not without a polemical sting. Following Turner, she explains the wish for integration of these churches by the interstitial position of their members in Dutch secular society. Many of their members are either under threat of expulsion as illegal residents or, if legal, unwelcome as black aliens. The marginalisation imposed on them at the secular level is neatly reflected in their exclusion at the religious level. The policy of the Dutch churches is a copy of that of the Dutch state and the European Community; and both are approved by the Dutch nation. By her innovating use of van Gennep and Turner, ter Haar shows that the rituals of these communities serve as coping mechanisms, both at the individual and group levels, in the face of the legal, economic and religious liminality imposed upon them. It creates a strong sense of *communitas ad intra*—for which the need is understandably great and to which the members of these churches are naturally highly receptive- and a strong desire for *communitas ad extra*.

Part two: The ritualization of the encounter

In the second part, three separate studies deal with very different examples of the ritualization of encounters between religions. The first, that of Nugteren, deals with an accommodative case, namely the rituals, by Buddhists of many different 'denominations', and Hindus, at the tree under which the Buddha is believed to have attained enlightenment. The second, by Sadan, deals with a remarkable exception to the fairly tolerant practice of 'protection' which Islam normally granted to non-Muslim religious communities in its territories. In the third, Platvoet shows that religious militancy may not be foreign to a religion generally regarded as the very paradigm of tolerance and accommodation.

Albertina Nugteren's paper begins with an examination of tree rituals in India and then describes those in Bodhgaya for the tree under which the Buddha Gotama is believed to have achieved liberating insight. Buddhists from all over the world, representing all its denominations, travel to Bodhgaya to circumambulate it in their distinctive apparels, venerate it in diverse other ways, and built their temples and pilgrim hostels around it. And Hindus also come; having performed their rituals for their ancestors at Gaya, a Hindu place of pilgrimage near Bodhgaya, many include a visit to Bodhgaya for a number of reasons. One is the incorporation of the Buddha into the Hindu pantheon as Vishnu's ninth *avatara* ('descent'). Another is that these two holy places form one cultic complex for them with strong morphological similarities in their ritual elements: at Gaya they circumambulate its 'immortality tree', and at Bodhgaya the tree of the Buddha's enlightenment; at Gaya they worship the footsteps of Vishnu, and at Bodhgaya those of the Buddha. Lastly, Bodhgaya had been in the care of a local Hindu *mahant* ('abbot') since the 18th century[7] and has several statues of Hindu deities and a stone altar which have all been placed under a secondary tree now but stood under the very tree of the Buddha's enlightenment in former times. They still receive regular offerings and brief worship from Hindu pilgrims.

Despite the general atmosphere of tolerance for the whole gamut of Buddhist denominational ritual and traditional Hindu worship, a touch of intolerance is not absent: Ambedkarite Indian Buddhists, recent converts from low castes, are inclined to lay monopolistic claims to Bodhgaya and not to tolerate Hindu worship of the tree of

---

[7] It entitles him to full membership of the committee responsible for the upkeep of Bodhgaya.

enlightenment with sweetened water and milk, for fear that these liquids will cause the roots of the tree to rot. Evidence, perhaps, that the communalist tensions of the last decade, described by Platvoet, have seeped through to even this place of pluralist ritual.

The second paper in this part is Sadan's contribution on the distinctive signs, colours and items of dress which Muslim authorities forced the Non-Muslims to wear, or forbade them to wear, in order to set them apart from their Arab overlords, and in an extreme case to humiliate them. This happened in Yemen, in the Arabian peninsula, in the late 17th century when the authorities of the time, reacting to a messianic movement among the Jews of Yemen which they took as a revolt, deprived them of their status as 'people of the protection' for some time, and forced them, as a group, by legal decree to act as latrine cleaners—a humiliating job which the Jewish community assigned to its poor in return for pay. Sadan summarizes the controversy among Muslim jurists in Yemen over this decree in the 19th century.

In the third paper, Platvoet examines the 'rituals of confrontation' in respects of the Babri mosque in Ayodhya, as part of a politically successful strategy of increasing 'communal' strife between Hindus and Muslims in India in the past decade. That policy, developed by some of a conglomerate of Hindu organisations, collectively known as 'the RSS family', aimed at de-secularising India and turning it into a Hindu nation in which the alleged privileges of communities professing a religion of non-Indian origin would be severely curtailed. Platvoet describes how new Hindu rituals were developed for use in the electoral mobilization campaign by RSS-related organisations. He shows that these rituals had the unitive effects *ad intra* and the divisive effects *ad extra* for which they were designed. Ritual may, therefore, also be non-customary symbolic behaviour in pursuit of overt political goals. It follows that ritual should be defined primarily from performance and pragmatic perspectives, as behaviour which is traditionalising but not necessarily traditional. On the basis of his analysis of the Ayodhya data, he defines 'ritual' as:

> collective, interactive, expressive, communicative, symbolic and performative behaviour with both customary, innovative and traditionalising properties, which uses multi-media forms of expression including aesthetic stylization and theatrical performance, directed implicitly or explicitly towards the achievement of strategic goals which are often integrative in nature but may also have, and be meant to have, explosive effects upsetting the balance of power in a given society.

Part three: Responses to internal and external religious plurality

The third part of this volume comprises five essays. They treat the responses of certain religions to two distinct situations of religious plurality: 'internal' and 'external'. 'External religious plurality' is the situation of the actual co-existence of different religions within a particular society or in some wider context, such as that created by modern communication technologies, by which they may be perceived as co-existing in some effective manner. It is the situation in which religions may meet each other on a more or less equal basis, as independent cultural institutions, each with its own community of believers and spheres of influence. 'Internal religious plurality', however, respects the situation of the prevailing diversity of beliefs, cults and practices within a religion, i.e. among its members, or in the society, or societies, in which that religion happens to hold a dominant position. Internal plurality is the normal state of affairs in 'community religions', the largest category of human religions. It comprises all the religions of mankind before the first millennium BC, and all those that developed since then which are co-extensive with a particular society and did not, or do not, articulate their beliefs into a unified doctrinal system nor espouse claims that their doctrine is exclusively true and that of other religions, or most other religions, false. The attitude that prevails in these 'community religions' is the pluralist ideology of religious receptivity and adaptability. This attitude has also become a mark of humanity's most recent religions. Though they do articulate their beliefs, they are highly synthetic, use revelation again, and do not usually hold exclusivist positions.[8]

Internal plurality is, however, a problem in religions of the doctrinal kind which espouse exclusive claims to the validity of their beliefs; they do not cultivate an attitude of religious pluralism. This numerically tiny category—the three so-called 'world religions'—entered the scene of the history of religions since the middle of the first millennium BC. They reject as idolatrous the religious beliefs and practices embraced and practised by many, indeed by most of their (in their eyes nominal) adherents who do not conform to their orthodoxies. The tolerance of these religions towards such perceived deviations varied, and varies, in periods and places. They might, and may, condescendingly tolerate them as the ineradicable superstitions of the ignorant. Or they might, and may, actively pur-

[8] Cf. Platvoet 1993.

sue their reformation by religious education. Or again, they might, or may, forcefully suppress them. Internal plurality, therefore, respects the ways in which an 'orthodox' religion, which has achieved a dominant or even monopolistic position in a society or number of societies, deals with its own internal variation in ('orthodox', 'less orthodox' and 'non-orthodox') beliefs and practices.

A very common source of this variation is the adherence of some, or often most, of its believers to beliefs and practices proper to one, or several, religions that were indigenous in that area before the current 'orthodox' religion gained its position of dominance. Internal plurality, therefore, often respects the 'left-overs' from the situation of external religious plurality which that religion found in a particular area and society when it entered them, and which it has tolerated or been unable to eradicate.

The third part of this book consists of four papers, by van der Toorn, Beck, Kaptein, and Wiegers, which deal with case studies of religions coping with internal plurality; and one by van Koningsveld which describes the symbolic means used to resist the 'encroachment' of external plurality.

Van der Toorn's paper describes a case in the crucial period of transition in the history of the religion of Israel in Palestine between 1200 BC when internal religious plurality prevailed as the normal situation and pluralism was the dominant attitude, to the earliest emergence of orthodoxy around 400 BC. It is the case of a kinship group, known as 'the house of the sons of Jehonadab ben Rechab', which protested in the late ninth century for political reasons against the official policy of religious pluralism in the state of North Israel, by adopting a nomadic style of life in an agrarian and partially urbanizing society. Having lost its high position in the political establishment, the group protested against its fall from grace by observing a rule imposed upon them by their apical ancestor forbidding them to live in houses, to reside in towns, to cultivate vineyards and fields, and to drink wine. By adopting this style of life they condemned themselves to the status of foreigners in the land of Israel. By the time their self-imposed isolation had become a self-fulfilling prophecy and they an insignificant group, their nativistic, puritanical and impotent protest had become a marker of their group identity. That emblem was, however, so stirring a symbol of fidelity that Jeremiah used it to chastise the Judaeans of his time for their infidelity to their Lord. Van der Toorn compares the Rechabite style of life substantively with youth counter-cultures prevalent in our own times and society, and functionally with the use of archaic vestiary codes by certain elite groups, such as academics and ecclesiastics, as a means of ritually affirming their high-ranking positions in society. Within the field of contemporary moral and religious movements, the Rechabites also invite comparison with puritanical abstention movements, such vegetarians, AA, and Moral Rearmament, or with religious ones, such as the Watch Tower Society and other millenarian movements. The nativism of the Rechabites bears comparison not only with the numerous prophetic movements of modern times which Köbben defined as movements of social protest[9], but also with the nativism of reform movements within the major doctrinal religions which usually aim to restore a religion's original purity by a 'return to its source', its earliest period, or its 'canonical' scriptures.

Beck's contribution analyses the compromise which Indonesia's largest Islamic reform movement, the *Muhammadiyah*, has struck between its reformist ideals and two major contingencies of its history: firstly, the intimate ties of its founder and most of its leaders with the court of the Sultan of Yogyakarta; and secondly, the political and cultural need of Javanese Muslims in general, and the Sultan's court in particular, of a ritual expression of Javanese Muslim identity. The most important expression of that identity is the major court ritual of *Garebeg Maulud*, dating from the early 17th century when kingship passed into the hands of a Muslim dynasty of doubtful origin. It is an Islamicized transformation of an earlier Hindu-Javanese kingship ritual in which Muslim beliefs about the Prophet as the perfect man, were merged with Javanese beliefs in the king as the semi-divine, perfect being at the centre of the universe. It was further integrated into official Islam by being celebrated on the Birthday of the Prophet (*Mawlid al-nabi*), and by the introduction into it of processions to, and recitations and blessings in, the grand mosque situated at the edge of the court area. The central part, albeit ritually somewhat disguised, is, however, a highly elaborate royal *slametan* (community meal) in which the Sultan himself is the central officiant, offering himself and his house in the shape of five rice mounds[10] as sustenance to the people and the court, and receiving, as the centre of their universe, from them their unquestioning loyalty in return. It is this part that cannot be reconciled with the demands of an Islam of pristine purity such as the *Muhammadiyah* intends to establish in Indonesia. This movement

---

[9] Cf. Köbben 1964a.

[10] Two of which are shaped after the ancient Hindu Shaiva symbols of *linga* and *yoni*, the 'male' representing the Sultan himself and the 'female' his spouse and consorts.

has not, however, condemned it as *bid'a*, unlawful 'innovation', *khurafa*, 'superstition', or *shirk*, 'idolatry'. Beck holds that the ritual has remained unscathed for two reasons: its centripetal, consolidating function for Javanese Muslim society, and the inability of the leaders of the *Muhammadiyah* to cut their ties with the court because it is at the centre of their world.

Kaptein's contribution deals with a different type of tension between a local Muslim custom in Indonesia, deemed less acceptable to orthodox Islam, and its standard form propagated from within the heartland of Islam. Kaptein describes two forms of circumcision which date back to pre-Islamic times and were practised, after Islam had arrived, by many Indonesian Muslims, a number of non-Muslim Indonesian peoples, and also by some converts to Christianity. They are the form of circumcision in which part of the foreskin is removed, and the incision method whereby the foreskin is cleft but not removed, the *glans* however being exposed in both cases. Starting his investigations in the late 19th century, Kaptein recounts the gradual replacement of this incision method in Indonesia by another form of circumcision in which the foreskin is partially or completely removed. An important role in this transition was played by the Indonesian Muslims who stayed for long periods in Mecca in the latter part of the 19th century for study purposes and asked for *fatwas*[11] in the matter of the licitness of circumcision by incision. They probably did so because their marriages into Meccan families caused their different manner of circumcision to become a matter of some dispute. Kaptein discusses ten such *fatwas* and concludes that cleavage of the foreskin was not acceptable: anyone refusing to undergo full circumcision was pronounced a sinner and therefore incapable of acting as a woman's legal guardian at her marriage or as a witness to a marriage. To avoid the grave moral, ritual, social, and even eschatological consequences of this state of impurity, many Indonesian Muslim residents of Mecca were circumcised a second time. As many thousands of pilgrims from Indonesia visited Mecca every year, this pronouncement soon began to be known in Muslim areas in Indonesia. By 1920, incision of the foreskin had become quite rare in parts of the country where it had once been normal practice, and today it seems to have disappeared completely. Apart from the increasing pressures from scripturalist and reformist movements in Indonesia, Kaptein also mentions three other factors that contributed considerably to the

[11] Authoritative statements on matters of Islamic law by a scholar of the law qualified to issue these.

disappearance of the practice of incision: the medicalisation of circumcision on grounds of hygiene; its collectivization; and its centralisation in specialised clinics.

If circumcision is an important identity marker of Muslims, the ritual use of Arabic, the language of the Qoran, is an even more important one. It is the required language of worship and learning throughout the 'abode of Islam', *ʿajami*, 'heathen language[s]' being the tongue of the 'abode of war' over which Islamic rule was yet to be established by military means. Muslim minorities in that 'abode of war' were however, often unable to master that minimal command of Arabic which would qualify them to fulfil the requirements for its liturgical use. Wiegers' paper examines the touchy issue of the use of 'heathen' language translations of the Qoran in Medieval Christian Spain which enabled the Muslim minority there to use it liturgically. That need became particularly pressing for the underground Muslim minority in Spain in the 16th century, when the use of Arabic in speech and writing had been officially forbidden and knowledge of Arabic had to be passed on secretly. In the second part of his article, Wiegers discusses the Islamic texts that were translated into Romance and Spanish from the twelfth century onwards until the expulsion of the Muslims from Spain in the period 1609-1614. He also dwells on the discussions which the translations provoked, particularly in the period of severe oppression which preceded the expulsion. Some Muslims defended it because the persecution had made the community totally ignorant of Arabic whilst others rejected it for that very same reason. After their expulsion from Spain, however, Muslims continued to use Spanish in North Africa for another century. Some of them defended the need, and even the duty, to provide religious instruction in it because so many of these Muslims were still not proficient in Arabic, and in the North Africa of the time—then under Ottoman rule—, Turkish was also used in religious education, even for people who knew Arabic.

In the last part of his article, Wiegers presents examples of modern developments in which the opposition of the 'abode of Islam' to the 'abode of war' was replaced by the peace (*daʿwa*) that should prevail between them. That transition was marked by fierce debates, particularly in the reformist camp, about the lawfulness of translating the Qoran and using translations for liturgical recitation. Wiegers discusses the positions of the Moroccan Salafists who argued in favour of the lawfulness of the translation of the Qoran into other languages, and those from the same movement who opposed it. The latter still reject it as a reprehensible 'innovation' (*biʿda*), whilst the former accept it on the grounds that a translation of the Qoran is no longer the Qoran, but that it is nonetheless an excellent instrument for the peaceful proclamation of Islam. It might be seen, they hold, as a spiritual *jihad* which replaces the military one by which Islam had been propagated in its early history.

The data presented in these last three essays tend to show that the success or failure of a strategy for eliminating internal plurality depend—in the case of traits that have a high value and prominent function as identity markers of the unified religious community—to a major extent on 'external', i.e. non-religious, factors. The reason for the failure of the *Muhammadiyah* leadership to censure the *Garebeg Maulud*, lies in its roots in the Sultan's court. The circumcision by incision disappeared because of the social pressure in marital matters on Indonesian Muslims in Mecca, and because of the medicalisation and collectivisation of circumcision in Indonesia itself. Opposition to the translation of the Qoran has been markedly diminished because modern international relations between states no longer permit doctrinal division of the globe into 'the abode of Islam' *versus* 'the abode of war'.

In the latter case, this fundamental shift was brought about by external factors: in the wake of increasing economic interdependence and the modern media reducing the world to a village, interpenetration of cultural and religious values and fashions is inevitable. This is also the context in which van Koningsveld examines a remarkable item in the last essay of this collection, the recent discussions in Sunnite Islam whether Muslim males may wear a hat and shave. Dress and shaving, or non-shaving, may be used as important identity markers and separators by ethnic and/or religious communities, particularly by minorities vacillating between integration and separation. What was ordinary and unremarkable attire 'back at home', unfit for emblematic use, may become dress with a highly distinctive value and function in a diaspora situation. Much more attention and money may be spent on it than before; it often becomes more refined; and in some cases it may even be invented[12]. Indeed, dress serves as a universal and major marker of gender, and the veil, or its diminutive version, the head scarf has become a hot issue as gender separator throughout the world of Islam and its diasporas.

---

[12] Cf. the essays collected in Hobsbawm & Ranger 1993, especially Trevor-Roper's on the invention of the kilt as marker of Scottish identity after incorporation into the United Kingdom (Trevor-Roper 1993).

Van Koningsveld, however, discusses the prescribed attire of the head of the Muslim male, an issue which provoked much debate in Sunnite Islam since the middle of the 19th century. Head covering has traditionally been prescribed for men also, and the specific forms developed for it in the course of Islamic history have served as important markers of Muslim identity. Predictably, the earliest discussions took place in Paris, the 'heart' of the most important diaspora for Sunnite Muslims from North Africa. At French universities, Muslim students and lecturers with an international frame of mind, pro-European attitudes, strong connections with the establishments and governments of their countries of origin, and taking what van Koningsveld terms the 'liberal' position, defended an accommodative position. They held that it was permissible for Muslims to wear the 'Christian hat' in stead of a traditional Muslim headdress because it was merely a matter of convenience rather than a strictly religious matter, the non-observance of which would constitute apostasy. Reformists also took that position. In response to a similar question about headdress from a Muslim in Transvaal, South Africa, Muhammad Abduh, founder of modern Sunnite reformism in Egypt, stated that as long as no apostasy was intended, the adaptation to local manners of dress was licit. From here on, the discussion entered the 'world of Islam' itself, where Western dress was becoming fashionable also. Liberals allowed males to fulfil their prayer obligations with their heads uncovered and in any dress customary or convenient in the particular society in which they found themselves, provided no religious assimilation was intended. The growing of a beard was also regarded as being merely the best of a number of licit alternatives. Reformists declared that a Muslim could dress in any type of attire.

These accommodating views were hotly contested by traditionalists who insisted that the *sunna* (customs) of the Prophet are destroyed by the change of headdress and the shaving of the beard. The wearing of a hat during the *salat* (prayers) also prevents a man from touching the earth with his forehead in the prostration. The practice of Western dress customs and other despicable habits, constitute mental 'emigration' from the 'world of Islam' into the 'world of war', and is therefore apostasy; it can be undone only by *hijra*, (mental) 'migration' back into the 'world of Islam'. A recent traditionalist movement in Morocco strongly inveighed against the shaving of beards, stating that prayers said with a shaven face are null and void, and that those who assimilate become unbelievers by their public propagation of doubt. They also defame religion, admire human reason, reduce religion to a private affair, remove it from the public sphere, allow the pernicious mixing of the genders in schools and social life, and mock traditional morality.

At issue is the status of the *sunna*, the 'tradition' of the Prophet, as a major fundament of Muslim life. Liberals and reformists sidestep the issue of its status, but their pragmatic approach effectively destroys much of the authority it had in the past. The traditionalists fight a loosing battle to restore it to its former status, because secularised citizenship has replaced religious communalism in the modern nation states also in 'the world of Islam'. Communalism was in need of distinctive dress; citizenship is not. The defeat of the traditionalists is covered up by the increasingly strict observance of the traditional norms in respect dress and coiffure by religious functionaries.

References

Hobsbawm, E., & T. Ranger (eds.) 1993[9], *The invention of tradition.* Cambridge: Cambridge University Press (1983[1]).

Köbben, A.J.F., 1964a, 'Profetische bewegingen als uiting van sociaal protest', in Köbben 1964b: 94-154.

Köbben, A.J.F., 1964b, *Van primitieven tot medeburgers.* Assen: van Gorcum.

Platvoet, J.G., 1993, 'De wraak van de "primitieven": godsdienstgeschiedenis van Neanderthaler tot New Age', in *Nederlands Theologisch Tijdschrift* 47, 3: 227-243.

Platvoet, J.G., 1994, 'Het religionisme beleden en bestreden: recente ontwikkelingen in de Angelsaksische godsdienstwetenschap', in *Nederlands Theologisch Tijdschrift* 48, 1: 22-38.

Trevor-Roper, H., 1993, 'The invention of tradition: the Highland tradition of Scotland', in Hobsbawm & Ranger 1993: 15-41.

PART ONE
CONTRIBUTIONS TO RITUAL THEORY

RITUAL IN PLURAL AND PLURALIST SOCIETIES

INSTRUMENTS FOR ANALYSIS[1]

Jan Platvoet
Leiden University

There is preciously little theory on ritual in the study of religions, understood here as the distinct academic discipline of *Religionswissenschaft*. In anthropology of religion, there is an abundance of it but it is, in my view, confused as well as confusing. In neither, however, has ritual theory been extended to ritual behaviour in situations of cultural and/or religious plurality and pluralism; i.e. to ritual behaviour in which groups co-existing in a society express their separate identities, boundaries, strife with, indifference to, or respect for, each other.[2] This article attempts to develop a ritual theory which may be applied also to cultural and religious plurality. It has two sections. The first develops a provisional operational definition of 'ritual', defined in a broad way to include religious as well as secular ritual behaviour. It is meant to serve as a heuristic instrument for general use in the study of ritual behaviour. In the second section, I tailor that definition for use in situations of religious plurality and pluralism.[3]

Towards a provisional operational definition of 'ritual'

An operational definition does not claim universal validity or applicability. It is expressly meant to be a hypothesis with heuristic qualities which should be tested, corrected and, if necessary, rejected.[4] It is, therefore, always provisional and to term it so is nec-

---

[1] I am grateful to Dr. J. Oosten for his incisive criticisms of an earlier draft of this study and that on the Ayodhya rituals of confrontation included in this volume below in Part II. They made me revise thoroughly the argument presented in this chapter as well as its application to the Ayodhya events.

[2] One of the very few and very recent exceptions to this rule is Baumann 1991; a few more, from political anthropology on inter-ethnic violence, will be noted below.

[3] In another article in this book, I will apply this operational definition to the political confrontation that unfolded in India between 1984 and 1992 when large numbers of Hindus pressed for the demolition of the Babri mosque in Ayodhya. That analysis will lead to a few anti-Durkheimian conclusions.

[4] Cf. Platvoet 1990: 181-183.

essarily tautologous. The one I propose below is, however, provisional in a stronger sense. Ritual, in fact, is found in such a great morphological diversity and serves so many different functions in human societies that scholars have not yet been able to define it in unambiguous terms.[5] Because it is a universal, polymorphous and multipurpose phenomenon, we need to develop much more theory before we can identify the analytically more important traits and functions of ritual[6] and separate them from the less significant ones.[7] For the time being I intend, therefore, to develop a fairly broad operational definition of ritual of the family resemblance type and accept it as a fuzzy category, in which one ritual may be defined by most of the traits or functions enumerated below, and another by a slightly different set of them, but each under the proviso that it is defined by a sufficient number of them. The virtues of such a polythetic definition are that it stays close to our prereflective use of the term, that it is flexible, and has a wide heuristic scope: it can accommodate a wide variety of rituals from very different cultures, periods and places. Its weakness is that it is a poor instrument of analysis. It should be seen, therefore, as only a first attempt to move away from the exclusively intuitive use of the category ritual which has been the normal practice in the study of religions until now.[8]

As many disciplines take a, and some even several different, theoretical interests in this broad and complex object of study[9], a broad variety of operational definitions of ritual has been legitimately developed. My interest is primarily morphological, or descriptive. I seek to develop a 'substantive'[10] operational definition of ritual for the comparative study of religions by which the more common basic traits of 'ritual' may be identified and this diverse type of human behaviour may be shown to possess the unity which we intuitively discern in it in both single societies and cross-culturally. My interest, however, necessarily includes also the functions of ritual, for the morphology of ritual cannot be studied apart from its functions, as ritual is a specific mode of interaction between hu-

---

[5] Cf. Tambiah 1979: 115-116.
[6] Cf. Grimes 1982: 117; Doty 1986: 80.
[7] Even so, several (operational) definitions of ritual have been proposed. I enumerate some of them in chronological order in appendix I.
[8] Cf. Lewis 1980: 6sq.
[9] Cf. Grimes 1982: 32; Doty 1986: 80-81.
[10] A substantive definition attempts to circumscribe what a phenomenon descriptively 'is' in contrast with a functional definition which tries to catch what it 'does' (in men or in societies).

mans which does certain things for and in them. In ritual, human society functions in the ritual mode.

Provisionally then, I define 'ritual' as

> that broad range of forms of social interaction between humans, and from one or several humans to other, real or postulated, addressable beings[11] which is marked by a sufficient number of the distinctive traits and functions set out below to merit classification as 'ritual' conceived as a fuzzy, polythetic category of the 'family resemblance' type.[12]

As the traits and functions of ritual cannot always be easily separated, they will, for the purpose of this paper, be combined under the term 'dimensions' in order to serve as the diacritical features by which we may identify a ritual, even if they do not always, strictly speaking, actually constitute it. They are, for the time being, the following thirteen typical 'dimensions'.

1. *the interaction dimension*

Ritual is a specific mode of social behaviour between addressable persons. This dimension restricts ritual to social behaviour acquired by learning in processes of socialisation and as part of a culture. It excludes compulsive repetitive behaviour which has no communicative intent, and instinctive interaction.[13]

2. *the collective dimension*

As interaction, ritual needs a minimum of two participants—a 'sender' and a 'receiver' in terms of communication theory—, either of whom, however, may belong to the class of putative be-

---

[11] By 'real' I understand beings whose existence and social activities can be verified by sense experience or its technological extensions. Examples of real, non-human, addressable beings, with whom men may ritually communicate, are domesticated animals such as dogs. Another category of real addressable beings of the non-human kind among whom ritual interaction is found, are the higher mammalians such as chimpanzees and gorillas who live in bands and teach their youngsters how to behave in them. Their ritual behaviour has not been included in this definition in order not to overburden it, though analytically it fully qualifies for inclusion. 'Postulated' refers to beings, the existence and activity of which can neither be verified nor falsified before a forum of neutral, competent observers but which believers believe to exist, and with whom they believe they may, and do, communicate through ritual behaviour. They may also be termed 'putative', 'meta-empirical', 'non-testable', or 'unseen' beings. Cf. also Platvoet 1983: 187.

[12] On definitions of the family resemblance type, cf. Clarke & Byrne 1993: 7, 11-16.

[13] Cf. Leach 1968: 520; Myerhoff 1977: 200; Kertzer 1988: 9.

ings.[14] All rituals are 'collective' in this minimal sense. Many rituals, however, are collective in a stronger sense when they engage, among the visible participants, actors of several kinds, such as officiants, those for whom a ritual is conducted, and a congregation. Rituals may be collective in the strongest sense when they engage a whole community, whether defined in terms of a secular or a religious cosmology. In the latter case, it is held by the believers to include both the visible, or verifiable, and the unseen, or non-verifiable, 'participants'.

3. *the customary dimension*

Ritual is an ordered 'flow'[15], or sequence, of social interaction, conventionalized and formalized by repetition and thereby made customary. It is constrained, given shape and structured by rules reflecting the relationships of sub- and super-ordination—and/or peer relationships—which exist between the participants, real and putative, and also by conventions how it ought to be performed.[16] The first group of rules are often accepted as 'normal' and may be practised without reflection and discussion, especially when the social distance between the participants[17] is great. It is then expressed in a rigorous enforcement of the 'proper' form, of precedence and protocol.[18] The second group may be the object of much discussion and even heated dissent.[19] As rule-governed behaviour, ritual is 'repetitive'. It normally proceeds along a set pattern established on earlier occasions and which has since become sanctioned as tradition.[20] As such, it tends towards formality, stereotypy, and rigidity

[14] Cf. also Moore & Myerhoff 1977: 8.

[15] Rite and ritual are etymologically connected with <ri>, the Indo-European root which means 'flow' (Turner & Turner 1978: 243-244), and so with e.g. rhyme, rhythm, river, as the ordered flows of words, music, and water. For analytical instruments for the comparative study of rituals as sequentially ordered processes of social interaction, cf. Platvoet 1982: 30-34, 101-117, 138-155, 166-170, 183-197.

[16] Cf. e.g. Goody 1977: 30-31; Tambiah 1979: 149; Lewis 1980: 11-12, 19, 22, 26; La Fontaine 1985: 11; for an example of the 'logic' ruling the order of Sinhalese exorcism rites, cf. Tambiah 1968: 176-178; 1979: 142-149.

[17] On 'social distance' as an important analytical element of the 'field', or network of relationships between the participants, in which a ritual takes place and by which it is constrained, cf. Platvoet 1982: 31, 32, 84-101, 121-138, 158-165, 175-183.

[18] Oosten 1990: 8.

[19] Staal (1979, 1986, 1989) holds that ritual is rule-governed behaviour without meaning. In his view, it does not have the expressive and communicative dimensions which I postulate. For a discussion of Staal's views, cf. Grapard 1991, Mack 1991, Strenski 1991, and the reply by Staal (1991).

[20] It may, in addition, be supported by other legitimations, such as having being instituted by the ancestors, or ordered by a deity (Lewis 1980: 23, 24, 34).

and has distancing effects upon the participants: it prevents spontaneous expressions (because they can be disordered) and private emotions when they do not express the public ones required by the ritual.[21] They also distance the participants from their spontaneous selves, and from their private motives for, or interpretations of, the ritual. For the duration of the ritual, the participants are reduced to the roles which it prescribes for them, and to the purpose and theory embedded in it.[22] If a ritual allows of spontaneity and chaos, it does so 'in prescribed times and places', manners and styles.[23]

4. *the dimension of traditionalising innovation*

Even though ritual behaviour is governed by rules and conventions, rituals are usually not static closed systems. A limited measure of change and innovation usually occurs as a result of a number of different factors. One is the plasticity of memory of the participants in respect of the traditional form of a ritual.[24] Another is the discussions of that form because of a conflict of interests among the participants who have a say in, or hold an opinion on, how a ritual ought be performed. There are also diverging interpretations of its meaning as different shades of the numerous meanings of the polyvalent symbols used in rituals are competitively stressed by some at the expense of others.[25] Complex rites may also have a stable core with fringes more open to innovation.[26] Innovation may also take place by the introduction of new core symbols[27], e.g. at times of religious or cultural revivalism[28], or of tense strife between groups.[29] Such innovation is, however, short-lived.[30] It quickly becomes normative[31] and is traditionalized by ritual's 'capacity for routinisation'.[32]

---

21 Tambiah 1979: 122-126. 'Ritual is not a free expression of emotions, but a disciplined rehearsal of right attitudes' (Tambiah 1979: 126).

22 Cf. Tambiah 1979: 127, note 1, 141; La Fontaine 1985: 14.

23 Myerhoff 1977: 7; for examples of comic episodes in Sinhalese exorcism rites, cf. Tambiah 1979: 144-146; Turner 1983: XXIII; Kapferer 1988: 74-75; 1991: 285-319.

24 Cf. Tambiah 1979: 136. In a few religious and secular traditions, some rituals and their rubrics have been written down and enforced by strict supervision. This has, of course, considerably fixed and frozen them, and has allowed for innovation and variation only in their more marginal elements.

25 Cf. also Tambiah 1979: 115.

26 Tambiah 1979: 136.

27 Rosaldo 1972: 361; for another example, cf. Tambiah 1979: 158-160.

28 Tambiah 1979: 165.

29 Kapferer 1988: 94sq.

30 Tambiah 1979: 166.

31 Rosaldo 1972: 361.

32 Smith 1980: 113.

A more speculative factor, but one with great explanatory powers, is the 'faculty' for judging competently the form of ritual, or the manner in which it is performed, which faculty cognitive anthropologists have recently postulated on the grounds that humans appear to 'learn much more than they are taught'[33] and are able to achieve great cognitive results with little cognitive effort.[34] This faculty would also explain why humans show creative facility in using and manipulating the cultural complexes in aesthetic, dramatic, rhetoric, or skilful ways when such special, often innovative, performances are required in specific contexts, such as those of aggregation, commemoration, or competition; as it would also explain why humans are able to judge whether newly devised ritual speech or behaviour patterns are well-formed, effective and proper expressions of the messages they are meant to convey.[35]

5. *the expressive dimension*

Society is reflected in a ritual by the very (f)act of its members taking part in it. The socio-structural or cosmological[36] relations obtaining among the participants in a ritual are normally 'revealed' in the positions and roles allotted to them in that event.[37] Following Robertson Smith and Durkheim, most anthropologists have focused on this expressive dimension of ritual as a means of studying society.[38] Leach identified it as its communicative dimension.[39] Lewis, however, distinguishes between expression and communication, as not all that is expressed in a ritual behaviour necessarily functions as a message to be communicated between the participants.[40]

---

[33] Boyer 1993a: 36.
[34] Atran 1993: 57, 59.
[35] Cf. Lawson & McCauley 1990; Boyer 1992; Boyer 1993b.
[36] By 'cosmological' I mean the putative social relationships which believers postulate between themselves and the meta-empirical beings whom they address in their religious rites.
[37] La Fontaine 1985: 11.
[38] For a brief survey of the history of anthropological theory on ritual as an expression of the structure of human society, cf. appendix II.
[39] Geertz (1966: 35) accuses Leach of 'vulgar positivism'. In his view, religious ritual describes the social order only very obliquely and very incompletely because (religious) ritual is not shaped by the social order but itself shapes it. Though Geertz does not hold a religionist point of view in the study of religions (cf. Geertz 1966: 28, 35, 39-40; 1973: 112, 119, 123), in this matter, he voices a point of view dear to religionists.
[40] Lewis 1980: 33-38.

6. *the communicative dimension*

As interactive behaviour, ritual also consists in the communication of messages of various kinds. They may be divided into explicit messages sent at the manifest level of the 'business at hand' that is transacted during a ritual[41], and more or less implicit ones transmitted at the latent, or less than latent, level. The latter messages mostly respect the socio-structural relations between the participants in a ritual and as such express society.[42] The explicit messages usually determine much of the content, or (apparent) matter of, a ritual[43]. The implicit ones may, however, constitute a more important agenda.[44] The way the participants receive these latter messages ranges from passing them over as if 'unnoticed'[45] to paying a great deal of attention to them and discussing them intensively. In the latter case, a socio-structural message, or the manner in which it is expressed, may 'intrude' into the manifest level of communication and compete for the attention of the participants with the emphatic messages of the business to be transacted.

---

[41] Cf. Lewis 1980: 23-24. The messages at this level may be subdivided into emphatic and phatic, depending on their content and their function in the communicative process. Emphatic messages have a precise, often urgent content and usually a pragmatic intention requiring a response from the receivers. Phatic messages have a more diffuse content and usually a socio-structural function, which the receivers are expected merely to perceive and receive as 'normal'—though they may comment on them disparagingly or approvingly if they are expressed in an unusual manner; cf. de Waal-Malefijt 1968: 198-199; Platvoet 1982: 29-34; Platvoet 1983a; Platvoet 1983b: *passim*.

[42] The expressive dimension, or function, of ritual at the latent, or socio-structural, level has been the central concern of most anthropological theories on ritual, as I set out in somewhat greater detail in Appendix II. Its communicative function at the manifest level was analyzed only by (neo-)Tylorian anthropologists who defined religion as communication between believers and their postulated beings (e.g. Horton 1960: 211-212; 1972: 358; Goody 1961: 157-158; Spiro 1966: 96; Platvoet 1982: 24-35; 1990: 189). They also stressed its explanatory function (Horton 1960, 1964/1972; Morris 1987: 300, 304-309).

[43] For the analysis of the content of explicit messages, cf. Platvoet 1982: 32-33, 105-111, 141-149, 167-168, 189-193.

[44] For their analysis, cf. Platvoet 1982: 31, 32, 84-101, 121-138, 158-165, 175-183 on the 'field', or network of relationships between the participants, in which a ritual is performed.

[45] I.e. noticing them subconsciously as 'normal', or 'ordinary', in an uncritical, pre-reflective manner and mood, because each participant's 'understanding' of them has been habituated to the use of these symbols by lifelong training in them. Cf. La Fontaine 1985: 12, and my remarks below on the power dimension of ritual.

7. *the symbolic dimension*

In rituals, expression and communication are achieved through symbolic action[46], in particular by the dense, core or pivotal symbols which present 'key aspects of a whole system of culture and belief' in an economic way by clusters of 'consonant' referents[47], the different meanings of which may become paramount at different times.[48] Apart from their polysemous meanings, these symbols also possess strong normative and emotive (or, in Turner's terms, *orectic*) aspects. Consequently, they carry and transmit a much heavier load than the multiple meanings they may, or may not, communicate as 'message'.[49] Lewis, therefore, prefers to discuss ritual as stimulating various responses rather than as only communicating messages.[50]

8. *the multi-media dimension*

The 'messages' and stimuli sent in a ritual may be expressed by the numerous, complex, polyvalent symbols that have been, and are constantly being, developed in each culture. They are clustered in e.g. verbal, facial, and other forms of body-language[51]; dress, ornaments and other symbolic modes of presenting oneself with ostentation, or apparent lack of ostentation[52], such as music, dance, trance, and comic drama[53]; gift-giving; the (ritual) objects used; the (self)ordering of the participants into specific groups; the places and roles they are allotted, or assign themselves, in the space and the diachronic order of the ritual; the manners in which the ritual space and time are ordered and adorned with the help of the plastic and pictorial arts; etc. La Fontaine points out that those who perform a

---

[46] Cf. Kapferer (1991: 4): 'in ritual, ideas [...] are objectified and reified so much that they are made controlling and determining of action.'

[47] On cultures as constituted by dense 'consonant', or 'replicating' complexes of symbols, cf. Douglas 1982³: 38, 64-71, 80-81, 149.

[48] Turner & Turner 1978: 246.

[49] Cf. Turner & Turner 1978: 243-251; Geertz 1966: 28sq; 1973: 113sq. Cf. also Tambiah (1979: 132-133): Ritual 'portrays many features that have little to do with the transmission of new information and everything to do with interpersonal orchestration and with social integration and continuity.'

[50] Lewis 1980: 34-35.

[51] Performance and performative approaches (see below) may single out two more 'dimensions' of ritual for separate analytical attention, that of the body as a central expressive device (e.g. Bocock 1974: 37; Myerhoff 1977: 200; Bourdieu 1990: 66-79; Parkin 1991: 12sq.; Bell 1992: 93); and that of the spoken word (e.g. Tambiah 1968).

[52] Cf. Sperber & Wilson (1986: 49) on ritual as 'ostensive behaviour' in which the sender encodes the messages which he or she deems relevant for his or her audience.

[53] Cf. Kapferer 1991: 10-11, 245-319.

rite of passage, and those subjected to it, 'are themselves representations of concepts and ideas, and therefore, symbolic. Like the performers in a morality play, the actors stand for something other than themselves'.[54] Having several levels, and being usable for many purposes, the symbols used in a ritual are often organized in sets of overlapping metaphors. They may, moreover, be expressed and sent as messages in many guises and along several different channels. In brief, they serve as the repetitive and redundant and/or condensed polyphonic transformations of each other[55], and are used not so much in order to transfer new information but to stimulate pattern recognition and configurational awareness and in order to produce 'total experiences'.[56]

9. *the performance dimension*

All rituals, even the 'solitary' ones of believers towards a postulated being, are collective events (in a weak, strong, or stronger sense). They need to alert and focus the attention of at least the addressees, or the audience, to at least the central parts of the message(s). Lewis has emphasized the alerting quality of ritual which he defines as conspicuous behaviour bound by explicit customary rules and enacted with a certain feeling for formality and aesthetics by which the attention of the participants is focused on the event, on the arena in which it takes place, and on the more than ordinary significance which gestures, actions and objects may have.[57] Likewise, Moore & Myerhoff reckon as one of the formal properties of ritual that 'most, if not all of it is self-consciously "acted" like in a play' by the use of stylization and an evocative, presentational style.[58] By the first they mean that 'special' behaviour which is constituted by 'actions or symbols that are extraordinary in themselves, or ordinary ones [that are acted or] used in an unusual way'. By the second, its alerting quality, producing not only an attentive state of mind in the participants but often also 'an even greater commitment of some kind [...] through manipulations of symbols and sensory

---

54 La Fontaine 1985: 13.
55 Cf. Leach 1972; 1978: 45-54; Tambiah 1968: 188-198; 1979: 130-149, 163-165; Ghosh 1987: 220; cf. also Douglas (1982: VII, XIV, XX, 38, 64-71, 80-82, 149) on the universal human drive to 'achieve [cognitive] consonance in all the layers of experience' in ritual behaviour by 'replicating' symbols at several 'levels' such as nature, the human body, society, cosmology, myths, etc.
56 Tambiah 1979: 134, 140-141; for examples, cf. Tambiah 1979: 142-149; La Fontaine 1985: 13-14; Kapferer 1991: XI.
57 Lewis 1980: 7, 8, 13, 19-20, 46, 97.
58 Moore & Myerhoff 1977: 7-8; cf. also Geertz 1966: 28-29; 1973: 112-114; 1983: 26-30.

stimuli'.[59] In some cases, they may 'produce a concentration so extreme that there is a loss of self-consciousness, and a feeling of "flow".'[60] They will also produce in the participants 'an awareness that they [*scil.* the ritual events, JP] are different from "ordinary" everyday events'.[61]

10. *the performative dimension*

Ritual may be performative in two ways. In a narrow sense, a part of social reality may be constituted by the 'illocutionary' use of speech acts, in the Austinian sense, and of other symbolic acts in rites of passages such as baptism, matrimony or installation into an office.[62] 'Simply by virtue of being enacted (under the appropriate conditions) [they] achieve a change of state, or do something effective' in human minds[63] and in society. In a wider sense, rituals may be seen as continually re-creating and re-constituting society, real and postulated, by the very fact and act of the actors participating in them. For in rituals society, real and postulated, is expressed by

---

59 Cf. also Douglas (1970: 78-80) on the 'framing function' of ritual. By providing the participants with a 'marked off time or place' which serve as the spatio-temporal frames that provide the participant with continuity from one session to the next and with 'a method for mnemonics' that 'links the present with the relevant past', ritual coordinates the brain and the body and 'alerts a special kind of expectancy' in the participants by which it creates and controls their experience. Cf. also Smith (1980: 113-116) on the sacred place as focusing lens in ritual because it is part of a symbolic map.

60 Cf. also Tambiah (1979: 140-142) on the psychological effects of intense ritual experiences such as 'submission to a compelling constraint', 'transportation into a supra-normal, transcendental "antistructural", "numinous", or "altered" state of consciousness', 'euphoric communion with one's fellow beings', 'subordination to a collective representation'. These transporting effects do not contradict the distancing effect of ritual, but are precisely effected by means of the distancing mechanisms operative in ritual.

61 Tambiah 1979: 117; cf. also Kapferer 1991: 6-11.

62 Cf. Tambiah 1973; 1979: 119, 127-129, 153-156; 1985; Ahern 1979: 7-16.

63 Tambiah 1985: 79; Ghosh 1987: 220-222. Cf. also Tambiah (1968: 202) where he contends that the magical rituals described by Malinowski, were not meant by the Trobriand to achieve effects in the external order of nature but in 'the minds and emotions of the actors'. Ahern (1979: 9-16), however, distinguishes between strong and weak illocutionary acts. The latter have weak social effects only. They improve social relations by the expression of phatic messages of well-wishing. The former may either be performed in order to effect changes in the prevailing social relationships, or in order to bring about desired effects in the external order, whether by the unseen beings that are explicitly or implicitly addressed or by virtues inherent in the ritual action itself. Whether effects in the external order are intended can only be established by accurate ethnographic research, Ahern holds, not by presumption.

the relationships between the participants being enacted, and time and again re-enacted, in them.[64]

11. *the aesthetic dimension*

From Leach's point of view, ritual is a formal, and therefore aesthetic mode of communication (about social structure).[65] Authors adhering to the performance and performative approach also stress that ritual as enacting and 'celebrating' society, or as performatively creating it, must be executed in not only traditional or 'proper' ways but also in felicitous, well-formed and pleasing manners in order that they may effectively alert, focus and hold the enraptured attention of the participant, and/or achieve its performative goal. It provokes participant criticism if its officiants fail to perform in a manner that is both well-styled and traditional.[66]

12. *the strategic dimension*

By the condensation of meaning, together with the moral and emotive aspects, in focal symbols, and by other mechanisms such as repetition, redundancy, formality, distancing and habituation, rituals cause the participants to fail to perceive the arbitrariness of the cultural order expressed in them and to take it for their 'natural world' and their normal situation. Ritual may cause them to experience as satisfactory a social condition which can objectively be shown to be oppressive and exploitive. In ritual, critical analysis is anathema. It must be suspended. The fiction must be maintained that rituals are not made-up productions.[67] Bourdieu has analyzed the mechanism of 'misrecognition' in the rituals of e.g. the educational institutions by which existing social divisions are maintained.[68] Bell, who defines ritual as the ritualization of social acts, takes it as an effective strategy of power. Ritualization is 'a particularly "mute" form of activity. It is designed to do what it does

---

[64] Geertz (1966: 29sq; 1973: 113sq; 1983: 26-30) stresses the constitutive role of rituals for the faith of believers and their community with their postulated beings through their rituals of communion with them: 'in these plastic dramas men attain their faith as they portray it' (1966: 29; 1973: 114); and 'reiterated form, staged and acted by its own audience, makes [...] theory a fact' (1983: 30). Cf. also Tambiah 1979: 139-140, 153-154; and de Coppet (1991a: 9): 'rituals create and construct [...] the social dimension'.

[65] Leach 1968: 523, 526; cf. also Lewis 1980: 16-17; Turner 1983: XXI; Kapferer 1991: 2, 10-11, 249-250.

[66] Lewis 1980: 20; Tambiah 1979: 127; Ghosh 1987: 221.

[67] Myerhoff 1977: 199.

[68] E.g. Bourdieu 1990: 26; cf. also Kapferer 1991: 5.

without bringing what it is doing across the threshold of discourse or systematic thinking'.[69] It produces 'expedient schemes that structure an environment in such a way that [it] appears to be the [objective] source of the [subjective] schemes and values that have created it', thereby preventing the actors from recognizing its arbitrary nature.[70] Bell, therefore, refers to that environment as a 'redemptive reordering'.[71] It 'implies and demonstrates a relatively unified corporate body' by suggesting 'more consensus [among the participants] than there actually is'.[72]

13. *the integrative dimension*

By the properties of ritual outlined in the foregoing and in several other dimensions, rituals often powerfully contribute towards the inclusion of members into their corporate groups. Moreover, many rituals, especially the collective or representative ones, express and re-create the solidarity, identity, and at times the boundaries, of a group or a society by their being performed at a particular time and place, in the special manner in which its participants are ordered, and by the prominent display and manipulation of objects which express the unity and distinctiveness of that group.[73] By thus expressing and stressing its solidarity, identity, and boundaries, these rituals are normally strongly unitive *ad intra* and weakly divisive *ad extra.*

As ritual is a special mode of social intercourse, most of the dimensions set out above are not exclusive to it, several being features of ordinary social commerce as well. That is certainly true of the interaction dimension as well as of the collective, customary, expressive, communicative, symbolic and multi-media ones, and also perhaps the power and inclusion dimensions. As ritual is a mode of symbolic interaction, all these dimensions are the necessary, but not sufficient marks of ritual. However, in ritual behaviour, these dimensions seem to feature in purer and more effective forms due to the presence of those other dimensions which seem more specific

---

[69] Bell 1992: 93.
[70] Bell 1992: 140-141.
[71] Bell 1992: 142.
[72] Bell 1992: 210. Cf. also Bloch 1985, and the discussion of Bloch's views by van der Veer (1994b: 81-83, 105), on ritual as an efficient means of legitimizing several sorts of domination by its traditionalising, highly authoritative modes of discourse and by its use, in religious rituals, of the supernatural for founding the social in it, making it inviolable by distancing it from everyday affairs.
[73] Cf. La Fontaine 1985: 11-12.

for ritual behaviour, to wit the performance, performative, and aesthetic dimensions as well as that of traditionalising innovation.

The definition of ritual in plural and pluralist societies

Due to the constraining legacy of Robertson Smith and Durkheim[74], the comparative analysis of ritual by anthropologists has almost exclusively been confined to ritual as conventional behaviour of unified corporate groups that maintains, or restores, solidarity, or order, or the established power relationships, within them. Rituals in which groups cultivating distinct identities and positions vis-à-vis each other express inter-group relations, and societies in which boundaries between groups are ritually expressed and maintained, have only lately begun to receive due ethnographic attention because of e.g. the atrocities of ethnic strife. This is not because such rituals and societies are recent phenomena. Ritual as an expression of group-predicated relationships has always been prominent in non-plural segmented kinship societies in which kin groups have cultivated their separate identities and solidarity *ad intra* and expressed and maintained boundaries *ad extra*.[75] Intergroup rituals

---

[74] Cf. also Baumann (1991: 98-99, 113-115), who maintains that this legacy is due to 'a narrow and one-sided reading of Durkheim rather than to Durkheim's position itself'.

[75] Cf. e.g. Horton (1972: 349): 'sectional and individual rites abound in African communities, and they are concerned as much with disruption as with harmony.' Cf. also Douglas (1982: 59-64), who distinguishes four types of societies and four corresponding attitudes to ritual with the help of her group—grid concepts: (1) high group—high grid societies which are ritualistic in a formal way; (2) low group—low grid societies which are a-ritualistic, or even anti-ritualistic; (3) low group—high grid societies which are ritualist for manipulative purposes; and (4) high group—low grid societies which are ritualistic for defensive purposes (Douglas 1982: 103-167). 'Grid' refers to the measure to which a society is internally structured, and 'group' to its degree of boundary consciousness (Douglas 1982: VIII, IX, 13-14, 24, 28-36, 57-61, 72-74, 82-106, esp. 103-105). I must point out, however, that Douglas is not interested in ritual in plural or pluralist societies. Being more Durkheimian than Durkheim, she is interested only in self-contained societies, particularly the well-integrated ones. She holds that 'the experience of closed social groups' is 'the most important determinant of ritualism. The better defined and the more significant the social boundaries, the more the bias I would expect in favour of ritual' (Douglas 1982: 14). Her comparative interest is in establishing how different types of 'societies', taken as reified social structures, condition their cultures, symbol systems and the ways in which these symbol systems are used in ritual. Cf. also Baumann 1991: 110-113 on the five manners in which the rituals of a group may implicate outsiders: bystanders, spectators, guests invited to enhance a ritual's prestige, witnesses from outside to validate legal proceedings, and outside beneficiaries. However, only in the last case does Baumann refer to intergroup rituals in the strict sense of the word.

have also been a marked feature of stratified societies in which social groups are hierarchically ordered after religious, social, economical, and/or political criteria. We meet them often also in 'plural'[76], or 'pillar', or 'apartheid' societies in which groups, living side by side, restrict interaction by cultivating social segregation attitudes and practices on the basis of colour, ethnicity, religion or other bars, and develop distinct and exclusive ethnic, 'racial', and/or religious identities and boundaries. We also find them in the 'pluralist' societies that cultivate an ideology of not imposing restrictions on the interaction between groups with distinct identities as well as in the global community of the modern, secular states, the leaders of which meet occasionally to express the relations between their nations in a ritual manner.

Because of the Durkheimian perspective, some empirical data about ritual have not yet been, or have only recently begun to be, faced in theory of ritual. One is that the context of ritual is often not the mono-cultural society with a unified ritual congregation, but rather a culturally plural or pluralist one which consist of several ritual constituencies that at least have windows on each other and in various ways make use of the 'others' in their rituals[77], or use their rituals for expressing their relations to them. Another is that ritual may be, and may be meant to be, explosive rather than unitive.[78] A third suggests that ritual need not always be the customary rehearsal of earlier ceremonies but may sometimes also be a one-time-only event, explicitly constructed for just one occasion and for one purpose.[79] A fourth reveals that the public rituals of modern plural and pluralist societies are situated within an 'imploding'[80] global context.

---

[76] This term was originally coined by Furnival (1948) for the analysis of the then colonial societies of Birma and Indonesia.

[77] Baumann 1991: 110-113.

[78] Cf. van Baaren (1983: 189): 'Ritual is always a form of communication, but this is not the same as a form of community. Ritual may be employed to establish community as well as to decline it, to prevent or break it off.'

[79] In Moore & Myerhoff (1977: 9-10), two one event only rituals are briefly described. They were both dedication ceremonies, one for a bridge and the other for an academic building. They brought together a 'motley' crowd in the apparent unity of an ephemeral occasion.

[80] The expression is Appadurai's. The technology of the modern media enables an increasing portion of mankind to witness live the major public events that occur on virtually any part of the globe. That again allows e.g. the diaspora Hindus in e.g. the USA and Canada to watch closely the political developments in India, and rears 'long-distance nationalisms' (B. Anderson, quoted in de Rijk 1994).

In order to analyse inter-group ritual adequately, additional[81] concepts need to be introduced for the analysis of some of the dimensions which have been set out above. They include four distinctions in the communication dimension with respect to the analysis of the messages, emphatic and phatic, which they carry. Firstly, we need to distinguish between the direct, or overt, addressee(s) of a ritual and its indirect, or implied, addressee(s): messages that seem to be addressed to e.g. the Hindu devotees of the god Ram at a rally may actually be meant for the Muslim section of the Indian nation. Secondly, therefore, between the overt, or stated, message(s) of a ritual and the implied message(s) it contained. It follows, thirdly, that a distinction has to be made between the field of direct ritual communication—that between the addresser and the direct addressee(s), whether they be real or postulated—, and the field of wider, indirect communication, between the addresser and his audience on the one hand, and those not present, the group indirectly addressed, on the other. That field may be established by the local rumours about the event. In most modern societies, however, it is established by modern communication technology and powerfully dominated by the modern communication media. That wider field of indirect communication is dormant until it is actualized by e.g. prevailing tensions and the interests of the modern media in dramatic news. The extent of this indirect field may vary in range, from a locality, a region, a nation to even the whole world after the different impact which the media expect from a ritual as a dramatic event, or from the messages expressed, or perceived, in it. Lastly, in competitive contexts, the implied messages for the indirect addressee sent through the wider communication context, may be the primary motive for that ritual behaviour and be given much more prominence, volume, and forcefulness of expression, coverage in the media, and attention by the direct and indirect addressees than the overt message to the direct addressee(s). In non-competitive contexts, the implied message for the indirect addressee may be only a minor side issue.

The manner in which a message is sent in plural or pluralist societies may also greatly affect the symbolic and the multi-media dimensions of rituals. The members of groups with different group identities may understand the messages expressed in a ritual very

---

[81] Additional to those needed for the analysis of 'ordinary' social and religious ritual communication in the 'face-to-face' encounter between social actors or between believers and the postulated beings which they believe to address.

differently, especially if they maintain strong cultural or other boundaries towards each other and perceive another group as competitor and threat. One reason for these differences in interpretation is that they may have different stocks of core symbols. Another may be that they may single out as relevant for them very different meanings from the spectrum of possible referents of a core symbol[82], or that they are differently, and even antagonistically, moved by its normative and emotive aspects. Ritual expression of boundaries and relative group status is particularly prominent when groups are engaged in competition.[83] They may be expressed directly in ritual behaviour, when members of different groups interact, or when groups interact as groups or through their representatives; or indirectly, when members of a group ritually display 'ostensive behaviour' in such ways that the members of another group cannot fail to notice the inherent messages, either because that behaviour is flaunted in front of their faces, as in provocative demonstrations, or because the media repeatedly spell it out for them.

Ritual in plural and pluralist societies, therefore, may also strongly affect the dimensions of power and of integration, and disintegration. Whereas rituals in mono-cultural corporate groups consolidate the established order by the mechanism which Bourdieu has termed 'misrecognition'[84], which operates through the blinding forces of convention and custom, rituals in situations of strife in plural societies may be one-time events constructed with disruptive intent. They may quite openly aim at the passionate, and at times violent, exclusion of 'non-members' in order to include 'members' in a total and, at times, totalitarian way. Only recently

---

[82] Cf. the discussion of Sperber & Wilson (1986)'s concept of 'relevance' in Wijsen 1994: 29-31.

[83] However, inter-group strife is not the only area of study for detailing the functions and morphology of ritual in plural and pluralist contexts. In my view, it needs to be balanced with an other important area of research, that of accommodative ritual by which a distinct group seeks to establish, or maintain, integration with, or subordination to, another and especially a dominant group, as in e.g. the ritual of 'resting in the (Holy) Spirit' which has caught on in charismatic groups in mainline churches in recent years for exactly that purpose. Time and space forbid the inclusion of an analysis of this contrasting class of intergroup rituals in this volume. For other examples of the accommodative use of ritual, such as Christmas rituals and birthday parties in England by non-Christian immigrants, cf. Baumann 1991: 97-110.

[84] Because ritual structures the field of action and the minds of the actors in identical ways—which causes the participants in a field of ritual behaviour to take that field and the ritual behaviour it requires as 'natural'. It prevents them from perceiving its arbitrary character and strategic effects. Cf. e.g. Bourdieu 1971/1972, 1977b, 1980, 1990; Verboven 1987; Robbins 1991; Bourdieu & Wacquant 1992; Jenkins 1992.

has attention focused on the long-neglected fact that ritual always had a prominent place in the combat between hostile orders[85], whether they be political, economical, military, religious, academic, etc. These orders are mental constructs rendered visible and reified in the symbolic behaviour, ritual and other, of the people in whose minds they are nurtured. The violence, inherent in master fictions such as nations, social orders or ethnic identities, may be concealed by e.g. the ritualization of 'invented traditions'—the myths about the legendary foundation, naturalness, antiquity, cultural distinctiveness, or historical achievement or other imagined 'foundations', which such constructs lack as historical facts but which are used effectively for furthering political aims or for bolstering political power[86], in particular the more recent examples, such as the one-party nations of post-colonial Africa.[87] Violence may also be openly expressed in rituals designed to incite the passions of ethnic strife.[88]

A provisional definition of ritual

Because operational definitions of ritual need not be universally valid, nor comprise all the traits that would have to be included if ritual were to be accounted for analytically in all its complexity and variety, they may also legitimately highlight in a selective manner those marks in this complex phenomenon that are central to the research aims of a particular discipline or scholar. That gives me the liberty to define ritual for my purposes[89] provisionally as

> that ordered sequence of stylized social behaviour that may be distinguished from ordinary interaction by its alerting qualities which enable it to focus the attention of its audiences—its congregation as well as a wider public—onto itself and cause them to perceive it as a special event, performed at a special place and/or time, for a special occasion and/or with a special message. It effects this by the use of the appropriate, culturally specific, consonant complexes of polysemous core symbols, of which it enacts several redundant transformations by multimedia performance, thereby achieving not only the smooth transmis-

---

85 Cf. Kertzer 1988: 2, 5-6, 178-179.
86 Cf. Hobsbawm & Ranger 1983.
87 Kertzer 1988: 178.
88 Kapferer 1988.
89 They are to test the heuristic utility of this provisional operational definition of ritual in an analysis of the ritual episodes at, or centring on, Ayodhya between 1984 and 1992 in the contest for power between a Hindu political movement and the Muslims and the secular government of India.

> sion of a multitude of messages—some overt, most of them covert—and stimuli, but also serving the strategic purposes—most often latent, sometimes manifest—of those who perform it *ad intra*, within unified congregations or *ad extra* as well as *ad intra* in situations of plurality.

This operational definition of ritual is sufficiently broad to allow the attribution to ritual of both communicative and strategic functions, and to stipulate for each a wider scope than attributed to them by Leach and Bourdieu.

Appendix One

Definitions of ritual, chronologically ordered

N.B. Two cautions must be registered. Firstly, no claim is made that this list is exhaustive. It is a bye-product of my study of the literature on ritual in the past year. I use it for analyzing the historical development of the central concept of ritual theory. Others with an interest in this field may find it useful in conjunction with the brief history of some of the theoretical developments in anthropology of religion presented below in appendix II, and may wish to develop it further. Secondly, although definitions are theories *in nuce*, they do not replace an author's full ritual theory.

1909 A. van Gennep (1909: 13-14, 16-17, 23-24, 275) termed rites of passage those 'ceremonial sequences' with the typical three stage structure of separation, margin, and aggregation, by which the passage of humans from one social situation to another, or from one cosmic or social world to another is effected; i.e. from some state, which van Gennep views as 'sacred' in relation to certain other 'profane' ones, to another state. Van Gennep saw 'ceremonies, rites, cult' (17) as praxis which is at once religious and technical; which he therefore termed 'magic' (17). Rituals are magico-religious acts. He discussed the theories about their presumed efficacy extensively and proposed a new division of them (5-13, 17-18).

1912 E. Durkheim (1912: 56): 'Enfin les rites sont des règles de conduite qui prescrivent comment l'homme doit se comporter avec les choses sacrées.'

1951 R. Firth (1951: 222): ritual is 'a kind of patterned activity oriented towards the control of human affairs, primarily symbolic in character with a non-empirical referent, and as a rule socially sanctioned.'

1951 Royal Anthropological Institute (1951: 175): 'Ritual, like etiquette, is a formal mode of behaviour recognised as correct, but unlike the latter it implies belief in the operation of supernatural agencies and forces.'

1954 E. Leach ($1954^1/1964^2$: 13): 'Ritual denotes those aspects of prescribed formal behaviour which have no direct technological consequence.'

1954 S.F. Nadel (1954: 99): 'When we speak of "ritual" we have in mind first of all actions exhibiting a striking or incongruous rigidity, that is, some conspicuous regularity not accounted for by the professed aims of the actions. Any type of behaviour may thus be said to turn into a "ritual" when it is stylized and formalized, and made repetitive in that form.'

1961 J. Goody (1961: 159): 'By ritual we refer to a category of standardized behaviour (custom) in which the relationship between the means and the end is not 'intrinsic', i.e. is either irrational or non-rational.'

1966 C. Geertz (1966: 1, 28-29; 1973: 87, 112-114) defines ritual as 'consecrated behaviour [in which the] conviction that religious conceptions are veridical and that religious directives are sound is somehow generated. [Ritual is] some sort of ceremonial form [in which] the moods and motivations which sacred symbols induce in men and the general conceptions of the order of existence which they formulate for men meet and reinforce one another. In a ritual, the world as lived and the world as imagined, fused under the agency of a single set of symbolic forms, turn out to be the same world, producing thus that idiosyncratic transformation in one's sense of reality to which Santayana refers [when he writes that religion opens vistas upon another world to live in]'. '[..] Religious ritual involves [the] symbolic fusion of ethos and world view'. It is the 'cultural performances [.. in] which the dispositional and conceptual aspects of religious life converge for the believer, [i.e. ...] the plastic dramas [in which] men attain their faith as they portray it.'[90]

1967 V.W. Turner (1967: 19; 1968: 15; 1978: 243) defined ritual as 'prescribed formal behaviour for occasions not given over to technical routine, having reference to beliefs in mystical (or non-empirical) beings and powers'; cf. also Turner (1974: 56): 'ritual [is] symbolic behaviour [which] actually creates society for pragmatic purposes'.

1971 J.W. Fernandez (1971: 56): ritual is 'the acting out of metaphoric predication upon inchoate pronouns which are in need of movement.'

1974 R. Bocock (1974: 37): 'Ritual is the symbolic use of bodily movement and gesture in a social context to express and articulate meaning'.

1978 R. Delattre (1978: 282): ritual is 'those carefully rehearsed symbolic motions and gestures through which we regularly go, in which we articulate the felt shape and rhythm of our own humanity and of reality as we experience it, and by means of which we negotiate the terms or conditions for our presence among and our participation in the plurality of realities through which our humanity makes its passage'.

1979 S.J. Tambiah (1979: 119; 1985: 28): 'Ritual is a culturally constructed system of symbolic communication. It is constituted of patterned and ordered sequences of words and acts, often expressed in multiple media, whose content and arrangement are characterized

[90] Cf. also Geertz (1983: 30): Ritual drama is 'reiterated form, staged and acted by its own audience [which] makes (to a degree, for no theater ever wholly works) theory fact.'

in varying degree by formality (conventionality), stereotypy (rigidity), condensation (fusion), and redundancy (repetition). Ritual action in its constitutive features is performative in these three senses: in the Austinian sense of performative wherein saying something is also doing something as a conventional act; in the quite different sense of a staged performance that uses multiple media by which participants experience the event intensively; and in the third sense of indexical values—I derive this concept from Pierce—being attached to and inferred by actors during the performance.'

1981 J. van Baal (1981: 162-163): 'A rite is a religious act, i.e. every act concerned with an unverifiable reality which is both feared and sought. [...]. Every ritual has two aspects: the one is turned to the realization of contact and communication with the supernatural, the other to the expression of awe by the observation of a respectful distance.'

1982 W.E.A. van Beek (1982: 13-14) defines ritual as 'stable patterns of activity in which men address the supernatural.' (translation J.P.)

1982 R.L. Grimes (1982: 55) proposes a 'soft' definition of ritual as 'ritualizing': 'Ritualizing transpires as animated persons enact formative gestures in the face of receptivity during crucial times in founded places.'

1983 J.G. Platvoet (1983: 187): '"Ritual" in its widest meaning may therefore be defined as any pattern of standardized behaviour for the purpose of communication between men and unseen beings, men and men, men and animals, animals and men, and animals and animals, which exhibit these formal properties [of *scilicet* repetition, self-conscious role or play acting, stylization (i.e. the use of extra-ordinary action or symbols, or the extra-ordinary use of normal action and symbols), order and organisation (with moments or elements of chaos and spontaneity at prescribed times and places), evocation (in order to attract attention) and a collective dimension {...} (Moore & Myerhoff 1977: 7-8)].

1983 Th.P. van Baaren (1983: 189): 'Ritual is the usual appellation of that variant of conventional relations which in mutual social relations between people as a rule is called ceremonial, but which in religion too can be found as sets of conventionalised rules for the relations between human beings and gods or beings venerated.'

1983 B. Kapferer (1991^2: 3): 'I define ritual as a multi-modal symbolic form, the practice of which is marked off (usually spatially and temporally) from, or within, the routine of everyday life, and which has specified, in advance of its enactment, a particular sequential ordering of acts, utterances and events, which are essential to the recognition of the ritual by cultural members as being representative of a specific cultural type.'

1985 J.S. La Fontaine (1985: 11): ritual is 'the acts performed in an ordered sequence which has purpose and meaning for the people concerned'.

1986 F. Staal (1986: 42-43): ritual 'is, like language, a *rule-governed activity*; [...] the assumption that rituals express meanings like language is not only unnecessary, but inaccurate and misleading'; cf. also 59: '[T]he chief concern of ritualists is with rules. They are constantly concentrating upon rules, and forms that are generated by rules. All their preoccupations illustrate the nature of ritual as rule-governed activity'; also 217-219; and the title of Staal 1989: rites are 'rules without meaning';

1987 E.M. Zuesse (1987: 405): 'For our purposes, we shall understand as "ritual" those conscious and voluntary, repetitious and stylized symbolic bodily actions that are centered on cosmic structures and/or sacred presences.'

1988 D.I. Kertzer (1988: 9): '[I define] ritual as symbolic behavior that is socially standardized and repetitive. [...] Ritual action has a formal quality to it. It follows highly structured, standardized sequences and is often enacted at certain places and times that are themselves endowed with special symbolic meaning. Ritual action is repetitive and, therefore, often redundant, but these very factors serve as important means of channelling emotion, guiding cognition, and organizing social groups.'

1991 D. Parkin (1991: 18): 'Ritual is formulaic spatiality carried out by groups of people who are conscious of its imperative or compulsory nature and who may or may not further inform this spatiality with spoken words'.

Appendix Two

A brief history of anthropological theory on ritual as expressing social structure

The history of anthropological theory on ritual as expression of structure and society may be divided into an early, a modern, and a recent phase. The early phase coincides with the period in which anthropology studied small societies in the colonial context. In this period (±1870-1960), ritual was equated by Durkheim (1912: 56) with religious, and by most other anthropologists, with religious and magical acts (van Gennep 1909: 5sq., 16-17) which they regarded as products of non- or irrational modes of thought (Tambiah 1968: 186). They opposed these to technological acts which they considered rational because they could be shown to achieve the results intended in strictly causal ways (e.g. Malinowski 1948: 17-92; Firth 1951: 222; Radcliffe-Brown 1952/1971: 123-124, 143, 153-177; Nadel 1954: 99; Goody 1961: 159-160; Leach 1968: 520-523; 1972: 334). Whereas technology was viewed as an instrumentally effective, rational and spontaneous means to a pragmatic end, ritual was perceived as a rule-governed, routinized, symbolic and, contrary to the views and intentions of the actors (cf. La Fontaine 1985: 12), as non-instrumental, as an arbitrary end in itself, and as expressing, reflecting, reinforcing and, with Gluckman and Turner, regenerating social structure.

After 1960, when decolonisation caused anthropologists to turn to the study of complex societies also, they found that sociologists, political scientists and historians, as well as ethologists and dramatists applied the term 'ritual' not only to religious acts but also to the secular ceremonial behaviour of modern man and to certain types of animal behaviour. It caused anthropologists to expand their field of study and to include secular ceremony in ritual (Moore & Myerhoff 1977). This inclusive definition caused anthropologists slowly to shed their preoccupation with the rational-irrational and the instrumental-expressive dichotomies and to shift towards the view that ritual is a mode, or aspect, of all social behaviour, characterised by either (increased) routinisation, formality and repetition (e.g. Goody 1977: 30-31), or by (the symbolic) communication (of social structure) (e.g. Douglas 1970: 78-89, 114-136, 148-153; 1982: 1-3, 8, 10-11, 20-21, 55; cf. also Bell 1992: 72-74). Both views attributed to ritual an integrative capacity as an 'all-purpose social glue' (Horton 1964: 349). Leach (1968: 523-524; 1972; 1978: 45-54) suggested that ritual be seen as acts that 'serve to *say* things' (Leach 1968: 523; his italics). He spoke of ritual as an 'unknown language' of which anthropologists must 'discover the rules of grammar and syntax' in order that they may 'decode' what ritual says about society (Leach 1968: 524; for an example, cf. Rosaldo 1968). In this quest, says Leach (1968: 523), 'the social scientist [...] can expect little help from the rationalizations of the devout' (cf. also Tambiah 1979: 120). Leach (1968: 524-525) refers only in passing and in a confusing manner to the power dimension of ritual.

This period also saw the emergence of new analytical paradigms. One was Tambiah's (1968, 1979: 119, 127-130; 1985; cf. also Ahern 1979; Ghosh 1987) performative approach to ritual. It was part of the performance approach, in which ritual is studied in analogy with other cultural performances such as drama, theatre, spectacle, festival (Geertz 1966: 29-35; Schechner & Schuman 1976; Schechner 1977, 1985; Turner 1982; MacAloon 1984; Schechner & Appel 1989), game, metaphor (Turner 1974; Fernandez 1977), and text (cf. Geertz 1983: 19-35; Sullivan 1986; Bell 1992: 37-46) (cf. also Moore & Myerhoff 1977: 7-8; Lewis 1980: 7, 8, 13, 19-20, 46, 97). From this markedly interdisciplinary approach, 'performance studies' as well as 'ritual studies' emerged in the late 1970s in North American universities as distinct disciplines, the first within the social sciences and arts (Turner 1983: XXI), the latter in the academic study of religion with its own *Journal of Ritual Studies* since 1987 (Grimes 1982: preface; Grimes 1987). In tune with the emphasis on style in the performance approach to ritual, Grime's concern is also with the several scholarly 'styles' in the study of ritual in the past (Grimes 1982: 1sq.).

In the last decade, attention shifted in particular to political rituals as the ritualization of power (e.g. Lane 1981, Bergesen 1984, Cannadine & Price 1987, Kapferer 1988, Kertzer 1988), and to the hidden power dimension of rituals (Bourdieu 1977, 1979, 1982; Oosten 1990). From these studies, it is clear that ritual may serve not only to achieve 'the peace and harmony typically promised to ritual participants' (Turner & Turner 1978: 244) by legitimising and extolling the existing order, but also to change and even overthrow it. Bell, who defined ritual as the ritualization of social interaction, has recently extended this view to all ritual: 'ritualization is first and foremost a strategy for the construction of certain types of power relationships effective within particular organizations' (Bell 1992: 197, 206). She defined 'ritualization' as that privileged form of interaction of a social body within a symbolically constituted spatial and temporal context in which value-laden distinctions are used in strategic ways in order to differentiate that social event by a variety of ways and means, which are specific to each culture, from other more quotidian forms of interaction as a more important, or more powerful, event. In Western cultural traditions, ritual has been differentiated from ordinary social intercourse by formality, fixity, and repetition, but these features are not intrinsic to ritualization or to ritual in general. They are 'frequent, but not universal strategies for producing ritualized acts' (Bell 1992: 8, 74, 90-93).

References

Ahern, E.M., 1979, 'The problem of efficacy: strong and weak illocutionary acts', in *Man* 14: 1-17.

Atran, S., 1993, 'Whither ethnoscience?', in Boyer 1993a: 48-70.

Baal, J. van, 1981, *Man's quest for partnership: the anthropological foundations of ethics and religion.* Assen: van Gorcum.

Baaren, Th.P. van, 1983, 'A short meditation upon the theme of ritual', in Platvoet 1983b: 189-190.

Baumann, G., 1991, 'Ritual implicates "Others": rereading Durkheim in a plural society', in de Coppet 1991b: 97-116.

Banton, M., (ed.) 1966, *Anthropological approaches to the study of religion.* London: Tavistock Publications.

Beek, W.E.A., 1982, *Spiegel van de mens: religie en anthropologie.* Assen: van Gorcum.

Bell, C., 1992, *Ritual theory, ritual practice.* New York, etc.: Oxford Un.Pr.

Bergesen, A., 1984, *The sacred and the subversive: political witch hunts as national rituals.* Storrs (Conn.): Society for the Scientific Study of Religion.

Bloch, M., 1985, *From blessing to violence.* Cambridge: Cambridge University Press.

Bocock, R., 1974, *Ritual in industrial society: a sociological analysis of ritualism in modern England.* London: George Allen & Unwin.

Bourdieu, P., 1971/1972, *Esquisse d'une théorie de la pratique; précédés de trois études d'ethnologie kabyle.* Genève: Droz, 1971; Paris: Éditions de la Minuit, 1972.

Bourdieu, P., 1977a, 'Sur le pouvoir symbolique', in *Annales E.S.C.* 32, 3: 405-411.

Bourdieu, P., 1977b, *Outline of a theory of practice.* Cambridge: Cambridge Un.Pr.

Bourdieu, P., 1979, 'Symbolic power', in *Critique of Anthropology* nos. 13/14: 77-85.

Bourdieu, P., 1980, *Le sens pratique.* Paris: Éditions de la Minuit.

Bourdieu, P., 1982, *Leçon sur la leçon.* Paris: Éditions de la Minuit.

Bourdieu, P., 1990, *The logic of practice.* Cambridge: Polity Press.

Bourdieu, P., & L.J.D. Wacquant 1992, *An invitation to reflexive sociology.* Chicago: University of Chicago Press.

Boyer, P., 1992, 'Explaining religious ideas: elements of a cognitive approach', in *Numen* 39, 1: 27-57.

Boyer, P., 1993a, 'Cognitive aspects of religious symbolism', in Boyer 1993b: 4-47.

Boyer, P., (ed.) 1993b, *Cognitive aspects of religious symbolism.* Cambridge: Cambridge Un.Pr.

Cannadine, D., and S. Price (eds.) 1987, *Rituals of royalty: power and ceremonial in traditional society.* Cambridge: Cambridge Un.Pr.

Clarke, P.B., & P. Byrne 1993, *Religion defined and explained.* New York: St. Martin's Press/London: The Macmillan Press.

Coppet, D. de, 1991, 'Introduction', in de Coppet 1991b: 1-10.
Coppet, D. de, (ed.) 1991b, *Understanding rituals*. London, etc.: Routledge.
Delattre, R., 1978, 'Ritual resourcefulness and cultural pluralism', in *Soundings* 61, 3: 281-302.
Doty, W.G., 1986, *Mythography: the study of myths and rituals*. Alabama: University of Alabama Press.
Douglas, M., 1970, *Purity and danger: an analysis of concepts of pollution and taboo*. Harmondsworth: Penguin Books (1966[1]).
Douglas, M., 1982[3], *Natural symbols: explorations in cosmology*. New York: Pantheon Books (1970[1], 1973[2]).
Durkheim, E., 1912, *Les formes élémentaires de la vie religieuse: le système totémique en Australie*. Paris: Alcan.
Eliade, M., (ed.) 1987, *The encyclopedia of religion*. New York: Macmillan.
Fernandez, J.W., 1971, 'Persuasions and performances: of the beast in every body ... and the metaphors of everyman', in Geertz 1971: 39-60.
Fernandez, J.W., 1977, 'The performance of ritual metaphors', in Sapir & Crocker 1977: 100-131.
Firth, R., 1951, *Elements of social organisation*. London: Watts & Co.
Geertz, C., 1966, 'Religion as a cultural system', in Banton 1966: 1-46.
Geertz, C. (ed.) 1971, *Myth, symbol, and culture*. New York: Norton.
Geertz, C., 1973, *The interpretation of cultures; selected essays*. New York: Basic Books.
Geertz, C., 1993[2], *Local knowledge: further essays in interpretive anthropology*. London: Fontana Press (1983[1]).
Gennep, A. van, 1909, *Les rites de passage; étude systematiques des rites de la port et du seuil, de l'hospitalité, de l'adoption, de la grossesse et de l'accouchement, de la naissance, de l'enfance, de la puberté, de l'initiation, de l'ordination, du couronnement, des fiançailles et du marriage, des funérailles, des saisons, etc.* Paris: Émile Nourry.
Ghosh, A., 1987, 'Tambiah on ritual', in *Contributions to Indian Sociology* 21, 1: 217-223.
Gluckman, M., & M. Gluckman 1977, 'On drama, and games and athletic contests', in Moore & Myerhoff 1977: 227-243.
Goody, J., 1961, 'Religion and ritual: the definitional problem', in *The British Journal of Sociology* 12, 1: 142-164.
Goody, J., 1977, 'Against ritual: loosely structured thought on a loosely defined subject', in Moore & Myerhoff 1977b: 25-35.
Grapard, A.G., 1991, 'Rule-governed activity vs. rule-creating activity', in *Religion* 21: 207-212.
Grimes, R.L., 1982, *Beginnings in ritual studies*. Washington (D.C.): University of America Press.
Grimes, R.L., 1987, 'Ritual studies', in Eliade 1987, vol. 12: 422-425.
Hobsbawm, E., & T. Ranger (eds.) 1993[9], *The invention of tradition*. Cambridge: Cambridge Un.Pr. (1983[1]).
Horton, R., 1960, 'A definition of religion and its uses', in *Journal of the Royal Anthropological Institute* 90: 201-226.
Horton, R., 1964, 'Ritual man in Africa', in *Africa* 34: 85-104.
Horton, R., 1972, 'Ritual man in Africa', in Lessa & Vogt 1972: 347-358 (abridged).
Jenkins, R., 1992, *Pierre Bourdieu*. London: Routledge.
Kapferer, B., 1988, *Legends of people, myths of state: violence, intolerance, and political culture in Sri Lanka and Australia*. Washington, etc.: Smithsonian Institute.

Kapferer, B., 1991[2], *A celebration of demons: exorcism and the aesthetics of healing in Sri Lanka*. Providence (R.I.)/Washington (D.C.): Berg/Smithsonian Institution Press (1983[1]).
Kertzer, D.I., 1988, *Ritual, politics, and power*. New Haven (Conn.), etc.: Yale University Press.
La Fontaine, J.S., 1985, *Initiation: ritual drama and secret knowledge across the world*. Harmondsworth: Penguin Books.
Lane, C., 1981, *The rites of rulers: ritual in industrial society—the Soviet case*. Cambridge: Cambridge Un.Pr.
Lawson, E.T., & R.N. McCauley 1990, *Rethinking religion: connecting cognition and culture*. Cambridge: Cambridge Un.Pr.
Leach, E., 1966, 'Ritualisation in man in relation to conceptual and social development', in *Philosophical Transactions of the Royal Society of London*, series B, no. 772, vol. 251: 403-408 (cited in this article as Leach 1972).
Leach, E., 1968, 'Ritual', in Shils 1968, vol. 13: 521-526.
Leach, E., 1972, 'Ritualisation in man in relation to conceptual and social development', in Lessa & Vogt 1972[3]: 333-337 (= Leach 1966).
Lessa, W.A., & E.Z. Vogt (eds.) 1972[3], *Reader in comparative religion: an anthropological approach; third edition*. New York, etc.: Harper & Row.
Lewis, G., 1980, *Day of shining red: an essay on understanding ritual*. Cambridge: CUP.
MacAloon, J.J., 1984, *Rite, drama, festival, spectacle: rehearsals towards a theory of cultural performance*. Philadelphia: Institute for the Study of Human Issues.
Mack, B.L., 1991, 'Staal's gauntlet and the queen', in *Religion* 21: 213-218.
Malinowski, B., 1948[1]/1974[2], *Magic, science and religion; and other essays*. London: Souvenir Press.
Moore, S,F., & B.G. Myerhoff 1977a, 'Secular ritual: forms and meanings', in Moore & Myerhoff 1977b: 3-24.
Moore, S.F., & B.G. Myerhoff (eds.) 1977b, *Secular ritual*. Assen: van Gorcum.
Morris, B., 1987, *Anthropology of religion: an introductory text*. Cambridge: CUP.
Myerhoff, B.G., 1977, 'We don't wrap herring in a printed page: fusion, fictions and continuity in secular ritual', in Moore & Myerhoff 1977b: 199-224.
Nadel, S.F., 1954, *Nupe religion*. London: Oxford University Press.
Oosten, J., 1990, 'Zin en macht in de studie van ritueel', in *Anthropologische Verkenningen* 9, 3: 4-15.
Parkin, D., 1991, 'Ritual as spatial direction and bodily division', in de Coppet 1991b: 11-25.
Platvoet, J.G., 1982, *Comparing religions, a limitative approach; an analysis of Akan, Para-Creole, and IFO-Sananda rites and prayers*, The Hague, etc.: Mouton.
Platvoet, J.G., 1983a, 'The study of rites in the Netherlands', in Platvoet 1983b: 177-188.
Platvoet, J.G., (ed.) 1983b, *Analysis and interpretation of rites; essays to D.J. Hoens*, The Hague: Boekencentrum (= *Nederlands Theologisch Tijdschrift* 37, 3 [July 1983] 175-277).
Platvoet, J.G., 1990, 'The definers defined: traditions in the definition of religion', in *Method & Theory in the Study of Religion* 2, 2: 180-212.

Radcliffe-Brown, A.R., 1952[1]/1971[7], *Structure and function in primitive society; essays and addresses*. London: Cohen & West.
Robbins, D., 1991, *The work of Pierre Bourdieu: recognizing society*. Milton Keynes: Open University Press.
Rosaldo Jr., R.I., 1968, 'Metaphors of hierarchy in a Mayan ritual', in *American Anthropologist* 70: 524-536; also in Lessa & Vogt 1972[3]: 359-369 (abridged).
Royal Anthropological Institute 1951, *Notes and queries on anthropology*. London: Routledge & Kegan Paul.
Sapir, J.D., & J.C. Crocker (eds.) 1977, *The social use of metaphor: essays on the anthropology of rhetoric*. Philadelphia: University of Philadelphia Press.
Schechner, R., 1977, *Essays on performance theory, 1970-1977*. New York: Drama Book Specialists.
Schechner, R., 1985, *Between theatre and anthropology*. Philadelphia: University of Philadelphia Press.
Schechner, R., & W. Appel (eds.) 1989, *By means of performance: intercultural studies of theatre and ritual*. Cambridge: Cambridge Un.Pr.
Schechner, R., & M. Schuman (eds.) 1976, *Ritual, play and performance: readings in the social sciences / theater*. New York: Seabury.
Shils, D., (ed.) 1968, *International Encyclopedia of the Social Sciences* (ed. by D. Shils), New York, etc.: Macmillan.
Smith, J.Z., 1980, 'The bare facts of ritual', in *History of Religions* 20: 112-127.
Sperber, D., & D. Wilson 1986, *Relevance: communication and cognition*, Cambridge (Mass.): Harvard University Press.
Spiro, M., 1966, 'Religion: problems of definition and explanation', in Banton 1966: 85-126.
Staal, F., 1979, 'The meaninglessness of ritual', in *Numen* 26: 2-22.
Staal, F., 1986, 'The sound of religion', in *Numen* 33: 33-64, 185-224.
Staal, F., 1989, *Rules without meaning: ritual, mantras and the human sciences*. New York: Peter Lang.
Staal, F., 1991, 'Within ritual, about ritual, and beyond', in *Religion* 21: 227-234.
Strenski, I., 1991, 'What's rite?: evolution, exchange and the big picture', in *Religion* 21: 219-225.
Sullivan, L.E., 1986, 'Sound and senses: toward a hermeneutics of performance', in *History of Religions* 26: 1-33.
Tambiah, S.J., 1968, 'The magical power of words', in *Man* 3, 2: 175-208.
Tambiah, S.J., 1973, 'Form and meaning of magical acts: a point of view', in Horton & Finnegan 1973.
Tambiah, S.J., 1979, 'A performative approach to ritual', in *Proceedings of the British Academy* 65: 113-169.
Tambiah, S.J., 1985, *Culture, thought and social action: an anthropological perspective*. Cambridge (Mass.), etc.: Harvard Un.Pr.
Turner, V.W., 1967, *The forest of symbols: aspects of Ndembu rituals*. Oxford: Clarendon Press.
Turner, V.W., 1968, *The drums of affliction: a study of religious processes among the Ndembu of Zambia*. Oxford: Clarendon Press.
Turner, V.W., 1974, *Dramas, fields and metaphors: symbolic action in human society*. Ithaca (N.Y.), etc.: Cornell Un.Pr.
Turner, V.W., 1982, *From ritual to theatre: the human seriousness of play*. New York: Performing Arts Journal Publications.

Turner, V.W., 1983, 'Foreword', in Kapferer 1991: XXI-XXVI.
Turner, V.W., & E. Turner 1978, *Image and pilgrimage in Christian culture: anthropological perspectives*. Oxford: Blackwell.
Veer, P. van der, 1994, *Religious nationalism: Hindus and Muslims in India*. Berkeley, etc.: University of California Press.
Verboven, D., 1987, 'Praxiologie en rituele analyse: epistemische opties', in *Antropologische Verkenningen* 8, 2: 1-7.
Waal-Malefijt, A.-M. de, 1968, *Religion and culture: an introduction to anthropology of religion*, New York, etc.: Macmillan.
Wijsen, F.J.S., 1993, *'There is only one God': a social-scientific and theological study of popular religion and evangelization in Sukumaland, Northwest Tanzania*. Kampen: Kok.
Zuesse, E.M., 1987, 'Ritual', in Eliade 1987, vol. 12: 405-422.

SIMILARITY AND DEMARCATION

Jan Snoek

The hypothesis

In discussing the theme 'pluralism and identity', we are dealing with different groups (pluralism) which have, and maintain, their separate identities, and thus are more or less similar, or different. The identity of a group can be maintained or stressed by demarcating the border between that group (the in-group) and a variety of other groups (the out-groups). However, the amount of attention paid to this demarcation seems to vary in relation to different out-groups. So, one of the first questions that pop up is whether there is a relation between similarity of, and demarcation between groups. I think there is, and I would, tentatively, formulate my hypothesis concerning this relation as follows:

> *The more the groups from which one wishes to distinguish oneself (the out-groups), are similar to one's own group (the in-group), the more rigidly will the distinguishing characteristics be formulated, and the more attention will be paid to these characteristics.*[1]

In other words: if there is a wish to distinguish the in-group from an out-group, then greater similarity between the two groups will stimulate a stronger demarcation by the in-group.

Support from group dynamics theory

A statement like this belongs to the domain of group dynamics. As such I have not found it stated there, but several, in that field of study, generally accepted points of view, help to make it plausible. To begin with,

> 'cohesive groups create intense pressures for conformity. Because of the attraction of the group, individuals value their group membership and are willing to conform to the group's norms and expectations. As

[1] Of course, this relation need not be symmetrical, i.e. a group B from which group A wishes to distinguish, need not feel that distinction necessary.

groups become more highly cohesive, group norms become more clearly specified, and the behaviour of group members conforms more closely to these norms. One of the ways cohesive groups enforce conformity is through greater communication. As they become more cohesive, they communicate more openly and create more explicit expectations regarding acceptable behaviour. In groups that are not very cohesive, members can sometimes express deviant views without repercussions or challenges. In a highly cohesive group, however, deviant attitudes are not acceptable, and other group members try to reform the deviant members. Those who refuse to change are ostracized.'[2]

However, this statement from Cherrington explains something related to demarcation (viz. stressing the group's more clearly specified norms) for *cohesive* groups. In other words, we have to ask whether the presence of similar groups creates cohesiveness. Here another observation from group dynamics may help, viz. that one of the sources of cohesiveness in a group are outside threats.[3] So, it would help if we could establish that more similar groups are more threatening. Again, group dynamics provides another insight that makes this plausible, viz. the so called 'realistic conflict theory', which 'maintains that intergroup conflict is caused by competition among groups over limited resources'.[4] Even though such competition is not necessary for conflict to exist,[5] it is easy to see that many groups, including religious groups, compete for members, and that the chance of loosing a member to another group is greater when the difference from that other group is smaller.

Another statement from group dynamics gives maybe even more direct support for my hypothesis. It says, in the first place, that

'by praising our own group more than others, we bolster our own self-esteem. By comparing our qualities to the qualities possessed by members of the out-group, we find evidence of our superiority.'[6]

But, secondly, and in our case more important, this is not restricted to the qualities of the persons in the groups, it holds equally for the 'products' of the groups:

'One ethnic group prides itself on its traditions and also views other group's traditions with disdain.'[7]

For religious groups, their 'product' is their particular brand of religion. How this relates to my hypothesis is easily seen when we

---

2 Cherrington 1989: 439-440.
3 Cherrington 1989: 439; Forsyth 1990: 400; Remmerswaal 1991: 127.
4 Forsyth 1990: 394.
5 Cherrington 1989: 448.
6 Forsyth 1990: 397.
7 Forsyth 1990: 405.

think of the way commercials are made. A commercial for beer, for example, will usually not stress how good cold beer in general is to satisfy your thirst on a hot summer day, but rather that this particular brand tastes better, gives a larger bottle, and yet is cheaper than any other. In other words, not the general qualities of the product, but rather those, sometimes really far less important, ones are emphasized that distinguish it from others. Now, obviously, the more similar the products of two groups are, the more importance the groups will attribute to those aspects in which their products differ, even if the general importance of these distinguishing elements is very minor. They simply have to be stressed all the time to remind both insiders and outsiders that there really is some difference and that this difference is important.

So, we see that group dynamics theory corroborates my hypotheses. To further increase its credibility I shall give some examples that illustrate it. Such examples are easy to find. The church fathers, for instance, were often more concerned with demarcating the border between 'true Christians' and heretics, than between Christians and infidels. However, I shall restrict myself here to only two examples, one that illustrates the main thesis, and another which shows what happens under extreme circumstances.

Freemasonry

My first example is the case of Freemasonry, which, as we shall see, illustrates my thesis nicely.[8] There are several texts which define what Freemasonry is. These set it off against all possible phenomena which are not Freemasonry. Besides that, however, a much larger volume of texts deals with what so called *regular* Freemasonry is, as opposed to so called *irregular* Freemasonry. As we shall see, ritual is of prime importance for both distinctions.

Shortly after the first Grand Lodge had been created in 1717 in London, it printed its *Constitutions*, as compiled by James Anderson. These contain no explicit definition of Freemasonry, but in the first 'Charge': 'Concerning GOD and RELIGION', the definition is hidden that: 'Masonry [is] the Centre of Union, and the Means of conciliating true Friendship among Persons that must have remain'd at a perpetual Distance.'[9]

---

[8] With thanks to E. Kwaadgras, curator of the collections of the Grand East of the Netherlands, for his assistance in locating the relevant publications.

[9] Anderson 1723: 50.

In 1813 the then existing two English Grand Lodges, the Premier Grand Lodge of 1717 and the Grand Lodge of the 'Antients' from 1751, merged into the United Grand Lodge of England and Wales. The Emulation Ritual, created at that occasion, states that Freemasonry is: 'a peculiar system of morality, veiled in allegory and illustrated by symbols'.[10] Probably this is the most famous definition of Freemasonry in existence, since the Emulation Ritual is still the official ritual of the English Grand Lodge.

However, Grand Lodges in other countries often use quite different definitions. The Grand East of the Netherlands, for example, uses the following:

> 'Freemasonry is the spiritual movement, born from inner urgency, which manifests itself in a continual pursuit of the development of all those qualities of mind and heart, which may elevate man and humanity to a higher spiritual and moral standard. Its application is found in the practice of the highest art of life.'[11]

All these definitions excel in vagueness. A little more instructive is the definition used by the Regular Grand Lodge of Belgium:

> 'Freemasonry is an initiation society which raises man spiritually and morally by its symbolic instruction, thus contributing to the perfection of mankind, by practising the ideals of peace, love and brotherliness.'[12]

This is parallelled by the statement by the Grand East of the Netherlands that 'it has its own working method, using symbols and rituals for expressing ideals and thoughts...'[13] And the Board of General Purpose of the Grand Lodge of England published in 1984 a leaflet entitled *What is Freemasonry*, which states that

> 'Freemasonry is one of the world's oldest secular fraternal societies ... a society of men concerned with spiritual values. Its members are taught its precepts by a series of ritual dramas, which follow ancient forms and use stonemason's customs and tools as allegorical guides.'

---

[10] The text of this definition is generally attributed to Samuel Hemming (cf., e.g., Carr 1967: 377). The definition is found at the beginning of the ritual for the second degree.

[11] *Grondwet 1917*, art. 2.1: 'Vrijmetselarij is de uit innerlijke drang geboren geestesrichting, welke zich openbaart in een voortdurend streven naar ontwikkeling van al die eigenschappen van geest en gemoed, die de mens en de mensheid kunnen opvoeren naar hoger geestelijk en zedelijk peil. Zij vindt haar toepassing in de beoefening van de hoogste levenskunst.' (in Anonymous 1990: 13).

[12] Constitutie van de Reguliere Grootloge van België, art. 2: 'De Vrijmetselarij is een inwijdingsgenootschap dat door zijn symbolisch onderricht de mens geestelijk en moreel verheft en aldus bijdraagt tot de vervolmaking van de mensheid door de toepassing van een ideaal van vrede, liefde en broederlijkheid' (in Anonymous [1993 (?)]: 35).

[13] *Grondwet 1917*, art. 3.2: 'Zij arbeidt ... op de haar eigen wijze met behulp van symbolen en ritualen als vertolking van idealen en gedachten ...' (in Anonymous 1990: 14).

Indeed, if we look for a single characteristic which separates Freemasonry (in general) from everything else, then probably the use of certain rituals for the admission of new members, based on a pattern of symbols derived from freestone masonry, would do. Besides, no one can become a Freemason without submitting himself to these rituals. In other words, the border between Freemasons and non-Freemasons is formed precisely by these rituals. For Freemasons, this is so obvious, that it seems not worth mentioning. Thus, when they try to define Freemasonry occasionally, they resort to poetic statements of widely different content. This shows how little they are in fact concerned with defining themselves as opposed to all others. Meanwhile, however, the differences in the formulation of definitions of Freemasonry, together with the strict observance of practising the required rituals, demonstrate that Freemasonry is characterised by an orthopraxis—a method, a pattern of action—while lacking an orthodoxy, a doctrine.

This orthopraxis is expressed in two ways: the rituals and the rules for the behaviour of Freemasons. These rules formed the contents of the 'charges' in Anderson's Constitutions. They were 'extracted' from the 'old manuscript constitutions' or 'Old Charges' of the Freestone masons, of which more than a hundred are known.[14] The oldest ones, the Regius Ms. and the Cooke Ms., date from about 1400.[15] Since the Grand Lodges, that emerged in other countries after 1717, usually adopted Anderson's Constitutions—if necessary translated—with only minor changes, and worked with the rituals their members had learnt at their initiation, there were originally no essential differences between the practices of Freemasons in different countries. Thus all Freemasons were recognised as such by all, and when a brother wished to visit another Lodge, wherever in the world, he would be admitted.

But even in 1720, George Payne, Grand Master of the Premier Grand Lodge, had commenced changing the rules.[16] The new 'General Regulations' were approved by Grand Lodge in 1721 and also published in Anderson's Constitutions of 1723. The last of these new regulations starts:

> 'Every Annual Grand-Lodge has an inherent Power and Authority to make new Regulations, or to alter these, for the real Benefit of this ancient Fraternity: Provided always that the old Land-Marks be carefully preserv'd ...'

---

[14] Knoop & Jones 1949: 62.

[15] Knoop, Jones & Hamer 1938.

[16] The Antients later accused the members of the Premier Grand Lodge, to whom they referred as 'Moderns', to have changed the rituals as well; this accusation is probably correct.

This introduced the concept of the 'Old Landmarks', without pointing them out, however. At first, no one seems to have bothered, but since the 'Old Landmarks' apparently comprise the criteria for what can be regarded Freemasonry proper, later generations felt a want for a precise enumeration. As a result, many collections of 'Old Landmarks' have been compiled since, the first and most authoritative list being that of 25 items, composed by Mackey in 1858.[17] No two lists are identical, however.

The subject became urgent only when 'in 1877 the Grand Orient of France in the expressive phrase of Anatole France "abolished God"'. Only then 'it first became necessary to consider whether organizations claiming to be Masonic were entitled to be counted as such'.[18] The next year the Grand Lodge of England withdrew its recognition from the Grand Orient of France, which thus became the first irregular Grand Lodge.[19] This implied a.o. that visiting a Lodge of one of these Grand Lodges by a member of a Lodge of the other Grand Lodge was no longer permitted.

Problems of this kind had occurred before, but had always been solved peacefully. For example, the Dutch Grand Lodge had, since its reconstitution in 1756, faced the problem that it was impossible for a Dutch citizen to comply with both of two masonic requirements: (1) that of taking the full traditional oath, including the imprecations, with the right hand on the Bible, and (2) that of promising in the same oath to obey the law of their country, since Dutch law forbade swearing, i.e. vowing imprecations with the right hand on the Bible. In 1770 the Grand Lodge of England recognized this contrariety and accepted that in Holland the oath was replaced by a promise.[20]

From 1878 on, however, the phenomenon of irregular Freemasonry did exist, and it has caused a lot of writing. Obviously, the Grand Orient of France had transgressed the 'Old Landmarks' so much too far that, even though no one could tell precisely what they were, it was obvious that they were violated. This, of course,

---

[17] Mackey 1966: 559, sub. Landmarks.

[18] Roscoe Pound 1956: 49.

[19] The relation between recognition and regularity is in fact more complicated. See, e.g., Ligou [1974: 1.086/7] sub. Régulier, Régularité.

[20] 'Que la Sublime Grand-Loge de la Maçonnerie séante à Londres sachant que les Maçons, plus que les autres hommes, doivent se conformer aux loi de leur pays n'a pu et ne peut désaprouver l'altération qu'à cet effet la dite Grand-Loge Nationale a cru devoir adopter dans notre formule d'obligation.' Agreement between the English Grand Master, Henry Sommerset, Duke of Beaufort, and the Dutch Grand Master, Baron van Boetzelaer of March 2nd, 1770, quoted in Van Loo 1967: 25-26.

asked for a guideline on how to decide in such cases in the future. But it was not an easy matter. It took until 1929 before the Grand Lodges of England, Scotland and Ireland set up identical 'Basic Principles for Grand Lodge Recognition', enumerating eight criteria to which each Grand Lodge should comply in order to be recognized. In 1949 the Grand Lodge of England formulated the 'Aims and Relationships of the Craft' in order to further clarify the 'Basic Principles'. I regard it worth mentioning the eight criteria from the 'Basic Principles' in full, since they show clearly that here again, orthopraxis rather than orthodoxy is involved, while most are of ritual nature. They are:

1. Regularity of origin: i.e. each Grand Lodge shall have been established lawfully by a duly recognized Grand Lodge or by three or more regularly constituted Lodges.
2. That a belief in the Grand Architect of the Universe and His revealed will shall be an essential qualification for membership.
3. That all Initiates shall take their Obligation on or in full view of the open Volume of the Sacred Law, by which is meant the revelation from above which is binding on the conscience of the particular individual who is being initiated.
4. That the membership of the Grand Lodge and individual Lodges shall be composed exclusively of men; and that each Grand Lodge shall have no Masonic intercourse of any kind with mixed Lodges or bodies which admit women to membership.
5. That the Grand Lodge shall have sovereign jurisdiction over the Lodges under its control; i.e. that it shall be a responsible, independent, self-governing organization, with sole and undisputed authority over the Craft or Symbolic Degrees (Entered Apprentice, Fellow Craft, and Master Mason) within its Jurisdiction; and shall not in any way be subject to, or divide such authority with, a Supreme Council or other Power claiming any control or supervision over those degrees.
6. That the three Great Lights of Freemasonry (namely, the Volume of the Sacred Law, the Square, and the Compasses) shall always be exhibited when the Grand Lodge or its subordinate Lodges are at work, the chief of these being the Volume of the Sacred Law.
7. That the discussion of religion and politics within the Lodge shall be strictly prohibited.
8. That the principles of the Antient Landmarks, customs, and usages of the Craft shall be strictly observed.[21]

These criteria form not a list of the Old Landmarks, as will be clear from the last one, though most of them would probably be considered as such by most Freemasons. The selection in fact reflects the cases that had to be dealt with. The Grand Orient of France was, in 1929, by far not the only irregular Grand Lodge. Some had been

---

[21] Anonymous 1993: 850.

excluded because they had replaced the Volume of the Sacred Law by a book with blank pages, others because they admitted women (either only women or both men and women), others again because they had taken overt political position, etc.

As a rule, the irregular Grand Lodges do not acknowledge the validity of the 'Basic Principles', of course. But what is more, some claim that they *are* regular, or even the really regular one. For example, a publication of the Grand Orient of France states verbatim:

> 'On est Franc-Maçon quand on respecte les Constitutions d'Anderson; on ne l'est qu'à ce prix. ... Les Loges françaises qui se groupèrent après 1773 dans le G.O.D.F. ont toujours été fidèles à la pensée et aux Constitutions d'Anderson.'[22]

However, if we compare 'Article premier' of the 'Constitution' of the G.O.D.F. (ibid.) with the first 'Charge' of Andersons Constitutions,[23] it becomes clear at once that there is a different attitude here with respect to 'God and Religion'. Be that as it may. This particular point is not of a ritual nature and thus of little concern to us now. But other ones, like taking the obligation on the Volume of the Sacred Law and the three Great Lights of Freemasonry being present in all Lodges at work, obviously are. And the 'Basic Principles' have been adopted, since the British Grand Lodges formulated them in 1929, by virtually all regular Grand Lodges all over the world.

Clearly then, Freemasons are much more concerned with the demarcation between regular and irregular Freemasonry—and do

---

[22] Anonymous [1979].

[23] G.O.D.F.: 'La Franc-Maçonnerie, institution essentiellement philantropique, philosophique et progressive, a pour objet la recherche de la vérité, l'étude de la morale et la pratique de la solidarité; elle travaille à l'amélioration matérielle et morale, au perfectionnement intellectuel et social de l'humanité. Elle a pour principes la tolérance mutuelle, le respect des autres et de soi-même, la liberté absolue de conscience. Considérant les conceptions métaphysiques comme étant du domaine exclusif de l'appréciation individuelle de ses membres, elle se refuse à toute affirmation dogmatique. Elle a pour devise: Liberté, Egalité, Fraternité.' (Anonymous [1979])
Anderson: 'On God and Religion: A Mason is oblig'd, by his Tenure, to obey the moral Law; and if he rightly understands the Art, he will never be a stupid Atheist, nor an irreligious Libertine. But though in ancient Times Masons were charg'd in every Country to be of the Religion of that Country or Nation, whatever it was, yet 'tis now thought more expedient only to oblige them to that Religion in which all Men agree, leaving their particular Opinions to themselves; that is, to be good Men and true, or Men of Honour and Honesty, by whatever Denominations or Persuasions they may be distinguish'd; whereby Masonry becomes the Centre of Union, and the Means of conciliating true Friendship among Persons that must have remain'd at a perpetual Distance.' (Anderson 1723: 50)

so much more precisely and explicitly—than with the demarcation between Freemasonry and something else. Furthermore, both borders are defined, at least partly, by ritual behaviour. The border between Freemasonry and non-Freemasonry is demarcated by the initiation ritual for an Entered Apprentice, which is a far more elaborate (ritual) practice than the (ritual and other) practices defining the border between regular and irregular Freemasonry. But the latter got much more attention as demarcating device, and are discussed and repeated time and again.[24]

Also, regular Freemasons often don't like to be grouped together with irregular ones as Freemasons; they usually regard themselves as the only true Freemasons, with exclusion of the irregular ones. Irregular Freemasons, on the contrary, don't make the distinction, and from the point of cultural studies, it would be a gross mistake to ignore them. After all, e.g. the Grand Orient of France is by far the largest Grand Lodge in France and a not negligible element in the cultural history of that country.

It seems then that the case of Freemasonry supports my hypothesis.

Pentecostal groups

To which one of two out-groups a given in-group is more similar can, to some degree, be objectively established by an outsider. Sometimes it is even obvious. The importance attributed to this smaller or larger similarity, however, is a subjective entity, which can shift in the course of time. Thus, 'similarity' is not only an objectively measurable entity, but also a phenomenon, subjectively experienced by the members of the group that wishes to distinguish itself. This perceived similarity can be influenced by changes in external circumstances. For example, a group with many members and a sound economic position may wish to distinguish itself sharply from a group that it experiences as similar-yet-different, whereas the same group may, when membership and economic position decrease, search for cooperation with precisely that same other group, now putting the differences in an other perspective. Under these circumstances, the experienced similarity shifts to the extreme end of the similarity-axis, the point of identity. Obviously, that process is accompanied by a loss of felt need to distinguish

[24] In the Netherlands most recently in: [de Boer Lzn.] 1992.

one's own group from the other. On the contrary, now the similarity is stressed.

An example of this process form the Pentecostal groups in the Netherlands, as described by Van der Laan.[25] From 1907 G.R. Polman and his wife were the first to lead the Pentecostal movement in the Netherlands. Polman did not intend to create a separate church, but rather to reform all existing churches. However, several churches regarded the movement as demonic. This forced the Dutch Pentecostal movement to form their own congregation, the *Pinkstergemeente* ('Pentecostal congregation'). In the 1920s, the *Gemeente des Heeren* ('Congregation of the Lord'), led by J. Orsel and later by A. Otten, split off this main group. It had a highly exclusive character. They claimed to be the only true believers, rejecting both science (especially medical treatment) and churches (including the other Pentecostal movements). It remained separated until this day.

When Polman resigned in 1930, he was succeeded by P. van der Woude, P.Klaver and N. Vetter. Rivalry between the three created factions in the *Pinkstergemeente*, but World War II brought them together again. In 1941 they formed the *Verenigde Pinkstergemeenten in Nederland* ('United Pentecostal congregations in the Netherlands'), which changed its name, first in 1944, and again in 1947, to *Volle Evangelie Gemeenten* ('Full Gospel Congregations'), and finally in 1952 to *Broederschap van Volle Evangelie Gemeenten in Nederland* ('Fraternity of Full Gospel Congregations in the Netherlands'). In 1960 it became an official church: *Broederschap van Pinkstergemeenten (in Nederland)* ('Fraternity of Pentecostal Congregations [in the Netherlands]').

After 1950 this group grew strongly, but simultaneously several factions emerged. Some of them were the result of the appearance of prayer-healers such as Tommy Lee Osborn or other charismatic leaders. Johan Maasbach, for example, created his own *Volle Evangelie Zending* ('Full Gospel Mission'), in 1968 renamed to *Johan Maasbach Wereldzending* ('Johan Maasbach World Mission'), which still flourishes.

One of these groups, *Stromen van Kracht* ('Streams of Power'), taught that speaking in tongues was not an action of the Holy Ghost, but of the believer. This was quite foreign to the teachings of other Pentecostal groups. In 1957, its leader, K.Hoekendijk, started celebrating the Last Supper and baptizing by immersion. This provoked not only a complete rejection by the churches, but also a

---

[25] The data in this paragraph are taken from Van der Laan 1990. I thank Jan Platvoet for drawing my attention to this publication.

schism within the group. W. Verhoef started a new movement of independent local congregations, 'free from whatever yoke of slavery and led by the Holy Ghost'; but *Stromen van Kracht* remained the more important of the two. Several local groups within *Stromen van Kracht* developed into independent congregations which, in 1972, united into the *Federatie van Volle Evangelie Gemeenten* ('Federation of Full Gospel Congregations'). In 1978, it merged with the *Volle Evangelie Gemeenschap in Nederland.*[26]

From *Stromen van Kracht* emerged yet another movement. In 1960 I. Roose took the initiative for the Beukestein conferences, which were held until 1968. They became the centre of a movement that would be associated with the periodical *Kracht van Omhoog* ('Power from Above'). The doctrine of the group was formulated by J. van den Brink in order to defend the practice of exorcism in the Beukestein conferences. This doctrine was rather controversial, also within the Pentecostal movements and isolated the *Kracht van Omhoog* group. Part of it moved to a milder attitude and in 1987 merged with the *Volle Evangelie Gemeenten [in] Nederland.*

In 1966 the *Broederschap van Pinkstergemeenten* was reorganised. As a reaction, several congregations left the organisation and formed the *Federatie van Volle Evangelie Gemeenten* ('Federation of Full Gospel Congregations'), but it was dissolved soon.

In 1969 another movement was founded: the *Volle Evangelie Gemeenschap* ('Full Gospel Community'), which was more successful. In 1972, eleven congregations from *Stromen van Kracht* created a new group, which named itself again *Federatie van Volle Evangelie Gemeenten* ('Federation of Full Gospel Congregations'). After a few years these two groups (*Volle Evangelie Gemeenschap* and *Federatie van Volle Evangelie Gemeenten*) proved so similar that they merged in 1978. The resulting group was called *Volle Evangelie Gemeenten in Nederland* ('Full Gospel Congregations in the Netherlands') to which was later added *en België* ('and Belgium'). It was registered as a church in 1980.

Van der Laan also describes the Pentecostal movements that came to the Netherlands in the wake of the proclamation of the independence of Indonesia and some others, but the data presented above should be enough to illustrate my hypothesis. Even though Van der Laan remarks that about half of the Pentecostal congregations is independent of any organisation, we see in those groups that are organized a complex process of splitting and joining. Sometimes a leader emerged who proclaimed ideas, incompatible

---

[26] According to Van der Laan, but this should probably be the *Volle Evangelie Gemeenten in Nederland* ('Full Gospels Congregations in the Netherlands').

with those of the group he belonged to, and a split was the result. At other moments, other leaders searched for cooperation and even merging, depending on how different, or similar, 'the others' were felt to be. This whole process took place in an area on the 'similarity axis', close to the extreme end of identity.

We see that all means available, ritual as well as others, were used to mark the distinction between groups. It might be a dogmatic issue, as stated by the leader of a group. As we saw, the leaders of the group *Stromen van Kracht* taught that speaking in tongues was not an action of the Holy Ghost, but of the believer. This was the issue that distinguished this group from the others. But such ideas alone seem hardly sufficient. They must be proclaimed in order to function as separators. Thus this group, as well as others, had its own periodical, called *Stromen van Kracht*, and the group can in fact be referred to only as the one whose members read this periodical. Indeed, the reading of the periodical was not the important thing; being a subscriber was. And when the issues of the periodical were overtly displayed in the houses of the members of the group, we are dealing with a kind of distinguishing behaviour that, I think, could well be referred to as ritual.

Similarly, the periodical *Kracht van Omhoog* formed the binding force of another group, which, however, had also another distinguishing feature which might well be regarded ritual: the Beukestein conferences. Annual meetings of all the members of the group had both a high potentiality for consolidating the group and for separating them from others. I think it is fair to compare this with the well known phenomenon that certain Roman Catholic parishes undertake a pilgrimage to a certain place each year. And we would not hesitate to refer to that as ritual behaviour. Other Dutch Pentecostal groups had—and have—such yearly meetings as well.

A last example of ritual behaviour as a marker of distinction which I want to mention is that of celebrating the Last Supper and baptizing by immersion, practised by the group of Hoekendijk. This separated it from the other Pentecostal groups. So I think that we can come to the conclusion that ritual behaviour functions as one of the ways to mark the distinction between the Pentecostal groups.

Membership of more than one group

It may be claimed that there are certain examples that form a rebuttal of my theses. One such example are the Australian tribes, who united in the performance of certain rituals. Another would be Polish refugees, living in Paris, going to the Mass together with French Catholics. Or another again, two councillors, members of two different political parties, who fight each other in the morning in the city council, but fully cooperate without friction in their masonic lodge in the evening.

I do not think these cases rebut my hypothesis. What we have here are examples of the fact that everyone is always a member of more than one group. The context of a specific occasion determines the group code according to which one should behave at that particular time. A French Catholic may well attend Mass on a Sunday morning and be a member of an extreme right wing group, demonstrating against the presence of foreigners in France, in the afternoon. During the Mass, all present are members of the same Roman Catholic Church, but that is a different context from the demonstration against immigrants.

So, when we discuss similarity versus demarcation, we have to compare 'comparable' groups. Indeed, the situations mentioned can be regarded as a confirmation of my hypothesis, when we realize that the conflicts, requiring demarcation, appear when the groups are more comparable, whereas no conflict exists between groups that are hardly comparable. In this case, French nationality can be compared with Polish nationality, but nationality cannot be compared with church membership. Thus, the French may have a problem with the Polish immigrants, based on nationalistic feelings, but, though they may have problems with the Roman Catholic Church personally, they will not have these problems as Frenchmen, or as Poles. The differences in the nationality context are not felt to involve the context of church membership in this case. The identical church membership, therefore, does not make the French feel more similar to the Poles, and, the other way round, their different nationalities do not separate them as participants at the Mass. It is clear, however, from the case described by Ter Haar in this volume, that the factors 'nationality' and 'church membership' are not always kept apart. Their independence in this case is, therefore, not an objective reality, but one that is subjectively chosen; and it is not even an obvious choice.

In fact, this point of membership of multiple groups is a different theoretical issue. As it requires a separate treatment, I shall not go into here.

Recapitulation and conclusions

What we have seen can now be represented graphically as follows:

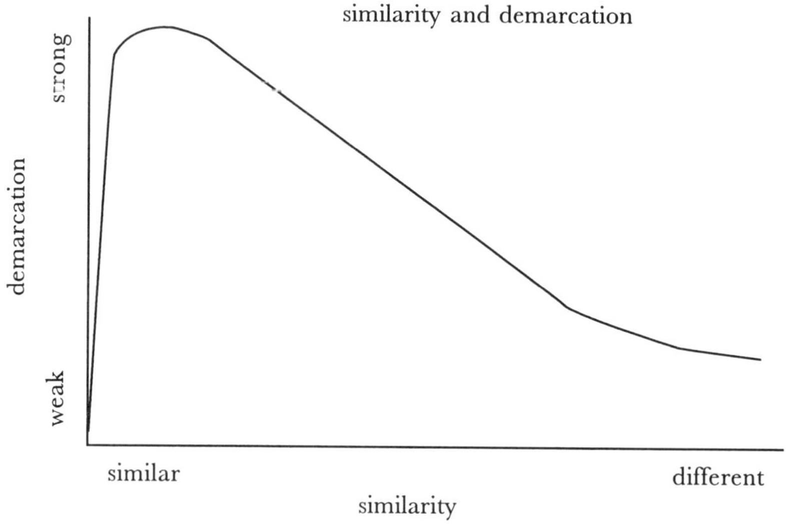

This figure should not be interpreted in a quantitative manner. The precise shape of the curve cannot be given. Neither dare I say whether the demarcation, when similarity decreases, finally goes to zero or remains at a low but constant level.

What it shows is what we have seen in the examples, viz. that, if a group has the wish to distinguish itself from another group, then, over a significant part of the similarity axis, demarcation increases with increasing (objective) similarity—in accordance with my hypothesis, formulated at the beginning of this text—but that, when (especially perceived) similarity approaches identity, demarcation sharply drops to zero.

References

[Anderson, J.], 1723, *The Constitutions of the Free-Masons*. London (= quoted from the facsimile edition, introduced by Lionel Vibert, London 1923: Bernard Quaritch Limited).

Anonymous, [1979], *Le Grand Orient de France*. Paris: Grand Orient de France (= leaflet).

Anonymous, 1984, *What is Freemasonry*. London: The Board of General Purpose of the Grand Lodge of England (= leaflet).

Anonymous, 1990, *Grondwet voor de Orde van Vrijmetselaren onder het Grootoosten der Nederlanden*, formulated in 1917, quotations translated by me from the edition of 1990. 's-Gravenhage: Orde van Vrijmetselaren onder het Grootoosten der Nederlanden.

Anonymous, 1993, *Masonic Year Book for 1993-94*, London: United Grand Lodge of England.

Anonymous, [1993 (?)], *De traditionele en reguliere Vrijmetselarij*. Brussel: Reguliere Grootloge van België.

[Boer Lzn., B. de], 1992, 'Commentaar: de essentie", in *Thoth* 1992, 2: 47-48.

Carr, H. (ed.), 1967[2], *The collected 'Prestonian Lectures' 1925-1960*. London: The Quatuor Coronati Lodge, No. 2076 (1965[1]).

Cherrington, D.J., 1989, *Organizational behavior: the management of individual and organizational performance*, Boston etc.: Allyn and Bacon.

Forsyth, D.R., 1990[2], *Group dynamics*. Pacific Grove (Cal.): Brooks/Cole (1983[1]).

Knoop, D., & G.P. Jones, 1949, *The genesis of Freemasonry*. Manchester: Manchester University Press.

Knoop, D., G.P. Jones, & D. Hamer 1938, *The two earliest Masonic Mss.*. Manchester: Manchester University Press.

Laan, C. van der, 1990, 'Historisch overzicht', in *Religieuze Bewegingen in Nederland* no 20: 7-28.

Loo, P.J. van, 1967, *Geschiedenis van de orde van Vrijmetselaren onder het Grootoosten der Nederlanden*. [Den Haag]: Ritus en Tempelbouw.

Ligou, D., (dir.), [1974], *Dictionnaire universel de la Franc-Maçonnerie*. tome 2 France [Paris (?)]: Editions de Navarre et Editions du Prisme.

Mackey, A.G., 1966[3], *Encyclopedia of Freemasonry, revised and enlarged by R.I. Clegg*. New York: no publisher (= edition Macoy; 1858[1], 1946[2]).

Remmerswaal, J., 1991[11], *Groepsdynamika I: inleiding*. Baarn: H. Nelissen. (1975[1]).

Roscoe Pound, M.W., 1956, *Grand Lodge recognition*. No place of publication: no publisher.

RITUAL AND IDENTITY IN ABORIGINAL AUSTRALIA

Wouter Belier

Introduction

Studies of ritual demarcations between socially and culturally divergent groups, presuppose such demarcations, either explicitly or implicitly. On the one hand, these studies deal with the internal relations within Western society, and relations between the dominant culture and subcultures of minorities stemming from non-Western societies. On the other hand, they also deal with the external relations between Western and non-Western cultures. These studies, of their very nature, are concerned with phenomena of a highly complex nature. The coincidence of differences in political power, different positions on the social-economic ladder, and developments arising from different religious-cultural systems, makes this a very difficult field of study.

For this reason then, I intend to focus on the intercultural relations in one, non-Western 'field of ethnological study' (FES). This needs some clarification perhaps. The term was coined by De Josselin de Jong, although the theoretical concept had existed for some time.[1] In his inaugural lecture in 1935, De Josselin de Jong presented his definition of what such a Field is, as follows.

> 'By this term we mean certain areas of the earth's surface with a population whose culture appears to be sufficiently homogeneous and unique to form a separate object of ethnological study, and which at the same time apparently reveals sufficient local shades of differences to make internal comparative research worthwhile.'[2]

The somewhat arbitrary confines of such a FES are determined both by homogeneity (separate object) and heterogeneity (internal comparative research), and in this context De Josselin de Jong suggests that the Australian Aboriginal cultures are a fine example. The concepts of culture and of intercultural demarcations, however, are also very vague, allowing several levels of in- and exclusion. It is quite possible, therefore, to discern several cultures within one FES.

---

[1] Cf. Mauss (1909: 133): 'province ethnographique'.
[2] De Josselin de Jong 1977a: 167f.

This last statement is easily reconcilable with the Australian Aboriginal *emic* perception of reality, in that many tribes discern highly divergent cultures within their surroundings. This paper is, in fact, an endorsement of that *emic* perception, and my purpose is to take a close look at the process of the religious, social and individual identities emerging in intercultural or intertribal situations. What kind of parameters are, or were, used by the participants of small cultural units to distinguish themselves from others? What role do, or did, their rituals play in this context? My aim is to answer those questions on the basis of two classical studies. The first contains a description of Murngin society in Arnhem Land by Warner, and the second of Arunta society in Central Australia by Spencer and Gillen. From each I will use data to describe how at the time of the fieldwork, the Murngin and Arunta viewed their identities at the tribal, local and individual levels, and how they expressed the borderlines of their cultures in supralocal rituals, warfare, trade, 'magic' and languages. These findings will be compared with those of two authorities in the field of Aboriginal Australian studies, namely Elkin and Berndt, and in my concluding section I will present a number of proposals.

Murngin identity

At the 'tribal' level

Between 1926 and 1929, W. Lloyd Warner made two trips to an area in the north-eastern part of Arnhem Land. The materials he collected were published in several journals and formed the basis for his 1937 study entitled: *A black civilization: a social study of an Australian tribe.* The black civilization referred to here is that of the Murngin. Warner used the term Murngin in two ways. In one meaning it referred to several tribes in the northern and eastern part of Arnhem Land, 'which may be referred to collectively as the Murngin'[3]; in another meaning he used it in a somewhat stricter sense. Warner's study concerned a combination of eight different tribes, of which the Murngin was the most important, hence his reference to the 'Murngin and surrounding people'[4], thereby distinguishing the Murngin tribe from the other seven.[5] Warner's map of

---

[3] Warner 1937: 3.
[4] Warner 1937: 15.
[5] The other tribes are the following: Yaernungo, Burera, Barlamomo, Djinba, Ritarngo, Yandjinung and Dai.

the area, seems to suggest that there are clear demarcation lines between the tribes.[6]

To the participants, however, this division into eight clearly defined tribal areas was completely without relevance. Clan members from different tribes intermarried or competed on the same matrimonial market and, what is more, Warner's list of clans which were supposed to prefer each other as marriage partners, also mentions clans from different tribes, e.g. members of the Birkili clan (from the Murngin tribe) had a preference for members of the Perango clan (from the Yaernungo tribe), whilst members of the Bringel clan (from the Ritarngo tribe) tended to direct their matrimonial ambitions more towards the Mandelpui clan (from the Yandjinung tribe).[7] The names used for the moieties were largely intertribal.[8] The Mandjikai language group comprised clans from the Murngin tribe, in strict terms, as well as clans from the Yaernungo and the Burera tribes.[9] Several rituals were intertribal and membership of the moiety was a criterion for participation. Tribal membership was of no relevance, indeed Warner suggested that : 'The tribe is almost a non-existent unit among these people'.[10] The term Murngin was more or less arbitrary too[11], and Warner referred to the tribes in his study as 'very weak social units, and when measured by the ordinary definitions of what constitutes a tribe fail almost completely.'[12] The tribe was not a belligerent group[13] and it enforced no laws.[14] Tribal clan membership in regions inhabited by two or more tribes was ambiguous, in the sense that some clans considered themselves to be members of two tribes, and the same was also true of clans situated more in the centre of the tribal area.[15] In this respect, we can perhaps make a functional distinction; in some situations a clan might be considered to belong to one particular tribe, whilst in other situations it might claim kinship to another tribe. The Yandjinung, for instance, regarded some clans as belonging to the Murngin, and the Murngin regarded those same clans as belonging to the Yandjinung. And, to confound the matter still further, members of those clans might sometimes even look upon themselves as belonging to the Yandjinung and sometimes to the Yaernungo![16]

[6] Warner 1937: 40.
[7] Warner 1937: 28.
[8] Warner 1937: 29.
[9] Warner 1937: 34.
[10] Warner 1937: 9.
[11] Warner 1937: 15, n.2.
[12] Warner 1937: 35.
[13] Warner 1937: 9, 35.
[14] Warner 1937: 9.
[15] Warner 1937: 35.

There were no clearly defined tribal units apparent in Warner's account, and there was no particular tribal identity. Tribal members did not think of themselves as being Murngin or Yaernungo etc.

At the local level

Identity established itself at the local level. Tribal membership was non-specific, whereas clan membership was a very clear concept. The clan was an exogamous, patrilineal group, living within a well-defined territorial area, and the totems were its religious expressions. The totems constituted the clan's identity—they, together with the sources in which the totems live, family ancestors and the living[17], made it what it is. The clans

> 'are the largest units of solidarity, and open conflict never occurs within them.... It is through his clan that a man establishes his totemic relations and identifies himself with the sacred world by virtue of a mystical experience of his father.'[18]

Membership of a clan was the most important reference for social identity. The approximately sixty clans were divided into two moieties, the Yiritja and the Dua, and nearly all the tribes classified by Warner as Murngin, generally use those same terms, with only one exception. This subdivision into Yiritja and Dua is the most radical principle of classification. Members of one clan might assist in performing another clan's rituals, provided the members of both clans belonged to the same moiety. Totemistic dances representing animals which did not belong to one's own clan, for instance, might be performed on condition that those animals were the totemic animals of a clan within the same moiety.[19] In many rituals, the only difference Warner refers to was that between Yiritja and Dua, with the exception of the burial rites. In some other exceptional cases the opposition was neutralized.[20]

The most important reference for social identity was thus a local one : i.e. the clan and its religious incarnation, the totem. Because the clan belonged to one of the moieties, local identity was incorporated into a supralocal structure.

---

[16] Warner 1937: 36.
[17] Warner 1937: 16.
[18] Warner 1937: 5.
[19] Warner 1937: 272.
[20] Warner 1937: 422, 424, 427.

At the individual level

Individuals did not simply derive their identity from clan or moiety membership, an intergroup label, so to speak. Members differentiated among themselves even within these groups. The higher the individual's social status, the higher his religious status. Through submission to certain *rites de passage*, men climbed the age-grade ladder[21]: in the first place the circumcision, followed by observance of the lower totems and finally the higher totems. Being the instigator of a blood feud and the father of many children increased a man's ordinary status in the secular family life, whilst authority to set foot on certain parts of the sacral ground and to participate in certain rituals increased his ritual status; under normal circumstances, these categories were, or were supposed to be, inter-dependent, i.e. a man could not attain the one without the other.[22]

Conclusion

One conclusion must be that identity in Murngin society was a local affair, the most important references being : 1) the clan; 2) a man's place in family life; and 3) his status in the age-grade system. Because 2) and 3) were supposed to be inter-dependent, or inter-related, and because clan and totem were inseparable, social and individual identity was pervaded with religious conceptions.

Murngin cultural borders

In this section, my aim is to describe the way in which differences between tribes and local groups were defined. Were rituals important for the demarcation of the borderlines? Was any other parameter used? To answer these questions I will examine in particular the situations in which culturally regulated supra-local encounters took place—i.e. those of rituals, war, trade and magic.

Supralocal rituals

The great *Gunabibi*, *Djungguan* and *Narra* totemistic ceremonials attracted participants from within a radius of several hundred miles or more.[23] The *Djungguan* ritual was a circumcision ritual of an

---

[21] Warner 1937: 124.
[22] Warner 1937: 115.
[23] Warner 1937: 111, 145.

interlocal character[24], as distinct from the *Gunabibi* ceremony which drew people from a wide area.[25] Warner wrote of a recently introduced ritual known as the *Ulmark*—again an age-grading ceremony, similar to the *Djungguan* and the *Gunabibi*—and to which members of others clans were also invited.[26] The interval between two *Djungguan* rituals might be so long, that a short interim circumcision ceremony, known as the *Marndiella*, was performed. Warner describes this ceremony but gives no information about the participants. The totemistic *Narra* rituals were also supralocal[27] and belonged to two mythological cycles, the *Wawilak* and the *Djungkao*, which tell the story of two women who travelled around the country, creating its scenery. The clans were given fixed places and became related to one another at a mythological level.

> 'The great rituals like the *Gunabibi* and *Ulmark*, which bring together, from widely separated clans and tribes, people who often have old scores unsettled and are ready to burst into open conflict, function as organizing units of these people during the period of the ritual.'[28]

War

War was a very important activity among the Murngin, the warring party being the clan and not the tribe. The primary causes were blood feuds or rivalries about women. An implicit result of this rivalry was that war between clans belonging to the same moiety was most common, with rivalries fought out on the matrimonial battle field being particularly fierce. According to Warner, war stood in direct opposition to ceremony.[29] The great ceremonials served to strengthen the solidarity between clans and tribes spread over a wide area, whilst war tended to increase the sense of solidarity within the clans themselves.

> 'Since both traits are necessary to the tribe's social organization, a nice periodical balance has been struck; at one period ceremonialism controls the people's activities, and later war is uppermost in the relations of the local groups.'[30]

For the Murngin, there were six kinds of armed conflict, and each conflict had its own name and its own code of behaviour. Conflict might arise between individuals in the camp or there might be a

---

[24] Warner 1937: 238, 250.
[25] Warner 1937: 280, 289, 292.
[26] Warner 1937: 304, 308.
[27] Warner 1937: 337, 352.
[28] Warner 1937: 382.
[29] Warner 1937: 145.
[30] Warner 1937: 146.

nighttime raid for which the whole clan was held responsible, or there might be a more overt surprise attack. There were also three kinds of battle between groups of warriors, and the fight itself could be waged between two clans or between regional combinations of clans. Each of the Murngin tribes had ritualized these forms of conflict in their own way.

Trade

Trade was also a form of supralocal contact. Trading products, such as stone spear heads, red ochre, pipe clay and *ranga* string, were carried over hundreds of miles, passing through the hands of many tribes along the way.[31] The relation between *waku* and *gawel* (i.e. ego and mother's brother) was central to this trading element. The *gawel* needed not actually be the real mother's brother, because the relationship was a purely classificatory one. Moreover, the mother's brother's son's son was also *gawel* to ego. The web of the *waku—gawel* relationship, therefore, was very extensive.[32] A reciprocal relationship with someone far away added to one's prestige.[33] Within another relationship web (*mari—kutara*, i.e. ego—mother's mother, mother's mother's brother), mainly ritual objects were exchanged. Both relationship networks stimulated intertribal economic activities.[34]

Magic

Magical conceptions present us with supralocal relations at a conceptual level. There were no magicians among the Murngin (in the narrow sense of the word) of the north, or among the Yaernungo, although the magician was very much a part of Murngin society in the south of the country, as he was also in the tribes to the west.[35] All tribes shared the same ideas about magic, but were believed to differ in their capacity to use it. 'It is analogous to knowing the effects of heavy artillery but not possessing it.'[36] Members of the clans of the northern Murngin and the Yaernungo, could ask the southern and western clans for assistance and treatment, although this would be unusual.[37] A person who fell ill as a result of a magic

---

[31] Warner 1937: 84.
[32] Cf. the scheme given by Warner 1937: 48.
[33] Warner 1937: 84, 134.
[34] Warner 1937: 135.
[35] Warner 1937: 183.
[36] Warner 1937: 213.
[37] Warner 1937: 213.

spell, would be treated in the south by a white magician[38] and in the north by means of a totemic ritual.[39]

Language

Religious concepts, therefore, did not operate very well as instruments of group demarcation, and we may in fact wonder if there were any other parameters available at all that may help us in the task. Warner points to the great variety of languages within the small local groups.[40] The language of each clan was indicated by a name 'that defines the language spoken by this people as different from that of all other clans.'[41] According to *emic* criteria, each clan spoke a different language and a separate language was sometimes even ascribed to both moieties. The Yiritja moiety spoke the Ko-par-ping-u language and the Dua moiety the Djam-bar-ping-u language. And here Warner faces a problem :

> 'Actually, vocabularies gathered by the author show no difference between the two so-called languages. Language, however, is a native criterion—the final test—used to differentiate local groups.'[42]

The latter subdivision was not used by all Murngin groups and at the empirical level one often found regional and dialectical variations which were extremely difficult to classify. In fact, adjoining clans might sometimes belong, although not necessarily, to the same tribes. The relation between identity and language was an important one at the conceptual level. Four Murngin clans (Warumeri, Wangurri, Wulkara en Gwiyamil) referred to themselves as the speakers of the Man-dji-kai language-group. In reality, however, the languages of these four clans differed greatly and every clan apparently claimed to have its own distinctive language, although 'they all insist that these languages are similar, and distinct and separate from those of all other clans.'[43] According to Warner, this was a rationalization and 'once again a use of the linguistic criterion which the native feels he must have to separate peoples as his own or as different.'[44] It could happen that the Kolpa clan of the Yaernungo tribe and the Wallamungo clan of the Burera tribe, both professed to be members of the Mandjikai group, and although they claimed to speak closely related languages they

[38] Warner 1937: 200 ff.
[39] Warner 1937: 217 ff.
[40] Warner 1937: 9.
[41] Warner 1937: 16.
[42] Warner 1937: 30.
[43] Warner 1937: 34.
[44] Warner 1937: 34.

could not understand each other at all. This confirms the symbolic character of linguistic borders and demarcations. Linguistic variation was a very important marker, 'all the clans consider themselves linguistically distinct, and members of the two moieties believe they speak different dialects.'[45] This relationship between clan and language was also evident at the mythological level, witness the Wawilak women in Murngin stories as they travelled around the country, crossing tribal borders and speaking the different languages of the various clans.[46] Yurlungur was believed to have conversed with some totemistic snakes; Yurlungur and the snakes identify themselves in relation to their own specific languages. We may conclude that totem, clan and language were directly related to one another.[47] The need for *Djungguan* initiates to learn a ritual totemic language, also illustrates the importance of language as an instrument of demarcation.[48]. And participants in the *Ulmark* ritual, used a kind of native pidgin, the *kidjin*, which was not the lingua franca of the tribe reserved for ritual use only. The secular language in the coastal areas was a kind of pidgin Malay.[49]

Conclusion

There seems little doubt, therefore, that intertribal contact and communication owed their existence to religious conceptions. Intertribal rituals, such as trade, war and magic, facilitated both inter-clan and inter-tribal communication. Religious notions did not define local cultural unities but offered instead, perhaps, a way of transcending the differences between them. We know of no ritual prescriptions which could be used as collective demarcation lines.

The Murngin, however, did consider themselves to be divisible into several cultural groups, language being one of the parameters. This linguistic boundary was more a concept, part of the ideology, than the result of everyday observation.[50] They were the religious

---

[45] Warner 1937: 38.
[46] Warner 1937: 241.
[47] Warner 1937: 245.
[48] Warner 1937: 278 f.; cf. also p.122.
[49] Warner 1937: 456.
[50] In general the interrelation of language and identity was a very important one, cf. C.H. Berndt (1961: 25): 'Language represents one means of self-other identification, one criterion for speaking in terms of "we" as against "they".' The relation between language and nationalistic ideologies also reveals the emblematic and ideological character of language (cf. Hobsbawm 1990: 51-63, 93-100). The often heard requirement for the integration of immigrants, viz. that they learn the language of the host country, is based most probably on other than merely practical grounds.

notions of these cultures that had to bridge the divides and make intercultural communication possible.

Arunta identity

At the 'tribal' level

In 1894 Baldwin Spencer was a member of the so-called Horn expedition, having been appointed as its biologist and photographer by W.A. Horn, the expedition's leader and sponsor. In the summer of 1896—1897, Spencer observed a number of important rituals—the so-called *Engwura*—and his study *The native tribes of Central Australia* published in 1899 in close collaboration with F.J. Gillen, was the ultimate fruit of his work. The authors described the culture of the Aborigines of Central Australia, focusing in particular on one specific group, referred to as the Arunta. The focus of attention was so specific in fact that Spencer entitled a later edition of this volume, together with their study about the northern tribes (viz., *The Northern tribes of Central Australia*, 1904) simply as *The Arunta*. As a matter of fact, this was as inaccurate as Warner's use of the term Murngin, because the Arunta apparently comprised a great number of different groups. Spencer and Gillen often presented interesting comparisons between the northern and southern Arunta groups; the southern Arunta groups, for instance, used four terms for the various age and marriage classes, whilst the northern Arunta groups used eight such categories.[51] Other customs such as that of an avenging party—the *kurdaitcha*—attaching small pieces of wood to their heads, was a practice common to the northern Aruntas but obsolete in the south.[52] There were also differences in vocabulary.[53] And in the south *churingas* made from stone no longer existed.[54] The ceremony of knocking out of teeth was exclusive to the north.[55]

The northern groups used a sacred pole called the *Nurtunja*, and the southern groups a ceremonial object known as the *Waninga*[56], whilst both objects were used in the central and western regions.[57] Spencer and Gillen also pointed out distinctions between the western and eastern Arunta; a western chief of a totemistic group, for

[51] Spencer & Gillen 1899b: 72, 74, 75.
[52] Spencer & Gillen 1899b: 477, 492.
[53] Spencer & Gillen 1899b: 26, n.1, 477.
[54] Spencer & Gillen 1899b: 152.
[55] Spencer & Gillen 1899b: 213.
[56] Spencer & Gillen 1899b: 226f..
[57] Spencer & Gillen 1899b: 234, n.1.

instance, was called an *Alatunja* whilst his eastern counterpart was called *Chantchwa* .[58] Implicitly, Spencer and Gillen distinguished five separate areas[59], attempting to consolidate their various descriptions by the somewhat indiscriminate use of material from the surrounding tribal areas, encompassing the Walpari, Warramunga, Kaitish, Ilpirra, Iliaura, Luritcha and Urabunna tribes. This lack of distinction was nonetheless a characteristic of supralocal activities, with adjoining groups meeting regularly for ceremonial purposes.[60] Spencer and Gillen described an *Engwura* ceremony performed by members of both the Arunta and the Ilpirra tribes.[61] They also observed that there were certain modifications of the class system in this ritual, the Arunta tending to borrow from Ilpirra customs.[62] The Arunta operated several systems for correlating the various groups practising inter-marriage, a prerequisite of course for inter-tribal marriages.[63] It is thus very difficult in this area of central Australia to make any clear distinctions between the separate tribal units, and it was a problem that Spencer and Gillen also faced in their efforts to characterize the specific local groups. They suggested that natives 'speaking of themselves, ... will refer to these local groups by the name of the locality which each of them inhabits.'[64]

An important identity reference at the supralocal level, was the membership of the moiety. On the one hand there were the Panunga and the Bulthara and on the other hand the Purula and the Kumara. When conflicts arose during supralocal meetings, it was the moiety membership that determined a person's position and status, the camp built for the *Engwura* ritual being constructed in accordance with this criterion.[65]

At the local level

The most important determinant for identity was a local one with two main aspects; i.e. socially the local group of the father, and ritually the totemic group. These two groups were not inter-dependent in Arunta culture. Membership of the first group was pre-

[58] Spencer & Gillen 1899b: 190.
[59] Cf. also Strehlow 1947: 47ff. Strehlow made the same distinction, however more explicitly.
[60] Spencer & Gillen 1899b: 14.
[61] Spencer & Gillen 1899b: 276.
[62] Spencer & Gillen 1899b: 72.
[63] Spencer & Gillen 1899b: 89ff.
[64] Spencer & Gillen 1899b: 8.
[65] Spencer & Gillen 1899b: 276.

determined by patrilinear rules, whilst membership of the totemic group was determined by Arunta ideas concerning conception. We may conceive of the Arunta area as a large totemic map, every part of it belonging to a certain totem and centred around one totemic sanctuary. The Arunta believed that the soul left the body at death and returned to its totemic area. Women were believed to become impregnated when such a soul entered her body, which would occur only in that area. It was, therefore, in this area that a woman was believed to become fully aware of her pregnancy. The area in which she realized that she had conceived a child thus determined the totemic group to which her baby would belong. If, at the time of her conception, she was not in the totemic area of the child's father, then the child would ultimately become part of a different totemic group from that of its father. According to Spencer and Gillen this happened very often, and the same was true of moiety membership. The patrilineal moiety and the various totemic groups were not always inter-connected, nor were these social and religious identities completely isolated—concurrent identities were more the rule than the exception. The first was considered to be the normal situation. The function of *Alatunja*, for instance, was not an hereditary one because other members of the totemic group could also become an *Alatunja*. Members of this totemic group from other local patrilinear groups, however, were excluded.[66] Members of other totemic groups were allowed to participate in the totem rituals, the roles allotted to them being determined by the moiety to which they belonged.[67]

Spencer and Gillen suggested that the performers of a certain totemic ritual did not necessarily have to belong to the totemic group or its corresponding moiety[68], but unfortunately the examples they gave as proof seem only to confirm the opposite. Participants in a totemic ritual, who were not members of the totemic group, nearly always belonged to the moiety to which the majority of the totemic group in question belonged. A ritual referred to in detail in Spencer and Gillen's writings, is the so-called *Intichiuma* ritual, which was reserved for members of the totem group only, although there were exceptional occasions when members of another totemic group, belonging to the right moiety, were allowed to be present.[69] Members of the group gathered and isolated themselves from the other groups before performing their rituals in the vicinity of the

---

[66] Spencer & Gillen 1899b: 126.
[67] Spencer & Gillen 1899b: 169, 176-179.
[68] Spencer & Gillen 1899b: 279, 283.
[69] Spencer & Gillen 1899b: 169.

totemic holy places. The purpose of this *Intichiuma* ritual is to increase the number of the totemic animals and plants.[70] In ethnographic literature, these rituals are referred to as increase ceremonies. Spencer and Gillen described some of these *Intichiuma* rituals in great detail (e.g. the *Intichiuma* of the *Witchetty* grub totem), whilst other ceremonies received more superficial treatment. Totem, totemic ritual and the totemic group all belonged to a confined universe, in striking contrast to other applications of totemic ritual and totemic symbols. Totemic rituals could be passed on to members of other totemic groups, or they might be inherited from the father, despite any totemic differences.[71] Many rituals were not confined exclusively to members of one particular group.[72] Those undergoing the initiation rites, for instance, were decorated with totemic representations, which might either belong to their own totems or to the maker of the representations, although this was not strictly necessary.[73]

At the individual level

Within the groups mentioned so far, each individual acquired his or her position according to the degree of initiation. For men there were seven initiation degrees and distinctive status terms, and for women three.[74] This status determined whether or not someone might participate in particular rituals. Climbing the status ladder actually constituted an increase in the sacred elements of an individual's life. Individual ownership of rituals was also an important marker. Spencer and Gillen made a distinction (theoretically, at least) between ordinary ceremonies, the *corroborees*[75], and sacred ceremonies or *Quabaras*.[76] The first were owned collectively and could be passed from one group to another. Spencer and Gillen referred to this as 'a constant circulation of these *corroborees* from group to group and from tribe to tribe..'[77] The latter, the sacred ceremonies, were private property, and

> '... the possession of such a ceremony is a mark of distinction, and it also gives the possessor a peculiar advantage over others ...... because he has something in his possession which enables him to confer a fa-

[70] Spencer & Gillen 1899b: 167ff.
[71] Spencer & Gillen 1899b: 341.
[72] Spencer & Gillen 1899b: 451.
[73] Spencer & Gillen 1899b: 376, 378, fig.87, 633.
[74] Spencer & Gillen 1899b: 638.
[75] Spencer & Gillen 1899b: 618f.
[76] Spencer & Gillen 1899b: 624.
[77] Spencer & Gillen 1899b: 624.

vour on some other man to whom he may decide to hand on the *Quabara*.'[78]

Conclusion

Arunta identity, therefore, was not formulated at the tribal level, and social identity was a local matter. An individual belonged at the local level, and at the same time, to one particular moiety and to one particular totemic group. The membership of a moiety and of the totemic group did not always coincide, but in practice they rarely failed to do so. The individual status within the groups could not be separated from the religious status.

Arunta demarcation

As with the Murngin material, I would now like to discuss the demarcations between local groups and tribes in Arunta society as presented to us in the literature. I will deal firstly with supralocal meetings and contacts, then with the functions of war and trade in the demarcation of identities.

Supralocal rituals

Arunta sacred ceremonies may be divided into two groups on the basis of their supralocal character. On the one hand, we have the very local *Intichiuma* rituals, for the exclusive participation of members of the appropriate totemic group. Those from other local groups who wanted to participate in these rituals, were allowed to do so provided they belonged to the right totemic group. The elaborate initiation ceremonies, on the other hand, were characterized by their supralocal nature and were even open to members of other tribes on invitation. Totemistic rituals performed during these meetings might vary, the most important factor being the chance composition of the group of male elders responsible for the actual organisation of the ritual. In addition to participation in supralocal rituals, there was a whole network of local groups lending and borrowing their very sacred *churingas*, sometimes for long periods of time. The borrowers and the lenders in this case did not have to belong to the same totem, and each act of borrowing and returning was accompanied by a good deal of ceremony.

---

[78] Spencer & Gillen 1899b: 294.

War

Spencer and Gillen did not deal explicitly with conflicts between groups and/or tribes, but they did describe various kinds of conflicts, very similar to the Murngin hostilities described by Warner. Spencer and Gillen treated us to vivid descriptions of highly ritualized forms of individual revenge when a case of manslaughter was suspected, the so-called *Kurdaitcha* for men[79] and the *Illapurinja* for women.[80] A similar form of ritualized revenge was also practised collectively by a group: it might, for instance, involve robbery of women or manslaughter. In this case one group could take revenge against another group—this was called *Atninga*. The groups involved might belong to the same tribe, although it was not unknown for inter-tribal conflicts to occur.[81] Full-blown fights between local groups could be intra-tribal as well as inter-tribal.[82]

Trade

Spencer and Gillen seem to have overlooked the existing web of trade relations among the tribes, although in their chapter on dress and arms etc., they did present a detailed list of what could and could not be traded. It is not clear whether there was any relationship between the trade in consumer goods and the exchange and presentation of ceremonial and ritual objects, as was the case in Murngin society.

Conclusion

Ritual in Arunta society created channels for supralocal and intertribal communication, and the exchange of ceremonial property and ritual objects created a supralocal and intertribal relationship network. The same is also true of the ritualized forms of revenge. Spencer and Gillen gave examples of differences in custom between the local groups and the tribes, but they did not indicate whether these differences were of any particular significance to the participants themselves.

This is very much in contrast to the many *Intichiuma* rituals which were performed by the various totemic groups and which, it must be said, were of particular interest to Spencer and Gillen. These rites were restricted exclusively to members of the local

---

[79] Spencer & Gillen 1899b: 476ff.
[80] Spencer & Gillen 1899b: 485ff.
[81] Spencer & Gillen 1899b: 489ff.
[82] Spencer & Gillen 1899b: 32.

groups. Exploring the belief systems of other tribes, Spencer and Gillen confined themselves entirely to questions about reincarnation and the *Intichiuma* ritual.[83] This was obviously based on their wish to study the religious character of totemism in Arunta society.[84] There may very well be a connection between finding an empirical phenomenon, viz. the exclusive character of the *Intichiuma* rituals, and already formulated basic theoretical assumptions on the origin and development of religion. During the course of their fieldwork, Spencer and Gillen exchanged frequent correspondence with Frazer.[85] In fact, Frazer—the 'self-assured armchair theorist who predicted what their fieldwork would reveal'—may well have exerted a very strong influence on their conceptions of totemic representations and the *Intichiuma* ritual.[86] They may also have fallen under the spell of Robertson Smith's thesis that the sacrifice of the totemic animal represented the rite that was most central to the original, totemic religion.[87]

Other comparisons within Australia

The question may now be asked whether or not our findings on the relationship between ritual and identity, were exclusively characteristic of Murngin and Arunta societies? The answer is, I think, 'no', and I base myself on the work of two authorities in this field of study, i.e. A.P. Elkin and R.M. Berndt. It has proved very difficult indeed to demonstrate the existence of clear tribal boundaries between many other groups of Aborigines in Australia, nor does there seem to have existed any demarcation between them through religious rituals.

Elkin pointed to the problems which arise if we really want to know whether we are dealing with a small tribe or with a sub-tribe, as the boundary lines between tribes and local groups were extremely vague. Elkin used as a working-definition:

> 'a tribe is a grouping of Aborigines who (i) inhabit and own a usually definite area of country; (ii) use a language or dialect peculiar to themselves; (iii) know themselves, or are known, by a distinct name, though sometimes it is difficult to learn what this is, and indeed, it may not exist; (iv) possess customs and laws which often vary in some degree

---

83 Mulvaney & Calaby 1985: 216.
84 Spencer & Gillen 1899a: 275; Marett 1932: 31f.
85 Marett 1932: 3-55.
86 Mulvaney & Calaby 1985: 190; cf. also Swain 1991: 173.
87 Kuper 1988: 103.

from those of neighbouring tribes; and (v) have their own rites and beliefs which frequently differ from those practised and held respectively by the peoples around.'[88]

The most important social unit however was not the tribe itself, but the 'several localized groups which are the real political and economic units'.[89] These local groups communicated with other groups in their area, regardless of tribal membership, and this was also the situation Spencer, Gillen and Warner found in the areas they were working in. And in all those areas, too, the most important cultural unit was the local group. Elkin seems to have been most impressed by the first of the five criteria[90], whilst the second criterion—'use a language or dialect peculiar to themselves'—is more problematical in its application, given the fact that Elkin himself quoted examples of tribes, divided into local groups but speaking very divergent dialects, and of different tribes speaking closely-related languages.[91] Elkin was unable to give any examples at all of the fifth criterion, suggesting a demarcation on the basis of rites and beliefs. Discussing this criterion, however, Elkin was only able to present examples of intertribal ceremonies. The elders of the different local groups, irrespective of their tribal membership, did deliberate on matters pertaining to the proper performance of totemistic, initiation and burial rituals.[92] This also confirms Elkin's statement that the same rituals could be performed in the same way over a vast area. Elkin did suggest, however, that there was a wide variation in circumcision and burial customs.[93] This also explains the rapid expansion of the *Kunapipi* cult (Warner: *Gunabibi*)[94]. In 1897 Roth described the so-called *Molong(l)o* ceremony, which was performed over an increasing part of Australia between 1893 and 1930.[95] Elkin also discussed a number of totemic myths. The old tribal heroes were believed to have travelled in mythic times across territories inhabited by several local groups[96], and these tracks were

'inter-group and inter-tribal in character, that is to say, they passed through the countries and territories of local clans and of tribes and in doing so served to bind these groups and tribes together.'[97]

---

88 Elkin 1956: 25.
89 Elkin 1956: 29.
90 Elkin 1956: 27 f.
91 Elkin 1956: 25 f.
92 Elkin 1956: 29, 30, 259.
93 Elkin 1956: 30, 31, 109, 132.
94 Elkin 1956: 215 f.
95 Elkin 1956: 260.
96 Elkin 1956: 143 f.
97 Elkin 1956: 145.

The myths surrounding these tracks, ensured the interdependent character of the cult life of those local groups and tribes. Elkin concluded that 'the groups and tribes are linked together by the cult-life.'[98]

Elkin's description of Aboriginal religion also showed that religious concepts were not derived from social relations. Religion is an autonomous area—it transcends group divisions and creates space for intertribal communication.

The work of R.M. Berndt would seem to support this view. He saw the spread of religious rituals and concepts as a relatively autonomous process. His work centred largely on the tribes of south eastern Australia, particularly the Dieri around Lake Eyre; they were tribes 'which can be regarded as being culturally intermediate .... particularly as regards ritual and myth, less as regards social organization'[99]. The Murray and the Darling rivers, he said, provided the geographical 'clue to religious differences and similarities'[100] and the spread of religious ritual. 'Religious patterns' from New South Wales have found their way into south eastern Queensland[101], leaving their mark on the initiation ceremonies (the *dora*)[102] in particular. In his chapter on northern Australia, Berndt pointed to the recent emergence of the *Kunapipi* ritual in Arnhem land, a ritual which had only been introduced into the area some thirty years before.[103] Berndt also devoted a separate paragraph to the northern fertility cults, which 'have spread across quite large areas'[104], the *Kunapipi* ritual ('their propensity to move'[105]) being a very good example of this trend.[106] The initiation ritual practised in the central Desert region is another good example of this steady territorial extension of rituals and religious concepts. Piercing of the nasal septum, tooth evulsion and cicatrization were innovations which entered the Desert from the east.[107] In his concluding chapter, Berndt presents a survey of the four most significant religious patterns and indicates the four areas from which these patterns spread uninterruptedly over the map of Australia.[108]

---

[98] Elkin 1956: 146.
[99] Berndt 1974: fasc.1: 24.
[100] Berndt 1974, fasc.1: 27.
[101] Berndt 1974, fasc.2: 1.
[102] Berndt 1974, fasc.2: p.6.
[103] Berndt 1974, fasc.2: 13.
[104] Berndt 1974, fasc.3: 1.
[105] Berndt 1974, fasc.3: 16.
[106] Berndt 1974, fasc.3: 4f.
[107] Berndt 1974, fasc.4: 3.
[108] Berndt 1974, fasc.4: 23.

A similar picture is found in the works of Charlesworth[109], Tonkinson[110], Kolig[111] and Gray[112], who were all studying changes in Aboriginal societies which were not caused by contact with Western cultures. The mechanisms which provoked these changes were of a more or less autonomous nature. Tonkinson distinguished four sources of change, namely : 'the diffusion of new rituals, songlines, and objects between groups'; 'ritual innovations at the local level'; 'discoveries of sacred objects' and 'the exploitation of the myth's inherent flexibility'.[113] There are also references to changes in the social structure.

Conclusion

We are now able to answer the questions posed in the introduction. It must be said, first of all, that socially and culturally differences between groups in Aboriginal Australia did not correspond exactly with the religious groups, and that religion seems to have been a very flexible expression of culture. Rather than using rituals for marking boundaries and demarcation, Aboriginal religion created space for intercultural communication. Rituals and religious concepts could spread their wings, so to speak, over wide areas and at high speed, penetrating ethnic boundaries with ease. It was therefore impossible to establish an unambiguous connection between someone's identity as a member of a group and his religious identity. The identity of the individual could be perceived at several levels, e.g. that of the person in an intra-group situation, who at the same time could identify himself with the smaller or the more encompassing groups to which he belonged. Religious ritual was present at all levels. The most important identity reference point was the local group. The notion of a relationship between ethnic identity and religion did not appear to be a very fertile one.

We did, however, see other parameters, such as elements of the material culture and language especially. As far as language is concerned, its intelligibility appeared to be a cultural concept and was not necessarily based on empirical observation. We should not be surprised by these findings. Stable inter-ethnic relations presuppose a certain structural interaction which Barth saw as:

---

109 Charlesworth 1984.
110 Tonkinson 1978.
111 Kolig 1981.
112 Gray 1978.
113 Tonkinson 1978: 113; cf. Charlesworth 1984: 385.

> 'a set of prescriptions governing situations of contact, and allowing for articulation in some sectors or domains of activity, and a set of proscriptions on social situations preventing inter-ethnic interaction in other sectors, and thus insulating parts of the cultures from confrontation and modification.'[114]

Religious concepts and rituals among the Australian Aborigines, therefore, fall under the prescriptions governing situations of contact.

This conclusion contrasts with the prevailing Western idea of religion as the most important parameter of identity. In Western society economical, social or cultural differences are usually defined in terms of religion. This conclusion also contrasts with some recent developments in Australia, where the Aboriginal liberation movement increasingly tends to develop a concept of Aboriginal Religion, perceiving and presenting it in direct contrast to Western Christianity. In this case Aboriginal Religion is in direct contrast to Western Christianity.

In my opinion, the religious definition of social differences is the result of colonial processes and not inherent in our humanity, because the notion of 'the' Aboriginal cannot be separated from colonial history, the various Aboriginal tribes being increasingly presented as representatives of 'the' Aboriginal. This concept should be studied in the light of 'a social and cultural formation, [as] an historical .... category'.[115] 'The' Aborigines emerged within a colonial context and the dichotomy of Aboriginal Religion and Christianity is a consequence of it.

The formulation of an Aboriginal Religion is already evident in the works of Elkin, who mixed the description of Aboriginal religions with prescriptions for an Aboriginal Religion (he proposed, for example, that the ritual exchange of *churingas* should take the place of the ritual exchange of women[116]). The contents of such a concept (Aborigines vs. White Australians) as well as the boundary line parameters (Aboriginal Religion vs. Christianity) appear to have been imposed by Western society. The aim—liberation from Western dominance—is pursued through the creation of an Aboriginal Religion, i.e. through a typically Western concept. The black response to white dominance is translated into white concepts.[117] Until the far-reaching changes in the Field of Ethnological Study brought about by Western colonialism had been felt, religious rituals in Aboriginal Australia had no meaning at all in terms

---

114 Barth 1969: 16.
115 Attwood 1989: 149.
116 Elkin 1956: 130, 179.
117 Cf. Broome 1982: passim.

of boundary line demarcations between the various cultural units. On the contrary, rituals and religious concepts were a necessary precondition for intercultural communication.

References

Attwood, B., 1989, *The making of the Aborigines*. Sydney: Allen & Unwin.

Barth, Fr., (ed.), 1969, *Ethnic groups and boundaries: the social organization of culture differences*. Boston: Little Brown.

Berndt, C.H., 1961, 'The quest for identity: the case of the Australian Aborigines', in *Oceania* 32, 1: 16-33.

Berndt, R.M., 1974, *Australian Aboriginal religion (Four fascicles)*. Leiden: E.J. Brill.

Broome, R., 1982, *Aboriginal Australians: black response to white dominance, 1788-1980*. London: Allen & Unwin.

Charlesworth, M. (ed.), 1984, *Religion in Aboriginal Australia: an anthology*. St. Lucia: University of Queensland Press.

De Josselin de Jong, J.P.B., 1977a, 'The Malay Archipelago as a Field of Ethnological study', in De Josselin de Jong 1997b: 166-182.

De Josselin de Jong, J.P.B., (ed.) 1977b, *Structural anthropology in the Netherlands*. The Hague: Mouton Publishers.

Elkin, A.P., 1956[3], *The Australian Aborigines: how to understand them*. Sydney, etc.: Angus & Robertson (1938[1]).

Gray, D., 1978, 'A revival of the law: the probable spread of initiation circumcision to the coast of western Australia', in *Oceania* 48, 3: 188-201.

Hobsbawm, E., 1990[2], *Nations and nationalism since 1780: programme, myth, reality*. Cambridge: Cambridge University Press.

Kolig, E., 1981, *The silent revolution: the effects of modernization on Australian Aboriginal religion*. Philadelphia: Institute for the Study of Human Issues.

Kuper, A., 1988, *The invention of primitive society: transformations of an illusion*. London: Routledge.

Marett, R.R & T.K. Penniman (eds.), 1932, *Spencer's scientific correspondence with Sir J.G. Frazer and others*. Oxford: Oxford University Press.

Mauss, M., & H. Hubert, 1909, *Mélanges d'histoire des religions*. Paris: Alcan.

Mulvaney, D.J. & J.H. Calaby, 1985, *'So much that is new': Baldwin Spencer, 1860-1929, a biography*. Melbourne: Melbourne University Press.

Spencer, B. & F.J. Gillen, 1899a, 'Some remarks on totemism as applied to Australian tribes', in *The Journal of the Anthropological Institute* 28: 275-280.

Spencer, B. & F.J. Gillen, 1899b, *The Natives of Central Australia*. London: MacMillan and Co.

Strehlow, T.G.H., 1947, *Aranda traditions*. Melbourne: Melbourne University Press.

Swain, T., 1991, 'A Bicentenary of the Study of Australian Aboriginal Religions', in *Religion and Religions* 21: 165-195.

Tonkinson, R., 1978, *The Mardudjara Aborigines*. New York: Holt, Rinehart & Winston.

Warner, W. Lloyd, 1937[1], *A black civilization: a social study of an Australian tribe*. New York, etc.: Harper & Row (1958[2]).

IDENTITY, RELIGIOUS PLURALISM AND RITUAL IN BRAZIL
UMBANDA AND PENTECOSTALISM

André Droogers
(Free University, Amsterdam)

Introduction

The aim of this contribution[1] is, first of all, to present a model for the study of religions in a plural society such as Brazil. It is suggested that religions can be compared in terms of three main dimensions: external, internal and supernatural. A religious group's identity, as well as the way it deals with religious pluralism, depends on the composition of these three dimensions. In the second section, I will comment on the Brazilian religious situation in general. In the course of time, Brazilian social and economic conditions have produced an idiosyncratic form of religious pluralism, and at the same time, it is emphasized that religiously motivated convictions and behaviour have contributed to this situation. The third section will take a closer look at two important Brazilian religions: Umbanda and Pentecostalism, their individual identities being defined on the basis of the model developed in the first section of this paper. Section four will be devoted to an analysis of these two religions in terms of how their religious identities have affected their attitudes toward religious pluralism, special attention being given their ritual behaviour as an expression of these attitudes. In the final section, I will summarize the comparative results, on the basis of the conceptual framework, focusing on the relationship between power and meaning-making. It will also be suggested that the social science explanation of religion and religious pluralism should concentrate more on the religious beliefs and rituals.

---

[1] I am grateful to the conference participants, Lucinda Dirven and Jan Snoek in particular, for their constructive comments. I also extend special thanks to my students, for their critical observations on an earlier draft of this contribution.

A framework

In order to facilitate the discussion of religious pluralism, an heuristic instrument would seem to be the most appropriate, and to that end I would like to present a model for the study of a single religious group.[2] This model focuses on the relation between power and the processes of meaning-making[3] or signification.

Religious pluralism derives from a situation in which two or more religions exist in the same society, and in which they are either complementary and inclusive, or competitive and exclusive. In both cases, religious differences are of paramount importance, and may provoke either the inclusion or exclusion of outsiders. It is necessary in the first place, therefore, to ascertain how a particular religious group positions itself in relation to other groups and to the wider society in which it operates. I will call this the external dimension of the group. In a situation of religious pluralism, this is the most apparent of the three dimensions I mentioned earlier.

It is, however, strongly linked to the two other dimensions of any religious group, which combine to form a three-dimensional model; the first of these two related dimensions I will call internal and the second supernatural. The internal dimension denotes the relationships among the believers themselves, including their religious specialists, if any. When I speak of the supernatural dimension, however, I refer to the relationship the group membership maintains with God, gods, spirits, saints, or other, less personal forces, including the beliefs which have a bearing on this relationship.

The nature of the core relationships in each of these three dimensions is, in my view, inherent in the group's own conceptions of power and meaning. Power, in this context, is defined as the capacity to influence a person's behaviour, and meaning as the conception of what reality is in all its various parts. An important aspect of a religion's exercise of power is its licence to control, or dictate, that meaning. In each of the three dimensions, power and meaning are connected in a specific manner, and I will try to illustrate this for each of them individually.

Externally, the core relationship is one which exists between believers and non-believers. The definition of who is a believer and who is not, depends in large part on a corpus of shared meaning, whilst, for a number of reasons, any distinction ultimately becomes a power issue. Believers differ from non-believers in that they con-

[2] Cf. Droogers 1989, 1994; Droogers & Siebers 1991.
[3] Cf. Crick 1976: 3.

sider themselves to be subject to the power exercised by supernatural entities and forces (the supernatural dimension), as well as by religious specialists (the internal dimension). By submitting themselves in this way, believers accept—often with great conviction—that others are empowered to exert influence over their behaviour. Non-believers do not submit themselves to such dictates and power, and are therefore 'outsiders', although they are, nonetheless, potential 'insiders'. If non-believers form a minority in society, the religion's power is likely to be spread to some degree over them as well. In any case, religious pluralism demands some form of boundary definition and corresponding behaviour codes, be they either explicit or implicit.

The nature of the two other dimensions will inevitably influence the discourse on external relationships, and vice versa. The way in which power and meaning are defined within each of the two dimensions has consequences for external relationships and thus for religious pluralism. External characteristics may, in turn, influence the form the internal and supernatural dimensions take.

The internal dimension refers to the way believers maintain relationships among themselves and this entails a certain exercise of power, depending on the extent to which the religious tasks are divided. Religious specialists of varying types are able to create and maintain a hierarchical social structure, at each level of which some members are subordinate to those above them, just as they themselves can exert power over those lower down the hierarchical ladder. The manner in which these power relationships are justified and legitimated, depends on the meaning construction processes. The link between meaning and power is thus established. The same process of signification may, of course, lead to subversion of the power structure prevailing at any given moment. The way power is organized internally, and the process by which it is justified or criticized, will have consequences for the religious group's own attitude towards religious pluralism. A group's identity may depend very much on its leaders, who act as the exclusive 'face' of the group. Internal religious pluralism may even be such that external pluralism is considered to be both normal and not problematical, an extension, as it were, of what is actually taking place within the religious group itself.

Much the same can be said with regard to the supernatural dimension. Power can be present in the individual believer's relationship with the supernatural, expressed both in his attitude of submissiveness towards it and in his efforts (often referred to as 'magic') to control it. The connection between power and the signification process, is again illustrated by the fact that the significance believers are expected to afford to supernatural forces, actually determines their attitudes towards them. What happens, here, therefore, has obvious consequences for religious pluralism. A strong emphasis on the absolute and unique power of the supernatural may, for example, create a sense of exclusiveness in the external dimension.

It should be clearly understood at this point, that attitudes towards religious pluralism are not only influenced by a summation of the views of believers on the question of power and meaning in the three dimensions. Rather than a juxtaposition, it is the three dimensions as a combined whole, which determines the group attitude, thereby putting the stamp on the group's total identity within the society around it. Religious identity is thus formed by external, internal, and supernatural dimensions.

This is not to suggest that there is a perfect integration and cohesion of the three dimensions. In fact, much of the dynamism in any religious group is nourished by the internal contradictions within and between the three dimensions. Believers simply do not behave in a consistent manner, despite the official, more or less homogeneous and integrated version of their religion, as represented by its religious figureheads. Time brings its own changes in the way people live their lives, and these changes cause them to modify their convictions, and to make strategical use of their beliefs. Nor should we assume that what happens within one dimension, is necessarily a reflection of what is going on within the others. Although consistency might be considered to be the ideal, exceptions do occur, despite official statements to the contrary.

The Pentecostal and Umbanda religions, which will be discussed below in more detail, will serve as our illustration. The central idea in Pentecostalism, essential to the supernatural dimension, is that the gifts of the Holy Spirit are available to all and should ideally, in terms of the internal dimension, create a fundamental equality between believers. It is obvious, however, that some people are more gifted than others, and that a group's expansion inevitably entails a certain degree of institutionalization and hierarchy—the result being inequality between leaders and followers. This often leads to conflicts and schisms, because adepts feel that the original source of inspiration is being neglected. A new church is founded on the basis of a return to the pure and authentic message of equality in the Spirit, until a generation or two later, the same process begins all over again. Similar contradictions occur among the Pentecostals; on the one hand, they derive sufficient inspiration within the supernatural dimension to condemn the world (the external dimension) as evil and 'dirty' and to avoid it, whilst on the other hand, it is in that same world that new believers are to be recruited and it is in that same world that they all have to work and make their livings.

Umbanda focuses on spirit mediumship with the accompanying possibility of consulting the spirits through their mediums. The properties of each spirit and its medium, are ideally viewed as being complementary to those of all the others. The whole spectrum of afflictions can thus be covered by the totality of the spirits, through the mediums. This central idea of the supernatural dimension should, ideally, create a sense of harmony and community at the internal level as well. Tensions between mediums or rival groups of mediums, however, are translated as conflicts between their spirits[4]; i.e. if the mediums themselves are in conflict, so too are their spirits. And this means that what is normal in the supernatural dimension does not necessarily find its parallel in the internal dimension and, conversely, conflicts in the internal dimension may temporarily produce a parallel in the supernatural dimension. Another example is the contradiction between the ideal of working externally, with the help of the spirits, for charity, and the practice of calling on the power of the spirits to harm other people.

In studying religious pluralism, the delicate inter-connection between the three dimensions, as evident in Pentecostalism and Umbanda, is an important aspect. All the partners in a context of religious pluralism introduce and defend their views, based on the relative identity of their own religious groups. A situation of religious pluralism, therefore, comprises a plurality of constellations and in studying each religious group's attitude towards religious pluralism, our three dimensional model can be helpful, its application revealing different ways of viewing power and meaning. The dynamism of the three dimension constellation will also differ from group to group and adds to the complexity of religious pluralism.

The resulting picture is not just one of what makes them different, indeed a surprising degree of similarity and overlap can exist between them, even though they are seemingly opposed and polarized. Much will depend on the members' conception of power and meaning, not only at the official level of the religious specialists but also, and particularly, at the popular level. At this point, it is important to remember that power as a concept does not refer to personal property, but to a relationship, indicating a give and take, a

---

4 Velho 1975.

process of negotiation. The influence one person may have over the behaviour of another is never total, even though the margins might be so small that the person over whom that power is exercised, is only able to think disagreement, rather than express it in words or deeds.

If overlap and similarities between religions do exist, however surprisingly, and at the popular level especially, then syncretism becomes an essential part of religious pluralism[5], and in this case we find another illustration of the connection between meaning and power. The term syncretism has been used disparagingly by religious specialists, in the Christian context in particular, as a means of condemning religious intermingling by believers under their supervision; an unwelcome practice, in their view, if boundaries are to be maintained. It is, after all, incumbent upon them to protect the group's boundaries against would-be trespassers. Syncretism has also been stimulated by religious specialists, such as Umbanda priests, in the belief that their religion does not essentially differ from all the others represented in the plural context. In both cases, although the consequences may be totally different, these attitudes depend on the constellation of the three dimensions.

Some observations must still be made in this regard, before we apply the framework developed in this section to the Brazilian situation. The manner in which the dimensions are related in a single constellation, depends on certain alternatives in each of the three dimensions. One way of understanding these alternatives, is to determine which side of a power relationship is stressed by the people involved in it. In each of the three dimensions, power is negotiated in a certain manner and the group's religious identity differs accordingly and can vary greatly. It should be borne in mind, once again, that there need be no consistency between the dimensions, in fact there is almost always some degree of contradiction and inconsistency. It is even possible that a clear choice is avoided in any one dimension and that traces of both are evident: there is thus an overriding need to steer clear of extremes.

As far as the supernatural dimension is concerned, we might see the emphasis being laid on how God, gods and spirits etc. manifest themselves, and we might call this a revelatory mode of religious identity construction. On the other hand, it might be the believer's ritual activity in seeking supernatural support which is given the greater emphasis. As we have observed already, this was referred to

---

[5] Droogers 1989.

as 'magic' for quite a long period of time, but because of its 'second-rate' or even 'illegitimate' connotations, I would prefer instead to speak of an explorative mode of religious identity construction.

The internal dimension presents the alternatives of a dominant leadership and a dominant laity, as opposites. If power is invested primarily in the hands of the religious specialists, we have what we call a hierarchical mode of religious identity construction, whilst its opposite, namely greater power in the hands of the laity, is described as inclusivist.

One of the criteria embodied in the external dimension, is the group's attitude towards the wider society. The hostile mode of religious identity construction, for instance, is characterized by a strong sense of dualism, whilst at the other extreme, we see a far greater tendency towards tolerance.

Brazilian religious pluralism

One might call Brazil a laboratory for religious studies, in the light of the fact that almost all the world's religions are represented there in one form or another. Christianity arrived with the Portuguese colonizers, Jewish immigrants imported Judaism, and African slaves took their tribal religions across the ocean and, in the course of time, their descendants transformed them into Afro-Brazilian religions. Other groups imported Islam into Brazil and were later reinforced by immigrants from the Middle East. Old and new Japanese religions came with the Japanese immigrant influx and spread among the Brazilian population as a whole. Spiritist Kardecism, as well as Umbanda, are the centres of *karma* and reincarnation thinking. And countless of smaller religions have also found their way onto Brazilian soil.

What gives Brazil its own particular brand of religious pluralism, however, is the combination of various factors and ingredients that has led in a specific historical context to a typically Brazilian religious practice, best represented in the Afro-Brazilian religions. I would now like to draw a brief map showing the historical background of these religions.

The pre-colonial Amerindian population has been literally decimated. Some elements of their religions live on, however, not only in the few Amerindian villages that still survive, but also more indirectly and in varying degrees, in the various forms of today's syncretic Afro-Brazilian religions. We must also not forget that Amerindians have become christianized on a wide scale.

It was, of course, the Roman Catholic church which made the greatest religious impact during the period of colonialisation. The Christian mission was the Portuguese king's responsibility and he had the right to appoint bishops. The end of the last century saw a period of 'Romanization' which brought the church province under Vatican rule once again. Brazil is known today as the country with the largest number of Catholics in the world; more than 80 % of the population declares itself to be Catholic, although only a minority of them, estimated at no more than 10 %, actually attends the Mass. For the majority, popular Catholicism is what matters : practical, festive and non-sacramental in nature, centred on the Virgin Mary and the saints. Within the Catholic church, itself, small groups are engaged in progressive 'base', or 'grass root' communities, taking their inspiration from various elements of liberation theology. Other small groups represent a Catholic version of the Pentecostal tradition within the charismatic renewal movement, and many Catholics participate in Afro-Brazilian groups without seeing any need to relinquish their Catholic baptism.

During the colonial period, the slaves brought from Africa were baptized, but their religious education was minimal. They continued the customs of their own religions, if for no other reason than that such practices helped them to cope with the terrible deprivations of slavery. A consequence of this was the emergence of syncretic forms of religion, comprising Amerindian, African and Catholic elements and patterns, to varying degrees and this, in turn, led to the rise of the Afro-Brazilian religions.[6] This was not a voluntary religious pluralism, but rather a response to historic pressures, the prevailing relations between social and economic power in particular. The white elite imposed Catholicism for the soul, while at the same time creating conditions in which all religious resources—primarily African and Amerindian—were called in to deal with afflictions of the body.

Although present for some time, it is not until approximately 1800 that the first institutionalized urban forms of Afro-Brazilian religions were established. Yoruba cosmology played a particularly important role in this, with its integration of Catholic elements, such as the identification of Catholic saints with Yoruba divinities, *orixás*, the use of statues and candles, and the altar as the central axis around which the rituals were performed. As we have seen already, Amerindian elements were also added. There are local

[6] Bastide 1978.

differences in the names given to these Afro-Brazilian religions, the best known being the Candomblé of Bahia, which is at once both very African and very Catholic. The Macumba of Rio de Janeiro version appeared later, making greater use of the Portuguese language rather than an African one. Spirit mediumship is central to all these different variations, with female mediums often occupying leadership positions, especially in the more African forms. Problem-solving is the main purpose; spiritual entities can, after all, be used for good and for evil. And, besides, who decides what is good and what is bad?—what is advantageous to one can be just as harmful to another.

These older forms of Afro-Brazilian religion persisted for some time, but the most successful to emerge in this century is the Umbanda.[7] It is estimated that about a third of the Brazilian population has some regular or irregular contact with one or other of the small Umbanda temples—to be found in practically all the poor and middle-class areas—particularly in times of need. Despite its African, Amerindian and Catholic roots, Umbanda has also been influenced by spiritism in the form of French 19th century Kardecism, and its success is probably best explained by its adaptation to the tastes of the white middle-class of the population.[8] This has meant that its most striking African elements, including animal sacrifice and prolonged initiation periods, have been abandoned. Its pantheon is characterized by a similar adaptation, i.e. spirits of Brazilian origin have been added to the Yoruba *orixás*. I will return to Umbanda later in order to illustrate religious pluralism in Brazil on the basis of the framework developed in the first section.

In bringing this short review of the Brazilian religious situation to an appropriate end, we have for a moment to consider the Protestant influences. Despite early, but abortive, efforts, the effects of Protestantism were not actually felt until the 19th century, following the influx of German Lutheran immigrants, and the work of Baptist, Methodist and Presbyterian missionaries from the United States and Great Britain. The churches which have emerged as a result of this process of immigration and missionary endeavour, differ enormously in theology, style and membership.

Nowadays, however, being Protestant means, in two thirds of the cases, being Pentecostal. The first Pentecostal churches had already been founded by missionaries from the United States as early as

---

[7] Droogers 1985.
[8] Ortiz 1978.

1910 and 1911, but it was not until the 1950s that Pentecostalism, as such, became a force to be reckoned with. Several churches were founded and mass evangelization and healing campaigns were held; Pentecostalism grew in line with the growth, in size and numbers, of Brazil's large-scale urban centres. Some of these churches are now working nation-wide, whilst others are one-pastor-temples with only a very small number of faithful followers. Some specialize in healing, and can be found near state clinics and hospitals, where they hold three healing services a day. Pentecostal churches differ in their styles and congregations, although all emphasize the dramatic role of the Holy Spirit in the lives of their converts. They work hard to attract new adepts—mostly from society's lower strata—and their church services are designed primarily to address these newcomers to the congregation. I will continue my discussion of the Pentecostal impact in the next section of this paper.

The concrete form which religious diversity takes in Brazil, reflects something of the general nature of the society in which it stands. Religious participation is partly the result of a combination of non-religious factors such as class, ethnicity, gender, migration and education. This is not to suggest that the explanation for religious plurality should be sought in non-religious factors, although they do sometimes make for striking differences. The scope must be widened, however, through the study of the dialectical interplay between non-religious and religious factors, in the growth of religious pluralism. The outline developed in the first section, allows for this double perspective, especially when it includes the supernatural dimension, and we will use it now in comparing two religious groups in Brazil in particular: Umbandists and Pentecostals. The central theme of this book dictates that I focus on the way in which these two groups, by means of their behaviour, beliefs and ritual, and thus their identity, define their attitudes towards other religious groups within their society.

Umbandists and Pentecostals

The supernatural dimension

The experience of, and belief in, supernatural power is present in both religions, although the contents of that experience and belief differ greatly. Both regard the onset of religious awareness as a very dramatic event in an individual's life. Only the Pentecostalists, however, speak of conversion, although the Umbandists do recognize the importance of similar events in personal histories, especially a person's first experience as a spirit medium. The supernatural power is thus experienced, very often in the context of problem-solving and healing, either through the Spirit (Pentecostals) or through the spirits (Umbanda).

In the Pentecostal act of conversion, the transition is expressed in the baptism by the Holy Spirit through the manifestation of charismatic gifts of healing, speaking in tongues, and prophecy, these gifts being a sign of God's power. This power is also available to believers in terms of mutual help, and conversion also means that God's power is exerted over the convert's moral life as well. Pentecostalism is a total religion, demanding complete dedication twenty-four hours a day, seven days a week.

In Umbanda, a god or spirit reveals itself directly through the medium, using his or her body, speaking through his or her mouth, and often healing that person through mediumship. The medium is considered to be god's, or the spirit's, 'horse', and sometimes a medium can literally be overpowered by the supernatural, entering a trance that is difficult to control. The art of mediumship lies in the ability to direct a trance, which although it may seem spontaneous, is in fact, in part, a learned behaviour. Experienced mediums are thus expected at all times to be fully in control of the situation. In the context of apprenticeship, we often hear the term 'baptism' although it is used in a different sense from that used in the Pentecostal churches, namely as the ritual washing, through which a person is formally invested as a medium.

What is particularly characteristic of Umbanda, is the syncretistic nature of its beliefs and rituals. As we have seen already in the history of Afro-Brazilian religions, African gods and Catholic saints have been fused into a double or even a single personality. Power relationships in society have played a central role in the development of these beliefs, as a result of African slaves having to adapt to the religious demands of their Catholic masters; they also defied them by calling on the powers of their African gods and rituals, particularly those connected with the West African trickster god Exu.[9] Meaning-making thus resulted in specific views on supernatural power.

In the course of the present century, social influences have resulted in yet another shift of meaning, with people from the lower-middle, white, classes adapting traditional African beliefs to their own. This process led to the rise of Umbanda from the 1920s on-

---

[9] Lapassade and Luz 1972.

wards and Ortiz called it 'the white death of the black magician'.[10] Throughout the history of Afro-Brazilian religions, there has always been a close relationship between power and meaning-making. Interestingly enough, the most common categories of the Umbanda spirits correspond to marginalized social categories, such as negro slaves, Amerindians, children, crooks and tricksters (called *Exus*, as a multiplication of the single West African trickster god), prostitutes and gipsy women. In contrast to how the wider society views them, these categories of people now find themselves promoted to the status of supernatural powers, and the dominant classes demoted to the needy client status. Since the mediums often come from the lower social strata, they obviously share in this inversion.

Rolim suggests that a similar situation has arisen within Pentecostal movement, where again power and meaning are inter-connected.[11] The lower strata disappropriated economically and religiously, became religion 'owners', producing their own lay religions, as it were, outside the sphere of influence of the religious specialists of the traditional churches. A loss in economic power is thus compensated by a gain in religious power.

The other side of divine power, namely the human effort to influence and use it, is also present in the two religions, although not always to the same extent. Pentecostalists use their charismatic gifts to solve their own problems and those of other people, whereby supernatural power is not only experienced but also used. Long prayer sessions beseeching God's help are common, and in Umbanda, almost all experiences of spirit possession are used by mediums and believers in gaining supernatural help for the solution of their problems. Among its opponents, Umbanda has gained the reputation of perpetrating magic rather than anything else. Mediums consciously seek possession and the aid of the spirits in order to help their clients. In some cases, this supernatural power is considered ambiguous, to say the least : it is seen as both harmful and destructive, as the defiant slaves of centuries past had already discovered.

The internal dimension

In both religions, internal power relationships cannot be understood without reference to the supernatural. They also contrast sharply to the hierarchical structures operating in society and the Catholic Church.

---

[10] Ortiz 1978.
[11] Rolim 1980.

In Pentecostalism, in the early stages at least of a Pentecostal church's history, hierarchical tendencies diminish in the face of all its people having potential access to the gifts of the Holy Spirit. Every Pentecostal church service is proof of the active role all its members play in giving and sustaining meaning. In a way, each Pentecostal believer becomes a religious specialist in his or her own right, the division of labour is highly diversified and all members share the gifts of the Spirit encompassed in healing, prophecy and glossolalia.

A church's success, however, can sometimes lead to emphasis being placed on organization and a hierarchical division of labour, their leaders often appealing to divine revelation in justifying their high status and their power. It goes without saying that charismatic authority helps to advance the careers of these leaders, although less charismatic leaders also come to the fore : every prophet, after all, needs an organizer. The result may be competition and schism, elements which in themselves have contributed greatly to the spectacular growth of the Pentecostal churches; new dissidents establish their own churches and attract a new following. Hierarchy and fission, therefore, are normal aspects of second and third generation churches. As has already been suggested, this process is not without its contradictions, a case in point being that between the supernatural and the internal dimensions.

In Umbanda, mediumship colours the structure of internal power relations; mediums by virtue of their capacity to intercede between gods or spirits and people, inevitably have the authority to exert power over their 'clients', and they do. Some mediums do better than others and attain positions of power above other mediums, success being measured by the size of the clientele network. Leaders of new temples are sought among the most experienced and successful of them, i.e. those who are able to 'reach' a wide range of spirits, have gone through all the stages of initiation in mediumship, and have fulfilled all the necessary obligations—and they are also often very charismatic figures. And here too, just as in the Pentecostal movement, conflicts often result in expansion; for instance, when a successful medium becomes a seeming threat to the current leader of a temple and breaks away to found another group. Again, the world of the spirits is believed to play a decisive role in such conflicts and schisms.

The external dimension

This dimension is clearly very closely associated with the other power relationship dimensions we have been discussing. The

Pentecostals, for instance, use every means available to spread their message, their experienced belief in the power of the Holy Spirit, the solver of all problems. It is the vocation of each member of the Pentecostal church to combat the devil, characterized as the master of the—evil—world and of the sinner, and they can regularly be seen preaching this message on the main squares of most Brazilian cities. An extreme example of Pentecostal evangelization are the commuter trains preachers, who deliver fervent testimonies on the radical rewards of conversion; they are their own models and they exhort their commuting audience to embrace a similar personal transformation.

Social scientists differ in their opinions as to the role Pentecostal churches actually play in society and in the process of modernization.[12] Some view Pentecostalism as a modern version of feudalism, the pastor being the new feudal master, and in that sense, we would expect to find a continuity between the rural setting the migrants have left behind them and the urban religious context in which they now find themselves. Others praise the enterprising spirit of the Pentecostals and see them as the Weberian Calvinists of our day, the vanguards of modernization. In any case, their respect for authority has given Pentecostalists the reputation of being model citizens and obedient workers, indeed Pentecostal representatives have recently been elected to the national and state parliaments. They are usually staunch defenders of strict moral codes and often take an anti-Catholic stance in their defence of policies designed to make Brazil a theocracy.

Umbandists do not consciously seek to influence society, even though some have opted for political careers. The mediums' societal role is normally limited to the help they offer their clients; they seek solutions, through their networks—and not only through their spiritual resources—and thereby intervene in the society around them. And by the same token, as we have seen already, Brazilian society has influenced Umbanda, a religion offering an interesting mixture of adaptation and resistance. The latter aspect is implicit—and therefore more symbolic—in the common categories of spirits, all belonging to marginal groups in society. In a sense, these spiritual outcasts return to society through the back door of the Umbanda temples.

---

[12] Droogers 1991a, 1991b, Hoffnagel 1978, Lalive d'Épinay 1969, Martin 1990, Willems 1967.

Umbanda, Pentecostalism and religious pluralism

Having described the two religions, we are now in a position to take a look at their attitudes towards religious pluralism. As has been suggested earlier, the constellation of the three dimensions has a direct influence on these attitudes. We will now look at this relationship in greater detail.

The external dimension

As far as their external relations are concerned, the two religions under discussion here both operate on the same market, with similar target groups in the lower strata of society, and both offer religious solutions to practical problems. This makes for a certain atmosphere of competition between the two, revealing striking differences. Whereas Pentecostals generally use public areas for their recruitment campaigns, and attract new adepts through private informal networks, Umbandists follow the latter approach only. Pentecostals generally seem to be more assertive and there have been recent signs that some groups are becoming aggressive in their attitudes towards Umbandists and Afro-Brazilian religion followers in general. A recent article on this subject[13] even refers to it in its title as 'The war of the Pentecostals against the Afro-Brazilian'. A few Pentecostal churches have taken the offensive against Afro-Brazilian religions to the extent of actually intervening in their ceremonies, especially the midnight rituals performed by Afro-Brazilian groups in cemeteries. These rituals are organized in honour of Exu, the trickster god, who non-Afro-Brazilian religions regard as the devil. The same ritual can also be dedicated to Exu's female counterpart, Pomba-Gira, the spirit of a prostitute or a gipsy woman. Exu and Pomba-Gira are morally ambiguous, sympathetic to the person who has commissioned the ritual, and at the same time unsympathetic to those purported to be his or her enemies. To Pentecostals these spirits are downright demonic.

Pentecostals generally speak quite openly against all Afro-Brazilian religions, without distinction, qualifying all divinities and spirits, even the unambiguously benign, as demons, forbidding contact with them and condemning spirit mediumship as idolatry. And yet, these same divinities and spirits are taken very seriously indeed, and criticism of them is based not, as in the Catholic and mainstream Protestant churches, on the assumption that spirits do not exist, are

[13] Soares 1993.

man-made idols or can be explained away psychologically, but on the belief that they do exist and are extremely dangerous.[14] Whereas the Catholic church for a long time regarded the Afro-Brazilian religions as backward and primitive, and even as pre-scientific, the Pentecostals take a very serious view of Afro-Brazilian spirit worship.

Umbandists will, in general, ignore such criticism and give no response to it. When pressed for an answer, however, they will usually say that all religions are true, and that all should have the liberty to manifest themselves. Having suffered decades of persecution as a consequence of Catholic clerical pressure on police authorities, Umbandists have become sensitive to any signs of aggression against them. Police action has led them in the past to organize themselves into regional federations of temples, whereby each temple had to surrender part of its fundamental autonomy. Their past unhappy and threatening confrontations with the authorities have undoubtedly contributed to their strong defense of religious freedom.

This same kind of tolerance is hardly evident at all in the Pentecostal churches; witness the assertive and even aggressive role they play on the religious *agora*. People who have been converted from Umbanda to Pentecostalism are the ones most ready to give witness to their move from the kingdom of the devil to that of Jesus. Several booklets are currently available which describe the religious careers of former Afro-Brazilian leaders and mediums, now Pentecostal pastors.[15]

In terms of power and meaning, Pentecostals are very conscious of the contribution they have made to the meaning-making process, and are eager to expand their share in this market. They are deeply convinced that they are right and cannot understand, therefore, that other people refuse to share their views. Their firm belief in the workings of the Holy Spirit stimulates them even more in their efforts to proclaim the message and draw others into the flock.

In the war against the Afro-Brazilian religions, the Pentecostal churches have made use of exorcism as their ritual weapon, exorcism in their view being closely related to the dramatic changes brought about by conversion. The conversion experience is ritualized in the Pentecostal church service or evangelization meeting, by stimulating one final trance whereby the 'demon' is incorporated for the very last time, and finally driven out by the power of the

---

[14] Soares 1993: 43, 44.

[15] E.g., Stevão 1975, with the title 'Umbanda Chief finds Christ'.

Holy Spirit.[16] The drama of the event is heightened by the responses of the congregation, singing short thundering songs against the devil, making arm gestures and shouting, for example, 'Sai, sai, sai!' (Be gone!) or 'Queima! Queima!' (Burn!). The irony is that in Umbanda, spirit mediumship is recommended as a means of healing, while in the Pentecostal churches it is exorcism, the final blow to mediumship, that is claimed to heal the person.

When speaking of the external dimension, we must of necessity take a look at Brazilian culture in general. DaMatta, in particular, sees a fundamental ambiguity in Brazilian history and culture, i.e. the dichotomy between hierarchy and equality, order and improvisation, authority and trickster god, rationality and irrationality.[17] Fry and Howe also encountered this in their study of Pentecostal and Umbandist groups.[18] Although both religions contain similar opposing elements, Pentecostalism exhibits a clear preference for the first (hierarchy, order etc.), whilst Umbanda tends to opt for the second (equality, improvisation etc.).

The Pentecostal war being waged against the Afro-Brazilian religions could perhaps be seen as part of a tidal movement in Brazilian society, between the two series of poles, leading sometimes to hierarchical structures and even dictatorship, and sometimes to greater equality and some form of democratization. It should not be forgotten, however, that Pentecostals have a very clear idea of what society should be—a sort of theocracy—and they are prepared to struggle and suffer for this ideal. It is not surprising, therefore, that the Pentecostal representatives in the regional and national parliaments we mentioned earlier, use their positions to propagate this view as far and wide as possible.

Umbandists and other Afro-Brazilians, however, do not have such an ideological view, even though their cosmology does have the potential of being translated into political action, particularly in respect of ecological and environmental issues, bearing in mind that the gods and spirits of nature are of fundamental importance to their religions. Despite the existence of regional federations of Umbanda temples, their fragmented organizational structure makes it almost impossible for them to manifest themselves at the national level. There are a few politicians, however, who are known to be Umbandists and to recruit their voters from Umbanda circles, but there is no doubt that the national Pentecostal churches have been much more effective at the political level.

---

[16] Soares 1993: 43.
[17] DaMatta 1979, 1991.
[18] Fry & Howe 1975.

The supernatural dimension

These external dimension differences cannot be understood fully, however, without relating them to the two other dimensions; we will examine the supernatural dimension first. The Umbandist pantheon is ever-expanding, incorporating more and more spirits as history goes on, to add to its already extensive record of famous popular heroes. It is also inclusivist in nature, the spirits of the past returning to life as they manifest themselves through the mediums. The various categories of Amerindians and negro slaves have, therefore, become marginalized heroes of Brazilian history; names like Lampião and Maria Bonita, for instance, famous popular rebels in North-East Brazil in the 1930s, killed by government troops, are still present both in altar statues and spirit mediumship in some of the Umbanda temples today. In fact, all the religious influences that merge in modern Brazil leave their traces on the altars. It will come as no surprise to find that even the Buddha is represented on the shelves of an altar in a Umbanda temple somewhere in the heartland of Brazil.

As far as the supernatural dimension is concerned, there are no clear-cut good and evil ethics in Umbanda; Exu and Pomba-Gira, for example, presenting a very ambiguous image in this regard. Umbanda temple leaders will always deny that they use these spirits against other people, but they will often point to others who do. It is a public secret that many Umbandist leaders and mediums execute rituals in the interests of harming individual people, and indeed it is a common fact that this kind of ritual is the most lucrative of the many.

If the pantheon is in continuous expansion and there are no strict views on what constitutes good and evil, religious pluralism will be more readily accepted as a normal phenomenon, with ritual serving as an expression of this pluralism. Spirit mediumship rather than exorcism is the ritual instrument for the appreciation of religious pluralism, a fact which became quite clear when the Yoruba *orixás* 'joined the realms' of the Catholic saints.

In contrast, the Pentecostals' supernatural dimension is characterized by strict monotheism, despite their separation of the three persons of the Holy Trinity, and their preference for the gifts of the Holy Spirit. Pentecostal cosmology is fixed, exclusive, and based on a more or less literal reading of the Bible. History, they say, is predestined until the end of time, when the devil will be slain by Christ—indeed, the chalked slogan 'Jesus is nigh' is a common sight on public buildings in Brazil.

There is also a strong emphasis on the contrast between good and evil—life is a constant war against the devil and midnight rituals in honour of Exu are condemned, and actively opposed, as idolatry. All people, including Umbandists, should be saved, they must be the objects of evangelization and they must be preached to, even at cemeteries in the midnight darkness. Once the Holy Spirit has manifested itself, the spirits must disappear; the life of the convert changes and a total claim is put on his or her behaviour. For once and for all, literally for eternity, the convert has passed to the side of the good and is now a soldier engaged in the war against evil, a war which viewed from a particular perspective, can also be seen as a war against religious pluralism.

The internal dimension

In the internal dimension, these religious pluralism options are both reflected and nourished. Umbandists will always welcome representatives from other religions and will, if necessary, try to solve their problems. The irregular visitor is a normal phenomenon in Umbanda temples, because so many only attend when they have problems. No claim is put on them, unless they show signs of a beginning mediumship, and Umbandists readily endorse personal freedom in attending both a church or an Umbanda temple, and even assert that their own activities are not religious at all : their religion is Catholicism. The fact that Umbanda is referred to as a 'non-religion' could be interpreted as representing a strategy to turn it into a national religion, in the sense that posing as something of a different order avoids having to compete with the other religions. Umbanda is viewed more as a kind of primary health care system, available at the nearest street corner, rather than a religion. National censuses have shown that few people actually call themselves Umbandist, a fact which might paradoxically indicate that many Brazilians do in fact consider themselves to be Umbandists. In any event, the boundaries between the internal and external dimensions are rather vague, for clients especially, although less so for mediums.

Pentecostals sometimes also see themselves as a kind of first aid post, albeit in a much more exclusive sense. The internal dimension bonds the believers into a community of persons touched by the Holy Spirit and available, therefore, to help a neighbour in need, never forgetting that that neighbour is always a potential candidate for conversion. Healing and other problem-solving methods, are manifestations of God's will for his people and his divine intervention is available to all, on request. The person thus healed is then presented with a commitment—and the commitment is total. Even in a more hierarchically-structured Pentecostal church, where some would seem to have greater access to the gifts of the Spirit than others, there is still ample room for the new convert to honour this commitment. Once the glory of the Lord has been fully recognized, religious pluralism becomes superfluous and syncretism an anachronism. The church is organized for the purpose of guiding as many people as possible onto the right path, to the safety of its confines. Those outside are lost unless they convert. The boundaries which separate the internal from the external dimension are clearly defined and strictly maintained, and they will only lose their relevance when all have joined the flock.

Conclusion

The framework developed in the first section of this article has helped us to make a comparison between two popular Brazilian religions and their attitudes towards religious pluralism. We have seen that it is the constellation of the external, internal and supernatural dimensions that produces a religion's identity and orients its followers in their attitudes towards religious pluralism. More particularly, the ritual expression of this attitude is a logical consequence of the convictions that characterize the supernatural dimension. A religion's approach towards religious pluralism results from a mixture of secular and religious factors, in dialectical interplay throughout history. The relationship between power and meaning-making is complex.

In terms of the various modes of religious identity construction set out at the end of the first section of this paper, both Umbanda and Pentecostalism seem to represent the revelatory type, employing both spiritual mediumship and the charismatic gifts as channels for the manifestation of the sacred. At the same time, however, believers also develop an active ritual attitude, typical of the explorative mode of religious production, in the sense that both religions see the sacred as a problem-solving instrument.

There are similarities too in terms of the internal dimension. In both religions the starting-point is inclusivist, whereby roles are allocated to all believers, and in both groups part of every congregation is there to seek relief from some kind of affliction or problem. In Pentecostalism those who become convinced that their problem has been solved, will often stay on as new converts, whilst they will only be integrated into Umbanda temples if they have shown signs of possessing mediumship capacities. In both churches, some members are considered more successful and therefore become more influential. If a group's success leads to a change in scale, as happens in the case of expansionist Pentecostalism, institutionalization can follow, as well as traces of a hierarchical structure. Under the firm leadership of its leader, bishop Macedo, one of Brazil's youngest Pentecostal churches, the Universal Church of the Kingdom of God, succeeded in opening more than 700 churches within a period of fifteen years. Umbanda, with rare exceptions, is much more directed towards small-scale face-to-face relationships, developing its patron-client relationships between mediums and visitors, the latter occupying a temporary and marginal position within the internal dimension—unless they prove to be instruments of spiritual mediumship.

The external dimension, the most important when the focus is on religious pluralism, shows definite differences between the two religions. Whereas Pentecostalism adopts a hostile and critical attitude towards society, Umbanda is much more tolerant and reflective toward the various processes in society, despite the fact that its main spirit categories imply an indirect criticism of society. As has been shown above, this difference can only be understood if the religious beliefs prevalent in the supernatural dimension are also taken into consideration. The active anti-syncretic exclusiveness typical of the Pentecostals, contrasts strongly with the passive, taken-for-granted, syncretism of the Umbandists. The ritual expression of these attitudes is accordingly reflected in the contrast between exorcism and spirit possession. Even though both religions extend practical services to the external dimension, and despite the fact that both have encountered resistance at that level, their main difference lies in their attitude towards society in general, and to religious pluralism in particular.

The application of the religious power relationships model as developed in the first section of this paper to two Brazilian examples of popular religion, has shown us that power and meaning are intricately interwoven and mutually influential. Power depends, in part, on the meaning-making process in which gods, spirits and people are viewed or experienced as powerful beings. Moreover, people who hardly play any role in society's power processes can, through meaning-making, find a way of creating their own world, real to them at least, and in which secular and religious power relationships, including religious pluralism, can be inverted and criticized. It has proved useful, therefore, not to have limited ourselves to the internal and external levels normally studied by social scientists, but to include the supernatural level of power relations in our treatment of Brazilian religious pluralism.

This should be a standard approach when studying religions, because it enables us to go beyond the functional questions and explain certain characteristics of the internal and external levels. It was for this reason, therefore, that the contents of beliefs and rituals have been included in our exploration of the relations between power and meaning in a situation of religious pluralism. The attributes of the supernatural have been shown to have an impact on the form and relevance of power relations in the internal and external dimensions. This does not, on the other hand, exclude the influence these relations may have on the form of power in the supernatural dimension; this is an aspect that has already been subjected to comprehensive analysis. The time has come to rehabilitate the explanatory role of the content of religious convictions and rituals—in the study of religious pluralism too.

References

Bastide, R., 1978, *The African religions of Brazil: toward a sociology of the interpenetration of civilizations*. Baltimore, etc.: The Johns Hopkins University Press.

Boudewijnse, B., A. Droogers & F. Kamsteeg (eds.) 1991, *Algo más que ópio: una lectura antropológica del pentecostalismo latinoamericano y caribeño*. San José (Costa Rica): DEI.

Crick, M., 1976, *Explorations in language and meaning: towards a semantic anthropology*. London: Malaby Press.

DaMatta, R., 1979, *Carnavais, malandros e heróis: para uma sociologia do dilema Brasileiro*. Rio de Janeiro: Zahar.

DaMatta, R., 1991, *Carnivals, rogues, and heroes: an interpretation of the Brazilian dilemma*. Notre Dame, etc.: University of Notre Dame Press.

Droogers, A., 1985, *E a Umbanda?* São Leopoldo: Sinodal.

Droogers, A., 1989, *Macht in zin: een drieluik van Braziliaanse religieuze verbeelding*. Amsterdam: Vrije Universiteit.

Droogers, A., 1991a, 'Visiones paradójicas sobre une religión paradójica: modelos explicativos del crecimiento del pentecostalismo en Brasil y Chile', in Boudewijnse, Droogers & Kamsteeg 1991: 17-42.

Droogers, A., 1991b, 'Bibliografia sobre pentecostalismo y movimientos carismáticos en Latinoamérica y el Caribe', in Boudewijnse, Droogers & Kamsteeg 1991: 137-176.

Droogers, A., 1994, 'The normalization of religious experience: healing, prophecy, dreams and visions', in: Poewe 1994: 33-49.

Droogers, A., & H. Siebers, 1991, 'Popular religion and power in Latin America: an introduction', in Droogers, Huizer & Siebers 1991: 1-25.

Droogers, A., G. Huizer & H. Siebers (eds.) 1991, *Popular power in Latin American religions*. Saarbrücken & Fort Lauderdale: Breitenbach.

Fry, P.H., & G.N. Howe 1975, 'Duas respostas à aflição: Umbanda e Pentecostalismo', in *Debate e Crítica* 6: 75-94.

Hoffnagel, J.C., 1978, *The believers: Pentecostalism in a Brazilian city*. Ann Arbor: University Microfilms International.

Lalive d'Épinay, C., 1969, *Haven of the masses: a study of the Pentecostal movement in Chile*. London: Lutterworth Press.

Lapassade, G., & M.A. Luz 1972, *O segredo da Macumba*. Rio de Janeiro: Paz e Terra.

Martin, D., 1990, *Tongues of fire: the explosion of Protestantism in Latin America*. Oxford: Basil Blackwell.

Ortiz, R., 1978, *A morte branca do feiticeiro negro, Umbanda: integração de uma religião numa sociedade de classes*. Petrópolis: Vozes.

Poewe, K., (ed.) 1994, *Charismatic Christianity as a global culture*. Columbia (South Carolina): University of South Carolina Press.

Rolim, F.C., 1980, *Religião e classes populares*. Petrópolis: Vozes.

Soares, L.E., 1993, 'A guerra dos Pentecostais contra o Afro-Brasileiro; dimensões democráticas do conflito religioso no Brasil', in *Comunicações do ISER* 12, no. 44: 42-50.

Stevão, G., 1975, *Chefe de Umbanda acha Christo (depoimento)*. Curitiba: Ed. Luz na Escuridão.

Velho, Y.M. Alves, 1975, *Guerra de Orixá: um estudo de ritual e conflito*. Rio de Janeiro: Zahar.

Willems, E., 1967, *Followers of the new faith: culture change and the rise of Protestantism in Brazil and Chile*. Nashville (Tennessee): Vanderbilt University Press.

RITUAL AS COMMUNICATION

A STUDY OF AFRICAN CHRISTIAN COMMUNITIES IN THE BIJLMER DISTRICT OF AMSTERDAM

Gerrie ter Haar
(Katholieke Theologische Universiteit, Utrecht)

Introduction

The research group 'Religious Pluralism' in the Theological Faculty of Leiden University has committed itself to investigating religious interaction in pluralistic societies, marked by the presence of a variety of religions whose adherents are living adjacent to one another.[1] This poses a basic question: given the situation of religious pluralism, how do adherents of one religion respond to adherents of a different religion and how do they articulate their relationships with them? In organising a symposium on pluralism and identity the underlying idea was that believers of any religion living in a plural society will design and use rituals, or ritual behaviour more generally, as an instrument for inter-religious demarcation. In other words, an important function of ritual behaviour in such a context is to emphasise religious identity and thus separate different believers by drawing strict lines between them.

In this paper I will argue the opposite. I will maintain that in the case which I intend to discuss, namely ritual behaviour among African Christian communities in the southeast district of Amsterdam, the purpose and function of ritual behaviour are essentially geared nòt to inter-religious demarcation but to intra-religious communication. Although the former idea may be a fruitful line of approach in many present-day cases, it is not a valid starting point for assessing the meaning of ritual in the communities under discussion. This is partly due to their diaspora status and partly also to their very short history in the Netherlands. Both are factors which influence ritual behaviour in these communities in such a way that, contrary to what one might expect in a context of religious pluralism, this is first and foremost aimed at creating and maintaining internal stability. The rituals designed in this context then become symbols for

[1] The present article was drafted in December 1993 and does not take account of developments after that date.

intra-religious communication within the Christian tradition.[2]

In my paper I will first describe the religious microcosm of the Bijlmer district of Amsterdam, paying particular attention to the African-led[3] churches and describing three different types of ritual behaviour in one of these churches. On the basis of that I will then analyze the situation of African Christian communities in the Bijlmer. In doing so, I will make use of the insights provided by van Gennep's classic study on rites of passage[4] and look at ritual behaviour in these communities in terms of a life crisis. Rites of passage are rites which can be found in all cultures and are connected to important phases of life. They mark the transition from one phase to the other and thus help in the resolution of a life crisis. Or, as van Gennep defines it, these are 'rites which accompany every change of place, state, social position and age'[5], or indeed a transition from one state into another. Rites of passage, according to van Gennep, comprise all ceremonial patterns which accompany a passage from one situation into another or from one cosmic or social world to another.[6]

This describes well the African communities under discussion. Their rituals have been designed basically to cope with a life crisis resulting from the transition from one social world to another. As van Gennep has pointed out, such drastic changes of condition do not occur without disturbing the life of society and individuals concerned, and it is the function of rites of passage to reduce the harmful effects of that change.[7] Van Gennep's concept of 'rites of passage' was designed to apply to small-scale societies or discrete social groups within a larger society. In the present text, I apply his theory to a secular situation involving large-scale social trends in order to explain the situation of African religious communities in present-day Western Europe. I am thus using existing social theory to explain the ritual behaviour under discussion in the belief that this provides the best available starting point for developing a deeper theoretical understanding of the phenomena described. Although van Gennep's theory is not applied here in its 'pure' and

---

[2] For definition of the terms used I refer to the discussions in the Leiden research group as reflected in the preparatory papers. See also the introduction to this volume.

[3] In using the term 'African-led' churches I follow the practice in the United Kingdom of referring to 'black-led' churches, in order to highlight the fact that these are churches under African leadership.

[4] Van Gennep 1975[7].

[5] See Turner 1969: 80.

[6] Van Gennep 1975: 10.

[7] Van Gennep 1975: 13.

original state, we can nevertheless still derive meaning from it when it is applied to modern times and circumstances.

I will further base myself on Victor Turner's analysis of ritual as a process.[8] His concepts of communitas and liminality,[9] which he developed on the basis of van Gennep's work on rites of passage and which he applied to both religious and secular situations,[10] shed a particular light on the meaning of ritual behaviour as presently practised among African Christian communities in the Bijlmer. The social context in which the ritual process takes place has changed, as has the nature of the life crises which many Africans face today. Nowadays such existential crises no longer affect small-scale and isolated communities, but concern communities world-wide, due to the globalisation of social and economic relations. This is clearly so with people affected by the large-scale migration processes of today, such as in the case of African migrants in Europe. At the same time, much of the social setting has been influenced by a process of secularisation which has reduced the meaning of rites in modern times, particularly in the Western world. But, as has been stated by others, there is no evidence that a secularised urban world has lessened the need for ritualized expression of an individual's transition from one status to the other,[11] and the same can be said of specific communities.

I will conclude my argument by showing that religious demarcation is not in the interest of the African communities in the Bijlmer (or elsewhere in Western Europe) but is a concept which favours the West.

The religious microcosm of the Bijlmer

In the southeast district of Amsterdam, commonly though somewhat incorrectly known as the Bijlmermeer or just 'Bijlmer'[12], we find a great variety of migrant communities, including many Africans. With almost 100.000 officially registered inhabitants,[13] the

[8] Turner 1969.
[9] Turner 1969: 80-118.
[10] E.g. to the 'beat generation' and the 'hippies' (Turner 1969: 99). See also the way Turner compares the American folk singer Bob Dylan to the Hindu musicians in Bengal known as Bauls (Turner 1969: 153-4).
[11] Kimball 1975: xvii.
[12] The southeast district of Amsterdam technically consists of three parts: the Bijlmermeer, Gaasperdam and Driemond, the largest of which is the Bijlmermeer.
[13] On 1 January 1992 the total number of people in the southeast district of Amsterdam was calculated at 91084 (Anonymous 1992c: table 162.14).

southeast district is the largest district of Amsterdam containing some minority groups large enough to deserve explicit mention in government statistics. About half of the Bijlmer population is of non-Dutch origin, the largest minority group being constituted by Surinamers.[14] Other groups explicitly mentioned in the statistics are Antillians, Turks, Moroccans (including other North Africans), and 'South Europeans', including Spanish, Portuguese, Italians, Greek and (former) Yugoslavs.[15] The many West Africans living in the Bijlmer and largely of Ghanaian origin, fall within the category of 'other foreigners' which in 1992 comprised slightly less than 10.000 people.[16] The number of different nationalities living together in this particular district of Amsterdam is said to be over sixty.[17] Depending on their size and substance these different groups have established their own networks which help them to survive in their new environment, which is full of difficulties. They are faced with unemployment, housing problems, and criminality at a time that the general atmosphere in the Netherlands is becoming increasingly hostile towards foreigners from the poorer parts of the world.[18]

One particular social network for many migrant communities in the Bijlmer is formed by the religious organisations, of which there were some 35 different ones in 1992.[19] Since the early 1990s the local council has become aware of the importance of these organisations in, and their contribution to, the process of social renewal of the Bijlmer.[20] Muslims and Christians of various sorts, Hindu groups and Winti adherents, can all be found in this particular district of Amsterdam.[21] The African Christian communities represent only one aspect of that kaleidoscope of religions, albeit an important one. There are at least ten different churches or church groups under African leadership in the Bijlmer, varying in size.

---

[14] The total number of registered Surinamers on 1 January 1992 was 23974 (Anonymous 1992c: table 162.14).

[15] Antillians: 5599; Turks: 851; Moroccans: 1005; South Europeans: 977 (Anonymous 1992c: table 162.14).

[16] The exact number is: 9603 (Anonymous 1992c: table 162.14).

[17] Anonymous 1992a.

[18] A sign of this is the nation-wide debate on the position of immigrants which was initiated by Frits Bolkestein, the leader of the liberal party in the Netherlands, the VVD.

[19] See de Jonge (1992). This is a report commissioned by the *Stuurgroep Vernieuwing Bijlmermeer*. However, the number of religious groups is still increasing.

[20] See Oomen & Palm 1994. This report will contain the results of a pilot project commissioned by the Ministry of the Interior.

[21] According to the latest known figures 25 Christian, 5 Muslim and 3 Hindu groups or organisations are active in the Bijlmer with a total number of some 15.000 members (de Jonge 1993).

They have all been founded by Ghanaians who constitute the largest African presence in the Bijlmer. Apart from these African-led churches, there are substantial numbers of Africans who belong to one of the Catholic churches or to other denominations such as the Seventh Day Adventists.[22] The presence of Ghanaians in the Bijlmer has received special attention from the local council which counted in 1991 an official total of some 2.500 Ghanaians here.[23] However, the total number of Ghanaians in the Bijlmer is estimated to be much higher and needs probably to be doubled.[24] To a large extent it is they who are responsible for the growth and flourishing of the Christian churches in the Amsterdam Bijlmer.

One of the major problems of all religious groups in the Bijlmer is the lack of space to worship. At the time that the Bijlmer district was built, in the 1960s, provision was made for one church building which would accommodate some of the traditional Dutch churches.[25] Almost thirty years later, a completely new picture has emerged as a result of the influx of non-Dutch people,[26] many of whom are adherents of some religion. To enable themselves to worship and fulfil their religious duties they have usually started to meet at private places, forming some sort of house congregation. With the increasing number of migrants the need for space became more and more urgent. Since 1991, therefore, representatives from different religious organisations in the Bijlmer which have no adequate meeting place have come together to discuss their space problem and find practical solutions to it.[27]

---

[22] For example, the so-called *All Saints Church* is a group of African Christians, mainly Ghanaians, within the Roman Catholic Church, while many Nigerians are known to attend the Bijlmer parish of the Dutch Catholic Church (*Nederlands-Katholieke Kerk*). The congregation of the *Seventh Day Adventists* in the Bijlmer consists for 75 % of Africans.

[23] The official figure is 2337, which includes 913 people with dual nationality (Anonymous 1992b).

[24] Recent research has estimated the total number of Ghanaians in the Netherlands, i.e. including non-registered ones, at 15.000, 10.000 of whom are believed to live in Amsterdam (van 't Hoff 1992).

[25] These were the two main Dutch Reformed churches (the *Gereformeerden* and *Hervormden*) and the Roman Catholic parish. Recently they moved into a new church building with the same name, *De Nieuwe Stad*, which is also used by the *Evangelische Lutherse gemeenschap*, the *Evangelische Broedergemeente*, and the Indonesian Christian community *Perki*.

[26] According to the introductory guide for newcomers, published by the council of Amsterdam, every year around 10.000 non-Westerners come to live in Amsterdam. Many of these settle in the Bijlmer.

[27] This circle is known as the '*Overleg Religieuze Organisaties*', an initiative of Jan de Jonge, in his capacity of leader of the Christian-Democratic Party (CDA) in the local council.

Groups which cooperate in this way include people from different faiths. They receive limited support from the local authorities. Some have come to share buildings on a temporary or permanent basis, others have been able to obtain their own space, usually at great financial cost, entirely paid by membership donations, while others are still coping with the present inadequate situation. The majority of groups are Christian, many of which have found shelter in one of the empty spaces under the multi-storey car parks, or in places such as an old shop or supermarket, or they may congregate on Sundays in one of the community houses in the Bijlmer. What they have in common is, literally, their invisibility. The only other religious building in the Bijlmer, apart from the above-mentioned church, is the Taibah mosque which was opened in 1985. It caters for a few thousand Muslim believers of different origin, particularly for Muslims from Surinam.[28]

African-led churches in the Bijlmer

To date, the lack of space to worship on Sundays and to engage in community-building activities during the week is one of the most pressing problems for the African Christian communities in the Bijlmer.[29] If we single out the self-governing churches under African leadership as a separate category, we find at the time of writing some ten different churches of varied size[30], all founded and led by Ghanaians, who are by far the largest single African community in the Bijlmermeer.[31] The rapid growth of their churches is a relatively new phenomenon which reflects the recent influx of Ghanaians into Dutch society. The beginning of this large-scale migration lies in the early 1980s and is connected to the political and economic

---

[28] De Jonge 1993. In practice there seems a tendency for different groups to worship in their own environment, if necessary outside the Bijlmer. However, this seems not to be the case on feast-days.

[29] Recently the local council has presented a provisional policy paper on the issue, which seems to indicate a change in policy from passive to active involvement in solving these problems for all religious organisations, implying a recognition of their role in society, especially in the process of social renewal of the Bijlmer.

[30] I cannot be more precise as the situation is one of constant change in which it is difficult to keep track of new developments. Membership varies from dozens in the smaller to hundreds of people in the larger churches.

[31] In 1991 Ghanaians were officially mentioned as the largest single nationality in the southeast district of Amsterdam, after Dutch and Surinamese (Anonymous 1992a).

changes in Ghana during that time.[32] Many of them found shelter in the Bijlmer where soon they also started to come together to satisfy their religious needs. In practice this often meant a small number of people congregating in an apartment and sitting around the kitchen table to pray together and read the Bible. The increasing numbers of participants forced most groups to look for more suitable accommodation in the sense described above. The emergence of full churches, therefore, is a very recent one, in fact a development of the last five years.

In the following I will describe one of these churches, the longest in existence and with the largest membership, the True Teachings of Christ Temple[33], which is also the one I know best. Although there are differences in style and structure between the True Teachings of Christ Temple and other African-led churches in the Bijlmer, the general pattern of religious belief and practice is rather similar. Some outstanding features of this from a Western perspective are the belief in the power of the Spirit, the importance of prayer and fasting, the intensive use of the Bible, the role of praise-giving during worship, the public testimonies and the overall pastoral care. All these are characteristics which we also find among African Christians in Africa.[34] An additional element, which is of importance in the European context, is that all these diaspora churches see themselves as charged with the task of evangelisation. In view of these similarities, the True Teachings of Christ Temple may be considered a model for African Christianity in the Netherlands.

There are also common features in the structural organisation. We will normally find the congregation under the leadership of a pastor, usually male[35], assisted by a number of church officials with varying responsibilities. A board of elders, a pastoral board and a welfare committee, as well as a financial board are among the most common structures, all made up of both men and women. Most of

---

[32] In recent years Ghana has been ruled by a military government and experienced two coups d'état, in 1979 and 1981, by the current president, Jerry John Rawlings. See further Nimako 1993.

[33] This is the official name of registration in the acts of the Chamber of Commerce. Nowadays a slightly different spelling is used, namely the *True Teachings of Christ's Temple.* In the present paper I will use the official name of registration.

[34] These are well-known features of African-led churches in Africa, better known as African independent or African indigenous churches.

[35] Sometimes also known under a different name or title, such as 'presiding elder'. One of the churches, at the time known as the *Resurrection Power Evangelistic Ministries,* was founded by a Ghanaian woman. Earlier this year she split off and started her own church which has now merged with another one.

them are known for their choirs and accompanying bands, and for their youth activities. They run their own crèches and organise Sunday schools and other activities, depending on their accommodation. Finally, and most significantly in the context of Dutch society, every one of their churches is always full on Sundays. The latter may be seen as an indication that the growth of one church does not necessarily take place at the cost of another.[36]

The True Teachings of Christ Temple was officially founded as a church when it was registered in 1988 by the Dutch Chamber of Commerce.[37] The leader and founder of the church is Reverend Daniel Himmans-Arday, commonly known as 'Brother Daniel', who comes from Accra, the capital of Ghana. In spite of his involvement with the Ghanaian migrant community in the Bijlmer his own presence in the Netherlands is not related to this latest flux of migration. It is the result of a religious experience as a young man in Ghana, when, during serious illness, he was promised recovery in a vision and received a divine call to preach the gospel overseas. 'You will be well, you will travel into the other continents and bring back lost souls (who will be made equally well on the account of your testimony) into My Vineyard'.[38] Following his vocation he arrived in the Netherlands in the late 1970s where during the years to follow he became involved in the lives of his fellow Ghanaians as they started to come and live in the Bijlmer. In the meantime he undertook theology studies with a Bible College in the United Kingdom which further prepared him for his task. His success as a pastor owes much to his charismatic personality which instils faith and confidence in people.[39]

Over the years the True Teachings of Christ Temple has grown from a small house congregation into a full-fledged church which is housed under one of the multi-storey car-parks that are located under the huge tower-blocks in the Bijlmer district. After experiencing several translocations, like other religious communities in the Bijlmer, in 1988 the True Teachings of Christ Temple bought this former accommodation of the Jehovah's Witnesses which could hold some 350 people. Five years later the hall has already proved far too small and an extension project is in full swing which should

[36] See also de Jonge 1993: 10.

[37] It was registered with the Chamber of Commerce on 18 April 1988 as a foundation for the formation of a church community.

[38] Information about the author in Himmans 1986.

[39] I am using the term 'charismatic' here in its common sense as well as in the religious sense of somebody believed to be endowed with a special gift of divine origin, in this case healing.

be completed in early 1994 and give room to some 600 people. Again, this is a trend we also find in other African-led churches, all of which have to make enormous sacrifices in order to obtain or build a place of worship.[40] The largest churches are visited by hundreds of people and have a corresponding membership. The True Teachings of Christ Temple, for example, has a membership of up to about one thousand[41], although precise indications are difficult to obtain as the African migrant community is very mobile. All churches declare themselves explicitly open to everybody who wants to visit or participate, or be a member. In practice, though for obvious reasons membership is largely defined by Ghanaians, many other Africans, particularly Nigerians, but also Antillians and Surinamese people, as well as some Dutch, frequent these churches. As a result, the services have become increasingly bi-lingual, held in both Twi and English to enhance communication among all present.[42]

Church doctrine and practice in the True Teachings of Christ Temple are derived from what is believed to be prescribed by the Bible and therefore seen, as the name indicates, as the 'true teachings' on which Christianity is based. The sermons, presented in the form of 'lessons' focusing on a particular theme, are a central element in the Sunday services. As in the other churches in the Bijlmer, a connection is always made between the lessons to be taken from the Bible and the present-day situation, and a line drawn from the universal meaning it entails to its individual application. In the True Teachings of Christ Temple two sermons are normally preached, the first in Twi by the second pastor with the rank of 'apostle' and simultaneously translated into English, followed by a sermon in English by the minister who elaborates further on some of the issues. The atmosphere is generally relaxed, joyful and attentive. People may come and go as they like although many will sit through the hours-long sessions of preaching, praying, reading, singing, dancing and music with ease and apparent pleasure. There is much attention for individual people's problems and ample time spent on addressing these.

---

[40] For example, the extension project of the TTCT cost over fl. 650,000 which had to be raised from membership donations and personal loans. Most churches practise tithing.

[41] See de Jonge 1992.

[42] Twi is one of the main languages of Ghana. The majority of people from Ghana living in the Netherlands are Twi-speaking. They are mainly Ashanti coming from Kumasi or surroundings. The pastor of the TTCT, interestingly, is Ga-speaking, which is the dominant language in Accra region.

Sunday worship will normally start with the latter during the 'morning devotion', when some of the junior pastors, known as the 'Holy Children', will lead the congregation into songs and prayer, encouraging people to put their requests before God. They wear white robes with a coloured trim, just like the pastor and the apostle. Often, the pastor himself, who is known for his spiritual gifts, will conduct special healing prayers and, if necessary, pray over individual people. As in other African-led churches, the awareness of the presence of evil as a potential threat to humankind is prevalent, and is a problem which will be openly addressed. Preventive action may be taken, for example by the use of incense in the building, as well as by using the rosary during prayers. These are practices which are unique to the True Teachings of Christ Temple and not always approved of by other congregations. The True Teachings of Christ Temple also lights candles during services, another individual characteristic which is disapproved of by some other churches.

Bible reading and the lessons to be taken from that are important aspects of the Sunday services. Christianity is preached not as a doctrine but as a way of life, with Christ as the perfect model. The leaders of the church are supposed to set an example for others by their life style. Through spiritual training they prepare themselves for this responsibility. To further spiritual growth the pastors and 'evangelists', a group of men and women who want to live up to the principles of the church and carry these further, engage in regular prayer and fasting. The male evangelists are called 'Faith Brothers' while the women are known as 'Divine Sisters'. Some of their tasks during services are to ensure order, to show people their seats, to answer any queries or to provide translation if needed, and to take care of the children. Like the pastors, they can be recognised by their special dress, the Divine Sisters usually wearing blue capes and the Faith Brothers a special badge.

Ritual practice is more developed in the True Teachings of Christ Temple than in any of the other African-led churches. It appears well-adapted to the needs of the congregation as related to their conditions of life in the Netherlands and, more particularly, in the Bijlmer. These are often conditions of uncertainty, anxiety and extreme concern, not knowing what tomorrow will bring. The majority of Africans in the Netherlands have come to find a job which will enable them to secure a future for themselves and their families.[43] However, they are increasingly made to feel unwelcome and

---

[43] This includes earlier labour migrants from North Africa, such as the Moroccans, who fall outside the scope of this paper. Apart from that, a substantial

many have to go underground as they are unable to legalise their presence. The church provides a place where they receive encouragement in all their endeavours by the spiritual underpinning of their lives.[44] At the same time it constitutes a community of equals where people in similar circumstances can share their experiences and lend each other practical support. That way the church provides a social network for basically marginalised people who depend on each other. Love and unity, mutual concern and understanding, compassion and solidarity are constantly stressed as important values to which every true Christian should adhere.

In the following I will give some examples of ritual behaviour in the True Teachings of Christ Temple, which involves the active participation of all ritual functionaries in the church.

Ritual acts of purification

Purification rituals or, more simply, ritual acts, may be performed in a number of ways. They are a symbolic expression of the awareness of the existence of evil which requires effective action to counter it. Evil forces can be warded off by calling upon the power of the good forces people believe in, that is the power of Christ or the power of the Holy Spirit. They may also seek protection by burning incense which spreads a pleasant fragrance and is therefore known in various religions as a cultic means to ward off evil forces or spirits and attract good ones. The True Teachings of Christ Temple bases the use of incense on various Biblical references, such as taken from Exodus 30 which gives prescriptions for the building of an altar for burning incense. The burning of incense is also seen as representing the prayer of good people in Christianity, as expounded in the Book of Revelations (Ch. 8: 3-5).

The most common and obvious symbol for purification in the True Teachings of Christ Temple, like in many religions, is the use of water. The sprinkling of holy water, that is water that has been blessed by an ordained minister, can take place on various occasions. One such occasion is at the end of the dedication ceremony, which will be described later in more detail. In this ceremony,

---

number of people from Africa have come to the Netherlands as political refugees, notably from the Horn of Africa.

[44] One may refer here to Edith Turner's view of ritual as the harnessing of spiritual power, based on a re-study of her husband's (Victor Turner) work which she corrected and complemented by developing an 'anthropology of experience'. See Turner 1992.

during which a new-born child is 'committed into the capable hands of the Lord', the sprinkling of holy water onto the congregation refers to the power of God as it is expressed through water and which is believed to work miracles. Evidence for such miracles is found in passages from the Bible, for example in 2 Kings 5: 13-16, which tells about the miraculous healing of Naaman, the army commander of the Syrian king. Purification and healing, the example shows, go hand in hand. The same is true for the use of water in the dedication ceremony. It is a symbolic act expressing the belief that God can heal people from whatever troubles they may have. In the context of a dedication ceremony it expresses the belief that he can also heal barrenness and use his miraculous powers to provide with children even those who may—humanly speaking—have no hope of conceiving. At the same time the sprinkling and washing with water as practised in the True Teachings of Christ Temple are meant as a symbol of love and equality in the sight of God. We find the clearest expression of that on New Year's eve, when, during a night-long service, every individual's feet are washed with water by the apostle and subsequently blessed with oil by the pastor. Purification and restoration are merging here into one final act that is to symbolise the love of God for all humankind, under all circumstances and irrespective of who and where they are.

The most common symbolic use of water, however, is through sprinkling as a simple act of purification. There is no particular time or moment during services set aside for this purpose, nor does it take place as a regular part of the weekly service. Rather different from traditional Dutch churches, much is said to depend on divine inspiration (which by definition cannot be channelled in the conventional way), while at the same time much room is left for improvisation within the broader framework of the service. The sprinkling with water may take place at the beginning of the service, before the morning devotion. One of the Holy Children goes around the church hall sprinkling water from a white plastic jar. Once the hall has been purified the necessary conditions have been created for the power of God to manifest itself during and through the prayers that will follow, conducted by the pastor. There is no set pattern, and the following is just an example.

The pastor enters the hall joined by the junior pastors. They kneel down in front of the hall, facing the congregation whose members follow their example. In the meantime the sprinkling of holy water continues. The pastor starts praying to purify the hearts and minds of everyone and to remove all evil. He calls upon the Lord to remove the evil forces which are believed to be acting against the well-being of individual people as well as of mankind as a whole. He will refer to Satan as the ultimate source of evil or otherwise express the belief in satanic powers which try to influence God's essentially good creation in a negative way. In his prayers the pastor shows an acute awareness of the fact that many people in his congregation are troubled physically or spiritually or otherwise under the pressure of forces they feel unable to control. He will therefore call upon the power of Christ and ask for 'spiritual blessings' for all in order to drive Satan away. He may address Satan directly by pointing out that the church is a holy place, sanctified and dedicated to the Lord and that therefore Satan is not wanted in this area. It is a powerful prayer which is said in the knowledge that as an ordained minister the pastor is not acting in his own right but on the authority of 'our Lord Jesus Christ'. This challenging of Satan may have a visible effect on those who indeed feel oppressed by evil in some way. Some of the members of the congregation may fall into a state of trance and start shaking, thus showing the tumultuous effect of the prayers for healing and purification.

When the prayers are concluded, that is when Satan is believed to have been effectively removed from this area, the pastor addresses himself to the congregation. He will assure them that the Lord has purified them and warns the congregation against going into any 'dark places', where Satan is believed to be active and where one can easily come under the influence of satanic powers. He emphasises the power of prayer and how the Lord is changing man's heart that way. He will call on the believers to open their hearts and to receive the Lord. All will then say the Lord's prayer together. This may be followed by a special prayer which is first said by the pastor and repeated by the congregation which is standing up with hands raised. It may go as follows: 'Unto you I commit my whole body; the forces from inside and outside have no control over me; let me walk free; because of your blood I am redeemed'. Once again, the congregation may call upon the Lord to cast out evil forces, with the words 'cast them out, cast them all out, I will be free'. Subsequently the congregation will submit itself to God by stating that 'I belong to you', and ask for his protection. 'Let me proclaim your glory, I need you always; protect me and protect my family; protect my feet, my eyes, my mouth, so that everything will be in glory to your name. Help me, touch me and set me free'. Often the session is ended with the Lord's prayer and what is called the 'song of togetherness', Psalm 133, which is in praise of brotherly love.

The dedication ceremony

As in all African-led churches, the True Teachings of Christ Temple pays special attention to the children. From a very young age parents take their children to church. Babies usually stay with their mothers for whom special seats are reserved in such a way that they can easily walk in and out to look after them during the service. The older children follow Sunday school classes in a separate room but participate during part of the service. Everything is aimed at preparing the children for a Christian way of life and instilling Christian values and principles from a very young age. In that context the first time a child enters the church after birth is seen as a very special and joyful occasion which is accompanied by a special ritual, called the dedication ceremony, of which the following is a description.

The dedication of a new-born child normally takes place after three months, when the mother has recovered from giving birth and will resume church attendance. Both parents will proudly present the child to the church community to which the new-born baby will also belong from now on. They will do so in the presence of a host of relatives and friends, who are not necessarily members of the church but may just accompany the parents for this special occasion in order to share in their happiness. To mark the festivity parents and other participants are dressed in their best clothes—the parents often in white—as for a party. During the service they will be seated on the front rows of the church, with the child that is going to be dedicated to God. At the appropriate moment, which is after the service has ended but before the closing prayer, parents and child with all who have accompanied them leave the church hall to re-enter again in procession. In the meantime the church mother announces the ceremony by reciting the relevant passage from the Bible which explains the need of dedication.[45] After that she also leaves the hall while the choristers rise from their seats and start singing and the congregation may join in.

Then, the Holy Children, preceded by the apostle, enter the hall solemnly in their white robes and without shoes.[46] They kneel down at the front of the church before the altar, facing the congregation.

---

[45] Reference is made to Lk. 2: 23 which speaks of the need to dedicate every first-born (male) to the Lord.

[46] The altar and its surroundings are considered sanctified space which may not be entered with shoes. In the same line of thought, women cover their hair in church. (It may be noted, in this context, that Ghanaian women's dress usually includes matching headscarf).

Once they have knelt down the full parade will enter, with the parents in front, the mother carrying the baby. They are preceded by the Faith Brothers and Divine Sisters and followed by other church functionaries such as members of the welfare committee. They enter in mixed couples through the centre aisle while the choir is singing and proceed to walk around the church hall. When they are back in front the Faith Brothers turn left while the Divine Sisters turn right, after which they kneel down joining the Holy Children. The parents remain standing in the middle, in front of the centre aisle with their backs to the congregation while facing the altar. The church mother positions herself behind them and takes the baby over from the mother. The pastor opens proceedings with a short speech, followed by prayer. The apostle will read from the Bible the section which speaks of Hannah who has been longing for a child and finally has her prayers answered.[47] Then the pastor leaves the altar while the choir starts singing again. He goes around blessing every individual who has knelt in front and those seated on the front rows, who are mostly family or friends. When he is finished the choir stops singing so that the actual dedication can take place.

The apostle takes the child over from the church mother while the pastor stands in front of the parental couple who have also taken off their shoes and knelt down. The apostle, who is standing behind the parents, hands the child to the pastor who hangs his rosary around its neck. He lifts the child up in the air for everybody in the church to see, walking from one side to the other, presenting the child to the congregation. He introduces the child as a gift from God to the community. 'Children of Israel', as he addresses the congregation in conformity with the Biblical base for the ceremony, 'here is the gift which the Lord has given us'. He then sprinkles the child three times—in the name of the Father, the Son and the Holy Spirit—with blessed water from a jar held by the Holy Head, the senior of the Holy Children. In the same way he blesses the child three times with blessed oil, applying the sign of the cross on the forehead. Finally (although this may also take place in a reversed order) he kneels down with the child to make it touch the floor with its feet, again three times in the name of the Father, the Son and the Holy Spirit. He directly addresses the child which for the first time in its life has literally set foot in the house of God, represented as the house of its Father. Although the actual wording may differ, the meaning of this act is clear: the church is introduced here as the

[47] 1 Samuel 1: 26-28.

ultimate place of security. It is presented as a place of asylum and a safe haven where she or he can always go and which will always be open to him or her even though the whole world may have abandoned the person. This is the house of God, where the power of God is believed to be present and all evil will be warded off, a place where Satan cannot enter. It is a moving and meaningful sign in an environment full of uncertainties.

At the end the pastor returns the child to the parents, pointing out once more that the newborn child is a gift from God and that they are its stewards. He impresses on them that the child has been entrusted to them by the Lord. Therefore they should take good care of it so that it will grow up in good health and prosperity. He then blesses both child and parents. Finally, he pronounces a blessing for the whole community, expressing the hope that the blessing of children may also be bestowed upon others. In doing so he may sprinkle the community with water as a symbolic act of purification and a sign of God's miraculous power and fatherly love.

All those who have knelt down will be getting up now and the thanksgiving part of the ceremony will start. The mother or both parents express their thanks to the Lord, usually introduced by a song. In doing so, and surrounded by all who have accompanied her, the mother may inform the congregation about eventual problems during pregnancy or at childbirth which were successfully overcome. She may tell about her longing for a child or her long waiting, or any other circumstance related to the new-born child. After giving this testimony there is singing and dancing to thank God. The choir and the band will contribute to the festivity which creates a party spirit throughout the hall. Finally the procession leaves the hall while still in a dancing mood. Parents and family then return to their seats in front. The whole ceremony will have lasted for about half an hour and will be concluded by the pastor with a final prayer. After that the service will be brought to an end as usual while soft drinks and cakes will be distributed among the congregation to celebrate the occasion.

The foot-washing ritual

Once a year, at the eve of the New Year, a special ritual is performed in the True Teachings of Christ Temple to mark the transition from the old to the new year. Following the example of Jesus as described in the New Testament the feet of every member of the church are washed and blessed with oil while the person is being prayed over. The service starts in the evening and lasts into the early morning, as a few hundred people need to be served this way. In order of arrival the individual names are written down on a list which will be worked through during the night-long service. The night is spent with singing, praying, Bible reading and preaching by the various evangelists. Tea and sandwiches are served through the night. From time to time a number of individuals' names are called out, some ten at a time, for the foot-washing ceremony. They queue up at the pastor's consultation room which they will enter barefoot. When it is their turn the faithful will enter the front room one by one for the apostle to wash their feet. To that purpose a plastic tub has been put in the room filled with water by some helpers who change it regularly. The person then enters into the tiny back room, which is the pastor's meditation room containing a small altar. This time the person steps into another little tub after which the pastor will bless his or her feet with oil making the sign of the cross. He does the same on the forehead while saying a short prayer for the person and blessing him or her. In case a person does not speak English, the language of communication used by the pastor, somebody will accompany him and translate what is said. Only when every individual has been served this way will the service be concluded. At the end of the service all the pastors and evangelists will queue up in front of the church hall to shake hands with every individual member to wish them happy New Year.

In practice this means that the service goes on for some twelve hours, during which most people will stay. In the prayers during the service regular references are made to the need to be washed anew by Jesus, and God's protection is sought against attacks from the 'Evil One'. The washing of the feet and the blessing with oil have symbolically prepared the congregation for the year to come. The washing has purified them from whatever evil they may have been affected by, or believe to have been affected by, while the blessing with oil is meant to provide protection against any Satanic attacks. The end of the year is seen as a particularly vulnerable period, during which Satan will try and strike a final blow. Spiritual protection, therefore, is needed more than ever.

Pluralism and identity in the context of the Bijlmer

I have been describing three types of ritual behaviour among African Christians in the Bijlmer as derived from the Bible and adapted to the specific conditions of modern Dutch society. At the same time, it is not surprising to note that several aspects of these ceremonies reflect the religious and cultural traditions of the peoples of Ghana, particularly the Ashanti.[48] The dedication of a new-born infant, for example, is a well-known practice in Ghana as indeed in many other parts in Africa. My main concern at the present juncture, however, is not to demonstrate the undoubted cultural precedents of ritual practices of African Christians in the Netherlands, but to demonstrate their meaning. Their meaning should not be understood by reference to the context of the past but rather by reference to the present, that is to the context in which African Christians live in the Netherlands today.

By taking this approach, we may see that the notion of demarcation is not a very helpful one. The situation in the Amsterdam Bijlmer is such that African Christians live easily with believers of other faiths, such as Islam and Hinduism, to mention two which are amply represented in the Bijlmer. There is no frequent formal interaction between the different religious communities, as they are all busy building up their communities in difficult circumstances. However, representatives meet regularly, in particular to solve a common basic problem, namely the lack of space to worship.[49] On occasion the different religious groups in the Bijlmer have also worshipped together, notably at the time of mourning the dead and other victims of the plane crash which took place on 4 October 1992.[50] In their present historical phase, it seems, the need to cooperate exceeds the need to demarcate which may develop over time. The variety of religious groups in the Bijlmer of non-Dutch origin is still increasing. All of them suffer from the prevailing political climate in Western Europe, including the Netherlands, which forces them into the margins of society. Marginalisation and the problems resulting from it are the main factors which define ritual behaviour in the most recent migrant communities in the Bijlmer, notably the African ones.

One may argue that, with Western Europe moving towards an effective European Union, the need for demarcation in all spheres

---

[48] For a classic study of the Ashanti people of Ghana, see Rattray 1955².

[49] See above, note 27.

[50] On that Sunday an Israeli cargo plane crashed into some of the tower-blocks in the Bijlmer, killing at least an official number of 43 people. Various joint services were held to commemorate the dead. A week after the tragedy a national service was held in the *RAI*, the largest congress hall in Amsterdam, which was broadcast live. One week later the various religious groups organised their own joint memorial service in the Bijlmer *Sportcentrum*, on 18 October 1993, a unique event in inter-religious cooperation.

of life manifests itself on the side of the Europeans rather than on that of the Africans. While the inner frontiers in Europe are gradually being removed in order to further integration among various peoples, new demarcation lines are being drawn at the same time in order to exclude certain other categories. The content and tone of the recent political debate in Europe on migrants and illegal workers is a logical consequence of this policy of demarcation. Significantly, the demarcation lines are largely racially determined, so that in practice a predominantly white community is consciously separating itself from largely black communities. These remarks apply to religion in the Netherlands. One of the most recent migrant communities to have established itself in the Netherlands is black people mainly from West Africa. Many of them, as we saw, are Christians. As such they identify with the Netherlands as a basically Christian country, and particularly with the Christian communities there. In such a context, they feel little need to emphasise their own identity—often ascribed to them by others—as Africans, or specifically African Christians. They have evidently understood that this would contribute to their isolation in society rather than bring them into the mainstream of Western Christianity. Therefore, Africans in the Bijlmer tend to stress their identity as Christians and not as Africans, while their congregations do not call themselves (as others do) 'African churches' but international churches. In other words, what we see in the African diaspora in Europe may well represent the beginning of a new trend in the history of African-led churches. Churches of this type became known at the beginning of the twentieth century as African independent churches (AIC's), a name given to them by others. Later, they changed their name into African indigenous churches, while retaining the same acronym. Now established outside the African continent, these churches refer to themselves as international churches. By using the same acronym (AIC's), but interpreting the 'I' with different words, one may see how the status of African churches has changed throughout the century. The changes of name are an eloquent statement of the dynamics of this particular history.

These African-led churches are international in that they explicitly declare themselves open to non-African believers, irrespective of race or colour. In practice however, these churches attract almost exclusively black people from various African countries, mostly from Ghana, and including people from Surinam and the Dutch Antilles. It is the Dutch Christians who, even in the context of the Bijlmer where they are living next door to African Christians, prefer to stay apart. A good example of this is provided by the Roman Catholic parish in the Bijlmer, the *Graankorrel.* African parishioners meet in a separate part of the church building for services in Twi and English every Sunday, and join the Dutch-speaking congregation in the main body of the church from time to time. The Dutch-speaking congregation, however, never goes to join the Africans for worship in their part of the church. Other Dutch Christian communities invoke various reasons for not mixing with African communities. The point is that by its behaviour, the Dutch community in general obliges African Christians in the Netherlands to stay apart. It is ironic that for African Christians in the Netherlands the relationship with their Dutch counterparts is very important but has so far proved a greater obstacle than the forced cohabitation with other faiths. I therefore propose to examine the issue under discussion—religious pluralism and identity—not in relation to other faith groups but specifically in the context of *Christian* pluralism and identity, arguing that the demarcation lines are drawn essentially not by the African Christians in the Netherlands, but by Dutch Christian communities.

We may, therefore, consider ritual behaviour in African-led churches from that point of view. The emphasis on purification, the need to ward off evil, the sharing in the power of Christ, and the offering of a secure place in the church are all ritual underpinnings of the teachings of the church. Church teachings and doctrines are all related, in one way or another, to the day-to-day situation in which people live. There is a constant awareness that the marginalisation of most Africans living in the Bijlmer, in itself already the most marginalised district of Amsterdam, can easily lead them into difficulties. Drugs, prostitution and its concomitant danger of contracting AIDS, drunkenness and theft, all social evils to be found in the conditions of a marginalised society, can easily turn from potential into real dangers for migrant communities. This is particularly true for young people who form the majority of the church members of the African-led churches. One of the most striking aspects of the True Teachings of Christ Temple, therefore, is the creation of a safe place, not just physically in the form of a church hall but, more importantly, in a ritual sense. The church constitutes a sanctified space which has been set apart as the place of the Lord and can neither be entered nor touched by Satan. Incense and holy water are means to secure the place's purity and sanctity, and to protect it against evil. Whoever enters the place under the spell of Satan, will be able to rid themselves of evil by the exposure of evil spirits in this sacred area, and by calling upon the power of Christ through the

Holy Spirit. The ritual is controlled by an ordained minister who is considered spiritually too strong to be affected by Satan. Rituals are performed in an orderly manner. Physical signs of spiritual presence, whether it is believed to be of a good or an evil spirit, signs of the presence of God or of Satan, are accepted as a normal effect of the ritual act that is performed and dealt with without disturbing the proceedings.

The aim of the ritual is to provide security and protection in a hostile and unstable environment. Hence the dedication ritual is particularly meaningful as it explicitly symbolises the idea of the church as a safe haven from the moment one is born. Love and unity, brotherhood and charity, caring and sharing are constantly promoted in word and action, including in ritual action. All ritual behaviour is designed to link people together by causing them to communicate with one another, literally and symbolically. For example, a 'chain of the Spirit' may be formed during or after healing prayers, when people join hands in order that they may be bound by the spiritual power. The healing referred to in the prayers is not limited to physical problems, but particularly addresses the social problems which have a disturbing effect on people, such as joblessness, homelessness, and the lack of formal identity papers. Jobs, housing, documentation problems, and so on, are all recurrent themes of prayer and preaching in church services.

Ritual in times of crisis

African communities like that in the True Teachings of Christ Temple are confronted with life crises which they try to solve by ritual means and which therefore may be usefully analyzed with the help of van Gennep's 'rites of passage' model. In the particular case which we are examining at present, the life crisis has been set in motion by some form of upheaval in the home countries in Africa: war, poverty, unemployment, lack of education, food shortages, etcetera. It is this type of life crisis which has motivated or even forced people to go through a transitional cycle, comparable to those described by van Gennep. It involves people separating themselves from their home countries, arriving in unknown and insecure places where they tend to live a marginal life, while preparing for full participation in their new environment. In other words, these migrant communities are going through an important transitional phase of life which, like other 'life crises' such as birth, puberty, marriage and death, require ritual or ceremonial validation. The rituals in church communities such as the True Teachings of Christ

Temple accompany this new type of life crisis and help in making the transition.

Van Gennep identified a regular pattern in the rites of passage which allowed him to develop a classification by distinguishing three major phases: separation, transition and incorporation.[51] I am particularly concerned with the second phase, the phase of transition or liminality which is vital to all rites of passage and marks the most sensitive phase in the ritual process. The African communities in the Bijlmer have gone through the phase of separation and are now in the most delicate phase of their life crisis, the transitional or marginal phase, which is marked by liminality. It is this phase elaborated upon by Turner—which is vital to their eventual successful incorporation into Dutch society. The crisis inherent in the transition from Africa to Europe has a disturbing effect on the community concerned as well as on its members as individuals. Ritual behaviour, therefore, is intended to restore the balance through spiritual empowerment, coupled with practical action to solve individual problems. Hence, we may argue, all ritual behaviour in these communities is aimed at achieving internal stability in order to overcome their liminality and prepare their members for entering the third and last phase, the phase of incorporation as an accepted part of Dutch society.

I will move to Victor Turner to explore in more detail the characteristics and consequences of the second phase, the liminal phase.[52] Characteristic of the liminal phase is the ambiguity which goes with it. Liminal persons belong neither to the community from which they have come, nor yet to a new community. Such is the case in the Bijlmer. Africans living in the Bijlmer have left their original communities in their home countries behind and—although there will continue to be links—they are not really part of these any more. Nor do they yet form part of the Western community where they have come to live. They are indeed, as Turner puts it, 'betwixt and between the positions assigned and arrayed by law, custom, convention, and ceremonial'.[53] Liminality, as he says, goes with marginalisation and structural inferiority, with low status and structural exclusion. The issue of demarcation lines being drawn by the European community is constantly and openly addressed in their churches.

---

[51] In English translation also referred to as stages of separation, margin or limen, and aggregation (e.g. Turner 1969: 80).

[52] Turner 1969: 81ff.

[53] Turner 1969: 81.

The characteristics of liminality can all be found among the African communities in Amsterdam.[54] Their marginality can be demonstrated from their social as well as their geographical position. They are concentrated in the least popular district of town where they live in the huge tower-blocks which in the 1970s-80s were left by many Dutch citizens who had come to find the living conditions of the Bijlmer intolerable. Socially the majority of Africans are equally marginalised, in the sense that most of them have unskilled jobs and relatively low wages while at the same time many are forced to live clandestinely as they lack the official papers which allow them a legitimate place in Dutch society. In other words, many of them have no recognised status in the wider society of the Netherlands, which is characteristic of their liminal situation: 'the passage from lower to higher status is through a limbo of statuslessness'.[55] The people concerned are aware of this and determined to turn things to their advantage during the liminal phase by moving away from their lower status towards a higher one in the Netherlands. The church communities in the Bijlmer play an important role in helping them to achieve that. They provide the institutional context for a type of ritual behaviour which is designed to help individuals make the transition from one stage to the other, from separation from an old community to incorporation into a new one.

Liminality, in given circumstances, as Turner has shown, is represented in various ways, for example by lack of possessions, passiveness or humility. Most significant, however, are the comradeship and egalitarianism which are promoted in this phase and which lead to a form of homogeneity which he has labelled 'communitas'. It stands for a model of society or a modality of social relationship which, according to Turner, emerges recognizably in the liminal period, representing a rather unstructured and undifferentiated community, or even communion, of equal individuals who submit together to the general authority of the ritual elders.[56] This is relevant to the case of the Bijlmer, where we can discern a similar pattern, with details varying according to the specific situation. The teachings in the various churches are clearly designed to emphasise this communitas aspect. The members of the church, although mostly coming from a specific region in Ghana, all bring

---

[54] There are, of course, individual exceptions, but as a group the statement holds true.
[55] Turner 1969: 83.
[56] Turner 1969: 82ff.

their different personal backgrounds, different individual experiences and their own hopes and expectations. They gather in these churches as individual beings in-between two communities: the one of the past and the one of the future. Love, equality, and sharing; firmness and discipline are among the qualities which recur in the 'lessons', as the sermons are often called, and other admonitions during church services. The authority of the church leadership is (as is normally the case in churches) generally accepted and followed, even if it is only because one cannot easily evade it. The leadership is clearly aware of the importance of promoting and cultivating communitas in these marginal communities as a prerequisite for successful integration in Dutch society. In order to do so, they need to find and develop a new identity. In the given circumstances this new identity does not lie in their being Africans, which sets them apart as a different and separate community in Dutch society, but in their being Christians, which allows them to become part of the world community or, indeed, the Western community.

Communitas, as Turner sees it, is essentially a relationship between concrete, historical, idiosyncratic individuals who are not segmentalized into roles and statuses but confront one another in the manner of Martin Buber's 'I' and 'Thou', that is in a mutual relationship between total and concrete persons.[57] That is precisely what one finds in these Bijlmer communities which in doctrine and practice favour an egalitarian model that, ideally, should lead to a form of solidarity which is not based on the contrast with others. The notion of demarcation is virtually absent, as the solidarity is with the marginalised, which also comprises members of other faith groups.[58] Christianity is preached not from a dogmatic point of view, but as a way of life which also offers the best solution to practical problems. Demarcation, by emphasising the differences among believers, offers no solution to the problems of these communities. On the other hand, stressing shared human values does help resolving their problems in life. Basing himself on a variety of sources Turner has shown the regular connection between liminality (as defined above) on the one hand, and universal human values such as peace, harmony, comradeship and brotherhood among all men, universal justice, fertility, equality before God,

---

[57] Turner 1969: 119, 124.

[58] One example is the concrete help given by the TTCT to a Turkish family which was homeless after a fire in the house. The notion of demarcation only comes in at times when Christian practices may literally get mixed with non-Christian ones, e.g. with certain traditional religious practices.

health of mind and body, etcetera, on the other. Christian values, therefore, are constantly preached and practised in the African Christian communities that have emerged in the Netherlands. The need for demarcation may be identified rather in the Dutch communities which so far have found it difficult to integrate African Christians into their wider Christian community, and continue to put emphasis on the African rather than on the Christian aspect of the believers. That is, Dutch Christians use culture as a mechanism to demarcate and separate, whereas the African Christians in the diaspora take the opposite view and aspire to use their Christian faith as a means of integration into Dutch society.

Communitas is the predominant element of one particular phase in the life process, the transitional or liminal phase, and as such not a permanent condition. The communitas that emerges during that phase is born out of a condition of crisis and may well be called a 'communitas of crisis'.[59] Turner makes a distinction between three different types of communitas, which represent three different phases in the transitional process: an existential, a normative, and an ideological communitas as it develops over time from a rather unstructured and spontaneous into a more structured and well-governed model.[60] The Bijlmer communities can best be compared to the normative communitas model, as they find themselves in a period where they need to mobilise and organise resources and require a degree of social control among members of the congregation in pursuit of these goals. Thus, from an existential communitas, often in the form of small house congregations, they have organised themselves into a more enduring social system, more structured and with an adapted institutional context. The step to an 'ideological communitas' has not yet been made but seems inevitable in the course of time.

Conclusion

My argument has, somewhat unusually, focused on the relations between two types of Christianity, of Dutch and African origin, in the context of modern Dutch religious pluralism. In doing so, I have been stressing similarities rather than differences between these two trends, for reasons I explained above. This is not to deny the meaning and influence of traditional African cosmology, as

---

59 Cf. Turner 1969: 143.
60 Turner 1969: 120.

some have suggested, but to bring out the dynamic interaction between tradition and modernity of African Christianity in new circumstances. In this case, these are not the circumstances of 'traditional' Africa, nor of modern Africa, but of modern Europe. The content of people's beliefs and the way they give expression to these are informed by the specific conditions of their life in respective circumstances. I have described these circumstances for Africans in the European diaspora (which are also quite different, for example, from those concerning Africans in the American diaspora), and I have looked at how 'traditional' Dutch communities respond to this latest process of social change. In other words, I believe that in order to try and understand ritual behaviour among African Christian communities in the Netherlands, particularly in the Bijlmer district of Amsterdam, one should not base the argument primarily on the African situation, but on the European situation, seeking points of references in the actual situation which involves and affects both African and Dutch communities.

The need for demarcation, I have argued, is a need of white Christian communities in the Netherlands which seek to separate themselves from black Christian communities in their midst. This may not be immediately apparent due to the intellectually liberal discourse often to be found in Western Christianity which stresses the right, or even the need, for Africans to maintain their own identity. This need is also expressed in the conventional view of many scholars of religion, or theologians for that matter, who use the same argument to describe and analyze the position of African Christians.[61] The demarcation argument prevents black Christians in the Netherlands from full participation in Dutch religious life. Thus institutional power remains with the Dutch in spite of the numerically growing importance of black Christianity in the country. This is equally reflected in academic debate inasmuch as theological faculties and institutes, or other places of religious studies, neglect to give institutional status to other than the traditional religious trends in the Netherlands and make no allowances for a serious input from non-Western Christians.

In practice, this means that it is Dutch Christians, or other non-Africans, who try and define for African Christians the nature of their identity, locating this in their African-ness. This in spite of the

---

[61] One may refer, in this context, for example to the debate at a recently held missiological congress on Africa, on 21-22 October 1993 in Heerlen, focusing on the question of inculturation, under the title: 'Abide by the otherness of Africa and Africans'.

latter's efforts to show that their identity lies first and foremost in their shared Christian-ness. Only when that has been accepted will they be able to emphasise their identity as African Christians. One may recall that the establishing of a new identity is one of the most important features of the liminal phase of the ritual process as Turner has described it. This is not different for African Christians in the Netherlands in their present phase. In this second phase of the transitional process it is more important for them to establish their identity as Christians, while in the third and last phase, that of incorporation into Dutch society, it may become more important to lay emphasis on the aspect of being African as part of their identity.[62]

For African Christian communities in the West, however, in present-day conditions, it runs against their interests to emphasise their African-ness as it helps to put up barriers rather than remove them, also considering their obvious presence as black people among whites. Instead, in their own discourse, they put great emphasis on the universal values, particularly stressing concepts of mutual love and unity, among Christians of all denominations and irrespective of race and colour, but also among all human beings, irrespective of their creed. Belief in Christ, rather than functioning as a strict line of demarcation, is stretched to encompass others who want to be part of the group, even if on an occasional or temporary basis. As such, African Christians in the Netherlands continue a religious practice characterised by openness and flexibility which is a hallmark of African religiosity in general. African religions are traditionally known for their capacity to incorporate others.[63]

Ritual behaviour in African Christian communities, I conclude, as I have described and analyzed it in the context of the Bijlmer district of Amsterdam, has a predominantly communicative character which expresses itself in two major ways. The building up of internal stability as a community is one important function of it, yet it is not an inward-looking affair solely aimed at strengthening group solidarity. Ritual behaviour in the African-led churches is open and flexible in character and should be considered in relation to the circumstances of Dutch society which Africans in the Netherlands aspire to join. Ascribing demarcating qualities to their rituals means ignoring their communicative qualities. Rather than func-

---

[62] We can observe a similar trend in other non-Western communities in Dutch society which settled there much longer ago, such as Turkish or Surinamese communities.

[63] See e.g. ter Haar 1993.

tioning as demarcation, ritual behaviour of African Christians in the case we have examined is a symbol for communication with the Dutch Christian community as they try to communicate to them their identity as Christians and their need to be incorporated into the wider Christian community in the West.

References

Anonymous 1992a, *Zuidoost in cijfers, 1991*. Amsterdam: Gemeente Amsterdam, Stadsdeel Zuidoost.

Anonymous 1992b, *Ghanezen in Zuidoost—een verkennend onderzoek*. Amsterdam: Stadsdeel Zuidoost.

Anonymous 1992c, *Diadam 1992; statische informatie: tabellen (1e deel)*. Amsterdam: Gemeente Amsterdam, Bureau voor Onderzoek en Statistiek.

Gennep, A. van, 1975[7], *The rites of passage*. Chicago: The University of Chicago Press, (1960[1]).

Haar, G. ter, 1993, 'Gemeenschapsgodsdiensten', in Weerdenburg 1993: 9-30.

Himmans, D., 1986, *Light on the scriptures*. London: Oval Press.

Hoff, G. van 't, 1992, *Migratie van Ghanezen* (Unpublished report of a *leeronderzoek*, Universiteit van Amsterdam).

Jonge, J. de, 1992, *Soms was er geen plaats in de herberg: een poging tot een religieuze kaart van de Bijlmermeer*. Amsterdam: Stuurgroep Vernieuwing Bijlmermeer.

Jonge, J. de, 1993, *Het wemelt hier weer van kleine luyden; scriptie ter afsluiting van de CDA-kaderschoolleergang 1992-1993*. Amsterdam (unpublished long essay).

Kimball, S.T., 1975, 'Introduction', in van Gennep 1975[7]: V-XIX.

Nimako, K., 1993, *Nieuwkomers in een 'gevestigde' samenleving: een analyse van de Ghanese gemeenschap in Zuidoost*. Amsterdam: Gemeente Amsterdam, Stadsdeel Zuidoost.

Oomen, M., & J. Palm, 1994, *Geloven in de Bijlmer: over de rol van religieuze groeperingen*. Amsterdam: Het Spinhuis.

Rattray, R.S., 1955[2], *Ashanti*. London: Oxford University Press (1923[1]).

Turner, E., 1992, *Experiencing ritual: a new interpretation of African healing*. Philadelphia: University of Pennsylvania Press.

Turner, V.W., 1969, *The ritual process: structure and anti-structure*. Harmondsworth: Penguin Books.

Weerdenburg, J., (ed.) 1993, *In grote lijnen: de godsdiensten van de wereld*. Utrecht: Universiteit Utrecht, Bureau Studium Generale.

PART TWO
THE RITUALIZATION OF THE ENCOUNTER

RITUALS AROUND THE BODHI-TREE IN BODHGAYÂ, INDIA

Albertina Nugteren
(Theologische Faculteit Tilburg)

The worship of trees in ancient India

The worship of trees is an ancient Indian custom and has been kept alive up to the present day.[1] We find traces of the special veneration for trees in pre-Aryan remains, such as in the stone seals of the Indus civilization.[2] There is an abundance of ritualistic, liturgical, philosophical, mythical and narrative references to trees in the scriptural tradition, from the Vedas to modern Indian literature. Many of the popular practices have been kept all over India, and many new ones have developed. Recently, as a result of growing ecological awareness, the multifunctional value of trees and their products has been emphasised all over again.[3]

In order to form an impression of the degree to which trees were part of the daily life in Vedic times, we have to think back 3500 years in time, and imagine a fruitful land in which rivers and forests abounded. The Aryans invading the Indus valley and proceeding forth to the Gangetic plains, must have stood in awe. The spirit of those Indo-Aryans must have been a compelling one, because not only did they drive the *adivâsins*, whoever they were, back into the other parts of the huge continent, they also made the land habitable, comfortable and profitable. Their aggressive attitude of subjugating the natural environment to man's demands secured sustenance for a growing population.

But at the same time, reverence for nature's presence and powers was never lost. On the contrary, the Vedic texts are full of references to nature, such as expressed in imitative magic, rites, charms, and laudatory hymns. Trees, in their material as well as

---

[1] The best systematic treatment of tree-worship in ancient India is found in Viennot 1954. Among the folkloristic studies, S.M. Gupta (1971) and S.S. Gupta (1965) provide the best information about the living cults in India today.

[2] Most of the studies concerned with tree-worship are written from the point of view of art-history. Of course, because wood is a perishable material, the relevant objects are mainly depictions of trees in stone.

[3] For a general introduction to the environmental issues in relation to trees, see Dargavel, Dixon, & Semple 1988.

their symbolic and cosmological aspects, played a prominent role in Vedic sacrifice. One of the ritual objects directly related to a tree is the sacrificial post (*yûpa*, *skambha* or *stambha*), to which the animals were tied in the middle of the sacred space. This wooden pillar deserved much veneration, because it stood there as the *axis mundi* between the micro-cosmic world of man and the macrocosmic realm of the elementary powers. Those powers were to be evoked, praised and cajoled in the course of the sacrifice, and the post was supposed to carry the sacrificial gifts to the gods. It is evident that, in the axial function of this pillar, the species of wood from which the post was made, was of crucial importance, as was also true of the type of wood of which the rubbing sticks, the fire drill, the firewood, the spoons, the bowls, and the *soma*-vats. The tree's power and special characteristics were thus transferred to its products.

But trees provided the Vedic priests not only with fitting implements and utensils for the sacrificial process, they also provided the people with amulets promising fertility for wife and cattle, as well as guaranteeing the exclusive love of a coveted person. The characteristic of certain trees (especially the creepers and epiphytes) were thought to be transmitted to the amulets made from them, so that pieces of the tree were carried by men who needed the power to strangle and choke their enemies, both literally and figuratively. Apart from the use of wood in sacrifice and magic, trees also had many functions in daily life; they provided shade, food, firewood and medicine. Farmers and herdsmen eked out a precarious living by cultivating the fields, which needed to be protected from wild animals by fences of thorny bushes. Certain trees were associated with *yakshas*, the servants of Kubera, the god of wealth, and all trees were the potential abode of sylvan deities (*vrikshakas*), who had to be honoured and fed on a regular basis.[4] There were trees said to be wishing-trees (*kalpavirksha*), and trees said to grant fertility to childless women (such as the *ashok*). And, of course, many trees showered the earth with flowers, thereby marking the passing of the seasons, and gladdening the hearts of young women.[5]

We see how forests and clusters of trees formed the backdrop of

---

[4] For a study of *yakshas*, see Coomaraswamy 1931.

[5] This connection between the flowering of trees and the lovesick moods of young girls, or the celebration of love by amorous couples under flowering trees, is abundantly depicted in Indian art. As elsewhere in the world, spring-festivals (*vasantotsava*) are joyous (and sometimes rowdy) occasions for celebrating the new vitality in man and nature.

the contemplative life as documented in the Âranyakas (literally: Forest Books) and Upanishads. We see hermits, sages, *sâdhus*, yogis and gurus there, in a forest clearing, where a couple of huts formed a hermitage. It was in this kind of sylvan context that the Indian leanings towards ascetism (*tapas*) and renunciation (*tyâga*) grew into a science, under these very trees. Mendicants often chose the roots of trees as their dwelling-place for the night; trees like the *banyan* tree with its hanging branches forming new roots, provided those thinkers with images of life as *samsâra* ('the cycle of existence'), whereas the symbol of the inverted tree between heaven and earth was often used to denote *brahman*.[6] At the same time, trees were often seen in mythology as the abode of Yama, who resided in them, together with the souls of the deceased. Because a tree is also potentially dangerous and malevolent, it was wiser in certain cases not to utter its name. Trees could be generous and fulfil wishes, but as well fiercely demanding; indeed, there are stories of human sacrifices being made to trees, the unsuspecting reader not being spared the gory details of human entrails hanging from the branches and serving as garlands.

We thus see that trees were awe inspiring in their cosmological functions, that they provided priests as well as lay people with all kinds of useful products, that they could fulfil wishes as well as guarantee fertility, that they were revered both for their beauty and majesty, and for their being the abode of a deity, and that they were loved and feared at the same time, because they were related to life (*samsâra*), immortality (*soma* and *amrita*) and death.

Trees in the Buddha's biography

Whereas all kinds of trees might claim a certain degree of sacredness in India, there is one particular tree that can boast of an ancestry dating back 2500 years, i.e. the *bodhi*-tree in Bodhgayâ, in the state of Bihar. In Indian history, we see one figure in whose life trees have played an unusually dominating role: the Buddha. In him the cyclic history of previous Buddhas found fulfilment under a specially prophesied tree, through him the Indian worship of trees has seen a remarkable continuity right up to the present day, and Buddhist iconography provides a wealth of information on the significant moments of his life in which trees played a part.

[6] For the symbolism of the inverted tree in India, see Coomaraswamy 1938.

As Siddhârtha Gautama, he was born under a flowering *sâl* tree, as a young prince he underwent his first meditative experience under a rose-apple tree (*jambu*), and as Shâkyamuni he practised rigorous ascetism under trees. After a long abstinence he received his first food from the hands of the daughter of the village-chief, Sujâta, as he sat under a tree, and he consciously chose the *pippala* tree from which he vowed not to rise before he had attained final enlightenment. And indeed, it was this very tree which towered over him during the assails of Mâra, when he made his victorious gesture of calling the Earth as witness (*mâravijaya* or *bhûmisparsha-mudrâ*), and during his final insight and awakening (*samyaksambodhi*). In the course of his long years as a mendicant preacher, he used to teach, sleep and meditate under trees. He emphatically prohibited his followers ever to harm or fell a tree. He even ordered a *bodhi*-tree sapling to be planted in the courtyard of one of his monasteries. The final moments before his death at the age of eighty, were spent in a grove of *sâl* trees, in full and miraculous bloom, their blossoms showering down over the dying master.

Of special interest here is the *bodhi*-tree, the tree which witnessed his enlightenment in a village now known as Bodhgayâ, a little more than ten kilometres to the south of Gayâ, the Hindu place of pilgrimage in the state of Bihar. It was in the immediate vicinity of Gayâ that the Bodhisattva (the Buddha-to-be), whilst sitting under a tree, received a bowl of specially prepared rice-porridge from the hands of Sujâta. Out of gratitude for her marriage and the birth of her son, this young woman had taken a vow to bring a ritually purified dish of rice and milk to the deity living in that tree. When the servant she had sent ahead to prepare the ground around the tree, noticed someone sitting beneath it, she thought that this time the tree-deity had come down personally to accept the annual gift from Sujâta. She hurried back to her mistress to recount the unusual event, whereupon Sujâta took extra care with her gift. With her golden bowl full of rice-porridge and a golden vase of perfumed water she proceeded to the tree, reverently greeted Siddhârtha, who was still seated there, and offered him her special gift. There are several versions of this story, but all agree that he accepted the food, and divided it into seven portions, of which he ate just one. After his meal of this particularly nourishing food, he went down to the river Nairañjana to bathe. He then chose his seat carefully: a fig-tree (*pippala* or *ashvattha*, Latin: *Ficus religiosa*), which he circumambulated while vowing that he would never rise from his seat again until he had attained final enlightenment. Facing east, he sat down on a cushion of special grass, the seat which is traditionally called *vajrâsana* (diamond throne) or *narasimhâsana* (man-lion throne).[7]

Indian iconography has portrayed the Buddha-to-be, sitting under that carefully selected tree, prepared as if for a sacrifice or a consecration. And indeed, having come to the end of his ascetic efforts without finding the answer to his quest, he had just abandoned the ascetic stage by taking a bath and eating some food, and was now on the verge of a new phase: the emergence of the answer to his all- encompassing experience of *duhkha*, ór, in case of failure, death. We are all familiar with the fact that he succeeded in fulfilling his own ultimatum, won, and became the Buddha, the Enlightened One. The phases which led to his final insight are also familiar: Mâra's attacks on him, the seductive efforts of Mâra's three beautiful daughters, Mâra's endeavours to lure him into world-sovereignty, etc. But all to no avail: when Mâra was beaten into defeat, the Bodhisattva called the Earth as witness to his victory. He was ready now for meditative interiorisation. With the help of his previously attained dhyânic experience he used his concentration to come to a series of final insights into the suffering which had put him on the path of probing the origins of suffering, six or seven years earlier.

This is what happened under that particular tree. We have focused on the moment of his enlightenment, but even without being equally elaborate on the other elements of his biography, this description illustrates the many ancient traditions, legends and narrative motifs that have combined to form a continuing line of cultural self-affirmation. We detect the tree-motif as well as the motif of royal consecration and sacrifice, and the tree-motif is present in all the important moments of his life. Whether one sees the Buddha as a world-sovereign (*cakravartin*), as a Buddha in a line of Buddhas, as a human teacher or as a god-hero, the narrative provides ample confirmation of it.[8] Through the figure of the Buddha, we see the amazing continuity of ancient Indian traditions, brahmanic as well as popular. Both in scriptural tradition and in Buddhist iconography, there is a remarkable wealth of details marking the continuity of pan-Indian motifs. Anticipating our analysis at the end of this article, we summarise by concluding that the tree-motif in the Buddha's biography forms a tight fabric of the sustained *caityavriksha*

---

[7] A free account of the Buddha's life is given in the romanticised narrative of Thich Nhat Hanh (1991).

[8] In Viennot 1954, only the second part deals with the Buddhist tree-worship, whereas Viennot 1946 deals with the iconographic representation of tree-worship in Buddhist art exclusively.

cult throughout Indian tradition. It might be that there are special Buddhist touches claimed by Buddhists as unique and special to them; yet, although the Buddha was a rebel in certain respects, opposed to the status of the priests, the efficacy of the ritual, and the social stratification of his time, he also carried the tradition forward. Whatever is mythical in his biography, and whatever small part of it is based on historic fact, both Hindus and Buddhists have adopted, and adapted, those loose strands of history and legend, and woven them into a shimmering fabric of continuity and cohesion.

The bodhi-tree in Bodhgayâ

Tradition has it that the tree under which the Buddha attained final enlightenment, was an *ashvattha* or *pippala* tree. This is a fig tree, with its easily recognisable heart-shaped leaves and long petiole, producing tiny fruits in November/December. In Indian tree-lore it was the *ashvattha* or *pippala* which was associated with *soma* (the sacred juice) and *amrita* (the juice of immortality). One of the pre-Aryan Indus seals even depicts a stylised *pippala* tree. The tree was associated with the East, and, thus, with the sun. There is also a seal on which the *ashvattha* is depicted in combination with a unicorn, and one in which it is being ritually worshipped by women.

The famous Rigvedic passage of the tree with the two birds in it, of which one is eating the fruits while the other just looks on, refers in fact to the same fig-tree.[9] Eating the fruit means: partaking of life. This belief in the life-giving function of the fig-tree, can also be traced back to the *ashvattha* fertility rites. This species of fig-tree is associated with life, sun and fertility. Trees were sprinkled with honey, milk and perfumed or sweetened water, as well as daubed with red powder. Sometimes music and dance were also incorporated into the worship, and the ritual always included a reverent circumambulation, a *pradakshina*. Women often wound cotton threads around the trunk, or suspended pieces of cloth from the branches, lighted candles, and offered flowers or other small gifts. In the iconography, we even see elephants and monkeys paying obeisance to the tree, and offering honey or lotus flowers.

The Buddhist chronicles, including the accounts of Chinese pilgrims, are not always consistent about the kinds of trees figuring in

---

[9] Rigveda I, 164: 22.

the Buddha's biography.[10] Some record, for instance, that it was a *sâl*-tree (*Shorea robusta*) under which the Buddha was born, whilst others say it was a *plaksha* (*Butea monosperma*) or even an *ashoka* (*Saraca indica*). In one of the Chinese records, it is said that every year, on the anniversary of the Buddha's enlightenment, the *bodhi* leaves withered and fell to the ground, after which the tree came to life again. It is recorded that on this day many pilgrims used to visit the tree and sprinkle the roots with perfumed milk. There would also have been music, flowers, incense, candles and other (sometimes costly and prestigious) gifts.

The first historical person named in connection with the worship of the *bodhi*-tree in Bodhgayâ, is emperor Ashoka, who reigned from 268 to 232 B.C., and whose Buddhist name was Piyadasi. His relationship with this tree was not without its problems, however; there are contradicting stories, the most interesting of which is that of the queen's jealousy. Following his conversion, Ashoka became so engrossed in the sacred tree, that the young queen, fearing that he had fallen in love with a tree-nymph, ordered a low-caste servant to cut it down, or, in an alternative reading, tried to let it die from within by wounding it with a *mandu*-thorn. Ashoka, shocked to find the tree dead, or at least dying, generously sprinkled the roots with perfumed milk, whereupon the tree revived. The chronicles further record that it was Ashoka who ordered the construction of the stone wall around it, as well as the laying of the slab called the *vajrâsana*. It was Ashoka too who ordered a twig, or shoot, from the tree to be taken to Lankâ, where it was received with much reverence and planted in the royal enclosure at Anuradhapura. And it was the same Ashoka who ordered the construction of gardens, shady avenues and water-wells for the well-being of men, animals and plants.

Now that the *bodhi*-tree began to attract Buddhist pilgrims, it had also become a potential menace for those with a fanatical belief in other gods and other religions. It is recorded that in the 7th century, the Gauda king Shasânka, ordered the tree to be cut down and the roots burned. The tree was replaced by a sapling brought from Anuradhapura. It might be this tree, or perhaps a later offshoot, which was blown down by a tempest in 1876. Then again, it might have been replaced by a sapling from Anuradhapura, or from its own surviving roots.

It seems that the Buddha himself had initiated, or at least sanc-

[10] See Legge 1965, Giles 1923, and Beal 1884.

tioned, the cults around the *bodhi*-tree, in addition to the construction of *stûpas* where his relics or ashes were to be preserved. There is a particular pilgrimage tradition between Bodhgayâ and Chinese, Birmese and Sinhalese Buddhists. The pilgrim tradition within India itself shows an interesting connection between Bodhgayâ and Gayâkshetra, the location of the present town of Gayâ where Hindu pilgrims traditionally came to deposit the ashes of their ancestors, and to offer *pindu* (balls of rice or flour) to the dead. There are curious parallels between the two sites: the *akshayavata*, or immortality tree (a *nyagrodha* or *Ficus bengalensis*) in Gayâ, and the *bodhidruma*, or enlightenment tree, in Bodhgayâ; the *Vishnupada*, or footsteps of Vishnu in Gayâ, and the Buddha's footsteps, or *paduka*, in Bodhgayâ.[11] From ancient times pilgrims have journeyed to Gayâ because of their obligations to the deceased, and they also made detours to the sacred precincts in Bodhgayâ. It might even be that the Buddha himself was attracted to that vicinity because of its sanctity. The textual evidence for his choice, however, is much more pragmatic in Pali: he considers it to be a good place, with a river close by and a village at a comfortable distance for collecting alms. The Mahâyâna texts, however, tend to emphasize that he hardly had a choice in the matter: the setting had been preordained by a line of former Buddhas.

Whatever reasons the Buddha may have had for choosing this particular tree at this particular spot, from the moment of his enlightenment onwards its sanctification was threefold: firstly, because of its nearness to Gayâ, secondly because of its traditional relation to the enlightenment of former Buddhas, and lastly and most importantly, because it was here that the awe-inspiring event of the Buddha's enlightenment took place. It may have been in the first century of the present era that the Mahâbodhi temple was built here. A tower was added in the 5th and 6th centuries, and in the 8th century the whole construction was expanded. It was demolished by Muslims in the 13th century, but rebuilt soon with Birmese aid. Four corner towers were added in the 14th century, but be-

---

[11] It is interesting to see how in the *Mahâbodhi* temple-complex, there are two places where the Buddha's feet are worshipped. On coming down the main stairs, approaching the entrance to the temple, on the left is a cluster of low buildings with a Shaivite *trishula* on top. In front of the first room is a stone depiction of the Buddha's feet. Those feet are eagerly pointed out to any new visitor by the Hindu priest in charge, exacting money from the baffled newcomer after a Blitz tour along the deities inside the dark room, whereas the other couple of feet, at the side of the main tree, just outside the new fence, evoke uncoerced devotion, constantly. It is from these very feet that the cloth imprints are made which are given or sold as sacred souvenirs.

cause Buddhism had practically disappeared from India by that time, the whole place fell into disrepair, and it was not until the 18th century that it was rediscovered by a wandering Hindu priest (*mahant*). He decided to settle there, laying Hindu claims to the temple, on the grounds that the Buddha had long since been incorporated into the Hindu pantheon by his having been accorded the status of the ninth *avatâra* (incarnation) of Vishnu. The sacred site must, however, have been a sorry sight for the few Western romantics who ventured there in colonial times.

At the end of the 19th century, during the Buddhist revival in Sri Lanka, the Singhalese monk, Anagarika Dharmapala, visited Bodhgayâ and saw the dilapidated state of both temple and tree. He resolved to make it his life's work to restore the place to its former ancient glory as the axis point in the Buddha's life and thus the centre of the Buddhist faith. He also founded the Mahâbodhi Society, but it was only in 1949 that it was decreed that the temple's management was to be placed in the hands of a committee of both Hindus and Buddhists. The second half of the present century, in particular, has seen an increase in restoration work on and around the site. In recent decades there has been construction activity at the periphery also, and several Buddhist denominations have built their own temples and pilgrim accommodations there. The inevitable trappings of tourism have also sprung up, such as stalls selling anything from Tibetan carpets to dried *bodhi* leaves, in addition to bronze statues and other kinds of religious paraphernalia.[12]

Rituals around the bodhi-tree

Buddhism had practically disappeared from India by the 13th century. Although the four most important sites mentioned in the Buddha's biography were revered by Buddhists and Hindus alike, it did not follow that they were kept in good repair. For some reason, it was Bodhgayâ which received the best care, both spiritually and materially. We have already noted that Hindu pilgrims on their way to or from Gayâ, used to make a detour to the sacred tree in Bodhgayâ, and that there has apparently been an almost constant trickle of visitors to the tree and the temple, during all these centu-

[12] The most complete information about the history of the Mahâbodhi temple complex is given by Barua (1981). An interesting collection of approaches is presented in Leoschko 1988.

ries. This trickle has increased considerably in recent times. Not only have people in India itself become more mobile, making it possible for growing numbers to visit both places, cross-cultural mobility has likewise increased and turned the trickle into a steady stream. First of all, there are the Hindu pilgrims to Gayâ who make a detour to Bodhgayâ, and secondly there are the newly-converted groups of Ambedkarites who lay a certain monopolistic claim to the place. Thirdly, Buddhists from the adjoining countries tread a pilgrim path to all the holy sites spoken of in Buddha's biography. Increasing numbers of Japanese Buddhists fly to India for an air-conditioned tour of the famous places, including the ruins of the once famous Buddhist universities. Tibetan Buddhists in exile are another special group, eager as they are, and in great numbers, to see the place, individually or in groups, and some of them even settle there. The fourth group of visitors consists of neo-Buddhists from outside Asia, from North America, Western Europe, and Australia in particular. Some come as monastics, wearing the orange, yellow, red, brown, grey or black robes of the many different denominations, or as lay Buddhists. Scholars and tourists constitute the fifth main group.

Factors which have contributed to Bodhgayâ's growing attraction, are possibly: improved mobility within India itself thanks to a steadily expanding transport system; the revival of Buddhism since the end of the 19th century; the scholarly work of translators, art-historians, archaeologists, ethnologists, anthropologists and social scientists, who have all helped to make the place known and attractive to a growing number of enthusiasts; the concept of pilgrimage has become fashionable again; and the world-wide and growing interest in our 'roots', and so too in the 'roots' of Buddhism.

Depending on the reasons for visiting Bodhgayâ, everyone assumes a distinct behaviour pattern there. One's stay might be long or short, one might be comfortably housed in one of the lodges, packed tightly and flea-bitten in one of the dormitories, or even huddled in a tent. Tourist, pilgrim or scholar, the pattern is the same for all: everyone leaves their shoes at the entrance to the precinct, everyone pays homage to the statue of Buddha in the main temple, and everyone stands reverently around the tree, in commemoration of Buddha's enlightenment. These are the general rules of behaviour for all who visit the place. The majority of visitors are Buddhists: monastics in orange robes from Sri Lanka, Thailand, Burma and Vietnam, in red robes from Tibet, Mongolia, Nepal and Bhutan, in black and grey robes from Japan and Korea, as well as lay people in their various colours and costumes, in addition to increasing numbers of non-Asian Buddhists and tourists from all over the world.

The rituals with which the various pilgrims pay homage to the *bodhi*-tree vary accordingly. The sacred complex of Bodhgayâ has become an intra-religious, as well as an interreligious, meeting point where pilgrims representing all the Buddhist traditions and denominations each practise their own particular rituals. Some circumambulate, some make the great prostrations, some count their beads and mutter *mantras*, some rotate their prayer-wheels, some sit in meditation, some come with small gifts, such as flowers, incense, oil-lamps and coins, some hang flags and banners around the tree and the temple, some apply gold-leaf to the trunk of the tree or to a Buddha statue, and some just sit or stand, revering the spot where the Buddha attained ultimate insight and entered *nirvâna*. In recent years especially, Tibetan pilgrims have flocked to Bodhgayâ in huge numbers. It is now Mahâyâna red which dominates this small place of pilgrimage in the dusty plains of Bihar. Several thousands of Tibetans live here, as monastics, as lay pilgrims, or by running one of the small family businesses in the Tibetan refugee market, where they sell devotional items, clothes, blankets, carpets or jewellery. Regular pilgrim routes from Bhutan and Mongolia are also being established, and it is not uncommon to see non-Asian faces, with their shaven heads, performing the same rituals and even wearing the same red robe. Whereas it was formerly the Theravâda monks from Burma and Sri Lanka who were most passionately engaged in the repair and management of the temple complex, they have now become almost invisible in the recent invasion of red-robed Vajrayâna Buddhists from Tibet, Bhutan and Mongolia.

The ritual they all have in common is the circumambulation. Some of them only make the three prescribed walks around the main temple, always clockwise, whilst others devote a whole day or even weeks to it. Their prayer-beads move constantly between their fingers, although this is a practice not performed by most of the Theravâdins. Buddha's footprints, the diamond-seat, and, of course, the tree are especially venerated, although the tree and throne have recently become practically inaccessible to visitors: the golden fence is usually locked, and only special delegations of pilgrims are allowed to enter. If a pilgrim earnestly wants to get closer to the tree, special permission can be obtained to climb an interior staircase to the second floor of the temple, an area usually reserved for meditation only; from there the visitor can look directly down into the heart of the tree. Pilgrims display a more individual type of religious behaviour in the wider area around the tree and temple; some unceasingly recite Tibetan texts or make the great prostrations, some sit in silent meditation, whilst others enjoy a picnic on the lawn, or simply sleep.

A few interesting phenomena should be noted here. Although the temple has been managed by a joint committee of Hindus and Buddhists since 1949, Buddhists definitely regard it as their own, whereas the Hindus, curiously enough, behave more or less as tourists. They are the ones who look bright and worldly, carrying cameras, and exhibiting only a minimum of ritual behaviour, namely revering the temple, the tree and the Buddha's feet, by touching them with their hands and forehead. Although theoretically the Buddha is one of the *avatâras* of Vishnu, the place does not provoke the same kind of fervent devotion they are used to display in Mathura, Vrindavan, Ayodhya or Benares.

A second phenomenon to be noted here is the daily activity taking place at the far ends of the temple complex. Here, groups of obviously poor people gather on the lawn or in the courtyard of the Mucalinda lake, where they are preached to by their own priests, and always with a note of violence. Some of the older women stand holding hands, with their backs against the high concrete pillar in the courtyard, moving around it and keeping in constant contact with it. I have, unfortunately, not been able to discover the meaning of this ritual. The air of furtiveness about it—the women usually stopped when a stranger happened to come into view—may mean that it has some kind of erotic undertone, similar perhaps to a Shaivite ritual in which the devotees pray for conjugal happiness well into old age. Later, those women, together with the men, partake in a common meal, after which the ragged group makes the obligatory walk around the main temple, throwing small coins at the Buddha's feet, the tree, and the golden Buddha statue inside. Some of them might well be followers of Dr. Ambedkar, the famous promoter of Buddhism among the lower-caste and outcast sections of the Indian population.

A third phenomenon worth mentioning here is a secondary tree at a little distance from the main tree, standing to the north of the main temple. This is a huge tree, a *pippala* too, surrounded by a broad stone platform. The statues beneath this tree somehow make a far more archaic impression than anything else in the whole temple compound. It is interesting that 18th and 19th century paintings, now in the museum of Calcutta, show how, in Hindu times, those very statues originally stood under the real *bodhi*-tree. When Bodhgayâ was transformed into a Buddhist place of worship once again, the statues were removed to this secondary tree, where they still stand today. White cotton threads have been wound around its trunk, and its roots are covered with red and orange powder as well as with the remains of food, honey, and other offerings. A stone altar with Hindu deities, of which the couple Shiva/Pârvatî, and Ganesha, are easily recognisable, stands in front of the tree today. The figure in the middle could be Vishnu. Although this place is visited by Hindus now and then, during my recent visit the platform was monopolised by a group of Bhutanese Buddhists. They usually arrived early in the morning, prepared the altar with butter-and-dough ornaments, incense, flowers, and oil-lamps, and remained there the whole day, performing a continuous rhythm of rituals, including prostration, recitation, and meditation. In fact, they used the place in a completely Buddhist way. Every other day they refrained from speech, communicating only in sign language. They drank tea together twice a day, and even then they had a ritual to perform: the twining of silk threads for ritual objects, such as the knots in prayer-*mâlas*. They formed a closely knit group, but were quite open to others, occasionally even allowing outsiders to join freely in their rituals. Every now and then, when the Bhutanese were engaged in one of their rituals, a group of Hindus would come to pay homage to the gods on the altar, but this never lasted more than a few minutes. Obviously, these Bhutanese Buddhists had taken over this ancient place for the duration of their stay in Bodhgayâ.

Each denomination has its own variations and peculiarities, as far as the ritual behaviour displayed in the temple, in front of the *bodhi*-tree, and in the larger area around it, is concerned. Theravâda Buddhists tend to make the gestures of *pranam* or *añjali* before the Buddha statue, make a *pradakshinâ* around the temple and a reverent greeting to the *bodhi*-tree. Some of them sit at a short distance from the tree and muse, while others stay closer to the tree and sit in meditation. Some practise walking-meditation, preferably close to the path where the Buddha himself is said to have walked in meditation. Mahâyâna Buddhists tend to be more exuberant in their ritual. It has become a common sight in Bodhgayâ for Tibetan Buddhists (or newly-converted Tibetan Buddhists from non-Asian countries) to perform their great 'prostrations' in public, sometimes alone, and sometimes in groups. Many of them make *pradakshinas*, by throwing themselves down to the earth and measuring the length of their body as one step, or by moving their prayer beads through their fingers while muttering *mantras*. Quite a few of them sit in the close vicinity of the tree and recite texts all day long;

others light candles on the altar by the tree, and some meditate. Some tie flags and banners to the tree or to the stone wall around it, and sometimes one of the monastics delivers a sermon, as an audience begins to gather in one of the open spaces. Singhalese Buddhists, especially, tend to bind pieces of cloth, flags, banners or even cleverly sewn patchwork lotuses to the trunk of the tree. Japanese Buddhists, on the other hand, tend to be more restrained and meditative when visiting the sacred tree, but all visitors clearly desire some kind of memento of their stay. Early in the morning, temple assistants sweep the pathways, and leaves from the *bodhi*-tree are gathered eagerly. Some of them are distributed among the faithful, and some of them are collected so that they can be dried and sold as souvenirs on one of the stalls.

There have been remarkable developments in the wider area around the tree, during the last decade. Buddhist conferences have been held here, and His Holiness the Dalai Lama has held two huge *kâlacakra* initiations here. Yearly eye-camps are also held in the immediate vicinity, as its association with the Buddha's eye-opening experience is regarded as helpful in this respect, too. The temples with adjacent lodges or dormitories have developed their own programme of religious and social activities. For those open to the many faces of Buddhism, it is possible to make a tour of the various temples and participate in the services or meditations. A gong is sounded several times a day in the Japanese temple, and one can hear the fine tinkling of the Birmese bells, or the impressive thumps from the Tibetan complex.

Hindu visitors stand in reverence before both the Buddha statue and the tree. Some overprotective and possessive Buddhists would prefer to ban them from the area around the tree, because they suspect the Hindus of being too generous in their sprinkling of sweetened milk and water. This is said to have caused some of the roots to rot away. There has been no open conflict with the Hindu *mahants* of the place, however, since it was decreed that the precinct is to be managed by a joint committee. Some over-zealous Buddhists, however, might feel that the *mahants* were irresponsible in neglecting the place for so long, and in allowing the statues, slabs and other precious objects belonging to the site to be removed, but they have to admit nonetheless that the *mahants* have also saved many objects by storing them in their own compound. These objects are still there, or are exhibited in the small museum.[13]

[13] The museum, situated next to the Ashok Hotel, does not charge entrance fees. The main statues are those of Hindu gods and goddesses, and of *Bodhisattvas*, mainly from the period between the 10th and 12th centuries. I noticed that the

It would be interesting to count the number of Buddhists coming to Bodhgayâ, who also visit the sacred site of the Hindus in the town of Gayâ itself. It seems that the Hindus are more inclusive than the Buddhists, in this respect. On the other hand, some of the local Hindus grumble amongst themselves about the hordes of Tibetan visitors with life-styles and social customs quite alien to their own. As with tourism anywhere in the world, local farmers profit from the market created by the influx of visitors, but despise the changes which follow in their wake.[14]

Bodhgayâ's ritual pluralism

For many reasons, pilgrimage in Bodhgayâ provides an interesting object of study. Since the reports of Francis Buchanan-Hamilton, Rajendralal Mitra and Alexander Cunningham, and the drawings of Thomas and William Daniell, attention has tended to focus on the archaeological remains. Sir Edwin Arnold, in his famous poem 'The Light of Asia', placed it in a very romantic light, but did not hesitate to use the medium of a newspaper article to complain about the sorry state of this once famous place. It was the Singhalese reformist and revivalist, Anagarika Dharmapala, who dedicated his later life to the struggle to restore the sacred site and return it to Buddhist ownership, rather than leave it in the hands of the *mahant*. In the last few decades, a number of Asian countries have erected temples, monasteries, dormitories and lodges in the area, donated money for restoration work, added votive *stûpas* and statues, and maintained religious congregations there.[15] The international character of the religious activity at Bodhgayâ today re-

visiting Hindu pilgrims reverently touched the threshold with their foreheads as if the museum was a shrine. Of course, to them it was a shrine, since it contained many *mûrtis*, statues of Hindu deities.

[14] It is not to be denied, however, that the local Hindus make a good business here. Not only the riksha-men or the street-vendors, but also the tour-operators who offer tours to the other Buddhist sites, the telephone-operator who often has the only telephone that really works (although mostly powered by a car-battery), the masseurs who offer their services in and around the hotels, and local *gurus* who make use of the boom and set up shop (usually a brightly coloured tent, *pandal*) in one of the adjoining fields, where they offer *darshan* (the special grace of a saint or sage communicating with his audience) and meditation courses. One of the most amusing ways of earning money from the pilgrims is done by boys, who sell small plastic bags with tiny fish. Those are to be set free in the Mucalinda tank, in order to gain merit. Of course, those very fish are caught and sold again the next day.

[15] An impressive addition is the huge Japanese Buddha statue (*Daibutsu*) overlooking Bodhgayâ, made by Indians, and dedicated by the Dalai Lama on 18th November 1989.

calls the Pâla period of a thousand years ago, when visitors from many parts of Asia travelled to the sacred site. Yet, part of the charm of the sacred places of Buddhism in India, is their air of transitoriness. Most of the important places quoted in the Buddha's biography, as far as they can be traced on today's maps of India and Nepal, lie more or less deserted and in ruins.[16] Those who insisted on restoring Bodhgayâ rather than abandon it to the natural process of decay, did so with more religious fervour than expertise, as far as style and taste are concerned. This, however, is an interesting phenomenon in itself.

In the wake of the Buddhist revival at the end of the 19th century, Bodhgayâ began to attract a regular flow of pilgrims and devotees. From the 1970s onwards, Buddhist pilgrims included individual visitors from non-Asian countries, coming initially as tourists but later increasingly as pilgrims too. The growing interest in Buddhism, worldwide, has created the new phenomenon of converts from Western countries, shaving their heads and donning the respective orange, red or black robes of the various Buddhist denominations. Some live in Asia in their first years as monks and nuns, and then return to their native countries where they hope to establish Buddhist centres. Visiting the Buddhist holy places is, of course, one of the main items on their programmes. This has meant that there has been a steady increase in the number of nationalities and languages to be found in Bodhgayâ today: this tiny dot in the Bihar landscape has certainly become a remarkably international place.

The rituals performed there show a huge variety of colours, gestures, utensils, positions, words and gifts. In certain ways, however, the national and denominational boundaries are clearly visible: the ritual customs of a Tibetan peasant are quite different from those of an orange-clad monk from Thailand or Sri Lanka, and the manner of a Japanese lay-pilgrim, with head shaven for the occasion, is totally different from that of a Hindu visitor who makes the detour from Gayâ. They all have their own habits and customs, and the various denominations are easily recognisable, both in terms of their individual dress styles or ethnic characteristics and in

---

[16] See Schumann 1992. It is no coincidence that the guided tours offered by the lay Buddhist Shantum Seth, to the places of the Buddha's biography in India and Nepal, carry the same title as Schumann's book. These tours are emphatically presented as pilgrimages: 'Experience the beauty and serenity of the places where the Buddha lived, while you journey at a slower pace than tourists usually do. Meditate, practise mindfulness and, at each sacred site, hear the stories of the Buddha's life.' Of course, the prices charged for these pilgrimage tours are well beyond the means of most of the Asian Buddhists.

terms of their ritual behaviour. New converts to Buddhism simply adopt the ways of their chosen denomination.

The tree and the temple both stimulate different kinds of ritual behaviour, the tree usually bringing the visitor into a more meditative mood: there is the tendency to go back some 2500 years and join in Siddhârtha's meditation, whilst the temple represents the greatness and values of Buddhism in general. In other words, whereas the tree points to, and reminds us of, the historical Siddhârtha Gautama, the temple is a monument to Buddhism in its entirety. The tree tends to create a meditative atmosphere, whilst the temple evokes devotion and awe in the hearts of its visitors. The mood of meditation, however, still leaves room for certain ritual acts as well. People approach the tree thoughtfully and reverently, and they walk around it with folded hands, or contemplate it from a short distance. Some stand in awe before the *vajrâsana*, and some gather a fallen leaf and store it away in the folds of their clothes. In comparison with earlier times, the tree has become rather inaccessible for more elaborate acts of ritual behaviour, and the place at times is too crowded to be able to sit in meditation right there. The early morning is the favourite time for gathering leaves, as well as for solitary meditation in close proximity to the tree.

Contribution to a theory of ritual behaviour in a pluralistic context

It is clear that Bodhgayâ is a place of pilgrimage. Although the small local Hindu population does visit the temple now and then, the activity in the temple compound itself is determined by devout believers who have come with the special zeal of pilgrims. Some have travelled long distances and at considerable cost. Others have adapted their normal behaviour pattern as a lay Buddhist into that of a Buddhist pilgrim, taking special vows, donning special robes, sometimes even shaving their heads. The whole day (and sometimes even the night as well) is spent inside the temple compound, with an intensified sequence of ritual and meditation. The idea of gaining merit by embarking on a pilgrimage, and even more so by specifically performing large numbers of prostrations and circumambulations, is very common in Buddhism. Some pilgrims proudly carry the mark on the forehead where, countless times, they have touched the wood of their prostration planks.[17] The continuous

[17] There is a way of counting the numbers of circumambulations or prostrations one has made, by making knots in the *mâla* (chain of prayer beads). I saw several pilgrims counting their prostrations by replacing a tiny heap of pebbles, but I also noticed a new technical device (made in Korea), giving the digital count.

recitation of canonical texts is performed both for personal benefit and for the benefit of all. However, despite this somewhat quantitative approach to the rituals, the place has a very special aura of devotion. It exudes an atmosphere of mildness, especially evident in the faces and gestures of the people themselves, which one can only marvel at.

Although on a normal day there could easily be twenty to thirty nationalities there, representing as many types of Buddhism, the only real demarcation line is that of language, both in terms of the daily or geographical language as well as the language in which the Buddhist canon is recited. Another identity mark lies in the colour of the clothes that are worn. Sometimes they are the every-day clothing common to each ethnic group, whilst some of them specifically designate the wearer as a pilgrim: those are worn during the liminal phase of the pilgrimage, but some, such as the red wraps and shawls, can be bought by anyone at one of the local stalls. Although some lay Buddhists might use these clothes as part of a conscious cultivation of their own identity, in order to distinguish themselves from those not subject to a special vow or from Buddhists of different denominations, a sense of ideological and existential communitas prevails. It is remarkable, however, that there are hardly any orange or grey robes to be seen during one of the huge Tibetan celebrations under the tree, such as the massive alms-giving ceremony performed by an American group of lay Buddhists I witnessed. Even more striking are the Bhutanese Buddhists who were seen to use the ancient Hindu altar for their rituals, although very few Buddhists would follow the example of the Hindus in making a special detour to Vishnu's footprints in nearby Gayâ, before proceeding to pay their respects to Buddha's footprints in Bodhgayâ.

Neither is Bodhgayâ the place for setting doctrinal demarcation lines. Although, in other instances, the discussion about the authenticity of the three *yânas* ('paths', or denominations) may, at times, tend towards self-proclamation, the locus where the Buddha attained enlightenment unifies rather than differentiates. Even when the three *yânas* and their various subsects are clearly distinguishable from each other in terms of dress, hair style, ritual behaviour and the language of their recited texts, the atmosphere of the place is such that those differences are not cultivated in any way, in fact the opposite is more likely to be true. A Korean woman, with shaven head and wearing the grey garb of a pilgrim, makes her prostrations shoulder to shoulder with a Tibetan nun and an Australian layman. When she has temporarily completed her prostrations, two Bhutanese child-monks may teach her how to intertwine silk for her string of prayer-beads, and she in her turn might massage the shoulders and skull of the Tibetan nun close to her.

As for the theoretical side of identity in a pluralistic context, it seems to me that identity is quite a relaxed and easy matter in Bodhgayâ. There are, of course, some obvious signs of ethnic and denominational differences, such as those mentioned above, but no one seems to make any conscious attempt to cultivate or exploit them, or to be aware of their potentially problematical aspects. There are several categories of visitors, and several categories of pilgrims. There are lay Buddhists and monastics, there are Buddhists from all over the world, and there are Hindus. They all have a right to worship here, and access is available to all. Although there might be some tension between born-Buddhists and the newly converted Ambedkarites, or between autochthonous Hindus and the hordes of Tibetan refugees and monastics, Bodhgayâ is a place where ritual unifies rather than divides. In the same way, the ancient tradition of tree-worship finds a remarkable continuity here, for Buddhists as well as for Hindus.

References

Agarwala, V.S., 1943, 'Kalpavriksha: the wishfulfilling tree', in *Journal of the Indian Society* 11: 1-8.

Ahir, D.C., 1989, *The pioneers of Buddhist revival in India.* Delhi: Sri Satguru Publications.

Ahir, D.C., 1991, *Buddhism in Modern India.* Delhi: Sri Satguru Publications.

Arnold, E., 1956, *The light of Asia, or the great renunciation.* Bombay: International Book Pvt. Ltd. (1879[1]).

Badiner, A. Hunt (ed.), 1990, *Dharma Gaia: a harvest of essays in Buddhism and ecology.* Berkeley: Parallax Press.

Barua, D. K., 1981, *Buddha Gaya temple: its history.* Bodhgaya: Buddha Gaya Temple Management Committee.

Beal, S., 1968, *Si-Yu-Ki: Buddhist records of the Western world; translated from the Chinese of Hiuen Tsiang (A.D. 629).* New York: Paragon (1884[1]).

Bhattacharyya, T., 1966, *The Bodh Gaya temple.* Calcutta: K.L. Mukhopadhyay.

Bloch, T., 1908-1909, 'Notes on Bodh-Gaya', in *Archaeological Survey of India, Annual Report 1908-1909.*

Brosse, J., 1989, *Mythologie des arbres.* Paris: Editions Plon.

Butterworth, E.A.S., 1970, *The tree at the navel of the world.* Berlin: Walter de Gruyter.

Cook, R., 1974, *De levensboom: symbool van het middelpunt.* Bussum: De Haan.

Coomaraswamy, A., 1931, *Yakshas.* Washington: Smithsonian Institution, Freer Gallery of Art.

Coomaraswamy, A., 1938, *The inverted tree*. Bangalore: (no publisher).
Cunningham, A., 1892, *Mahabodhi or the great Buddhist temple under the Bodhi Tree at Bodh Gaya*. London: W.H. Allen.
Dargavel, J., K. Dixon, & N. Semple (eds.) 1988, *Changing tropical forests; historical perspectives on today's challenges in Asia, Australasia and Oceania*. Canberra: ANU/University of Canberra Centre for Resource and Environmental Studies.
Das, R.P., 1988, *Das Wissen von der Lebensspanne der Bäume: Surapâlas Virkshâyurveda kritisch editiert, übersetzt und kommentiert*. Stuttgart: Franz Steiner Verlag Wiesbaden GmbH.
D'Oyly, C., 1830, *Sketches of the New Road on a journey from Calcutta to Gyah*. Calcutta: (no publisher).
Dumoulin, H., (ed.) 1976, *Buddhism in the modern world*. New York/London: Collier/Collier Macmillan.
Dutt, S., 1962, *Buddhist monks and monasteries of India: their history and their contribution to Indian culture*. London: George Allen & Unwin.
Emeneau, M.B., 1949, 'The strangling figs in Sanskrit literature', in *University of California Publications in Classical Philology* 13, 10: 345-370.
Falk, N.E., 1972, *The study of cult: with special reference to the cult of the Buddha's relics in Ancient South Asia*. Chicago: University of Chicago Press.
Fergusson, J., 1868, *Tree and serpent worship*. London: W.H. Allen.
Fiske, A., 1969, 'Religion and Buddhism among India's new Buddhists', in *Social Research* 36.
Fiske, A., 1976, 'Buddhism in India today', in Dumoulin 1976.
Gandhi, M., & Y. Singh 1989, *Brahma's hair: mythology of Indian plants*. Calcutta: Rupa & Co.
Giles, H.A., 1923, *The travels of Fa-hsien (399-414 A.D.); or record of the Buddhist kingdoms*. Cambridge: Cambridge University Press.
Gupta, S.M., 1971, *Plant myths and traditions in India*. Leiden: E.J. Brill.
Gupta, S.S.. (ed.) 1965, *Tree symbol worship in India: a new survey of a pattern of folk-religion*. Calcutta: Indian Publications.
Gupta, S.S. 1980, *Sacred trees across cultures and nations: a new study for greater understanding of tradition*. Calcutta: Indian Publications.
Huntington, J.C., 1985, 'Sowing the seeds of the lotus: a journey to the great pilgrimage sites of Buddhism; part I (Lumbinî and Bodhgayâ)' in *Orientations* 16, 11: 46-61.
Huntington, S.L., & J.C. Huntington 1990, *Leaves from the bodhi tree: the art of Pâla India (8th-12th centuries) and its international legacy*. Seattle/London: The Dayton Art Institute/University of Washington Press.
James, E.O., 1966, *The tree of life; an archaeological study*. Leiden: E.J. Brill.
Jha, V.N., (ed.) 1991, *Proceedings of the National Seminar on Environmental Awareness reflected in Sanskrit literature*. Poona: Centre of Advanced Study in Sanskrit, University of Poona.
Lal, R.B., 1953, *Bodh Gaya: past and present*. Patna: Department of Public Relations of the Government of Bihar.
Legge, J. 1965 (repr.), *A record of Buddhistic kingdoms; being an account by the Chinese monk Fa-hsien of his travels in India and Ceylon (A.D. 399-414)*. New York: Paragon Book Reprint Corporation.
Leoschko, J., (ed.) 1988, *Bodhgaya: the site of enlightenment*. Bombay: Marg Publications.
Ling, T., 1980, *Buddhist revival in India: aspects of the sociology of Buddhism*. London: Macmillan Press.

Macy, J., 1991, *World as lover, world as self.* Berkeley: Parallax Press.

Majupuria, T.C., & D.P. Joshi 1988, *Religious and useful plants of Nepal and India: medicinal plants and flowers as mentioned in religious myths and legends of Hinduism and Buddhism.* Lashkar (Gwalior): M. Gupta.

Mitra, R., 1972, *Buddha Gaya: the great Buddhist temple; the hermitage of Shâkya Muni.* Delhi: Indological Book House.

Monier Williams, M., 1876, 'Sraddha ceremonies at Gaya', in *The Indian Antiquary* 5: 200-204.

Morinis, A., (ed.) 1992, *Sacred journeys: the anthropology of pilgrimage.* Westport (Conn.), etc.: Greenwood Press.

Nikam, N.A., & R. McKeon (eds. and trsl.) 1959, *The edicts of Asoka.* Chicago: University of Chicago Press.

Philpot, J.H., 1897, *The sacred tree, or the tree in religion and myth.* London: McMillan & Co.

Przyluski, J., 1967, *The legend of Emperor Ashoka in Indian and Chinese texts.* Calcutta: K.L. Mukhopadhyay.

Randhawa, M.S., 1977, 'The cult of trees and tree-worship in Buddhist-Hindu sculpture', in *Roopa-Lekha* 33, 1: 1-42.

Schumann, H.W., 1992, *Auf den Spuren des Buddha Gotama: eine Pilgerfahrt zu den historischen Stätten.* Olten/Freiburg im Breisgau: Walter-Verlag.

Thich Nhat Hanh, 1991, *Old path, white clouds: walking in the footsteps of the Buddha.* Berkeley: Parallax Press.

Thomas, E.J., 1927, *The life of Buddha as legend and history.* London: Routledge & Kegan Paul.

Viennot, O., 1946, *L'arbre dans l'iconographie bouddhique.* Paris: Bulletin des Musées de France.

Viennot, O., 1954, *Le culte de l'arbre dans l'Inde ancienne.* Paris: Annales du Musée Guimet.

THE 'LATRINES DECREE' IN THE YEMEN VERSUS THE DHIMMA PRINCIPLES

Joseph Sadan
(Tel Aviv University)

The principles of 'protection'

The legal and social status to which the non-Muslims are subjected in the Muslim world is known as the Pact of 'Umar. The institution of this system is ascribed to the caliph 'Umar the first (d. 644). The rules constituting the pact (*al-shurût al-'umariyya*)[1] were in fact formulated at a later period; historical evidence, hopefully authentic, from the days of 'Umar the first, at the time of the major Muslim conquests (*futûh*), reveals only basic conditions such as are usually imposed by victors on the vanquished. In the case of the Muslim conquests, the vanquished population was required, for example, to supply the garrison with provisions, such as fat (*wadak*), as well as to be obedient, and not to guide or pass any information to the opponents of Islam, nor allow entry to any of their agents. The latter stipulation, for instance, often appears even in late versions of the Pact; the context which emerges if one examines the text closely is that of the termination of war and the subsequent semi-military rule of the newly conquered country.[2] However, not every detail in

---

[1] Since the present study is not addressed solely to Arabists and 'Orientalists', it will be suitable to provide, in these notes, a general bibliography rather than references to primary sources. A special emphasis is put in the footnotes of this first section, on the interpretation of the *dhimma* rules by modern scholars, so as to meet, for instance, the needs and the background of the contribution by P.Sj. van Koningsveld to this volume. See Cahen 1965; Chehata 1965; Perlmann 1965. The most extensive study on *dhimma* matters remains: Tritton 1930. The richest mediaeval sources are Ibn Qayyim 1961; Ibn Qayyim 1981. Cf. Strauss 1944-1951: 1: passim, esp. 79ff, 84-116, 127ff, 202-205 (about the question, which will interest us later: the illegality of employing non-Muslim officials), 206ff, 2: 58ff, 173-179 (the above problem of state officials) 204ff, 263ff, 298-309; Zaydân 1982; Baron 1952-1983: 3: 97-98, 120-172, 5: 95ff; Stillman 1979: esp. 25-27, 167-168, 255-258 (this document, studied by Goitein, has been reprinted in Goitein 1983: 288-299, and studied again by Nini 1983, with some parallel documents), 273-274; Noth 1987; Stillman 1991a: 4-6, 225-226; Cohen (forthcoming), esp. ch. I, on the *dhimma* principles and the distinctive attire and signs imposed on the minorities. For details on further studies by the same authors and by others, see *infra*, nn. 5, 6, 8, 9, 12, 14: Bat Ye'or, Cohen, Goitein, Kister, Lewis, Qâsim, Stillman, Strauss.

[2] See Hill 1971. The studies written on these issues rely, to a great extent, on Balâdhurî (al-) 1866; see also Balâdhurî (al-) 1916, Belâdorî (el-) 1917. Cf. Sadan 1980: 105.

the series of conditions in the various versions of pacts signed with the vanquished population should be deemed authentic. For example, the status of the conquered land is often determined by evidence provided by Arabic historiography; Islamic law distinguishes between land conquered by the Muslims by force and land surrendered without a fight, and the distinction is taken into account in determining ownership and taxes. These items, however, were sometimes influenced by political or agrarian situations which came about long after the conquest; such items may even have been interpolated at a later stage.

The non-Muslim subjects of the Muslim realm are known as *ahl al-dhimma* (literally: the 'people of the protection', namely the 'protected ones' (or the 'protected population'). The use of this term implies that the population under discussion, mainly adherents of the monotheistic faiths, Christians and Jews, should enjoy safety and protection for both their lives and their property, and that they be allowed to maintain their various religious practices. One of the theoretical difficulties concerning the definition of *ahl al-dhimma* in Islamic jurisprudence is whether or not to include in this category idol worshippers, or those (such as Buddhists) who might conceivably be taken for idolaters; another complicated case is that of the Zoroastrians, minutely described by B. Spuler.[3] In practice, Islam tolerated the existence of the latter, and usually treated them as 'protected ones'. Unfortunately, this is not the occasion on which to elaborate on these delicate issues.

Throughout the centuries, large non-Muslim communities managed to exist in the Muslim world, although processes of conversion to Islam gradually thinned their ranks. The protected minorities living under Muslim rule are known as *dhimmîs* (or *kitâbîs*).[4] Modern Muslim scholars and several of the most eminent orientalists are inclined to see in the Muslim protection (*dhimma*) the expression of a relatively liberal and tolerant spirit. Orientalists such as Goldziher and Massignon reached this conclusion, despite the heavy poll-taxes levied from the *dhimmîs*, despite the obligation to wear garments different in form and colour and even, occasionally, a special type of belt, or a yellow badge, all in accordance with decrees issued from time to time, but in certain periods not strictly enforced. In addition, there were limitations concerning the erecting of new houses of worship, the riding of horses and the manner in

---

[3] Spuler 1952: 294(n.)ff, 449f, 494f.

[4] *Kitâbî* is derived from *kitâb* = a book, a revealed book, Scripture, i.e., one who belongs to a community which possesses a revealed text. See, for instance, Lazarus-Yafeh 1992: 22ff.

which the 'protected ones' might ride their beasts. These orientalists had in mind the situation of the Jews throughout the history of Europe, by comparison with which the rule of Islam seemed to them relatively tolerant.[5]

Arab scholars praise the tolerance of Islam towards the 'protected population'. The Egyptian Qâsim 'Abduh Qâsim, for instance, who has published several works on the *dhimmîs* in Muslim lands in general, and Egypt in particular, emphasizes the positive attitude of Muslims towards non-Muslims, even under the regime of the eleventh-century Fâtimid caliph al-Hâkim, known for his persecution of the minorities, especially the Christians.[6] The opposite point of view is represented by a number of researchers, notably a writer who the pseudonym Bat Ye'or, i.e. Daughter of the Nile. She has managed to select from the body of historiographical evidence, chronicles and documents, only that material which portrays the negative aspects. Some such materials can occasionally be found, relating to various episodes, periods and areas; it is therefore no wonder that she has succeeded in filling a complete volume, now published in several languages, on the maltreatment of the *dhimmîs* by Muslims.[7] Bat Ye'or has recently published a new book dedicated exclusively to the long history of Christians under Muslim rule; this book is characterized by the same spirit as her previous book on the *dhimmîs*.[8]

Does the truth lie in the viewpoint which attributes a relative degree of tolerance to Islam or in the attitude denouncing Muslim behaviour towards minorities? It seems that the truth lies somewhere in between, although one may differ regarding the precise emphasis. The life of the *dhimmîs* in the shade of Islam was certainly not easy, but at least their physical security (*amân*) and the safety of their property were assured, almost without exception. Such a prudently revised standpoint is expressed both in *The Jews of Islam* and

---

[5] Goitein 1964: 65-66 chooses Goldziher 1920 as an example of a favourable attitude towards the status of minorities under Muslim rule, whereas Cecil Roth is chosen by Goitein as an 'anticlimax' (the reference given by Goitein: *Jewish Forum* 1946: 28-33, is mistaken and we have been unable to correct it). One of the first symposia in which an effort was made to refute the generally accepted opinions of the 'Orientalists' is: Brinner 1974: passim, esp. 1-6 and cf. Ma'oz 1974 (these two booklets contain contributions by various scholars, such as Brinner, criticizing the favourable attitude of some orientalists towards the status of non-Muslims under Islamic rule). For a division of the views of 'Orientalists' into 'favourable' and 'unfavourable', see: van Koningsveld, Sadan & Samarrai 1990: 87; the delicate problem is the subject of a fierce controversy between Cohen 1991 and Stillman 1991b.

[6] Qâsim 1979.

[7] Bat Ye'or 1979, 1980a, 1980b, 1985, 1986.

[8] Bat Ye'or 1991.

Semites and Anti-Semites by Bernard Lewis[9], and in a popular book by Lazarus-Yafeh, as well as in other recent works.[10]

A.S. Tritton and others[11] have already discussed the phases in the evolution of distinctive designs for hairdressing, and of the form and colour of certain items of clothing which were used to differentiate the appearance of the Muslims from that of the 'infidels'. In the period following the Arab conquests, the conquerors arriving from Arabia at first kept their characteristic clothing, hairstyles and so on, and were still distinct from the conquered in their appearance at that early stage. The situation became more complicated when their styles began to resemble, in certain details, those of the sedentary population of the newly conquered countries. A series of traditions (*hadîth*)[12] and recommendations preserved in Muslim religious and moral literature which can plausibly be ascribed to that period of transition, instruct the Muslims to 'be different' (a verb from the Arabic root: *kh.l.f.*) and to refrain from 'resembling' (a verb from the root: *sh.b.h.*) the non-Muslims. It was only when the religious leaders failed in their attempt to stop the Muslim community from following certain non-Muslim fashions that there was no alternative but to issue the first decrees preventing the non-Muslims from imitating the characteristic Arab-Muslim attire, and imposing distinctive signs on the occupied population. The linguistic aspect is instructive: the expressions 'being different' (from the above-mentioned root: *kh.l.f.*) and trying not to 'resemble' (*sh.b.h.*) are both forms referring to the Muslims' conduct, whereas the *ghiyâr* (from the root: *gh.y.r.* to 'be different', to 'make different', to 'differentiate') is a definitive term referring to the distinctive signs, colours and items of attire imposed by the authorities on non-Muslims.

These verbs and verbal forms indicate that we have here the

---

9 Lewis 1984: ch. 1 (on the Middle Ages), ch. 3 (esp. 135ff, on the attitude of the Ottomans towards Jews roughly defined as tolerant, whereas pp. 107-148 treat both the advantage and frailty of the Jews' status within the Ottoman empire). Cf. Lewis 1986: 121ff.

10 It is important to examine general works on Islam addressed to the wide public of various countries (especially where one encounters cultural sensibility or political confrontation) and written in a somewhat popular style; we shall be content here with a reference to one text, originally broadcast as a series of radio talks: Lazarus-Yafeh 1985: 52ff (for instance: 58: '... there is no doubt that the situation of the Jews in the Muslim Orient was better, during most of the periods, than their situation in the West. This fact is due mainly to theological reasons. But there certainly were social reasons as well, due to which the Muslim attitude towards minorities was never harsh as the attitude of Christian Europe toward its Jews.' On the other hand, the author does not overlook (*ibid.*) 'riots and persecutions against Jews and the humiliation of the latter; an entire theory on the humiliation issue was even developed and applied, especially during the last centuries.' Scholars of this opinion give no indication of the frequency and proportion of riots (often, rarely, etc.).

11 Tritton 1930: esp. 5ff, 115ff.

12 Kister (forthcoming). Cf. Vajda 1937.

unquestionable origin of the concept of self-demarcation versus imposed differentiation, and they enable us to see an entire gamut: identity, self demarcation,[13] imposed demarcation, reservation, impurity, humiliation (for instance, the term *saghâr* which we explain below, in connection with the Latrines Decree). Each of these terms should be used only where it is appropriate.

The authorities imposed distinguishing signs not only between Muslims and non-Muslims, but also between the various non-Muslim communities; there were periods during which the minorities were differentiated from each other by means of a sign or a certain colour. E. Strauss, who was the first to emphasize the importance of the 'social isolation of *ahl al-dhimma*',[14] attributed the differentiation between the non-Muslim minorities of Egypt to the influence of certain twelfth century North African political and religious movements (the Almohads); however, it has been shown that a decree imposing on minority communities the wearing of distinctive colours had been issued in the eleventh century by the Fâtimid caliph of Egypt, al-Hâkim.1[15]

A particular case, constituting an extreme example of the effects of such demarcation, is that of the 'Turban Decree' imposed on the seventeenth century Yemenite Jews, whose special situation will be discussed below. The prohibition of the wearing of turbans symbolized a major change in the attitude of the Yemenite authorities towards the local Jews, following the first phase of the evolution of a Messianic Jewish movement: the Jews were now denied the right to *dhimma* status. This decree, as well as additional measures taken by the authorities in reaction to further phases of the evolution of the Messianic movement, caused the deterioration of both the social and the economic status of the Jews,[16] as we shall see.[17]

---

[13] Issues of humiliation (*saghâr*), impurity etc. will be treated below in the section on the controversy over the Latrine Decree.

[14] Strauss 1950: esp. 77. See also Strauss 1956.

[15] Proved in Sadan 1986: 366-367; cf. Sadan (forthcoming), both studies relying on al-Nâbulusî's treatise against the behaviour of the *dhimmîs*, of which the paragraphs dealing with Christians were published by Cahen 1958-1960 and those dealing with Jews by Sadan 1986.

[16] Van Koningsveld, Sadan & Samarrai 1990: 53-57, 80, 125-126, 164; Sadan 1990: 113, 119-120, 123. The text by Ahmad ibn Nâsir published and translated in these two studies not only provides almost the precise date (around 24.4.1667) on which the 'Turbans Decree' was issued, but also proves that this took place at the end of the first Messianic movement (perceived by the Yemenite authorities as a revolt deserving punishment and which, according to the text, could easily lead to the abrogation of the *dhimma* status granted to the Jews, which is a most important piece of information; see also *infra*, the section on the Latrines Decree) and not at the end of the second one. As to the various opinions expressed in relation to this issue before the latter text was published, see Ratzaby 1958: 292-293; Goitein 1983: 166; Klorman-Eraqi 1983: 51; Ahroni 1986: 104, 111 (two contradicting dates), Tobi 1986: 44, 105ff, 114ff, 117-141, esp. 134 (cf. Tobi 1979: 51-52).

[17] See *supra*, n. 13.

A hypothetical question

I should like to quote here an unpublished fourteenth century text resembling, at least externally, a legal opinion, a form which will be explained below. The text was written by Ibn Durayhim al-Mawsilî.[18]. As far as we can tell, the work that Ibn Durayhim composed and which interests us here has not been edited, nor have the two manuscripts that we shall use here, one from the British Library[19] and the other from Istanbul[20], been taken into account or reported in any study or bibliography:

Question: Islamic jurisprudence generally attempts to prevent or, at least, to limit major damage. It is clear that the damage to be expected from the infidels among us is greater than the benefit of the poll-tax levied from them; this damage is more serious than any benefit from all the taxes in the world. Why, then, does Islamic jurisprudence content itself with a levy on the worthless, and not oblige us to exterminate the infidels and, in this manner, wipe out their wickedness?

Answer: The present issue is a good example of the policy of limiting major damage and, consequently, enabling the Muslim world to draw a much more important benefit from the infidels' existence. For, if one had chosen to kill the infidels and not to provide safety and security [*amân*] to them—*one would not expect them to live safely and happily among us.* After all, God himself[21] formulated the duty of levying poll-tax, out of His hope that the infidels would convert to Islam in the future. And they would do it after recognizing the merits of living in the shade of Islam. Even if they die as infidels, there is still hope that their direct descendants or the descendants of their descendants will embrace Islam, one day in the future, till the Last Day [the Day of Doom]. *An hour of belief is better than an eternity of infidelity!*[22]

---

[18] Or with 'al': Ibn al-Durayhim. See Brockelmann 1937-1943: 2: 165, and Suppl., 2: 213. Brockelmann knows our author and some of his other works, but does not know the tract against the *dhimmîs* which interests us here (see the complete title, *infra*, n. 23), whereas Steinschneider 1877: 102, many years before Brockelmann, knew the title of the tract (relying on Khalfa [Khalîfa] 1835-1858: 6: 221, item No. 13280) but could not identify the author. However al-Ziriklî 1980: 5: 6 identifies both the author and the title (referring to two other unpublished MSS of the treatise, from Damascus and Cairo, not the ones used by us here; see *infra*, nn. 19, 20). Cf. Kahhâla 1957-1961, 7: 210 (very partial information).

[19] Ibn Durayhim MSa. Not to be found in any catalogue of the BL (except the hand-written acquisition registers).

[20] Ibn Durayhim MSb.

[21] *Quran*, Sûra 9, verse 29.

[22] Italics JS. The (rather freely) translated passage is taken from: Ibn Durayhim MSa: fols. 42a-42b. The spirit of this text is present in other sources of Muslim law

This pseudo legal opinion, while seemingly revealing a most positive attitude towards minorities living under Muslim rule, is frightening by reason of the very posing of the question of extermination. Fortunately, the question should be deemed purely hypothetical and is not included in any collection of legal opinions (*fatâwâ*). It appears in Ibn Durayhim al-Mawsilî's book *The right path demonstrating the ugliness of employing Non-Muslims as officials*[23], in which the author occasionally poses questions as a methodological ploy aimed at convincing his readers. (Even questions which would require a jurist to give 'authoritative' *responsa* are not always presented to him by members of the public, by the authorities or by his colleagues; in many instances, one may imagine that the questions were formulated by the scholar himself, and then presented as if someone had actually posed them.) In the present case, it seems that our scholar has formulated an entirely hypothetical question, in order to be able to demonstrate to the readers, in a new way, a principle encountered in older Islamic sources; the question has been minutely and artistically shaped to fit the following answer by the same hand that provided the response. The "matching" answer amplifies Ibn Durayhim's seemingly humane and liberal opinions, but one must not forget that this traditional Islamic view is expressed here in the framework of a treatise composed in order to bring about the deterioration of the status of non-Muslims by preventing them from filling administrative positions in public service.[24] On the other hand, the apparently severe character of the question about extermination should not be stressed, since the question is merely a stylistic device skilfully employed to display what the author considers a most positive side of the Islamic attitude towards the "other".

---

and it is connected with the legal opinions on the latrines decree written by the opponents of al-Shawkânî (cf., *infra*, the section on the latrines decree). For instance, according to Mâlikî (Ms), fol. 86b, the Muslims should respect and cherish Yemenite Jews, 'leave them in their religion, but make them observe, at the same time, the stipulations and restrictions (concerning attire, building, etc.) due to the conditions of the 'protection' (*dhimma*). And 'any tendency to disregard these rules cannot but cause trouble and suffering'.

[23] The complete Arabic title, in both MSS, is: *Manhaj al-sawâb fî qubh istiktâb ahl al-kitâb*.

[24] Granting 'superiority', such as an administrative post, to a non-Muslim is strictly forbidden by the Pact of 'Umar (see *supra*, n. 1).There are several tracts against employing non-Muslims as officials; Steinschneider 1877: 55, 102, 104-105, 393-394, provides a list of such tracts; published works are, for instance, Belin 1851-1852; Gottheil 1921; Perlmann 1940-1942; Perlmann 1948-1958; a source mimeographed in Saudi-Arabia (a relatively late tract of the Ottoman period): al-Wâridânî 1983. For the historical and socio-economic background of the wave of criticism against employing non-Muslims in certain posts (the fact that graduates of many newly erected Islamic *madrasas* looking for employment in the administration; growing religious feelings of the public and the ruling class, etc.), see Baron, Cahen, Sadan, and esp. Strauss, *supra*, nn. 1, 15.

In the spirit of the genuine tradition and sources of Islam, as well as in the ambience (Mamlûk Egypt and Syria) in which the author lived and worked, posing a question relating, in an overt way, to the extermination of *dhimmîs* can hardly be imagined in any but a hypothetical context.

The controversy over the Latrines Decree

When dealing with issues concerning the status of Yemenite Jews between the seventeenth and the nineteenth centuries, one must emphasize the commonplace that everything is relative. Whereas in other countries the existence of the *dhimma* might be the subject of deliberations among Muslim scholars and orientalists as to its merits and faults, in the Yemen of the late seventeenth century the attainment of *dhimma* status would be unequivocally considered a remarkable achievement on the part of the Jews. This is due to the fact that, at a certain stage of their history, the Jews were denied *dhimma* status, their lives were exposed to perilous threats and they were almost expelled from the Yemen.[25] (As we know from Muslim and Jewish chronicles, the Jews of San'a were banished for a number of years to the region of Mawza', in the Yemen itself, where many of them died.)[26] When the concept of *dhimma* status for the Jews was reinstated by the Yemenite jurists and authorities, it was not officially declared or publicly recognized. For reasons which will be explained below, the Yemenite Jews still found themselves worse off at that stage than they had been formerly at the time when they enjoyed the status of "normal" *dhimma*, granted by the Zaydî Shî'î authorities in the Yemen.[27]

---

[25] For detailed deliberations about the right or absence of right that the Jews have to live in the Yemen, and whether the *hadîth* traditions attributed to the prophet Muhammad and his Companions forbidding non-Muslims to live in the Hijaz (or the entire Arabian Peninsula, according to some versions) include the Yemen or not, see Ibn al-Wazîr and Ibn Nâsir in the following note.

[26] Ibn al-Wazîr 1985: 352-353; Tâzî (al-) 1981: 15-35; text and background, various views in Ibn Nâsir and parallel authors on the apparent duty to expel the Jews from the Yemen, see in van Koningsveld, Sadan & Samarrai 1990: 103-112, 114-115, 125 ('The Imam, however—peace be upon him—said: Do not say the Protected Ones; do not call them *dhimmîs*, but say: the Jews'), 133-134, 152-155 (Jewish sources are mentioned as well). See also studies by Goitein 1964: 74; 1983: 143-144, 166; Ratzaby 1958, 1961, 1971-1972; Zadoq 1967: 54-60; Serjeant 1983: 399b-418b; Amri 1985: 164; Ahroni 1986: 121ff; Tobi 1986: 37, 45-46, 76, 112-113, 149; Jirâfî (al-) 1987: 235-236.

[27] Van Koningsveld, Sadan & Samarrai 1990: 99, 112-117.

It should be added here that the requirement of humility on the part of non-Muslims is rooted in the Quran. The humility, often interpreted as a duty to humiliate non-Muslims when they come to pay taxes, is mentioned in a famous Quranic verse[28] demanding that non-Muslims pay by their own hand, in a state of complete obedience or humility (*saghâr*, often compared with the parallels *dhull* and *dhilla*). A study treating the expression 'by their hand' (*'an yadin*) by M.J. Kister,[29] and a recently published study by U. Rubin,[30] refer to the original significance of the Quranic expression according to old traditions and commentaries, which could denote paying according to one's means, paying a progressive tax, etc. However, we are interested here in the concept of *saghâr* (humility, humiliation; see below), as seen through the eyes of Yemenite scholars in relatively late periods.

The decree with which we are concerned, the Latrines Decree (or the Scrapers Edict, or the Dung Gatherers),[31] is related, among other things, to the issue of *saghâr*. There was in addition a series of decrees which rendered the status of the Yemenite Jews vastly infe-

---

[28] *Supra*, n. 21.

[29] Kister 1964.

[30] Rubin 1993.

[31] Ratzaby 1971-1972: 200, 206 (a passage in ornate prose, from the end of the 17th century, and which proves that the removal of dead horses and camels was occasionally imposed on the Jews; do we find the beginnings of the spirit of the Latrines Decree there?); Ratzaby 1969: 57-59, 68ff (references to Jews collecting dead animals and excrement, this task apparently corresponds to the that of the *mashâ'ilî* described by Lapidus, *infra*, n. 36); Ratzaby 1989; Habshûsh in Qâfih 1958: 274-275; Zadoq 1967: 82-83; Nahum and Tobi 1975: 131-133; Tobi 1979: 29-30; Tobi 1986: 22, 150 (n. 46); Ahroni 1986: 115-117, 146, 149, 151; Nini 1991: 23-26, esp. 67. Gamli'el 1986-1987, 2: 150-154 reports that towards the middle of the twentieth century the task of removing filth (performed by the Jews) 'was not compulsory' (cf. *infra*, the end of the article and n. 53). Gamli'el's observation should be applied solely at the individual level. Ratzaby and others have shown that towards the end of the nineteenth century, the Muslims imposed this duty on the Jewish community as a whole, but the Jewish dignitaries compromised with the authorities and formulated an agreement according to which the latter would not interfere with the selection of workers, so that the community would be able to give these jobs (paid by the community) to needy Jews. In this respect, at the individual level, emptying the latrines was not enforced without distinction. However, sometimes (on rare occasions of harshness on the part of the authorities, inner disputes within the community and so on) the compromise was not respected and even dignitaries were forced, as a punishment, into this humiliation. In a document published in Ratzaby 1969: 68-70, a distinction is made between compelling 'on the whole' and compelling 'individually'. In spite of the vague hints concerning the existence of the 'Latrines Decree' towards the end of the seventeenth century, most of the information refer to the eighteenth and especially the nineteenth centuries. It is more important to remember that the controversy between Muslim scholars described in the present chapter took place in the nineteenth century. See also *infra*, n. 36.

rior to that of minorities subject to the *dhimma* in other Islamic countries. A typical example of such a decree is that Jewish orphans were to be taken from their families and brought up as Muslims.[32] Al-Shawkânî, a nineteenth century Muslim scholar, with whom we shall be dealing in the following lines, dedicated a special epistle to this issue[33] but, unfortunately, the text is lost or, maybe, hidden in the dim recesses of some uncatalogued library in the Yemen.

In the second half of the seventeenth century, a significant Messianic movement succeeded in attracting and engaging many circles within the Jewish community in the Yemen. The Muslim authorities perceived this movement as an insolent revolt against the rule of Islam. Consequently, they officially abrogated the legal and social status (the *dhimma*, or Protection, granted by Islam to non-Muslims) of the Jews. This act was followed by other steps taken by the authorities against the Jewish community, such as confiscation of land and the expulsion of the Jews of San'a for a period of several years; this expulsion caused many losses among the Jews.[34]

Later, the *dhimma* was gradually restored, but a series of decrees continued to erode the status of the Jews. One of these was the 'Latrines Decree' (*iltiqât al-azbâl*, or *Gezerat ha-meqammesim*, i.e.'The decree concerning those who are compelled to clean and remove dung from the Muslims' latrines').[35] It should be noted that this decree does not reflect the common attitude of other Muslim countries towards Jews.

There are more than a dozen terms[36] to denote sewer cleaners and dung removers in the Muslim world:

---

[32] Tobi 1984-1985: 120; Ahroni 1986: 117-120; Nini 1991: 21-23, 60, 160..

[33] Hilâl 1969: 44, item No. 85; 1979: 36, item No. 72.

[34] *Supra*, n. 26.

[35] Shawkânî (al-) MSa; concerning this tract and the continuations and reactions to it (*infra*, nn. 43-51), see the following bibliographical details (some given by the author himself) Shawkânî (al-) 1929-1930, 1: 391-392, 2: 220-221; Zabâra 1931-1932, 2: 94; Mawi 1970; Habshî 1978; Serjeant 1983: 394b; Amri 1985: 196 and the long bibliographical lists contained in the works of Hilâl (*supra*, n. 33).

[36] Collected from the Yemenite tracts discussed below (esp. Mâlikî [al-] MS: fols. 86a: *multaqit azbâl*, 89b: *kannâf*), as well as the following compositions: Jahiz (al-) 1964-1979: 1: 389-390; Jâhiz (al-) 1969: 3: 13-15; Jâhiz (al-) 1981: 114; Abî (al-) 1983: 213; Isfahânî (al-) 1961: 1: 460; Subkî (al-) 1983: 146, No. 110 and n. 2 ; and the following studies: Mez 1922: 392; Brauer 1934: 236, 237; Colin et Lévi-Provençal 1943: 67; Lévi-Provençal 1947: 108; Lévi-Provençal 1955: 48; Qâsimî 1960: 136, 363; Qâfih 1961: 238; Lapidus 1967: 83-84; Sa'd 1983: 89; Serjeant 1983: 395a (n. 29), 429b (and n. 289, 562a (explanation of verse 24 in the poem); Gamli'el 1986-1987: 2: 153; Ratzaby 1989: 133; Nini 1991: 67. Prof. M. Gil has documents on a similar trade, *fajjâl* (the 'collector' of urine), who produces ammoniac out of this liquid. See also *supra*, n. 31.

hâmil mâ fî 'l-kunuf; kannâf; kannâs; kâsih; kassâh; mashâ'ilî; meqammes[37]; *mijahhif; mukabbî; multaqit azbâl; mutayyib; qumaymî; zabbâl.*

In the Yemen, excrement was customarily collected from the houses and used as fuel in baths or even carried to the fields, where it was used as natural fertilizer. The practice of confining this work to non-Muslims, following the religious restrictions on touching impure materials such as dung, is to be found in other Muslim countries (Morocco,[38] Muslim Andalus[39] and the region of Bukhara[40]), but it was rarely a matter of compulsion. In the Yemen, however, the Jewish community was, on several occasions (up to the beginning of the twentieth century), compelled to provide a specific number of workers to perform this task. It would be wrong to assume that the practical reason for the imposing of such an unpleasant assignment on the Jews was merely an ardent desire to humiliate them. The special structure of Yemenite latrines, and the need to empty them occasionally, were the real motivation for the proclamation of the Latrines Decree, whereas the humiliation of the infidels, as well as the reticence to employ Muslims in impure works, were the official, legal and religious justification for the decree; nevertheless, there were numerous theologians and rulers for whom the issue of deliberate humiliation was real. The duty of emptying filth from latrines was not imposed personally on every Jewish individual; a small group of poor Jews was chosen by the community to perform this menial task, while the costs were covered by the community as a whole. The majority of the community did not feel humiliated, but preferred to ignore, or to psychologically minimize the effect of the Decree. On the other hand, while apparently not suffering from contempt felt by Muslim society for them, they themselves showed contempt for the those Jews who actually carried out the latrine emptying; rich Jews and the families of rabbis and of other learned people did not allow the latrine

---

[37] The Hebrew term *meqammes* requires some explanation. It is a rare Talmudic word used by the Yemenite Jews, who were probably ashamed to use a common Arabic term understood by the non-Jews. Even the pure Arabic word *mutayyib* means simply *perfumer*, one 'who scents', not one who deals with malodorous materials; we can sympathize with this euphemism of the local Jewish idiom.

[38] We know that in 1884 the Sultan of Morocco defended the Jews and ordered a ban on the imposition of various tasks, such as cleaning latrines (a task performed by them before this ban); see Leven 1911-1920: 243-244 (I thank Dr. P. Fenton for this reference); Bat Ye'or 1985: 325-326, document No. 78.

[39] See *supra*, n. 36, references to Lévi-Provençal.

[40] Ibn al-Fuwatî 1932-1933: 69; Bat Ye'or 1985: 191-192. However, in this case it is not clearly stated that they were forced to do it.

cleaners to pray with them in the same synagogues, and refused to marry members of their families.[41]

The Latrines Decree became an issue of juridical controversy. One should examine carefully the following list and compare it with some data published by R. Serjeant in his exhaustive book on San'a; he based his description on information that he found in a catalogue, without seeing or checking the MSS themselves. He confused the various authors, ascribing to al-Shawkânî, for instance, writings of his opponent, and vice versa; he also defined authors who in fact attacked al-Shawkânî as supporters of the latter.[42] The following list reflects the true relations between the various extant compositions:

1. Al-Shawkânî, *Resolving the difficulties related to the [justification of] obliging the Jews to collect filth.*[43]
2. (Against 1:) al-Kawkabânî, *Delivering an [oral or written] speech against the epistle 'Resolving the difficulties'.*[44]
3. (Against 2:) al-Shawkânî, *Directing [or, in another version: Spreading] high arrows against [the epistle] 'Delivering a speech'.*[45]
4. (Against 3:) al-Kawkabânî, *Addressing straight spears against [the epistle] 'Directing [Spreading] high arrows'.* This polemical tract is lost or hidden in the dim recesses of some unknown collection in the Yemen.[46]
5. (Against 1:) 'Alî ibn 'Abdallah al-Jalâl, *Elucidating the various confusing aspects in [the epistle] 'Obliging the Jews to collect filth'.*[47]
6. (Against 5:) al-Shawkânî, *Refutation of those who claim the existence of confusing aspects in the epistle 'Obliging the Jews to collect filth'.*[48]
7. (Against 1 and treating 2 as well): 'Abdallah ibn Mubârak (another reading: Bârik) ibn Bashîr al-Mâlikî (the only one jurist who is not Shi'î), *Investigating the arguments and settling the controversy [between the epistles] 'Resolving the difficulties' and 'Delivering a speech'.*[49]
8. (Against 7): al-Shawkânî, *Analyzing [or: proving the sickness of the epistle] 'Investigating the arguments'.*[50]

---

[41] Ratzaby 1969; Ratzaby 1989; for more details about it, see *supra*, n. 31.
[42] Serjeant 1983: 394a-395a.
[43] Shawkânî (al-) MSa, and see *supra*, n. 35.
[44] Kawkabânî (al-) MSa.
[45] Shawkânî (al-) MSb.
[46] References to this apparently lost tract of al-Kawkabânî, see Zabâra, *supra*, n. 35.
[47] Jalâl (al-) MS.
[48] Shawkânî (al-) MSc.
[49] Mâlikî (al-) MS.
[50] Shawkânî (al-) MSd.

The written form of the long disputation regarding this issue dates from the 19th century, but its origins are older. It caused confrontation between Muslim scholars (such as al-Shawkânî and al-Kawkabânî) almost all of whom belonged to the dominant Zaydî Shî'a, but at least one of the participants was a Sunnî jurist (of the Mâlikî school of law). Most of them criticized the Decree, arguing that nothing can be added to or modified in the *dhimma* status dating to the time of the prophet Muhammad and his Companions (or, according to some modern scholars, attributed to them). According to this line of argument, non-Muslims should be treated neither more leniently nor more harshly than determined in the Traditions (*hadîth*) which are believed to reflect that period. Al-Shawkânî, on the other hand, believed that Islamic jurisprudence can be modified, strengthened and augmented (relying on the *ijmâ'* principle).[51] Another issue involved in the series of polemical tracts was that of impurity: may a Muslim touch human or animal waste? Some scholars claimed that even certain Companions of the Prophet used to manure their fields with their own hands (the manure is called here: *'ura*[52]), and that some well-known, pious and learned Yemenite figures of later periods used to empty their own latrines. However, al-Shawkânî insisted that such impure tasks should be left to non-Muslims—namely, the Jews. The latter have no right to dwell in the Arabian Peninsula (al-Shawkânî disregards all the Traditions restricting this prohibition to the Hijaz, and argues firmly in favour of the Tradition and commentaries which speak about the entire peninsula), cannot enjoy the *dhimma* status and should at least be kept continuously humiliated, as prescribed by Islamic sacred texts; moreover, they deserve this humiliation, due to their behaviour. The phases that can be clearly distinguished in the written polemics are as follows (we do not observe in the exact order of the arguments presented in the original texts):

1. Al-Shawkânî writes in favour of the duty of compelling the Yemenite Jews to empty latrines.
2. His opponents reveal that the Companions of the Prophet touched filth and manure. Thus, nothing should prevent Muslims from emptying latrines and there is no need to compel non-Muslims to perform this task, unless they agree to do it.

---

[51] The entire work of Hilâl 1969 is dedicated to this religious issue and see also Amri 1985: 140-171; al-Mawrawî (al-) 1992: passim, esp. 15 of the introduction (on al-Shawkânî). See also Dharawî (al-) 1983.

[52] Cf. Kister 1991: 301: *'ura*.

(3. A discussion takes place as to whether any of the examples from the time of the Prophet are applicable to San'a of the authors' time; this kind of question is typical of the deliberations of jurisprudence [*fiqh*] deliberations: Were there latrines in the time of the Prophet? Were these latrines constructed in the same way as those of San'a in the authors' time, i.e., latrines in which filth is accumulated in a special hollow place[53] that has to be emptied regularly? If there are in fact differences between the various kinds of latrines, can one, relying on the 'principle of analogy', draw from the earlier examples with respect to the needs of the present?)
4. Al-Shawkânî's riposte is that manure is different from human excrement.
5. His opponents retort that among their religious masters were pious and reliable figures who used to empty their own latrines.
6. Al-Shawkânî insists that his opponents' references were to pious men who touched their own excrement, whereas the issue was of emptying other people's latrines, some of which may contain impurities, such as infidels' filth.

The deliberations contained in this series of polemical tracts display the various attitudes of Yemenite Muslim scholars towards the delicate issue of the rights of the "Other". We may conclude that some of these scholars felt they could not stand aloof while seeing the ardent wish of al-Shawkânî and the authorities to worsen the *dhimma.* stipulations, by imposing on the Jews the Latrines Decree, although in everyday life, these initiatives were often local, as has been suggested, for instance, by Y. Ratzaby (relying on Jewish documents).[54]

---

[53] Some of the references quoted *supra*, n. 36, demonstrate various types of latrines and various ways of emptying them. As to the special case of the latrines in San'a and their structure, see Serjeant 1983: 440a-441a, 469a (also 515b, on using excrement as fuel in baths).

[54] *Supra*, nn. 31, 40. Our enriched and more detailed study of some of these texts, with quotations in Arabic, technical terminology, etc., will be included in a forthcoming book (in Hebrew) in honour of M. Gil. For further information concerning the impurity of various kinds of excrement used as fuel in bakeries, etc., see Ibn Taymiyya 1987: 464 (for instance, sheep's droppings are apparently 'pure', whereas donkey's dung is 'impure'); Râgib (forthcoming), who deals with the controversy concerning the 'impurity' of pigeons' dung (*fiente, colombine*), sold as manure in medieval Egypt.

References

Abî (al-), Abû Sa'd, 1983, *Nathr al-durr; al-juz' al-sâbi'; edited by 'U. Bughânmî.* Tunis: al-Dâr al-Tûnisiyya lil-Nashr.

Ahroni, R., 1986, *Yemenite Jewry*. Bloomington: Indiana University Press.

Amri, A., 1985, *The Yemen in the 18th and 19th centuries; a political and intellectual history*. London: The Centre for Middle Eastern and Islamic Studies, University of Durham.

Anonymous (ed.) 1983, *Studies in Aggada and Jewish Folklore*. Jerusalem: Centre for Folklore Research, Hebrew University (= Studies published by the Centre for Folklore Research, 7).

Balâdhurî (al-), Ahmad, 1866, *Futûh al-buldân; Liber expugnationis reginorum; Auctore: Imâmo Ahmed ibn Jahja ibn Djâbir al-Belâdsorí; edited by M.J. De Goeje*. Leiden: E.J. Brill.

Balâdhurî (al-), Ahmad, 1916, *Futûh al-buldân: The origins of the Islamic state; translated by Ph. Hitti*. New York and London: Columbia University and Longman Green.

Baron, S., 1952-1983, *A social and religious history of the Jews*. Philadelphia: Columbia University Press & The Jewish Publ. Soc. of America.

Bat Ye'or (pseudonym) 1979, *Juifs arabes ou dhimmis juifs*. Geneva: Éditions de l'Avenir.

Bat Ye'or (pseudonym) 1980a, *Le dhimmi*. Paris: Anthropos.

Bat Ye'or (pseudonym) 1980b, *Dhimmi Völker*. Geneva: Éditions de l'Avenir.

Bat Ye'or (pseudonym) 1985, *The Dhimmi*. Rutherford (N.J.): Fairleigh Dickinson University Press.

Bat Ye'or (pseudonym) 1986, *Ha-dhimmim* (Heb.). Jerusalem: Cana.

Bat Ye'or (pseudonym) 1991, *Les chrétiens d'Orient entre jihâd et dhimmitude*. Paris: Éditions du Cerf.

Beladorî (el-), 1917, *Futûh al-buldân; translated by O. Rescher*. Leipzig: Harrassowitz.

Belin, M., 1851-1852, 'Fetoua relative à la condition des zimmis', in *Journal Asiatique*, série 4, 18: 417-516; 19: 97-140.

Brauer, E., 1934, *Ethnologie der Jemenitischen Juden*. Heidelberg: Carl Winters.

Brinner, W.M., (ed.) 1974, *Islamic aspects in the Israeli-Arab conflict* (Heb.). Jerusalem: The Hebrew University.

Brockelmann, C., 1937-1943. *Geschichte der Arabischen Literatur*. Leiden: E.J. Brill.

Cahen, Cl., 1958-1960, 'Histoires coptes d'un cadi médiéval', in *Bulletin de l'Institut Français d'Archéologie Orientale au Caire* 59: 130-150.

Cahen, Cl., 1965, 'Dhimma', in *Encyclopédie de l'Islam; nouvelle édition* (Leiden: Brill), 2: 234-238.

Chehata, Ch., 1965, 'Dhimma', in *Encyclopédie de l'Islam; nouvelle édition* (Leiden: Brill), 2: 238.

Chelhod, J., 1984-1985, *L'Arabie du Sud*. Paris: Maisonneuve & Larose.

Cohen, M.R., 1991, 'Neo-lachrymose conception of Jewish-Arab history: have present-day politics distorted our understanding of the Jewish-Arab past?', in *Tikun* 6, 3: 55-60.

Cohen, M.R., (forthcoming), *Under crescent and cross: the Jews in the Middle Ages*. Princeton: Princeton University Press.

Colin, G.S., & E. Lévi-Provençal (eds.) 1943, *Un manuel hispanique de hisba*. Paris: E. Leroux.
Dharawî (al-), A., 1983, *Nazariyyat al-ijtihâd*. Jedda: Dâr al-nashr.
Gamli'el 1986-1987, *The Jews and the king in the Yemen* (Heb.). Jerusalem: Shalom Institute.
Goitein, S.D., 1964, *Jews and Arabs*. New York: Schocken.
Goitein, S.D., 1983, *The Yemenites: history, communal organization, spiritual life* (Heb.). Jerusalem: Hebrew University, The Ben-Zvi Institute for the Study of Jewish Communities in the East.
Goldziher, I., 1920, *Vorlesungen über den Islam*. Heidelberg: Carl Winters.
Gottheil, R., 1921, 'An answer to the Dhimmîs', in *Journal of the American Oriental Society* 41: 383-457.
Habshî (al-) 1978, *Masâdir al-fikr al-Islâmî fî al-yaman*. San'a: [?].
Hilâl, I.I., 1969, *Wilâyat allâh wal-tarîq ilayhâ*. Cairo: Dâr al-Kutub al-Hadîtha.
Hilâl, I.I., 1979, *Al-Imâm al-Shawkânî wal-ijtihâd*. Cairo: Dâr al-Nahda.
Hill, D.R., 1971, *The termination of hostilities in the Early Arab conquests*. London: Luzac.
Ibn Durayhim (MS)a, *Manhaj al-sawâb*. British Library. MS Or.9264.
Ibn Durayhim (MS)b, *Manhaj al-sawâb*. Topkapi Saray. MS A III, 1404.
Ibn al-Fuwati, 'A.R., 1932-1933, *Al-Hawadith al-jâmi'a*. Baghdad: al-Maktaba al-'Arabiyya.
Ibn Qayyim, al-Jawziyya, 1961, *Ahkâm ahl al-dhimma*. Damascus: Damascus University Press.
Ibn Qayyim, al-Jawziyya, 1981, *Al-Shurût al-'umariyya* (extract from the preceding item, with a commentary). Beirut: Dâr al-'ilm lil-malâyîn.
Ibn Taymiyya, Taqî al-Dîn, 1987, *Ahkâm al-tahâra; edited by 'A.-Q. 'Atâ*. Beirut: Dâr al-Kutub al-'Ilmiyya.
Ibn al-Wazîr, 'A., 1985, *Tabaq al-halwâ; edited by M. 'A.-R. Jâzim*. Cairo: Dâr al-Masîra.
Isfahânî (Isbahânî [al-]), R., 1961, *Muhâdarât al-udabâ'*. Beirut: Maktabt al-Hayât.
Jâhiz (al-), 1964-1979, *Rasâi'l; edited by 'A.-S. Hârûn*. Cairo: al-Khanjî
Jâhiz (al-), 1969, *Kitâb al-hayawân; edited by 'A.-S. Hârûn*. Cairo: Dâr al-Kitâb al-'Arabî.
Jâhiz (al-), 1981, *Kitâb al-bukhalâ'; edited by T. al-Hâjirî*. Cairo: Dâr al-Ma'ârif.
Jalâl (al-), Jamâl al-âl 'A., (MS), *Tawdîh wujûh al-ikhtilâl fî izâlat al-ishkâl fî ijbâr al-yahûd 'alâ iltiqât al-azbâl*, in microfilm No. 2216 at al-Hay'a al-Misriyya Library (Cairo) of a MS in the al-Siyâghî (or al-Sayâghî) collection: fols. 74a-78a.
Jirâfî (al-), 'A., 1987, *Al-Muqtataf min ta'rîkh al-yaman*. Beirut: Manshûrât al-'Asr al-Hadîth.
Kahhâla, 'U.R. ,1957-1961, *Mu'jam al-mu'allifîn*. Damascus: Matba'at al-Taraqqî.
Kawkabânî (al-), 'Abdallâh ibn 'Îsâ, (MS), *Irsâl al-maqâl 'alâ izâlat hall al-ishkâl*, in microfilm No. 2216 at al-Hay'a al-Misriyya Library (Cairo) of a MS in the al-Siyâghî (or al-Sayâghî) collection: fols. 49a-58a.
Khalfa (Khalîfa), Haji (Hâjjî), 1835-1853, *Kashf al-zunûn: lexicon bibliographicum et encycopaedicum; edited by G. Flügel*. London and Leipzig: Oriental Translation Fund.

Kister, M.J., 1964, 'An yadin', in *Arabica* 11: 272-278.
Kister, M.J., 1991, 'Land property and jihâd', in *Journal of Economic and Social History of the Orient* 34: 270-311.
Kister, M.J., (forthcoming), 'Traditions of the Prophet concerning the dhimma', an article in preparation, following an oral contribution on this topic, at the Israel Academy of Sciences and Humanities (Jerusalem: Jan. 11th. 1994).
Klorman-Eraqi, B.-Z., 1983, 'The Sabbatian movement in the Yemen' (Heb.), in *Pe'amim—Studies in the Cultural Heritage of the Oriental Jewry*, fasc. 15: 47-57.
Komlos, O., (ed.) 1950, *Etudes orientales à la mémoire de P. Hirschler*. Budapest: Gewirtz.
Koningsveld, P.S. van, J. Sadan, & Q. Samarrai 1990, *Yemenite authorities and Jewish messianism*. Leiden: University of Leiden, Faculty of Theology.
Lapidus, I.M., 1967, *Muslim cities in the Later Middle Ages*. Cambridge (Mass.): Harvard University.
Lazarus-Yafeh, H., 1985, *Religious thought and practice in Islam; more talks on the Islamic religion* [Heb.]. Tel Aviv: University Radio Broadcasting.
Lazarus-Yafeh, H., 1992, *Intertwined worlds*. Princeton: Princeton University Press.
Lazarus-Yafeh, H., (ed.) forthcoming, *The attitude of Islam towards Jews* (Heb.). Jerusalem: The Shazar Centre.
Leven, N., 1911-1920, *Cinquante ans d'histoire: l'Alliance Israélite Universelle*. Paris: Félix Alcan.
Lévi-Provinçal, E., 1947, *Séville musulmane; le traité d'Ibn 'Abdûn*. Paris: Maisonneuve.
Lévi-Provinçal, E., 1955, *Documents arabes inédits: trois traités hispaniques de hisba*. Cairo: IFAO.
Lewis, B., 1984, *The Jews of Islam*. London: Melbourne & Henley.
Lewis, B., 1986, *Semites and anti-Semites*. New York & London: Norton.
Löwinger, S., A. Schreiber, & J. Somogyi (eds.) 1948-1958, *Ignaz Goldziher memorial volumes*. Budapest, etc.: Globus & R. Mass.
Mâlikî (al-), 'Abdallâh ibn al-Mubârak Bashîr, (MS), *Tahqîq al-maqâl waqat' al-jidâl 'alâ hall al-ishkâl wa-irsâl al-maqâl*, in microfilm No. 2216 at al-Hay'a al-Misriyya Library (Cairo) of a MS in the al-Siyâghî (or al-Sayâghî) collection: fols. 84a-90b.
Ma'oz, M., (ed.) 1974, *The aims of the Arab struggle* (Heb.). Jerusalem: The Hebrew University.
Mawi, Abd al-'Al, 1970, *Jews in Yemen in the 17th-19th centuries* (Unpublished Ph.D. dissertation, University of St. Andrews).
Mawrawî (al-), M. al-Rûmî, 1992, *Al-Qawl al-sadîd fî ba'd masâ'il al-ijtihâd wal-taqlîd*. Kuweit City and Cairo: Dâr al-Da'wa and Dâr al-Wafâ'.
Mez, A., 1922, *Die Renaissance des Islams*. Heidelberg: Carl Winters.
Nahûm, Y.L., & Y. Tobi 1975, 'The epistle: life of the Yemenites', in *Yesha'yahu* 1975: 115-143.
Nini, Y., 1983, 'Protection certificate' (Heb.), in Anonymous 1983: 157-186.
Nini, Y., 1991, *The Jews of the Yemen (1800-1914)*. Chur: Harwood Academic Press.
Noth, A., 1987, 'Abgrenzungsprobleme zwischen Muslimen und nicht-Muslimen: die Bedingungen Umars'. in *JSAI* 10: 290-315.

Perlmann, M., 1940-1942, 'Notes on anti-Christian propaganda', in *Bulletin of the School of Oriental and African Studies* 10: 843-861.
Perlmann, M., 1948-1958, 'Asnawi's tract against Christian officials', in Löwinger, Schreiber & Somogyi 2: 172-208.
Perlmann, M., 1965, 'Ghiyâr', in *Encyclopédie de l'Islam; nouvelle édition* (Leiden: Brill) 2: 1100.
Qâfih, Y., 1961, *Customs of the Yemen; life of the Jews in San'a and the environs* (Heb.). Jerusalem: Ben-Zvi Institute.
Qâfih, Y., 1958, 'The Qorot Yisra'el be-Teman, by Rabbi H. Habshush', in *Sefunot* 2: 246-286.
Qâsim, 'Abduh Q., 1979, *Ahl al-dhimma fî misr al-'usûr al-wustâ.* Cairo: Dâr al-ma'ârif.
Qâsimî, M.S., 1960, *Qâmûs al-sinâ'ât al-shâmiyya.* Paris, etc.: Mouton.
Râgib, Y., (forthcoming), 'Une vente à livrer de colombine', in *Ars Orientalis; hommage au Professeur Claude Cahen.*
Ratzaby, Y., 1958, 'Documents concerning the history of the Jews in the Yemen' (Heb.), in *Sefunot* 2: 287-302.
Ratzaby, Y., 1961, 'The Mawza' exile' (Heb.), in *Sefunot* 5: 237-295.
Ratzaby, Y., 1969, 'The Yemenite Jewry under the Turks' (Heb.), in *Sinai* fasc. 64: 52-77.
Ratzaby, Y., 1971-1972, 'The Mawza' expulsion in the light of new sources' (Heb.), in *Zion* 37: 197-215.
Ratzaby, Y., 1989, 'Urban Jewish life in Central Yemen' (Heb.), in *Sefunot* 19 (new series 4): 123-164.
Rubin, U., 1993, 'Quran and *Tafsîr*', in *Der Islam* 70, 1: 134-144.
Sa'd, F., 1983, *Al-'Âmma fî Baghdâd.* Beirut: al-Ahliyya.
Sadan, J., 1980, 'Community and extra-community as a legal and literary problem', in *Religion and Government in the World of Islam* (= *Israel Oriental Studies* 10): 102-115.
Sadan, J., 1986, 'Some literary problems concerning Judaism and Jewry in Mediaeval Arabic sources', in Sharon 1986: 353-398.
Sadan, J., 1990, 'The chronicle of Ibn Nâsir' (Heb.), in *Pe'amim—Studies in the Cultural Heritage of the Oriental Jewry* fasc. 43: 111-135.
Sadan, J., (forthcoming), 'Polemics as literary writing' (Heb.), in Lazarus-Yafeh (forthcoming).
Serjeant R. B., (*et alii*) 1983, *San'â'—an Arabian Islamic City.* London: World of Islam Festival Trust.
Sharon, M., (ed.) 1986, *Studies in honour of Professor David Ayalon.* Jerusalem, etc.: Cana & E.J. Brill.
Shawkânî (al-), M., (MS)a, *Hall al-ishkâl fî ijbâr al-yahûd 'alâ iltiqât al-azbâl,* in microfilm No. 2216 at al-Hay'a al-Misriyya Library (Cairo) of a MS in the al-Siyâghî (or al-Sayâghî) collection: fols. 44a-48a.
Shawkânî (al-), M., (MS)b, *Tafrîq* [or *tafwîq,* in another version]*al-nibâl ilâ irsâl al-maqâl,* in microfilm No. 2216 at al-Hay'a al-Misriyya Library (Cairo) of the above MS: fols. 59a-73b.
Shawkânî (al-), M., (MS)c, *Al-Ibtâl li-da'wâ al-ikhtilâl,* in microfilm No. 2216 at al-Hay'a al-Misriyya Library (Cairo) of the above MS: fols. 79a-83b.
Shawkânî (al-), M., (MS)d, *Al-I'lâl li-tahqîq al-maqâl,* in microfilm No. 2216 at al-Hay'a al-Misriyya Library (Cairo) of the above MS: fols. 91a-96a.
Shawkânî (al-), M., 1929-1930, *Al-Badr al-tâli'.* Cairo: Matba'at al-Sa'âda.
Spuler, B., 1952, *Iran in früh-islamischer Zeit.* Wiesbaden: F. Steiner.

Steinschneider, M., 1877, *Polemische und apologetische Literatur*. Leipzig: Abhandlungen für die Kunde des Morgenlandes.
Stillman, N., 1979, *The Jews of Arab lands*. Philadelphia: The Jewish Publ. Soc. of America.
Stillman, N., 1991a, *The Jews of Arab lands in modern times*. Philadelphia: The Jewish Publ. Soc. of America.
Stillman, N., 1991b, 'Myth, countermyth and distortion', in *Tikun* 6, 3: 60-64.
Strauss (Ashtor), E., 1944-1951, *History of the Jews in Egypt and Syria under the Mamlûks* (Heb.). Jerusalem: Rabbi Cook Institute.
Strauss, E., 1950, 'The social isolation of Ahl adh-Dhimma', in Komlos 1950: 73-94.
Strauss, E., 1956, 'Saladin and the Jews', in *Hebrew Union College Annual* 27: 305-326.
Subkî (al-), Tâj al-Dîn, 1983, *Mu'îd al-ni'am*. Cairo: Dâr al-Hadâtha.
Tazî (al-), 'A.-H., 1981, 'Al-Nusûs al-zâhira fî ijla' al-yahûd al-fâjira' li-Ibn Abî Rijâl', in *Majallat al-bahth al-'ilmî*, 32: 15-35.
Tobi, Y., (ed.) 1979, *The history of the Jews of Yemen from their own chronicles* (Heb.). Jerusalem: Shazar Centre.
Tobi, Y., 1984-1985, 'Histoire de la communauté juive du Yémen aux XIXe et XXe siècles', in Chelhod 1984-1985, 2: 119-137.
Tobi, Y., 1986, *Studies in Megillat Teman* (Heb.). Jerusalem: Hebrew University at the Magnes Press.
Tritton, A.S., 1930, *The Caliphs and their non-Muslim subjects*. London, etc.: Humphrey Milford.
Vajda, G., 1937, 'Juifs et musulmans selon le hadîṯ', in *Journal Asiatique* 229: 57-127.
Wâridânî (al-), Mustafâ ibn Muhammad, 1983, *Al-Nahy 'an al-isti'âna wal-intisâr fî umûr al-muslimîn bi-ahl al-dhimma wal-kuffâr; edited by T. al-'Alawânî*. Jedda: al-Manhal.
Yesha'yahu, Y., & Y. Tobi 1975, *The Yemenite Jewry: studies and research* (Heb.). Jerusalem: Ben-Zvi Institute.
Zabâra, M., 1931-1932, *Nayl al-watar*. Cairo: al-Matba'a al-Salafiyya.
Zadoq, M., 1967, *The Jews of the Yemen: their history and customs* (Heb.). Tel Aviv: Am Oved.
Zaydân, 'A.K., 1982, *Ahkâm al-dhimmiyyîn wal-mu'taminîn fî dâr al-islâm; reprinted from the 1963 edition*. Baghdad: Maktabat al-Quds.
Ziriklî, Khayr al-Dîn, 1980[5], *Al-A'lâm—qâmûs tarâjim*. Beirut: Dâr al-'Ilm lil-Malâyîn.

RITUAL AS CONFRONTATION

THE AYODHYA CONFLICT[1]

Jan Platvoet
(Leiden University)

On 6 December 1992, Hindu devotees of the god Ram destroyed the Babri mosque[2] in Ayodhya[3] because it stood on a spot which they venerated as *Ramjanmabhumi*, 'Ram's birthplace'. That mosque had been built there in 1528 by Babur Shah, founder of the Muslim Moghul empire, after a Hindu temple dedicated to Ram had allegedly been torn down.[4] This article deals with the ritual elements in the conflict over *Ramjamnabhumi* in Ayodhya. It was the focal point in the nation-wide troubled political relationships between the Hindu and the Muslim 'communities' and the central government of India in the last decade. I deal first with Ayodhya as the dense symbolic complex with a primarily cultural and religious quality as it has developed over the past millennium. I will then describe it as an arena of political strife, at first of local importance, but with a national impact in the past decade when it was made the focus of a nationwide struggle for power. These events and their background are described because they serve as the historical data on which to test the heuristic utility and analytical clarity of the concepts for the analysis of ritual in religiously plural situations developed in a previous chapter of this volume. Their application to the Ayodhya rituals of confrontation leads me to bring this study to a close on an anti-Durkheimian conclusion. It will show that the emphases on the integrative functions of ritual in anthropological theories and on ritual as standardized sequences of behaviour, must be complemented by theory that is able to account for the different kinds of ethnographic data presented in this chapter.

---

[1] I thank Dr. A. Nugteren and Drs. N. Bonouvrié for their help.

[2] It is termed 'Babar mosque' by van der Veer in his publications; Babri mosque seems, however, the more current designation.

[3] Ayodhya is a suburb of Faizabad, a major town in Uttar Pradesh (the 'United Provinces') in the northern part of India.

[4] That such a temple existed is asserted by Bakker (1986, I: 44sq., 133sq.; II: 146sq.; 1991: 91) and others but disputed by Panikkar (1992: 107; 1993: 27-33), Srivastava (1993: 47-49), Bhan (1993) and found 'far from conclusive' by Champakalakshmi (1993: 232); cf. also Muralidharan 1992b; 1992c.

Ayodhya as a ritual complex

Ayodhya is a small, picturesque temple town[5] on the river Sarayu in the state of Uttar Pradesh in North India. This important Hindu centre of pilgrimage has some 3000 Hindu temples. At the height of the pilgrimage season, its floating population may be well over 1 million. As a place of devotion, it has evolved slowly since 'the early second millennium AD'[6], and rapidly in the last three centuries[7], into a multi-layered consonant complex of dense religious symbols[8] which holds a strong appeal to Hindus of many walks of life, particularly in Northern India. This place of pilgrimage is, however, of special significance to Hindus of the high, or 'twice-born' (*dvija*), castes who support 'cultural' movements like the RRS[9] and political parties like the BJP[10]. Both belong to the *Sangh parivar*, the 'family'

---

[5] Ayodhya has some 4360 houses and a resident population of 30,000 (van der Veer 1989: 468-469).

[6] Thapar 1993: 155; cf. also Bakker 1984/1986, part I: 1-150.

[7] See Bakker 1984/1986, p. I: 150-153, van der Veer 1985: 308; 1988: 34-42, passim; Thapar 1993: 153-156.

[8] On cultures as constituted by dense 'consonant' symbolic complexes, cf. Douglas 1982³: 38, 64-71, 80-81, 149.

[9] The *Rashtriya Swayamsevak Sangh*, 'National Volunteer Corps', was founded in September 1925 by the Maharashtra *brahmin* and medical doctor Keshav Baliram Hedgewar (1889-1940) at Nagpur at a time when a wave of violent Hindu-Muslim riots was sweeping across India (Andersen & Damle 1987: 26). It was launched during the *Dasara* festival which celebrates Rama's victory over Ravana. The RSS made its first public appearance in April 1926 at the *Ram-Navami* festival in honour of Ram's birthday in a village near Nagpur. The RSS was meant to remove what Hedgewar considered the root cause of British colonial rule over the Indian subcontinent: the lack of national consciousness and cohesion among Hindus. It was to serve as a cadre of dedicated *pracharaks*, 'missionaries'—most of them celibate, as was Hedgewar himself—, and laymen with a militant Hindu national consciousness through political and martial training in *akharas*, 'gymnasia', and devotion to the god Maruti (= Hanuman, Rama's general), who aimed to regenerate, redefine, and defend the 'ancient Hindu nation'—as distinct from, and opposed to, the modern Indian state—on the sub-continent of India (Embree 1994: 619-628, 631). *Akharas* had been prominent institutes among Maharashtra *brahmins* who had cultivated a martial tradition as rulers and soldiers; they became popular again during the communal violence of the 1920s (Andersen & Damle 1987: 34-35). When the RSS was banned after the destruction of the Babri mosque on 6 December 1992, it had 35.000 *shakhas*, local units, and two and a half million active members (Ghimire & Pathak 1992: 51; Embree 1994: 649). Cf. also Gold 1991a: 533-535, 540-542, 546-549, 553-555, 559-563, 566-569, 571-583; 1991b; Embree 1994, esp. 635-642; van der Veer 1994: 655; Frykenberg 1994: 603.

[10] The Bharatiya Janata ('Indian People's') Party was founded in April 1980 when the RSS affiliated Jana Sangh section seceded from the Janata Party. The Janata Party itself was a merger, in May 1977, of the Jana Sangh, the 'political arm' of the RSS which it had founded in 1951, and some other parties (Andersen & Damle 1987: 8, n.5, 224-237); on the relationship of the Jana Sangh and the BJP to the RSS, cf. also Embree (1994: 637-638).

of RSS affiliated organisations[11] which oppose the secular constitution of India[12] and strive after a Hinduisation of Indian society. The RSS does this at the ideological level by training Hindu cadres, and the BJP by carrying the RSS goals into the political arena in order to wrench political power from the Congress Party, the traditional defender of the secular order as laid down in the constitution[13].

Ayodhya combines, in a way that is both complex and consonant, and full of different religious and political options, at least three distinct, interlocked complexes of symbols that may be used in ritual behaviour. It is firstly a major *tirtha* (place of pilgrimage); secondly, the centre, in terms of sacred history and sacred space, of the cult of Ram, the most popular god of North India; and thirdly, the seat of the one of the largest Indian orders of *sadhus* (ascetics), the Ramanandis. The order is composed of three very different, and each very loosely organised, groups of *sadhus*: the *tyagis*, or peripatetic 'abandoners'; the *nagas*, or 'naked' warriors, who live in *akharas*, military camps and castles; and the *rasiks*, who are the 'enjoyers of the bliss' of serving the divine royal couple, Rama and Sita. They dwell in the temples which they beautify for them.[14]

---

[11] Cf. Andersen & Damle 1987: 2-4, 37-38, 96, 116-117, 143, 250; Hansen 1993; Jaffrelot 1993: 521-523. The *Sangh parivar* is said to consist of 38 organisations by Janssen (1989: 15). Others give even larger numbers. Its other most important affiliates, apart from the BJP, are the *Rastriya Sevika Samiti* (National Women's Volunteer Corps), its female branch, founded in 1936; the BMS, *Bharatiya Mazdoor Sangh*, its trade union, founded in 1955; the VHP, *Vishwa Hindu Parisad* (Hindu World Alliance), its religious organisation, founded in 1964; the *Bajrang Dal*, the RSS youth movement, formed in 1985 (Sridhar 1993: 17); the *Akhil Bhartiya Vidyarthhi Parishad*, its student wing; the *Krishak Sangh*, its farmers' union; its *Hindu Jagran Mach*, its lawyers' association; an *Adivasi* (Aboriginals') wing; etc. To the *Sangh parivar* also belong more than thirty newspapers, published in twelve languages, which interpret the news from RSS perspectives. Cf. also Pande 1992; Thakur 1993: 657; Embree 1994: 635-642, esp. 638-642; Frykenberg 1994: 603.

[12] On the secularism of the Congress Party and India's constitution, cf. Embree (1994: 633): 'The Indian usage of "secularism" does not mean rejection of the transcendental values of religion; on the contrary, there is an insistence that all religions are true and that all have an equally valid place within the nation.' It is precisely this constitutional guarantee of equality entitling all religions to 'an equally valid place' within the Indian state to which the *Sangh parivar* vehemently objects and causes it to oppose the Hindu 'nation' (*rashtra*) and the 'state' (*raj*) of India (Embree 1994: 619-620, 622-623, 629-635, 637, 643); for a more Western interpretation of Indian secularism, cf. Becke 1994: 3, 22-24. Cf. also Baird 1975 for a discussion of the provisions for freedom of religion in the Constitution of India and the problems the Supreme Court [of India] has had in applying them.

[13] See e.g. Hiebert 1982: 301. Chatterjee 1993a, 1993b; Chengappa 1993; Ghimire 1993; Shridhar 1993; Yechury 1993.

[14] Burghart 1982: 362-363; see also Burghart 1983: 643-648; van der Veer 1982; 1987; 1988: 66-182; 1989; on *nagas*, see also Lorenzen 1978; Bakker 1991: 85-89.

As a *tirtha*, 'ford' or 'crossing', on the river Sarayu, Ayodhya is a place of pilgrimage (*tirtha*) primarily because for Hindus every *tirtha* represents, and presents, a connection between heaven and earth, life and death, and the living and their ancestors. A *tirtha* is believed to allow humans to 'cross over' to spiritual realities by the performance of *tirtha* rituals. One reason for such belief is that sacred rivers, like the Ganges and Sarayu, are believed to have originated in heaven.[15] Another is that like all sacred rivers, the Sarayu is a goddess whose life-giving waters purify believers of all kinds of impurity. Its banks are, therefore, also a most appropriate place for the cremation of corpses, for feeding the ancestors, and for the nightly rituals by which the recent dead are assisted in the crossing of Vaitarani, the river of death, which stinks of blood and bones and which they can cross only by holding on to the tail of the cow that must guide them to the opposite shore.[16] Two groups of *pandas*[17], or *tirthpurohits*, Brahman pilgrimage-priests, vie in Ayodhya, not without violence, for serving the ritual needs of the hundreds of thousands of pilgrims that annually arrive by train and other means of transport: to be set free from impurity, sin and sickness; to gain merit by 'worshipping' the river Saraju and bathing in her; to cremate a corpse; to guide the dead across the river of death; or feed the ancestors.[18] This is what van der Veer calls the brahmanical complex of Ayodhya.

But the pilgrim may also have travelled to 'behold' (*darshan*[19]) and worship Lord Rama in order to gain liberation for his soul by ardent devotion (*bhakti*) of him.[20] This is the 'spiritual' complex of

---

[15] One myth tells how Shiva, moved by the penance and devotion of Bhagirath, induced Mother Ganges to descend to earth from a lake in heaven. In order to forestall the world being destroyed by her descent, he brought her down to earth by holding her in the coils of his matted hair. Another relates how Brahma moved Vishnu to tears of affection for him by worshipping him immediately after his, Brahma's, birth from a lotus which had sprung from the navel of Vishnu. Brahma caught Vishnu's tears in the hollow of his palm and treasured them for ages in a wooden vessel close to his heart until he granted them, as a reward for great devotion, to a son of Manu, the king of Ayodhya. They now flow on earth as the river Sarayu (van der Veer 1988: 2).

[16] Van der Veer 1985: 304-305; 1987: 285; 1988: 2-4.

[17] From the Sanskrit word *pandita*, 'he who has knowledge', particularly of rituals and sacred texts. It is a common term of address for Brahmans.

[18] Van der Veer 1985; 1988: 79, 183-272; on *tirthayatra*, 'pilgrimage', see also Fuller 1992: 205-223.

[19] In Hinduism, *darshan*, 'beholding (a god)', is a 'sacramental' act that is believed to be full of salvific effects in itself. The god may be 'seen' in either his statue, when it is worshipped in the temple or when it is carried in a procession through a town, or in a human form—e.g. an avatar, like Sai Baba of Putaparthi, or in one's *guru*, or in a brahmin.

[20] In the *Skanda Purana*, Ayodhya is reckoned to be one of the seven places in which one may find liberation (*moksha*) for one's soul (van der Veer 1985: 308).

Ayodhya, for which the pilgrim will visit the many temples of Ayodhya, the *sadhus* who run them, perhaps choose one of them as his *guru* and become either his lay disciple, or enter into one of the many Ramanandi communities in Ayodhya in order to practise the discipline of the 'wandering' (*tyagi*), wrestling (*naga*) or doting (*rasik*) devotees of Ram. That spiritual complex takes two main forms: the *nirguna* and *saguna* devotion to Ram.[21] The first is the 'advanced', monistic *bhakti* mode: the worship of *Ram nirguna*, 'Rama unqualified', as the supreme, transcendent reality (*brahman*). It is believed that he may be beheld in that state by those who practise *jnana*, disciplined contemplation. It is also held that the essence of *Ram nirguna* is contained in his name, *Ram Nam*. Its constant repetition in the mantra *Ram Ramaya Namah*, 'I bow to Ram'[22], is believed to bring liberation[23], for that mantra is the 'phonic body' of the Lord for the believer. The *tyagi* Ramanandi ascetics, who in particular practise this monistic form of *nirguna bhakti*, do not worship Ram in a statue (which presents him in one of his *saguna* forms) by *murti-puja* ('worship of the form'), but in the shape of small face- and formless *shalagram* (black ammonite) stones.[24] They carry these with them on their annual peripatetic tours, when they travel as 'itinerant monasteries'[25] to the nine major Vaishnavaite centres of pilgrimage in North India in order to take part in the major festivals there, some of which celebrate events in the lives of Rama and Sita.[26] Or they accommodate them in their temples in Ayodhya during their stays there, or have become resident there, as most *tyagi* communities have.[27]

Apart from devotion to *Ram nirguna*, the *tyagi* Ramanandi *sadhus* use another major complex of ritual symbols which centres on ashes (*vibhuti*) and fire. A candidate is incorporated into a *tyagijamat*, an itinerant group of *tyagis*, by his *tyagiguru* smearing ash into the palm of the left hand of the disciple, writing *Om* in it, whispering into his ear the *guptmantra*, the secret mantra on which he must constantly meditate, and smearing him all over with ashes. A *tyagi* applies ashes to his body each morning, taking them from a live fire. That fire symbolises Brahman/Ram as ultimate reality; the god Agni,

---

[21] Cf. van der Veer 1988: 80-81.

[22] Cf. van der Veer 1988: 71, 81.

[23] 'To die with the name of Ram on your lips, as Mahatma Gandhi did, is the only way to reach salvation' according to *tyagi* Ramanandi ascetics (van der Veer 1988: 94-95, 122-123).

[24] Van der Veer 1988: 94-95, 124, 285, note 9; Burghart 1982: 371.

[25] Burghart 1982: 363.

[26] Cf. Burghart 1982: 364-367.

[27] Van der Veer 1988: 126-130; also 1982: 60-61, 69-70, 75.

who conveys sacrifices to the gods; the Vedic fire-sacrifices, small and large, which they and Brahmans perform; the hearths with the burning fires, which symbolise the state of householder; and the fire of the desires (*kama*) for procreation and wealth (*artha*) which go with that state and which *tyagis* have renounced. To *tyagis*, renunciation of that state and its passions consists in the interiorisation of fire by ascetic practices; it enables them both to be *anagni*, 'without fire', and *alamgi*, 'without fixed abode', and to build up in themselves *tapas*, 'spiritual heat', and acquire the special powers (*siddhis*) which *tapas* is believed to bestow.[28]

The other major mode of *bhakti* to Rama, held to be of equal value by his devotees, is the 'common' way: the worship of *Ram saguna*, 'Rama qualified', i.e. in the 'phenomenal' forms (*murti*) in which he is believed to have appeared in the course of Hindu salvation history. It is the ardent devotion to Rama as an *avatar*, or 'descent' of the god Vishnu on earth[29], as a god in heaven[30], and as he reveals himself in the statues in the temples built to house him on earth. Vishnu took human shape as Rama long ago by being born to Dasara, king of Kosala, who ruled from Ayodhya, as that king's eldest son by his first wife.[31] Rama won Sita, daughter of the king of Videha, in a contest. Dasara's second wife, however, tricked Rama from acceding to the throne upon the death of his father. Rama, Sita and Lakshman, Rama's full brother, went into exile in the forest for fourteen years, where Rama battled with Ravana, king of Lanka (the South), and his army of *ashuras*, when Ravana had abducted faithful Sita to Lanka in his aerial chariot.[32] Sita was

---

[28] Van der Veer 1982: 65; 1988: 94, 114-120, 126.

[29] As recorded in the *Ramayana*, in the revised standard version of Valmiki (cf. Thapar 1993: 145-147), about Rama as *dharmaraja*, or ideal king, and in the *Ramcharitmanas*, 'The lake of the deeds of Ram', a version of the Ramayana in Hindi by Tulsidas (1532-1623) which became very popular in North India. The latter work formulated the doctrinal basis for the *bhakti* cults of Ram in both its *nirguna* and *saguna* forms (van der Veer 1988: 80-84). However, many more versions of the *Ramakatha*, 'story of Ram' had appeared all over India by 1000 AD and as far as Bali and China by 1500 AD. Their analysis is important for the history of the evolution of the Rama-complex in different religious, historical and regional settings (cf. Thapar 1993).

[30] Rama devotees hold that Rama did not die but ascended to heaven at the *Svarvadgar ghats*, the 'Door to heaven' stone steps on the river in Ayodhya (van der Veer 1988: 5, 17, 19). The Ramanandi order developed the cult of Rama as a deity in the early second millennium (Thapar 1993: 151, 153).

[31] Cf. Thapar 1993: 144 for another summary.

[32] These themes are also sources of inspiration to *tyagis* who see Rama's as a wandering ascetic. They think of his and their sojourns in the forest, and the captivity of Sita, as representing the cosmic journey of the soul away from, and back towards, supreme reality, and liken his battles with the *ashuras* as the soul's fight against the fires of attachment (van der Veer 1988: 83-84, summarizing Gross 1979).

liberated and Ravana defeated with the help of the monkey-god Hanuman, minister and general of Sugriva, king of the monkeys. On his return to Ayodhya, Rama ascended the throne, which had been faithfully kept for him by his half-brother Bharat, and ruled as the very paradigm of the *darmaraja*, the king whose strict observance of the prescriptions of *dharma* brings order, peace, prosperity and happiness to everyone in his realm.

In Hindu time reckoning, however, Rama reigned over a million years ago, in the *treta yuga*, when men were much more virtuous than they are in the present *kali* age.[33] His reign, *Ramaraj*, is now regarded as the perfect model for every ruler and subject. Likewise, the matrimonial relationship between Rama and Sita serves as the true paradigm for husbands and wives, the first to be as loyal and respectful to their wives as Rama, the latter to be as unquestioningly obedient and subservient to their husbands as Sita.[34] The relationships, however, between the courtiers in the palace and Rama and Sita as the royal couple dwelling there (of Laksman and Hanuman who had been Rama's companions in his battles against Ravana; of Bharat who had faithfully kept Rama's throne for him;

---

[33] Hindu cosmogony covers an immense span of time. It seems designed to reduce the span of a human life to total insignificance. It is very complex. An important unit in it is a *kalpa*, or a day in the life of Brahma. It is 4,320,000,000 years long and is followed by a night of Brahma of the same length. Brahma is believed to live one hundred years of 360 Brahma days and nights each. The largest cosmogonic cycle, therefore, lasts 311,040,000,000,000 years. After the life of Brahma, the universe disappears into the *nirguna* supreme reality until, from it, a new creator god appears. During each day of his life, the creator god re-creates the universe; during each night, he gathers it back in into his body to keep it there in potentiality. Each such a day, or *kalpa*, consists of fourteen *manvantaras*, secondary cycles of 306,720,000 years each. Each mantanvara begins with the appearance of a new Manu, who is the progenitor and lawgiver of the human race. Each *kalpa* also contains one thousand *mahayugas*, and each *manvantara* seventy-one. Each *mahayuga* is divided into four *yugas*, or aeons, declining progressively in length. They are the *kritayuga*, lasting 1,720,000 years; the *tretayuga*, which lasts 1,296,000 years; the *dvaparayuga*, with a duration of 864,000 years; and the *kaliyuga* which lasts only 432,000 years. The decline in time span by a quarter in each *yuga* is matched by an equal decline in the observance of *dharma* by men. As piety and morals diminish, order and peace in society, and the prosperity and happiness of its citizens also deteriorate.

Humanity is currently believed to live in a seventh *manvantara* and in its *kaliyuga*. Vishnu descended as Rama at the close of the *tretayuga* preceding this one. After that he appeared as Krishna, his eighth incarnation. Krishna again appeared as *Arjuna* in the *Bhagavadgita*, the centrepiece of India's other major epic, the *Mahabharata*, the story of which is set in the *dvaparayuga* when morality was already much lower than in Rama's aeon, and war therefore more frequent (Kinsley 1982: 25-36; van der Veer 1988: 5-6).

[34] See Kinsley 1982: 25-30; van der Veer 1982: 75-76; 1987: 285-286; 1988: 4-5, 80-84, 92-95, 174; Bakker 1991: 89-90. In e.g. Shakta versions of the *Ramakatha*, 'Rama story', Sita plays a very different role (Thapar 1993: 154).

and of Sita's female companions (*sakhis*) who served Rama and Sita in unobtrusive ways and prevented their every wish) became the models of completely self-less, non-erotic devotion for the *rasik* and *naga* Ramanandi *saddhus* and their lay disciples. The *rasiks* in particular imitated the relationships of Sita's female companions towards Rama by beautifying (*sringar*) his temples with rich cloth and fine scents as their part in *Ramlila*, the 'play of Ram', whilst the naked *nagas* took their inspiration especially from Hanuman and his army of monkey soldiers.[35]

The religious use by Hindu believers of these relationships, which the texts set out for them as models of their 'world' and models for their lives[36] determines the sacred geography of Ayodhya with its thousands of temples, ponds and tanks connected with the Ram-Sita story. Apart from the temples, in which the *rasik sadhus* reside, it has many *chauks* ('places of ashes'), *chaunis* ('army camps') and *akharas*, 'training camps', in which the *tyagis* and *nagas* live; and several *ghats* (stone steps) on which Brahman *pandas* perform rituals on the riverside for their pilgrim clients. The most important temple for 'seeing' (*darshan*) Rama and Sita is the splendid *Kanak Bhavan* ('Golden Palace') temple, which represents the palace where Rama and Sita spent their married life.[37] It stands on *Ramkot*, or *Ramadurga* ('fort of Ram'), the steep hill in the centre of Ayodhya that served as its citadel. The fortress *Hanumangarhi*, which vies with *Kanak Bhavan* for fame, is also on *Ramkot* and is the central residence of the *nagas* and the temple of Hanuman who is 'even more revered than Ram-Sita'.[38]

The most famous, because most contested, place in Ayodhya, *Ramjanmabhumi*, 'Ram's place of birth', is also on *Ramkot*. Traditions emerging in Ayodhya from the middle of the 19th century claim that until 1528 a small temple stood on that site, to which Hindu pilgrims flocked, perhaps from the eleventh or twelfth century onwards when *Ramabhakti*, the cult of Ram, had begun to catch on in North India. Babur Shah (1483-1530), the founder the Moghul empire in 1526, is said by these same Ayodhya traditions to have visited Ayodhya in 1528 and to have ordered that the Ram temple be demolished[39] and a mosque built on that site. He is said to have

---

[35] Van der Veer 1988: 22-23, 71, 75, 78, 81-84, 149-150, 159, 161-165, 168-172.
[36] Cf. Geertz 1966: 7; 1973: 93.
[37] Van der Veer 1988: 22-23, 161, 273-274.
[38] Van der Veer 1988: 23; also 19-27, 151-159; 1982: 59-60.
[39] Cf. above note 3.

given these orders at the request of two Muslim *fakir*[40] residents of Ayodhya in order to gain their political support.[41] Traditions also has it that another temple, the *Janmasthanamandir*[42], was built on *Ramkot* nearby the Babri mosque shortly after it had allegedly been built on *Ramjanmabhumi*; and that Hindu pilgrims were allowed to visit *Sitarasoi*, 'Sita's kitchen', located in the outer enclosure of the Babri mosque, and to throw flowers in the *Ramchabutra* pit in front of the mosque over which the sanctum of the former temple was said to have stood.[43]

From the early eighteenth century onwards, when the Moghul empire was in decline, the cult of Rama spread widely and attracted many pilgrims to Ayodhya. Local warring Shi'a rulers entered into alliances with Hindu *rajputs* and employed thousands of *nagas*, 'warrior ascetics', in their armies. Tulsidas (1532-1623) had just written his *Ramcharitmanas*. It is in this period that Hindu *diwans*, ministers of Shi'a rulers, began to build temples for Ram and Sita in Ayodhya and became important patrons (*jajmans*) of its *pandas* and *sadhus*.[44]Till that time, most religions of North India had had some stake in Ayodhya.[45] It was a place of pilgrimage, for instance, for Jains who believe that the first of their 'preceptors' (*tirthankaras*, 'ford makers'), Rishhabdev, was born in Ayodhya. Jains had six temples in Ayodhya till the close of the nineteenth century[46]. Bud-

---

[40] They are named as Khwaja Fazal Abbas Ashikhan, who is said to have become a disciple of *sadhu* Syamanand in order to be taught methods of meditation by him, and Jalal Shah (van der Veer 1988: 20). *Fakirs* were the Muslim *sufi* counterparts of Hindu *sadhus* in North India. They taught doctrines and practised disciplines very similar to those of the monistic forms of *nirguna bhakti* which developed in North India at that time (see van der Veer 1982: 68-69). The so-called *Sanyasi* rebellion in Bengal, quelled by the British in 1765, was actually by Muslim *fakirs*, known as Madaris, whose outward appearance and behaviour were virtually identical to those of wandering Hindu warrior ascetics (Lorenzen 1978: 72-75).

[41] Van der Veer 1987: 285-286; 1988: 11, 19-21; Bakker 1991: 90; cf. however note 3.

[42] *Ram Janmasthan* was often identified by early British authors with the Babri mosque and *Ramjanmabhumi* (Srivastava 1993: 38-42). In many modern press reports, *Jamasthan* serves as a synonym for *Janmabhumi*.

[43] Cf. van der Veer 1988: 21, 22, 37-38. This is the *Ramchabutra*, the raised platform under a tree in the eastern part of the outer enclosure of the *Babrimashid*. Near, in the far corner of the same outer enclosure, stood images of other Hindu gods in recent years: Nandi, Ganesh, Parvati, Panchmukhi and Mahadev, which received regular worship (cf. Panikkar 1993: 33; Noorani 1993: 59, 94-95; Ramakrishnan 1993d).

[44] Lorenzen 1978: 69-72; van der Veer 1982: 67-73; 1987: 287-288; 1988: 11, 36-38, 143-145, 150-151, 211-214; Panikkar 1993: 30-31; Srivastava 1993: 39-40, 46, 47.

[45] Cf. also Hasan 1993: 112.

[46] Srivastava 1993: 38, 46.

dhists came to Ayodhya because of traditions that the Buddha meditated there. They identify it with Saketa, a town mentioned in Buddhist scriptures[47]. Muslims believed that Noah had been buried in Ayodhya and they also identified Hanuman, as worshipped in *Hanumangarhi*, with Hathile, one of the five *pirs* (Muslim saints) whom they venerated on Hanuman hill.[48] The traditions which Tieffenthaler, who visited Ayodhya between 1766 and 1771, recorded about a Hindu fortress *Ramakota* having been destroyed by Aurangzeb or Babur and a mosque with three domes having been built in its place[49] may reflect the increasing strength of *Ramabhakti* in the Ayodhya of that time. Until 1853, Hindu-Muslim relations seem not to have been strained in Ayodhya; the religious strife in Ayodhya before 1800 was between Shaiva Sanyasins and Vaishava Bairagis (i.e. Ramanandi *tyagi* ascetics) rather than between Hindus and Muslims.[50]

Ayodhya as local confrontation, 1853-1980

In the period between the Muslim and the British rule, 1853-1858, however, Hindu-Muslim relations in Ayodhya deteriorated gravely for a few years. Sunni Muslims, then an assertive 10% minority[51], proclaimed in 1853[52] that a mosque had stood in the precincts of *Hanumangarhi* and demanded that Muslims be permitted to pray there.[53] When they attacked *Hanumangarhi*, a pitched battle ensued with its Ramanandi *nagas* who drove them back into the Babri mosque, killing seventy. Muslim unrest spread through the whole of Awadh (Oudh)[54]. To quell it, the British appointed a commission of

---

[47] Cf. Bakker 1984/1986, I: 1-48.

[48] Van der Veer 1988: 1, 2, 10, 11, 149-150.

[49] Gopal 1993a: 11. Panikkar (1993: 32), however, holds that this tradition dates from 1855 only, originating as a ploy by the *Mahant* ('abbot') of Hanumangarhi to counter the claims staked out by Sunni Muslims on Hanumangarhi. This tradition also became established opinion among the British in Awadh soon after 1866 when they were led to believe that Babur Shah had actually visited Ayodhya in 1528 on the basis of documentary 'proof' provided by Leyden in 1819 and Erskine in 1826 (Srivastava 1993: 47, 55, notes 59, 60).

[50] Cf. Srivastava 1993: 46-47, 54, note 54.

[51] In 1869, the Muslim residents of Ayodhya numbered 2,500 and formed one-third of its population; two-thirds of them were Shi'a, and one-third Sunni (Srivastava 1993: 38-39, 51, note 7). They had 26 mosques in Ayodhya in 1989 (Roy 1989c: 27).

[52] Srivastava (1993: 42) argues that *Hanumangarhi* was attacked in 1853 and not, as is stated by most authors, in 1855.

[53] Panikkar 1993: 31-33; Srivastava 1993: 51-52, note 23.

[54] Then an independent kingdom in North India under British 'protection'.

Hindu and Muslim noblemen to look into the claims of the Sunni Muslims with respect to *Hanumangarhi*. It concluded that the Muslim claim was unfounded. This provoked the Muslims of Awadh into forming an army of 2000 to wage a *jihad* against the *nagas* of Ayodhya; it was stopped by a British regiment before it was able to reach Ayodhya, and there were heavy losses on both sides in the three hour battle that followed.[55] After the annexation of Awadh on 13 February 1856, the British immediately put up an iron railing between the Babri mosque and the *Ramchabutra* to ensure a separation of worship.[56]

During the remainder of the colonial period, relations between Hindus and Muslims in Ayodhya remained relatively peaceful[57], notwithstanding the 1855/1856 events and the general rise of tension between Hindus and Muslims in Northern India then under British rule. When, from 1893 onwards, the 'Cow Protection Movement', *Gaurakshina Sabha*[58], tried to prevent Muslims from slaughtering cows on major Muslim feasts, there was violence in several towns in Northern India of which Ayodhya had its share in 1912 and 1934.[59] Other movements that increased tensions between Hindus and Muslims in the region were the *shuddhi* (reconversion) movement launched by Arya Samaj preachers in the mid-1890s[60]; the struggle for the recognition of Hindi as an official language in courts and schools next to Urdu, and of *Devanagari* script[61]; the resistance of *Hindu Shabha* (Hindu Forum) movement after 1907 against the perceived pro-Muslim bias of the British authorities, who instituted separate electorates for Muslims throughout India, even in areas like the Punjab where Muslims formed a majority[62];

---

[55] Cf. Panikkar 1993: 30-31; Srivastava 1993: 42-44.

[56] Van der Veer 1987: 289; 1988: 38-39; Bakker 1991: 93-94.

[57] Hasan (1993: 110-114) reports that Faizabad and Ayodhya remained relatively free of Hindu-Muslim strife between 1858 and 1949. Cf. also Roy (1989c: 27-28): 'Not one communal incident has taken place in Ayodhya since 1934'. Cf. also below on the relative lack of interest which van der Veer (1987: 290-291) found in Ayodhya in the *Ramjanmabhumimuktiyagna*, the 'sacrifice for the liberation of Rama's place of birth', in late 1984. Only after the demolition of the Babri mosque on 6 December 1992 were the Muslim quarters in Ayodhya attacked by Hindu *kar sevaks* ('volunteers'). Ten Muslims were killed and a hundred houses and shops burned (Ramakrishnan 1993: 13).

[58] See Lütt 1970: 134-147; Freitag 1980; Yang 1980; Becke 1994: 10, 11; Embree 1994: 638-639. Cow riots, however, have a longer history. The earliest one on record occurred in Ahmedabad in 1714 (Janssen 1989: 7).

[59] Van der Veer 1987: 289; 1988: 40; Noorani 1993: 67.

[60] Cf. Gold 1991: 552, 564-565; Jaffrelot 1993: 519.

[61] Cf. Lütt 1970: 37-52, 148-154; Becke 1994: 10.

[62] Jaffrelot 1993: 519.

Hindu resistance to forced conversions to Islam on the Malabar coast in the wake of the *Khilafat* movement of 1921[63]; etc.

These tensions were part and parcel of the wider process of the emergence of 'communalism' in the public and political life of colonial India when 'communities' of believers of the several religiously organized corporate groups of India emerged as distinct power blocks.[64] These 'communities' have a long history in India[65], but were made much more visible in the colonial era (1858-1947) when the British administration registered each person's caste and/or religious affiliation and mentioned these on the identity cards which it issued. The British also gave these 'communities' additional profile, firstly by allocating jobs in the colonial civil service, army, police, courts, schools, universities, and hospitals to each community according to each community's relative size; secondly, by creating in 1935 special electorates and constituencies for the Hindu and Muslim 'communities' and reserving seats for them in the legislative bodies[66]; thirdly, by granting some their own personal law; and fourthly, by 'caring' from above for the other 'legitimate' interests of the lower communities.[67]

---

[63] Jaffrelot 1993: 520.

[64] They were those of the (high caste or 'twice-born') Hindus, the Muslims, the Sikhs, the Parsis, the Christians, the Jains, the low castes Hindus (*shudras*, Dalits), the untouchables (pariahs, Harijans), the so-called 'tribals' or 'scheduled tribes' or 'aboriginal' (*adivasi*) communities not integrated into Indian society (some of which live as food gathering nomads in forested hill country) and, much later, the Ambedkarite converts to Buddhism. The Hindus were not one 'community' because Hindus are stratified by the four *varnas*, each of which is divided into numerous *jativads* (caste-communities). Due to the wide gulf separating the 'twice-born' Hindus of the three upper *varnas* from the lowest castes and outcastes (cf. also Mahmood 1993: 732-734; 1994), a united Hindu 'community' is more a political projection, and programme, of high caste and upwards-mobile Hindus (Frykenberg 1994: 603) than a social reality. It has been termed 'organized Hinduism' by Gold (1991a) and 'syndicated Hinduism' by Thapar (1985; 1993: 160). The RSS followed a policy of disregarding caste distinctions within its own rank after the tradition of Indian world renouncers in order to create a more inclusive Hindu community. In Jaffrelot (1993: 521-522)'s view, this RSS policy does not affect the Hindu 'community' at large. Recent developments, presented below, however, seem to indicate that the RSS does have some unifying influence on the Hindus of India.

[65] Cf. Mahmood (1993: 723), who offers a strong defense for the view that communalism and religious intolerance have deep roots in upper caste Hinduism and 'present a far more intractable problem than most current dialogue admits' (Mahmood 1993: 737; 1994; cf. also Saberwal 1991: 348-350).

[66] Gold 1991a: 358-359; Thakur 1993: 647; Vithal 1993: 337.

[67] Cf. e.g. Gold 1991a: 535-537. The British followed a policy of reforming and reconstructing Indian society in line with their own moral values, by forbidding customs such as *sati* ('widow burning') and child marriages, and by strengthening the social position of disadvantaged groups, like the low- and out-castes, measures which considerably reinforced the vertical divisions of Indian society along lines of religious identities.

Moreover, these communities also gained prominence in Indian public life by the activities of their political and ideological leaders who deliberately fostered these emerging ideologies of separate identity by pursuing policies of 'strategic syncretism'[68], both by politicising the distinctiveness of the 'communities' in matters of religion[69], language, social organisation and other elements of culture[70], and by creating organizational structures for mobilizing masses in order to convince their 'communities' that they were constantly under threat of unequal treatment, opportunity or privilege and so force them into constant competition with other groups[71]. At the same time, these new opportunities allowed the leaders of the Hindu communal movement, who all came from the upper castes, to reinforce the leading positions of high castes when these were endangered by reforms or changes in the balance of power between the various social groups.[72]

Until recently, this Indian 'communalism' was very much an urban phenomenon which, by using 'religion as the dominant form of identification'[73], increased boundary consciousness among co-believers[74] for political competition with groups defined by a differ-

---

[68] Jaffrelot (1993) shows that early leaders of the Hindu communalist movements developed the building blocks of Hindu nationalism by imitating and assimilating the perceived strong points of others. The Brahma Samaj and the Arya Samaj invented the traditions of the golden dawn of Vedic civilisation, and of the Upanishads or the Vedas as Hindu scripture, and started the *shuddhi*, re-conversion, movement. The RSS and VHP began to attempt to develop means and structures, including an ecclesiastic structure, by which they might unify the Hindus as a nation and as a religion. Cf. also Thapar 1989; 1993: 159-160; Mahmood 1993: 729.

[69] Gandhi e.g. often appealed to *Ramarajya*, the perfect rule of Rama, in his speeches. Hindu symbols were often used by the leaders of the Indian National Congress before 1947 (Janssen 1989: 4, 7).

[70] Cf., e.g., Becke (1994: 11-12, 14-16) on the roles played by Vinayak Damodar Savakar (1883-1966) who coined the notions *Hindutva* ('Hindudom') and *Hindu rashtra* ('the Hindu nation'), and by Mohammed Ali Jinnah (1876-1948) who in 1940 declared that India contained two separate 'nations', the Hindus and the Muslims, thereby laying the foundation for the partition of 1947.

[71] Mansingh 1988: 179; see also Bakker 1991: 95. Reform movements like the *Arya Samaj* played a prominent role in these processes; cf. e.g. Lütt 1970: 99-123.

[72] Cf. Chatterjee 1993a: 5-6; 1993b: 4, 6, 7; Chibber & Misra 1993; Ghimire 1993: 50; Jaffrelot 1993: 519; Sarkar 1993: 164; Vithal 1993: 337; Yechury 1993: 18, 19. Hansen (1993: 2271), however, contests the view that the Hindu communalist movement of the RSS *sangh parivar* is mainly carried by, and serves the interests of, the *brahmin* and *bania* (trader) communities.

[73] Freitag 1980: 599, note 7. Rudolph & Rudolph (1988: 78) define communalism as 'the exclusive identification with and commitment to one's religious or social community'. In their, rather polemic, view, it 'destroys civil society and the state'; for other such definitions, cf. Becke 1994: 13-16, 22-24.

[74] Cf. Becke (1994: 23): 'Identities are built by demarcation' (*Identitäten werden gebildet durch Ausgrenzung*).

ent religion which were seen as political opponents.[75] In the colonial era (1856-1947), these clashes were mainly between Hindus and Muslims. Though Gandhi tried to prevent rifts between the colonized communities and to use communalism for anti-colonial ends, he failed to prevent communalism's inherent divisiveness from ending in the bloody partition of the colony into what are now the states of India and Pakistan.[76]

In Ayodhya, cow protection riots had taken place on a large scale in 1912 and again in 1934, when Muslims were prevented from slaughtering bulls at *Bakr-Id*, the Babri mosque was attacked and major damage was done to one of its domes. Hundreds of Muslims were killed and the British army had to intervene.[77] The Partition also caused Hindu-Muslim relations in Ayodhya to become more tense again, which caused the Indian government to declare *Ranjanamabhumi* and the *Babrimashid* out of bounds for both Hindus and Muslims and place a guard outside the mosque.[78] Tensions increased further in 1948, when local Congress politicians used the cult of Ram for electoral purposes, thereby reviving 'the Masjid-Mandir issue which had lain dormant for decades'.[79]

The stage was thus set for the events of late 1949, when, after nine days of continuous reading from the *Ramayana* in front of the *Babrimashid*[80], statues of Ram and Sita[81] were smuggled into the

---

[75] On these processes, see also Björkman 1988, Rudolph & Rudolph 1988, Saberwal 1991, Khare 1991, Caplan 1991, Juergensmeyer 1991, Madan 1991; Becke 1994: 13-18; Frykenberg 1994: 600ff.

[76] Rudolph & Rudolph 1988: 79; Mansingh 1988: 182-183; Becke 1994: 14-18.

[77] Van der Veer 1987: 289; 1988: 40; Noorani 1993: 67.

[78] Van der Veer 1994: 662.

[79] Hasan 1993: 113.

[80] Noorani 1993: 68.

[81] Noorani 1993: 67, 78, 79, 80, 94, 95. Most authors, however, refer only to that of Rama (Van der Veer 1987: 289; 1988: 40; Hasan 1993: 114; Thakur 1993: 645) as do the reports (e.g. by the District Magistrate Nayar) quoted in Noorani 1993 (68, 70-71). Others speak of 'the idols (*sic*) of Rama Lala' (Rama as a child) without mentioning Sita (Roy 1989c: 27; Vyas 1991: 12; Chatterjee 1992; Anonymous 1993b: 22; Ram 1993). Anonymous (1993a: 134), however, has a picture of the makeshift temple, erected on the rubble of Babri mosque in the night of 6-7 December 1992, which clearly shows two images, and, unclearly, perhaps a third one. The two shown clearly are likely to be those of Rama and Sita. Apart from the statues in the mosque, another number of images of deities were kept and given regular worship in the outer enclosure of the mosque (Noorani 1993: 94; Ramakrishnan 1993d).

mosque during the night of 22 December.[82] On the following morning they were presented to the public as having miraculously revealed themselves there; an armed guard was posted near to watch over them. After the riots, which followed, had been quelled by the police and the army, both Muslims and Hindus were forbidden by court orders to enter into the Babri mosque. However, when the District Magistrate, K.K. Nayar, who was an RSS supporter, was ordered to remove the statues from the mosque, he refused to comply[83], and they remained in the mosque. Litigation was started by Muslims to regain, and by Hindus to gain, entrance to the mosque for worship, but the courts never reached a verdict on these appeals. The *Ramjamnabhumisevaksamiti*, 'Committee of the servants of Ram's place of birth', was, however, granted permission to perform rites for the Ram statue in the Babri mosque once a year, on the night of 22 December. In addition, this committee had a *sadhu*, Ram Lakhan Saran, organise uninterrupted devotional singing in front of the Babri mosque until the hoped-for liberation.[84]

Ayodhya as national confrontation, 1984-6.12.1992

After independence, the more violent clashes in the national arena changed for some time from Hindu-Muslim to Hindu-Sikhs, in particular in the Punjab and Delhi from early 1980 onwards, by Bhindranwale's violent bid for an independent Kalistan, followed by Operation Blue Star on 1st July 1984 aimed to drive him out of the Golden Temple in Amritsar, and the murder of Indira Gandhi by her Sikh bodyguards on 31 October 1984.[85]

A number of 'incidents' in the national arena in the early 1980s,

---

[82] In an interview in Ayodhya on 7 April 1993 granted by the President of the Ramjanmabhumi Temple Construction Trust at Ayodhya, Paramhansa Ramachandra Das, to Andreas Becke, Ramachandra said: 'The Ram Janmabhoomi movement is not new. I started it in 1949 with the assistance of the District Magistrate of Faizabad. We introduced the Ram idols into this very mosque and brought a petition into the District Court of Faizabad to safeguard our rights to worship Rama [there] and perform our rituals' (Becke 1994: 20; translated from German by JP).

[83] Cf. Noorani 1993: 70-72.

[84] Van der Veer 1987: 289-290; 1988: 40-41; Bakker 1991: 97; Noorani 1993: 67.

[85] Wallace 1988; Juergensmeyer 1991.

however, caused the VHP[86], the RSS affiliate for religious affairs[87], to develop strategies for making Ayodhya the nationwide focus of Hindu-Muslim tensions. These incidents included the conversion to Islam of untouchables in Meenakshipuram in South India in 1981[88]; the violent reactions of Muslims in India to the killing of more than one thousand Muslims by 'tribals' at Nellie in Assam in 1984; the agitation of Muslims against the ruling of the Supreme Court in 1985 on the Shah Bano case which they perceived as a secular threat to the *shari'a* in matters of personal law[89]; and Muslim agitation in 1988 demanding that Rushdie's *Satanic Verses* be banned as blasphemous of Islam.[90] Muslim agitation against the ruling of the Supreme Court in the Shah Bano case in particular proved a watershed in Hindu-Muslim relations, in that it exposed the inconsistent secularism of the ruling Congress Party.[91] Hindus began to perceive it in terms of demands being made on them to

---

[86] The *Vishva Hindu Parisad* (Hindu World Federation) was founded in 1964 in order to unify Hindus in India and abroad, and to promote RSS/VHP goals through an order of missionaries (Andersen & Damle 1987: 133; Janssen 1989: 18; van der Veer 1994: 553-554sq.; Embree 1994: 638). It propagates the views that Sanskrit is the oldest of all languages', that Hindu *dharma* is the eldest of mankind's religions, and that Sanskrit should be compulsory teaching in Indian schools; it organises courses in Sanskrit. It holds that Jains, Buddhists, Sikhs, and *Lingayats* are Hindus; that the slaughter of cows must be forbidden by law; and that all mosques and churches in India were originally Hindu *mandirs* (Janssen 1989: 18-19; cf. also van der Veer 1994: 657). *Ramjanmabhumi* is to the VHP only the most obvious example of a general fact of history. In 1964, 1966, 1979, and 1982, it organized meetings to which leaders of all Hindu 'sects' were invited. The first such *dharmasansad* met in New Delhi from 7 to 9 April 1984 and was attended by 558 delegates from 76 different Hindu religious groups. One of the items discussed was the *Ramjanmabhumi* controversy (cf. Janssen 1989: 17). The basis for the participation of Hindu religious leaders of very different hue in the *Ramarathayagna* campaign of late 1984 was laid at this meeting.

[87] Van der Veer (1994: 655) warns against the common view of the VHP as merely an instrument of the RSS, because it 'underestimates the extent to which the VHP goes beyond the RSS in its articulation of what I call "modern Hinduism"'. In his view, the VHP propagates a fundamentally modernist conception of Hinduism that is strongly influenced by Western Orientalist understanding of India (van der Veer 1994: 656-660). Though it rejects the secular state, it does not reject capitalist development, science, technology, and nationalism, and claims that the 'majority community' should rule the country (van der Veer 1994: 656, 660-661, 666).

[88] These conversions caused the VHP to make the reconversion (*paravartan*) of Muslim and Christian lowcastes, pariahs and 'tribals' its major objective. It began to provide these '170 million down trodden brethren' with schools, hospitals, orphanages, etc. (Janssen 1989: 22; van der Veer 1994: 654, 655-656, 660).

[89] Andersen & Damle 1987: 134, 238; Rudolph & Rudolph 1988: 84; Madan 1991b: 396-397; Embree 1994: 618.

[90] Thakur: 1993: 653-654, 655.

[91] Thakur 1993: 650, 655; see also Andersen & Damle 1987: 236; Embree 1994: 619-620, 622-623, 629-635, 637, 643.

accept reforms of their religious customs in accordance with the secularism of the state, and allowing the Muslims to continue to be governed by the *shari'a*, immune from similar secular reform, for fear of losing the Muslim bloc vote in elections. This became especially apparent when Rajiv Gandhi in 1986 forced the Muslim Women (Protection of Rights on Divorce) Act through parliament, overruling the decision of Supreme Court in the Shah Bano case.[92]

Between 1984 and 6 December 1992, when the Babri mosque was demolished, the VHP and the BJP planned and executed three nationwide politico-religious manifestations with Ayodhya as their focus.[93] Their aim was to mobilise the Hindu 'community', in order to liberate Ram from his 'imprisonment' in the *Babrimashid*, to demolish the mosque, to regain *Ramjanmabhumi*, to built a temple on it for him, to gain electoral victories for the BJP, to reduce the Muslims to their proper place, and so promote the Hinduisation of *Hindutva*, i.e. of India as a nation of Hindus.[94]

The 1983 preliminary: the 'marches' for national integration

The foundation of these campaigns was laid by the success of the month-long *Ekatmata yagna*, 'sacrifice for unity'[95], from 16 November to 16 December 1983. It was a nationwide fund-raising drive for VHP-missionary and social work under the untouchables.[96] This first major VHP exercise in mass mobilization brought in 30 million rupees[97]. It was organized by a council of eighty-five religious leaders who represented

> 'virtually every major sect and sub-sect—starting from the followers of Shankara (8th Century AD), the Jains, the Naths, the Vaishava sadhus

---

[92] Thakur 1993: 646-650, 658-660.

[93] Van der Veer (1994: 655, 663) presents data which demonstrate 'a direct coordination of rituals, agitation, and political maneuvering by a high command made up of BJP, RSS, and VHP leaders and in fact an important overlap of functions', in particular after the electoral victory of 1989.

[94] The Babri mosque, however, served as *pars pro toto*, as the paradigmatic example of what was in the RSS interpretation of Indian history common Muslim practice: it drew up a list of over two thousand mosques erected on the ruins of Hindu temples (Embree 1994: 632).

[95] Van der Veer 1987a: 292; 1994: 653, 661-662. Mitra (1983: 34) translates it as 'integration rite'. It was also termed *Ekmatayathra*, 'unity pilgrimage' (Andersen & Damle 1987: 135, 238; Janssen 1989: 23).

[96] The VHP termed it *paravartan*, the 'return to [their] original position' of those *Harijans* (untouchables) and *Adivasis* (aboriginals) who had been converted to Islam or Christianity (Badhwar 1986: 35-36); cf. also Embree 1994: 638; van der Veer 1994: 654, 659, 660.

[97] Andersen & Damle 1987: 154; see also 141, 238.

to Sikhs of the Namdhari sub-sect and Buddhists from Ladakh, Sikkim and Arunachal Pradesh. [...] Others represented [...] the Arya Samaj' (Mitra 1983: 36).

It consisted of three major *yathras*, 'marches', from, and to, the four corners of India, and some ninety subsidiary ones (*upayathras*)[98] which at some point joined one of the major marches. Most of them traversed the regions with the highest incidence of Hindu-Muslim strife[99]. At stops in 1700 places[100], taped religious music was played, prayers were said, and speeches given by VHP-affiliated religious leaders on the dangers to Hinduism by politicians pampering the Muslims.[101] The three major marches and a number of regional ones, all converged on the RSS headquarters in Nagpur where they arrived on 29 November to celebrate 'the confluence of the three pilgrimages'[102]. The major processions then continued to their destinations at the other end of India from where they had started out.[103] The processions are said to have covered some 85,000 kilometres with something like 60 million participants (Andersen & Damle 1987: 135).

The central features of these processions were two trucks[104], one with an eight foot high brass vessel (*kalasha*) containing four hundred litres of *gangajal*, water from *Gangamata*, Mother Ganges, India's holiest river,[105] as well as the portrait of *Bharat Mata*, 'Mother

---

[98] Van der Veer (1994: 661) gives their number as 'at least forty-seven'.

[99] And received with greatest enthusiasm in precisely those regions (Mitra 1983: 34; Janssen 1993: 33-34).

[100] Janssen 1989: 6-7, 24-25, 31-37. Mita (1983: 34) gives 1.800.

[101] With local variations (cf. e.g. Janssen 1989: 41-42); for the content of the speeches, cf. also the VHP pamphlet *India in danger*, appendix II to Janssen 1989 (43-47).

[102] An explicit reference to the confluence of the Ganges, the Yamuna, and the (invisible) Sarasvati rivers at Prayag, the most important *tirtha* on the Ganges (Janssen 1989: 28, 34; Eck 1991: 146).

[103] They followed traditional routes: the *Bahgirath rath* from Hardwar, near Gangotri in the Himalaya, to Kanyakumari on the southernmost tip of India; the *Kapil rath* from Gangasagar in Bengal, where the Ganges pours into the Indian Ocean, to Somnath on the western coast of Gujurat; and the *Pasupati rath*, from Kathmandu in Nepal to Rameshvaran, the other southernmost place of pilgrimage (Janssen 1989: 31-37; van der Veer 1994: 661).

[104] The procession from Kathmandu consisted of one truck, two matador vans, and three jeeps (Mitra 1983: 35).

[105] *Kalashas* and (water from the) Ganges both represent immortality as liberation from the cycle of rebirths. The Ganges is the supreme *tirtha*, 'ford' (to immortality), and therefore the supreme goal in life for many devout Hindus. *Kalasha* refers both to the myth of the gods churning the milk ocean in order to obtain the nectar of immortality, and to its association with blessing, and to its manyfold use in rituals, e.g. as aniconic representation and residence of any god (cf. Janssen 1989: 27-30).

India' sitting astride a lion[106], and the other with a smaller *kalasha* with water from all the other main rivers (Mitra 1983: 34). The water was distributed to temples along the way for use in the ritual bathing (*abhisheka*) of its deities in a *puja*, and sold in bottles, thus bringing the water of the Ganges to poor Hindus who might never have the opportunity of travelling to the Ganges itself. It was replenished with water from the local or regional holy rivers, lakes and temple water-tanks. This mixing of holy water from all over India 'symbolized in an immensely direct way for Hindus the unity of Hindu India'.[107] The great success of these processions enabled the VHP to strengthen its network of local branches throughout the country.[108]

The VHP Ramarathayagna, 1984-1986

The first VHP Ayodhya-centred mass-mobilisation was the *Ramjanmabhumimuktiyagna*, the 'sacrifice for the liberation of Rama's place of birth', in late 1984, for which it founded the *Sri Rama Janmabhumi Muktiyagna Samiti*, a council of leaders of diverse 'Hindu' religious traditions. It chose the form of a *Ramarathayathra*, pilgrimage procession along the road which Ram had travelled in his chariot[109] in mythical times.[110] It departed from *Sitamarhi*[111] in Bihar on 25 September 1984 and traversed the length of Uttar Pradesh, with Ayodhya and Lucknow, the capital of Uttar Pradesh, as major campaign sites, on to Delhi, the national capital. Its primary pur-

---

106 Mitra 1983: 34. In other posters, she has the lion as her mount at her right side, a flying banner in her left hand, her right hand in the posture of teaching, her head surrounded by flames. Thus she stands before the Indian subcontinent without the boundaries of Pakistan, Bangladesh, Nepal, Tibet, etc. (Janssen 1989: 26-28). Thousands of these posters were sold (Mitra 1983: 35).

107 Van der Veer 1987a: 292; 1994: 662.

108 Van der Veer 1987a: 300. He regards these marches as 'a ritual of national integration' (van der Veer 1994: 661). He points to the parallel of Bharat Mata being taken by chariots for a ride throughout her domain, India, to the traditional temple-chariot processions in the major Indian temple towns in which (an image of) the god is taken over his domain in a chariot to confirm his sovereignty over it.

109 *Ratha*, (war) chariot. The use of the chariot as a symbol complex, also evokes in the minds of Hindus associations with Krishna, another incarnation of Vishnu, in his role as the charioteer of Arjuna in the *Bhagavadgita*. When gods are taken out of a temple for a procession, they are also carried on *rathas*.

110 Noorani 1993: 77-78.

111 *Sitamarhi* is the place where Sita is believed to have been 'born' according to some versions of the Rama-story complex, or more precisely where she was found in an earthenware pot in the ploughing fields. Sitamarhi was also the scene of the last major riots, in October 1992, before the Babri mosque was destroyed on 6 December 1992 (Thakur 1993: 656).

pose was to put pressure on the political parties in the coming general election of December 1984 and make them promise that mosques would be cleared from sites held sacred by Hindus, and the ground restored to Hindus for worship. The procession consisted of a number of trucks and cars manned by VHP activists and *sadhus* from all over India. Its main feature was a truck carrying large statues of Ram and Sita and a banner saying *Bharat Mata ki jay*, 'Mother India, hail'. On its way through Bihar and the eastern parts of Uttar Pradesh, it met with considerable enthusiasm[112] and its arrival at Ayodhya, in the evening of 6 October 1984, was witnessed by van der Veer.[113] The procession appeared neither particularly impressive nor militant to him and was given only a lukewarm reception; Ayodhya stirred emotions more in the region than in Ayodhya itself.[114] The mass rally on the banks of the Sarayu on the following day drew only some seven thousand people—which reports in the papers and on t.v. inflated to fifty thousand and even one hundred thousand—, who listened to speeches from VHP officers and 'a seemingly unending row of religious leaders'[115] from many different religious orders and from regions as far apart as the Punjab and Kerala. These *sadhus* were seated on a platform in front of a large painting representing a fight between Muslims armed with swords and unarmed ascetics. The local religious leaders were conspicuously absent except for one, the abbot of an *akhara* of *nagas* in Ayodhya, who accused the absentees, in a powerful speech, of indifference to Ram's captivity 'in a Muslim jail'.[116] The other speakers urged the audience to vote in the coming general election for parties which would pledge to remove mosques from *Ramjanmabhumi*, Krishna's birthplace in Mathura[117], and from the *Viswanath* temple of Shiva in Benares, and restore them to Hindus. Remarkable, in view of the long history of violent competition between the orders of Hindu ascetics, was the unanimity among the leaders of the

---

[112] Van der Veer 1988: 42.

[113] Van der Veer 1987a: 290-291.

[114] Cf. also Hasan (1993: 113). This ties in with the fact that Ayodhya is not on a map of districts and towns with a high incidence of Hindu-Muslim violence in Janssen (1989: 7).

[115] Van der Veer 1987a: 293.

[116] According to van der Veer (1987a: 295-297), the Ayodhya religious leaders feared gross loss of income if *Ramjanmabhumi* were liberated. Moreover, the *nagas* of Hanumangarhi supported the Congress Party. Another notable absentee, the chairman of the *Ramjanmabhumiseva* Committee in charge of the annual worship of Ram and the singing in front of the Babri mosque, had made a political deal with the Congress Party.

[117] Another major Vaisnava pilgrimage centre in Uttar Prades situated on the river Jumna.

Vaisnava, Shaiva and Tantrist orders present, 'peacefully gathered under the banner of a goddess not worshipped by any of them: *Bharat Mata*, Mother India'.[118] On its journey from Ayodhya to Lucknow, the capital, where a petition was presented to the Chief Minister of Uttar Pradesh, the procession met again with a great enthusiasm. Then, on 31st October, Indira Gandhi was murdered by her Sikh bodyguards, causing a dramatic change in the national political arena for a brief time, replacing Hindu-Muslim strife with the antagonism of both against the Sikhs. Further 'sacrifice for the liberation of the place of birth of Ram' was pointless. The petition delivered in Delhi in early December had no impact. Rajiv Gandhi won a landslide victory in the elections. The BJP lost heavily. It retained only two of its sixteen seats in parliament.[119]

Although the first results of the *Ramjanmabhumimuktiyagna* were very disappointing for the VHP, a major success followed in early 1986. The VHP Ramjamnabhumi Liberation Committee resumed the *Ramarathayathra* from twenty-five places in Uttar Pradesh and Bihar on 23 October 1985, organizing six processions through the rural areas of Uttar Pradesh and one in Bihar.[120] The portraits they carried of Lord Ram in jail, had an electrifying impact on the Hindu-Muslim tensions in the region.[121] The committee had also received support from the first *Dharmasansad*, a 'parliament' of major Hindu national religious leaders which the VHP had convened in Delhi on 7-8 April 1985.[122] Politicians from several parties had also been nominated on the committee and D-day for the liberation of Ram was fixed on 9 March 1986. The committee also contended that the wide support from the people, religious leaders and politicians had enabled it to play a significant role behind the scenes in the legal proceedings early in 1986 in which the young lawyer U.C. Pandey obtained a court order from the Faizabad judge K.M. Pandey on 1 February 1986 for the gates of the fence around the Babri mosque to be opened.[123] When they were opened, within an

---

[118] Van der Veer 1987a: 293. Cf. also Andersen & Damle 1987: 135-136; Janssen 1989: 26-27; Bonouvrié n.y.: 9.

[119] Van der Veer 1987: 297-299; Andersen & Damle 1987: 234.

[120] Sankar 1991: 14; Noorani 1993: 78.

[121] Cf. Badhwar 1986: 30-32, 36, who also reported that militant Hindu youths increasingly began to sport the *trishul*, the trident as the emblem of the god Shiva; cf. also Roy 1989c: 29; Awasthi & Aiyar 1991: 14; Sankar 1991: 14; Awasthi 1992: 15.

[122] Cf. Badhwar 1986: 34.

[123] Cf. Noorani 1993: 78-79. Thakur (1993: 665; Becke 1994: 6) and several other commentators hold that Rajiv Gandhi himself had instructed the judge to grant permission for worship in order to appease the Hindu 'community' for having given in to Muslim agitation over the Shah Bano case.

hour, Hindus streamed into the mosque to worship Lord Ram in his jail. The court order sparked serious communal violence in the North Indian cities.[124]

The 1989 brick production campaign

In the election year 1989, the VHP launched its second nationwide campaign to liberate Ram from his jail. It installed *Ramajanmabhumi muktiyagna samiti* action committees in all cities and villages of India[125] with more than two thousand inhabitants, as also in the Hindu diaspora, to supervise the solemn consecration by ancient Vedic *shilapuja* of the *Ramshilas*, bricks for 're-building' Ram's temple on *Ramjamnabhumi* carrying the inscription *Jay Shri Ram*, 'victory to Shri Ram', and also to collect donations (*shila yagnas*) for the project from every Hindu household.[126] They were to be transported back to Ayodhya in solemn processions. The first stone was to be laid with due pomp and circumstance on 9 November 1989 to mark the beginning of the re-building of the temple of Ram[127]. No plans, however, were announced for the demolition of the *Babrimashid* in which thousands of Hindus daily had unobstructed *darshan* of the images of Ram and Sita, though militant Hindu youth movements were publicly demanding that the mosque be destroyed.[128] The BJP openly backed the VHP brick production campaign and 300,000 bricks were sent out all over India.[129] In Gujurat alone, *shila pujas* were reported to have taken place in 20.000 villages. After the bricks had thus been 'sanctified' in the village temples, they were taken from door to door on decorated palanquins, donations being collected in exchange for coupons with a picture of the proposed Rama temple. After the bricks had been collected at the block level centres for *maha yagnas*, ceremonies for

---

[124] Andersen & Damle 1987: 135-136; van der Veer 1987a: 300, note 5; Bakker 1991: 98; Noorani 1993: 78-80.

[125] The RSS and other *Sangh parivar* affiliates had grown considerably in most regions of India since 1983. In some, they had doubled the number of their local branches (Bardhwar 1986: 34-35).

[126] Roy 1989: 26.

[127] The model for this action was borrowed from the successful campaign in the previous year in Somnath where, as a result of a similar action a large Hindu temple had been built on a spot where Muslim rulers in the past had destroyed Hindu temples on several occasions (Bakker 1991: 98).

[128] Roy 1989: 27.

[129] Some were also sent to the Hindu diaspora. *Shilapujas* were held in, and 'sanctified' bricks were sent back by airmail from Canada, the United States, the Caribbean, South Africa, etc (van der Veer 1994: 664). One brick was also sent from the *Rammandir* in The Hague (de Rijk 1994).

the presentation of major donations, they were taken in processions to district centres for their solemn transportation to Ayodhya in the first week of November 1989.[130] Their passage through Muslim districts and villages led to bloody riots, particularly in Bihar, with hundreds being killed on both sides.[131]

In an attempt to counter the rising tide of support for the BJP, Rajiv Gandhi's ruling Congress Party gave permission for *shilanyas*, the solemn ritual of laying the foundation stone for the new temple for Ram, to be performed on 9 November 1989.[132] The stone was to be laid at a distance of sixty meters from the front gate of the Babri mosque. Permission for the building of the temple was, however, refused.

The *shilanyas* ceremony was performed with due ceremony on 9 November. In order to stress the RSS stated policy that caste divisions must take second place in order that a united Hindu nation be achieved, 'the honour of laying the first brick for the foundation [of the Ram temple] went to a *Harijan* [untouchable, JP] from Bihar, Rameshwar Chopal'.[133] Rajiv Gandhi himself also performed *shilanyas*.[134] To celebrate this victory, Hindu youths marched through the streets of the towns of North India, chanting:

> That Hindu whose blood does not boil has water in his veins, youth that does not serve Ramjanmabhumi is youth lived in vain.

Rajiv's concession and his performing *shilanyas* did not, however, bring the electorate back to fold of the Congress Party which suffered a major defeat in the November 1989 elections. The BJP went from 2 to 88 seats in the national parliament.[135]

The 1990-1992 Ramarathayatra and kar sevak campaign

In September 1990, the third nationwide mobilisation campaign was launched using Hindu cultural and religious symbols, this time by the BJP itself as a means of gaining votes in the coming elections. With Ram still in his Muslim jail, the BJP party leader Advani led a 10,000 kilometre long *Ramrathayatra*, 'pilgrimage in the

---

130 Roy 1989b: 18. 19; Sankar 1991: 14.

131 In Bhagalpur, in Bihar, the Muslim population was almost wiped out (van der Veer 1994: 663).

132 Thakur 1993: 655-656.

133 Roy 1989c: 31. However, after the destruction of the Babri mosque had been achieved, a section of the Hindu religious leaders, united in the VHP, began to voice dissent from this RSS reformist aim (Chatterjee 1993b: 4, 6; Ghimire 1993).

134 Thakur 1993: 656.

135 Bakker 1991: 98-101; Fuller 1992: 258-259; Thakur 1993: 655-656.

war chariot of Ram', in a jeep painted as a war chariot on which the lotus flower, the BJP iconic symbol[136], was prominently displayed. Starting out from Somnath on the Gujurath coast in West India, the march took him through eight states and the Union Territory of Delhi to Ayodhya.[137] Advani exhorted his audiences along the way to demonstrate *Rambhakti*, fervent devotion to Ram, and *lok shakti*, 'people's power', and to follow him to Ayodhya for *Sri Rama kar seva*, 'voluntary service for Sri Rama', for 'rebuilding' his temple at *Ramjanamabhumi*.[138] The procession's slogan was *mandir wohin banayenge*, 'we will build the temple there, and only there', and it did indeed incite many thousands of volunteers to join him on his *Ramrathayatra*.

When Advani reached Ayodhya on 30 October 1990, he had gathered over one hundred thousand *kar sevaks*[139] around him, many of them members of the recently established *Bajrang Dal*, the militant RSS youth movement. Upon entering Ayodhya, they tried to storm the Babri mosque but their path was blocked by the thousands of troops which had been posted there in its defense by the government of Uttar Pradesh.[140] Thirty *kar sevaks* died at their hands. Some *kar sevaks*, however, managed to break through, scramble onto the top of the major dome of the mosque, and wave flags from it, an event which received worldwide media coverage the next day.[141] Advani was arrested and in the communal violence that followed, hundreds more died.[142]

In the elections in May-June 1991, however, the BJP proved to be riding on popular acclaim[143], especially in North India where it won a majority in four states: Himachal Pradesh, Madhya Pradesh, Rajasthan, and Uttar Pradesh. It also did well in the national elections, increasing its number of seats in parliament from 88 to 119,

---

[136] The lotus is also the traditional symbol of liberating knowledge (cf. e.g. Klostermaier 1989: 271-273).

[137] Vyas 1991: 12; Sankar 1991: 15.

[138] The latter two symbols were united by the *kar sevaks* often being encouraged to carry a *trishul*, trident, the symbol of the terror inspiring god Shiva (Bonouvrié no year: 9).

[139] Inflated to half a million in Becke (1994: 7).

[140] That government was headed by Mulayam Singh Yadaw, leader of an upwards mobile 'backward' caste (van der Veer 1994: 664).

[141] Reproduced in Anonymous 1993: 24; Gopal 1993b: cover.

[142] Bakker 1991: 101; Thakur 1993: 653.

[143] The VHP and BJP effectively exploited the events of 30 October 1990 by circulating videos and cassettes about the attack on the mosque and claiming that the police had killed many more *kar sevaks*. After their cremation, the bones and ashes of those who were killed were taken through the country in ritual pots before their immersion in a sacred river (van der Veer 1994: 664).

gaining one-fifth of all the votes.[144] After the elections, the BJP government of Uttar Pradesh began to put pressure on Muslims to convert to Hinduism. It refused to order the *kar sevaks* to stop their work at Ayodhya as requested by the central government and as it was ordered by the Supreme Court. On October 31 1991, a small number of *kar sevaks* managed to slip through the security guarding the Babri mosque, hoist a safron flag on its domes, and inflict minor damage on the building.[145] The BJP moreover announced that it would conduct another nationwide *Ramarathyagna* in late 1991, from Kanyakumari, on India's southernmost tip, to Srinigar in its utmost North in order to increase pressure on the central government.[146]

In the course of 1992, a deadlock ensued between the central government and the state of Uttar Pradesh, now controled by the BJP. That put the troops guarding the mosque in an ambiguous position, because they knew that the Uttar Pradesh government was privately committed to destroying the mosque.[147] On 30 and 31 October 1992, a *Dharam Sansad* of over 5000 religious leaders, which had gathered in Delhi, announced that *kar seva* for the construction of the Ram temple on the spot of the Babri mosque would be resumed on 6 December. All over Northern India, ritual fire services (*Agnishapath divas*) were held at which *kar sevaks* pledged that they would continue to engage in *kar seva* till the temple was completed.[148] On the first of December, Advani and the BJP president M.M. Joshi undertook a six day mini *Ramrathayatras*, Advani starting out from Varanasi, Joshi from Mathura, in order to 'mobilize people against the Centre's injustice'.[149] In this they were greatly assisted by two RSS female leaders, Sadhvi Rithambara and Uma Bharati, who in fiery speeches, which were widely circulated, charged Hindu men who were unwilling to shed their blood for Hindu India, that they had water, not blood, in their veins.[150]

The destruction of the Babri mashid

These developments, as well as the Hindu sympathies and the known corruption among politicians and senior police officers, were

---

[144] Cf. e.g. Awasthi & Ghimire 1992: 15.
[145] Pande 1991: 12, 16.
[146] Vyas 1991: 12.
[147] Thakur 1993: 656, 658.
[148] Ramakrishnan 1992b: 18; Ghimire 1992: 33.
[149] Ramakrishnan 1992c: 10; 1992d.
[150] Embree 1994: 647.

the main reasons for the troops guarding the Babri mosque[151] to offer at first only a little resistance, and soon to become passive 'spineless spectators'[152] when on 6 December 1992, shortly after 11.00 a.m., some of two to three hundred thousand *kar sevaks*[153], many armed with *trishuls*, the metal tridents of Shiva, began to filter through the cordons and slip over the walls towards the mosque. In particular, the 40,000 *kar sevaks* of the RSS youth movement Bajrang Dal functioned as the 'storm troopers' in taking possession of the mosque and assisting a specially trained force of 1,200[154] which destroyed the mosque in less than six hours[155]. While that night many *kar sevaks* fanned out into Tehri Bazar, the main Muslim quarter of Ayodhya, killing ten Muslims and burning nearly a hundred houses, others built a makeshift temple on the rubble of the mosque and installed the images of Ram and Sita in it.[156] They completed their job on the following day, December 7, by building a five foot high brick wall around it. In the evening of that day, some *kar sevaks* already began to leave Ayodhya by special trains. Only in that night, at 3.00 a.m., did the troops of the central government arrive to take possession of the disputed area. They met with only a brief show of resistance from a few *kar sevaks*. By the end of the next day, all *kar sevaks* had left Ayodhya by special trains and busses.

Communal violence, however, ensued nationwide, with seven-

---

[151] The Central Government had also sent quite a large force in November 1992, but that had been quartered in cantonments in Faizabad, at a few miles' distance from the Babri mosque (Awasthi 1992b). On December 6, four battalions of the special Rapid Action Forces were called out at 1.30 p.m., two and a half hours after the attack on the *Babri masjid* had begun. At 2 p.m., when they were at a distance of 2 k from it, the Uttar Pradesh Prime Minister Kalyan Singh ordered the Faizabad District Magistrate R.N. Srivastava to send them back to their barracks. They never arrived at the scene of destruction (Ramakrishnan 1993b: 13; Awasthi & Mahurkar 1992; Sidhu & Awasthi 1992).

[152] Sidhu & Awasthi 1992.

[153] Embree (1994: 647) reports their number as 'about sixty thousand' (apart from a motley crowd of *sadhus*, shopkeepers, peasants, and students). Among the *kar sevaks* was a separate contingent of five thousand females whose very effective contribution was that of spurring on their male counterparts (Embree 1994: 646-647). Becke (1994: 9, 24) again inflates the number of *kar sevaks* to half a million.

[154] Cf. Ramakrishnan 1993a; Awasthi & Mahurkar 1992; Badhwar & Ghimire 1992; Thakur 1993: 657. Four of them fell to their deaths and six hundred got injured in the demolition of the domes (Ramakrishnan 1993b: 13; Shankar 1992).

[155] Between 11.00 and 16.49 hours. The first dome collapsed at 1.55 p.m.; the second at 3.30 p.m.; and the main dome at 4.49 p.m. For the chronology of these and the other events on 6, 7, and 8 December 1992, cf. Awasthi 1992: 26-27; Sidhu & Awasthi 1992; Ramakrishnan 1993.

[156] Ramakrishnan 1993b; the statues had been removed from the mosque by the *kar sevaks* during the demolition,.

teen hundred dead and over five thousand wounded.[157] The central government dismissed the BJP governments in the four states it ruled and banned the RSS, the Bajrang Dal, and the VHP. It arrested key VHP and BJP leaders, among them Advani, and forbade worship of the images of Ram and Sita the 'temple' on top of the destroyed Babri *mashid.* The District Magistrate of Ayodhya, however, lifted the ban on the worship of Ram at *Ramjanmabhumi* already on 2 January 1993; and the central government released Advani and the other leaders within a month.[158]

Ram had been freed from his jail. His place of birth had been restored to the Hindus at a price which Ram, the perfect model of *dharmaraja*, might not have been willing to pay. But then Ram reigned in the *tretayuga*, not in this *kali* age, in which Hindus converted Rama, traditionally represented as a powerful, but restrained and tenderhearted man, into an aggressive, masculine, warrior god.[159]

An anti-Durkheimian conclusion

Seven conclusions may be drawn from this description of the VHP/BJP rituals of confrontation[160] of 1984, 1989, and 1990-1992 if the analytical perspectives developed in the chapter on 'Ritual in plural and pluralist societies' are applied to them. Some of these clash with the traditional emphasis in Durkheimian sociology on the integrative function of ritual.

1. The Ayodhya rituals of confrontation show that rituals may not only express, maintain, and restore a society's solidarity, as discovered by Durkheimian sociology, but may also be used to destroy it. A ritual may not only (re-)unite a society—even if only temporarily, as in unstable social systems such as Turner's Ndembu—but it may also be used in power contests in order to achieve significant readjustments in the balance of power among a society's various factions, as was the case in the Ayodhya 'rituals of confrontation' described above, or even to banish some group permanently from

---

[157] Cf. Anonymi 1992; Thakur 1993: 645; Embree 1994: 648.
[158] Ghimire & Pathak 1992; Ramakrishnan 1993c; Ram 1993; Ghimire 1993: 49; Thakur 1993: 645, 653-654, 656, 658-659.
[159] Bhattarcharya 1993: 129; cf. also Sarkar 1993: 166, and Hansen (1993: 2271-2272) on the 'Kshatriyaisation' of the image of 'the angry Hindu' through the Ram campaigns.
[160] Sankar 1991: 14; Bhattarcharya 1993: 130.

their midst, as in the rituals of exclusion which Chidester (1988) has analyzed.

The Ayodhya rituals served both unitive and divisive intentions. They were meant, on the one hand, to overcome the traditional fragmentation of Hindu piety into the numerous traditional *sampradayas* or 'traditions' of the past such as the highly different religiosities of high, low, and out-caste groups; of town and village religion; of the hundreds of religious orders of *Shaiva*, *Vaishnava*, and *Shakti* persuasion; of traditional and reform Hinduism; of the North-South divide; and even of Hindus and 'heterodox' religious communities of Indian origin, like the Jains, Buddhists, and Sikhs. The *Sangh parivar*'s policy was to replace all these with one, sub-continent-wide[161], and even worldwide, *sampradaya*, Hindu 'community'[162], culturally and politically united[163] against the religious communities of non-Indian origin, the Muslims and the Christians. It had to be strong enough to stop the conversion of more Indians to their folds, and to dictate to them the terms on which they would be suffered as residents in India, once the Hindu majority, politically operating as a militant *Hindutva*, 'Hindu-dom' inspired by 'Hinduness', had turned India into *Hindu rashtra*, the strong, modern and unified Hindu nation-state.[164] Bharat Mata, and Ram imprisoned in the *Babrimasjid* in his own capital city of Ayodhya, served as the symbols with which the VHP and BJP were to forge a political front against the Muslim 'community' and against liberal, or disinterested Hindus in favour of the secular state. That front, established

---

[161] Cf. also Ramachandra Das' statement in his interview with Andreas Becke on 7 April 1994: 'We want India to be re-united just as Germany achieved its re-unification. We want Bharat [= the present state of India, JP], Pakistan, and Bangladesh re-united, because these countries constitute India' (Becke 1994: 20; translation JP).

[162] Cf. the answer in VHP pamphlet *India in danger* (Appendix 2 in Janssen 1989: 43-47) to the question 'Who are Hindus?': 'The followers of any religion originated in India, like Sanatan Dharma, Jainism, Sikhism, Buddhism, etc., though they may be residing elsewhere in the world, are Hindus'. However, the VHP definition of 'Hinduism' is identical to the one in section 25 of India's Constitution of 1951 (Frykenberg 1994: 609; cf. also Yechury 1993: 16).

[163] Cf. also Chengappa (1993: 32) on the use of the Shaivaite *trishul* in Ramjamnabhumi campaigns, and the additional demands for the demolition of mosques at Mathura and Kashi/Varanasi in order that temples for Krishna and Shiva might be (re-)built there.

[164] Cf. Klostermaier 1989: 33, 173; Gold 1991: 546-551; Bhattacharya 1993: 129-131; Chengappa 1993; Embree 1994: 619, 620, 644; Becke 1994: 11-13, 222-23. On the role of M.S. Golwarkar, the second *Sarsanghchalak* (Leader for life, 1940-1973) of the RSS, in the formulation of the *Hindutva* ideology and in development of the *Sangh parivar* as the RSS multi-purpose instrument for achieving its goals, cf. Yechury 1993.

during the 1984-1986, 1989, 1990-1992 campaigns, instilled in Hindus the feeling that they were 'a majority who must act like an embattled minority'[165], and its unexpected success[166] is likely to prove to have been a watershed in India's political history.

2. The Ayodhya rituals of contest also show that ritual need not necessarily be a form of customary, conventionalised behaviour merely repeating earlier identical sequences and utterly constrained by them. They show, on the one hand, that rituals may be designed for particular, one-time purposes as events which are not meant not to be repeated after their purpose has been achieved; and on the other hand, that the new rituals may be constructed by selecting rather freely and selectively from a large stock of older as well as younger, but never completely new complexes of dense consonant core symbol systems. Upon this ritual repertoire, one draws intuitively and selectively the contents as well as the forms of the new rituals, being both constrained to a degree by these complexes from the past as well as fairly free because they are full of replicating redundancies. Moreover, innovations in form and content are made possible by recent technological developments in e.g. communication and transportation facilities, and are demanded by the new contexts of cultural communication or political competition. The descriptions presented above of the Ayodhya complex, in which a brahmanical *tirtha* is combined with the Ram cult of the Ramanandis, and of the 1983-1992 events show that the VHP and BJP inventively combined elements from the older but far from stagnant Rama-Ayodhya complex and Ganges-water traditions, with the recent and still evolving *Bharat Mata* symbolism; and that they used them for their one and only purpose: the political unification of Hindus.[167]

The *Sangh parivar*, the RSS family, was quite familiar with the symbolism of the *Ramarajya*, 'the rule of Rama', representing the ideal Hindu society. It had in *Rama* a perfect symbol of the divine king who not only maintained the perfect social by the justice of rule but had also established it by his victories over Ravana and by

---

[165] Gold 1991: 577.

[166] 'The power unleashed by the Ram mandir agitation took everybody by surprise, also the RSS and BJP' (Hansen 1993: 2270). In Hansen's view, the success of the *Sangh parivar* is not due to careful planning, but to its 'more belligerent, majoritarian and populist' answer to the structural transformations of the Indian polity in the 1980s.

[167] Cf. van der Veer 1994: 661-662.

liberating Sita[168]. The *Sangh parivar* might, therefore, well have confined itself in propagating the Hindu nation it sought to build, to the use of Rama symbolism. But the VHP in particular accorded a large role to *Bharat Mata*, the 'Mother India' of India's national anthem[169], which it projected onto the divine plane, thus according her, in the form in which she had been created during the independence struggle as a politico-religious symbol, a new lease of life in the struggle for the Hinduisation of India. She was useful as a symbol of India as a unified nation precisely because she was, as yet, a goddess virtually without temples, cult, traditional myths, or groups of devotees after the traditional, divisive Hindu patterns.[170]

Two reasons seem to have inspired this use. Firstly, the need to project the new political phenomenon, the modern nation-state, and the RSS aspirations as to how it should be ordered, in a traditional manner onto the divine plane without linking it to any already existing religious complex connected to past and present Hindu divisions, in particular those between the high and the low castes, and between *Sanatan Dharm* and the other religions of Indian origin: Jainism, Buddhism, and Sikhism. And secondly, the need to link the struggle for Hindu unity to the powerful symbols of femineity and motherhood in order to connect it with that other major symbol at the heart of the 1983 *Ekatmata yajna* campaign, the sacred rivers of India, in particular the Ganges, which is worshipped as a major deity in its own right, as life-giving and purifying, thus suggesting *ad intra* to Hindus of all castes and even to the untouchables who were converting to Islam, that a unified Hindu India would shelter and protect them as a caring mother. However, the iconography used also projected martial traits onto her: the

---

168 See e.g. Andersen & Damle 1987: 34, 35, 93, 229; Gold 1991: 548.

169 The symbol of Bharat Mata was created in 1882 by B.C. Chatterjee as a representation of his motherland Bengal. It was given wide circulation by Aurobindo Ghose who republished it. After Tagore had put it to music and it had been made popular by the use which Nehru made of it in the election campaigns of the National Congress Party on the eve of independence, it was chosen as India's national anthem despite protests from the Muslim League (Janssen 1989: 26-27; van der Veer 1994: 661-662; cf. also Embree 1994: 647).

170 However, Shraddhananda, a radical Arya Samaj protagonist of a unified *Hindu rashtra* (cf. Gold 1991: 564-566), proposed as early as 1926 'to build one Hindu Rasthra mandir in every city and important [...] devoted to the worship of the three mother-spirits, the Gautama [Mother Cow], the Saraswati [Goddess of Knowledge]-mata, and the Bhumi-mata [Motherland goddess]' (quoted in Jaffrelot 1993: 524, note 34). The VHP actually may have begun a cult for *Bharatmata.* It built a temple for her in Hardwar, a famous place of pilgrimage on the upper reaches of the Ganges in North India, in 1976. Indira Gandhi is reported to have participated in a ritual in that temple on May 15, 1983 (Badhwar 1986: 28) and to have inaugurated it in October 1983 (Muralidharan 1992a).

banner in her left hand, the lion at her side, the flaring flames around her head, and her standing before an undivided subcontinent and projecting herself far beyond it.[171] In Hindu minds, these associate *Bharat Mata* with demon-killing Durga[172]. By these associations, *Bharat Mata* also served as another, and therefore redundant transformation of messages sent through the Rama complex, who is also depicted as strong as well as gentle as he is both the powerful martial hero and the perfectly just and impartial king, and Sita's tender-hearted husband.

The ideal of *Ramarajya*, the proleptic symbol of *Hindu rashtra* as a unified Hindu India, was ritually expressed by further replicating redundancies in the mixing of all its sacred waters and in the nation-wide *yathras*, converging on Nagpur in 1983 and on Ayodhya in the VHP/BJP *Ramrathras* of 1984-1986 and 1989, the bricks sent back to Ayodhya in 1986, and the *kar sevaks* converging on it for the rebuilding of the *Rammandir* in 1989-1992.[173] The desired unity of a Hindu India was also expressed, and to some extent realised, by the remarkable success of the VHP in uniting religious leaders across virtually the whole breadth of non-immigrant Indian religious diversity, and organizing them into councils and committees that either authorized and supported the VHP-BJP campaigns or took an active role in them.

Another reason why the VHP complemented the Rama-complex with that of *Bharat Mata*, is that Rama could not, by virtue of his 'imprisonment' since 1949 in his 'Muslim jail', serve as the mythical hero who leads the battle for a unified Hindu nation. Whereas in the *Ramayana* Rama had liberated Sita, it was now Rama who must be liberated. The first campaign to set him free,

---

[171] On the use of the symbolism of *Bharatmata*, 'Mother India', as the Divine Mother and as the motherland which extends from Iran to the Malay Peninsula and from Tibet to Sri Lanka which has been raped by marauding Muslim invaders, cf. Andersen & Damle 1987: 77; Janssen 1989: 26-27; Gold 1991: 547-548; van der Veer 1994: 666-667; Becke 1994: 12-13.

[172] Bonouvrié n.y.: 9. Durga is a form of Devi, the mother goddess who killed the buffalo demon in mythical times (Klostermaier 1989: 261-261). Cf. also Gold (1991b: 361-367), who 'explains' the RSS combination of carefully planned mass mobilisation campaigns with sporadic outbursts of anti-Muslim mob violence in what he takes, in Durkheimian terms, as the compelling need of Hindus to identify with the encompassing collectivity of the Hindu nation by occasional outbursts of religious frenzy. These, he holds, have received mythological legitimation in the Shiva-Kali polarity and in that inherent in Shiva himself; cf. also Embree 1994: 647; Becke 1994: 13, citing Klimkeit 1981: 243-247, 303-305.

[173] The ideal pilgrimage is the clockwise circumambulation of India by a visit to the four divine *dhamas*, 'abodes': Badrinath in the Himalaya in the north, Puri on the eastern coast, Rameswaram on the southern coast, and Dwarka on the western coast (Fuller 1992: 206).

therefore, set off from 'Sita's place of birth' (Sitamarthi) in Bihar. The caravan of *sadhus* and VHP-officials represented both Sita, Ram's bride, travelling to be married to him, and Hindu India, as *Bharat Mata*, on her way to liberate her Lord and restore him to his throne and kingdom. *Ramarajya* would be re-inaugurated by Bharat Mata defeating 'Ravana' and freeing Ram. The equation of the secular government and the Muslim community with Ravana, the king of the *ashuras*, demons, was clearly implied[174], as was the comparison of their manner of rule and political influence with the forest, Ravana's kingdom, as the realm of chaos and the inversion of *Ramrajya*. The large painting of armed Muslims slaughtering unarmed *sadhus*, used in the 1984 *Ramjanmabhumimukhtiyagna* replicated the message of the image of the Muslims as the demonic enemy, as did the use of the war chariot in the 1991 BJP *Ramarathayatra*, and the appeal for *kar seva*, sacred service in the 'war' to be fought for the conquest of *Ramjanmabhumi*. They served as the consonant and redundant spatio-temporal frames for focusing experience on parts of the mythological and historical past: those in which Hindus, and particularly Hindu temples and ascetics, had suffered at the hands of Muslims in power; others in which Hindus had fought Muslim rulers; and again others in which the monkey army of *Hanuman* assisted Ram in defeating Ravana. They also marked Muslims, whether or not in power, as alien intruders, and Indians who had converted to Islam as traitors.

Even though we have little detailed information about the actual religious rituals that were performed in all these campaigns, the messages which were implicit in them and in the wider mobilisation contexts were clear and forcefully transmitted, both *ad intra* and, especially, *ad extra*. Whether the messages *ad extra* were expressed in dignified rituals, in devout or inflammatory speeches, in provocative marches, or in bloody riots, they all forcefully transmitted the overt or implied message, through the indirect and direct fields of ritual communication, that India should be de-secularised and that Muslims should accept the privileged position of Hinduism in India in the form the *Sangh parivar* sought to establish. Or, as an Indian journalist concluded on 6 December 1992, when the last of the

---

[174] E.g., in July 1992, the then Prime Minister of India, P.V. Narasimha Rao, was depicted as Ravana in speeches of VHP leaders to the odd 20.000 *kar sevaks* then in Ayodhya (Ramakrishnan 1992: 13, 15); cf. also Embree (1994: 631-635) on the construction by the RSS of its four categories of enemies: Indian adherents of foreign religions, Communists, Westernized Indians, and unfriendly 'foreign powers', destabilizing India with the help of the first three categories.

three domes of the Babri mosque had collapsed: the BJP political goal was not primarily the building of the *Ram mandir*, but the razing of the *Babri mashid*.[175]

3. From the foregoing analysis, it is clear that these rituals not only served as power strategies, and open ones at that, but also as communicative events. Indeed, they were, in this case, effective strategies of power by the very fact that they sent out loud and clear messages, to 'friends' as well as 'enemies'.[176] The messages and their diverse interpretations in accordance with the various codes, Hindu, Muslim, secular and other, in the minds of the groups addressed, were an essential part of these strategies of power. Apart from overt political aims, they did, of course, also serve covert aims, such as e.g. the RSS ideal of the controlled emancipation of women[177], and the less covert one of narrowing down the wide gap in Indian society between the upper and lower strata.

4. The Ayodhya rituals confirm the heuristic usefulness of an inclusive operational definition of ritual that does not separate religious 'ritual', as addressing of postulated beings, from secular ceremony. In the Ayodhya rituals, the two categories are so completely intertwined, morphologically, content-wise as well as functionally, that they can hardly be separated, either descriptively or analytically. This is very much in line with the Durkheimian concept of the social as the sacred, but belies Durkheim's analytical dichotomy between the sacred and the secular, or profane.

5. The Ayodhya rituals prove the analytical usefulness of the performance and performative approaches to ritual. Ritual behaviour enables symbolic complexes to be dramatically enacted on the political stage for evoking powerful sentiments and attitudes, of diverse and even highly antagonistic sorts, in the different groups addressed, and for creating, and at least temporarily constituting,

---

175 Badhwar 1992: 35.

176 Cf. Embree (1994: 646): 'They [the Muslims, JP] read the demand for the destruction of the Masjid as a code word for the RSS assertion that they were an alien element in India, surviving on Hindu tolerance, not on their rights as people of the land.'

177 Cf. Hansen 1993: 2272. On the attitude of the *Rashtra Sevika Samiti*, the RSS organisation of women, towards the emancipation of women, cf. Embree 1994: 640-642.

significant political 'realities'.[178] The Ayodhya rituals not only effectively alerted and focused attention onto themselves and the political messages they proclaimed, but also proved also more successful than their planners, or their opponents, ever expected.[179] Ritual not only expresses, sustains and restores the social order, it can also reshape it by performatively constituting new relationships between the persons or groups involved, for shorter or longer periods of time.

6. The family resemblance, or synthetic, type of operational definition which I have proposed is borne out by the Ayodhya rituals. They do not contain data refuting that ritual is in fact

> collective, interactive, expressive, communicative, symbolic and performative behaviour with both customary and innovative, as well as traditionalising qualities, in which multi-media forms of expression are used including aesthetic stylization and theatrical performance, and which is implicitly or explicitly directed towards the achievement of strategic goals which are often integrative in kind but may also have, and be meant to have, explosive effects upsetting the existing balance of power in a given society.

---

[178] However forcefully sent, ritual messages are not by themselves performative. Performative utterances constitute social relationships only by the consent of all involved, the sender, the receiver and the congregation, i.e. by the 'community' as a whole. The *ad extra* messages in the Ayodhya rituals of confrontation were instruments of pressure for achieving a political vision. On their success, opinions differ. Van der Veer (1987: 299) correctly holds that 'Hindu feelings and values are not [static] givens; rather they are the product of a political process'. Chhibber & Misra measured the support for communalism immediately after the destruction of the *Babrimasjid* at Ayodhya by a survey conducted in Delhi and three cities in Uttar Pradres with a sizable Muslim population. Measured in terms of castes, support for communalism was highest among the non-Brahmin upper-castes (*dvijas*) (55%), high among the Brahmins (50%) and lowest (45%) among the *non-dvija* castes; measured in terms of class and occupation, support was high among the middle class, particularly the traders and small businessmen (62%) and white collar workers (60%), but low among students (32%) and labourers (28%); measured in terms of age, it was highest amongst those over 45 years who had witnessed the partition (63%), and lowest (47%) amongst those below 45 years of age who had not. They conclude that 'communal feelings are most pronounced among [...] particular occupations, age cohorts, and those who believe that the government favours some groups over others. [...] These sentiments are [however] not as widespread as assumed, especially among the younger, post-independence generation' (Chhibber & Misra 1993: 671-672; Embree 1994: 638, 640, 645). Cf. also and van der Veer (1994: 664, 665-666) on the growing economic and political significance of India's middle class as a major factor in the Ayodhya events, in particular by its growing share in indigenous tourism, especially to such places as Ayodhya, and the strong boost which that again received from India's media industry which has produced many Hindu mythological plays in the past few years, the undisputed high point being the serialisation of the *Ramayana* on Indian television in 1987.

[179] Cf. Hansen 1993: 2270.

7. The analytical extensions of this operational definition of ritual for the historical and comparative study of ritual in plural and pluralist societies (developed in the chapter on the analysis of ritual) proved useful in the case of the Ayodhya rituals. Apart from the direct messages they carried, e.g. that the secular government 'pampered' the religious minorities, the Muslims in particular, these rituals also sent out messages which clearly demonized the Muslim community. The concepts of indirect addressees, indirect messages, and indirect, or wider, field of ritual communication, proved useful in the analysis of the Ayodhya rituals, and may be helpful in similar situations of religious plurality. This is also true of the ways in which these direct and indirect messages were received in diverse quarters and the manners in which they were interpreted there on the basis of the different codes of interpretation by which each quarter is ruled. These differences in interpretation, often rooted in past experiences and hopes or fears of the future, were an essential mechanism in the unfolding process of the political confrontation between the Hindu and Muslim 'communities', the Indian government, the press, and the Hindus disinclined to support communalism.

In conclusion, the rich Ayodhya data presented in this chapter show that it is heuristically more fruitful not to separate religious ritual from secular ceremony. But they also establish that the historical data for the comparative analysis of ritual are so rich in complex forms, functions and usages, that we are at present still very far from a sure grasp, in terms of definition and division, of the complex phenomenon of 'ritual'. We are, in brief, still in the pre-paradigmatic stage in the science of ritual, and we are likely to remain there for much longer if scholars of religions continue to regard ritual as a self-evident term not in need of definition, classification and theoretical analysis.[180]

---

180 One of the few exceptions is Snoek 1987.

References

Andersen, W.K., & S.D. Damle 1987, *The brotherhood in saffron: the Rashtriya Swayamsevak Sangh and Hindu revivalism*. New Delhi: Vistaar Publications.

Anonymi 1992, 'Bloody aftermath', in *India Today*, December 31, 1992: 40-43.

Anonymous 1993a, 'Picture feature: the saffron invasion', in *Frontline*, January 1, 1993: 129-134.

Anonymous 1993b, 'The Hindu upsurge: the road to Ayodhya', *The Economist*, 6 February 1993, 21-24.

Awasthi, D., 1992, 'A nation's shame', in *India Today*, December 31, 1992: 15-24, 26-27.

Awasthi, D., & S.A. Aiyar 1991, 'RSS-BJP-VHP: Hindu divided family', in *India Today*, November 30, 1991: 14-21.

Awasthi, D., & Y. Ghimire 1992, 'Politics of opportunism', in *Frontline*, August 15, 1992, 14-16, 18-21.

Awasthi, D., & U. Mahurkar 1992, 'Orchestrated onslaught', in *India Today*, December 31, 1992: 36-37.

Badhwar, I., 1986, 'Militant revivalism', in *India Today*, May 31, 1986: 30-39.

Badhwar, I., 1992, 'Masters of deception', in *India Today*, 31 December, 1992: 35.

Baird, R.D., 1975, 'Religion and the secular: categories for religious conflict and religious change in independent India', in *Journal of Asian and African Studies* 11, 1-2: 47-63.

Bakker, H.T., 1984 (1986), *Ayodhya; part I: the history of Ayodhya from the 7th century BC to the middle of the 18th century, its development into a sacred centre with special reference to the Ayodhyamahatmya and to the worship of Rama according to the Agastyasamhita; part II: Ayodhyamahatya, introduction, edition, and annotation; part III: appendices, concordances, indexes, and maps*, Groningen, Institute of Indian Studies, University of Groningen; also Groningen, Egbert Forsten, 1986.

Bakker, H.T., 1991, 'Ayodhya, a Hindu Jerusalem: an investigation of "holy war" as a religious idea in the light of communal unrest in India', *Numen*, 38, 1: 80-109.

Basu, T., *et alii* 1993, *Khaki shorts, saffron flags*. Hyderabad: Orient Longman.

Becke, A, 1994, 'Fundamentalismus in Indien?: Säkularismus und Kommunalismus am beispiel von Ayodhya', in *Zeitschrift für Missionswissenschaft und Religionswissenschaft* 78: 3-25.

Bhan, S., 1993, 'A comment', in Gopal 1993: 225-228.

Bhattarcharya, N., 1993, 'Myth, history, and the politics of Ramjanmabhumi', in Gopal 1993b: 122-140.

Björkman, J.W., (ed.), 1988, *Fundamentalism, revivalists and violence in South Asia*. Riverdale (Maryland), The Riverdale Company.

Bonouvrié, N.C., no year, *Communalisme in India* (unpublished manuscript, 14 pp.).

Burghart, R., 1982, 'Wandering ascetics of the Ramanandi sect', in *History of Religions* 22, 4: 361-380.

Burghart, R., 1983, 'Renunciation in the religious traditions of South Asia', in *Man* 18, 4: 635-653.

Caldarola, C., 1982, *Religion and societies: Asia and the Middle East*. Berlin, etc.: Mouton.
Caplan, L., 1991, 'Christian fundamentalism as counter-culture', in Madan 1991a: 366-382.
Champakalakshmi, R., 1993, 'A comment', in Gopal 1993: 228-232.
Chatterjee, M., 1993a, 'The fascist face, and the BJP's bid to cloak it', in *Frontline*, January 15, 1993: 4-7, 9.
Chatterjee, M., 1993b, 'Strident saddhus: contours of a Hindu rashtra?', in *Frontline*, January 29, 1993: 4-10.
Chengappa, R., 1993, 'Dangerous dimensions', in *India Today*, February 15, 1993: 31-33.
Chibber, P.K., & S. Misra 1993, 'Hindus and the Babri masjid: the sectional basis of the communal attitudes', in *Asian Survey* 33: 665-672.
Chidester, D., 1988, *Salvation and suicide: an interpretation of Jim Jones, the Peoples Temple, and Jonestown*. : Bloomington: Indiana Un.Pr.
Eck, D., 1991, 'Kashi: city of all India', in Madan 1991a: 138-155.
Embree, A., 1994, 'The function of the Rashtriya Swayamsevak Sangh', in Marty & Appleby 1994: 617-652.
Freitag, S.B., 1980, 'Sacred symbol as mobilizing ideology: the North Indian search for a "Hindu" community', *Comparative Studies in Society and History* 22: 597-625.
Frykenberg, R.E., 1994, 'Accounting for fundamentalisms in South Asia: ideologies and institutions in historical perspective', in Marty & Appleby 1994: 591-616.
Fuller, C.J., 1992, *The camphor flame: popular Hinduism and society in India*. Princeton (N.J.): Princeton Un.Pr.
Furnivall, J.S., 1948, *Colonial policy and practice*, Cambridge, Cambridge Un.Pr.
Geertz, C., 1966, 'Religion as a cultural system', in Banton 1966: 1-4.
Geertz, C., 1973, *The interpretation of cultures; selected essays*. New York: Basic Books.
Ghimire, Y., 1992, 'Confused aggression', in *India Today*, November 30, 1992: 30-33.
Ghimire, Y., 1993, 'The rise of the saddhus', in *India Today*, January 31, 1993: 49-51.
Ghimire, Y., & R. Pathak 1992, 'Too much, too late', in *India Today*, December 31, 1992: 50-53.
Gold, D., 1991a, 'Organized Hinduisms: from Vedic truth to Hindu nation', in Marty & Appleby 1991: 531-593.
Gold, D., 1991b: 'Rational action and uncontrolled violence: explaining Hindu communalism', in *Religion* 21: 357-370.
Gopal, S., 1993a, 'Introduction', in Gopal 1993b: 11-21
Gopal, S., (ed.) 1993^{2}b, *Anatomy of a confrontation: the Babri masjid—Ram Janmabhumi issue*. New Delhi: Penguin Books India.
Gross, R.L., 1979, *Hindu ascetism: a study of the sadhus of North India*, Ann Arbor, University Microfilms International.
Hansen, T. Blom, 1993, 'RSS and the popularisation of Hindutva', in *Economic and Political Weekly*, October 16, 1993: 2270-2272.
Hasan, M., 1993, 'Competing symbols and shared codes: inter-community relations in modern India', in Gopal 1993b: 99-121.
Hiebert, P.G., 1982, 'India: the politicization of a sacred society', in Caldarola 1982: 289-331.

Jaffrelot, C., 1993, 'Hindu nationalism: strategic syncretism in ideology building', in *Economic and Political Weekly*, March 20-27, 1993: 517-524.
Janssen, F.H.P.M., 1989, *Het Ekâtmatâyajña van de Vishva Hindu Parisad: een case-study van communalisme in India.* Unpublished long essay, Utrecht University, Department of Oriental Languages.
Juergensmeyer, M., 1991, 'The logic of religious violence', in Madan 1991a: 382-383.
Khare, R.S., 1991, 'The radical and protesting ascetic', in Madan 1991a: 351-365.
Kinsley, D.R., 1982, *Hinduism: a cultural perspective.*Englewood Cliffs (N.J.): Prentice Hall.
Klimkeit, H.-J., 1981, *Der politische Hinduismus: Indische Denker zwischen religiöser Reform und politischer Erwachsen.* Wiesbaden.
Klostermaier, K.K., 1989, *A survey of Hinduism.* Albany (N.Y.): State University of New York Press.
Lorenzen, D.N., 1978, 'Warrior ascetics in Indian history', in *Journal of the American Oriental Society* 98, 1: 61-75.
Lütt, J., 1970, *Hindu-Nationalismus in Uttar Prades, 1867-1900.* Stuttgart: Klett.
Madan, T.N., (ed.), 1991a, *Religion in India.* Delhi: Oxford University Press.
Madan, T.N., 1991b, 'Secularism in its place', in Madan 1991a: 394-409.
Mahmood, C. Keppley, 1993, 'Rethinking Indian communalism: culture and counter-culture', in *Asian Survey* 33, 7: 722-737.
Mahmood, C., 1994, 'Ayodhya and Hindu resurgence', in *Religion* 24: 73-80.
Mansingh, S., 1988, 'The political use of religious identity in South Asia', in Björkman 1988, 170-193.
Marty, M.E., & R.S. Appleby (eds.) 1991, *Fundamentalisms observed.* Chicago, etc.: University of Chicago Press.
Marty, M.E., & R.S. Appleby (eds.) 1994, *Accounting for fundamentalisms: the dynamic character of movements.* Chicago, etc.,: University of Chicago Press.
Mitra, S., 1983, 'Road to revival', in *India Today*, November 30, 1983: 34-36.
Muralidharan, S., 1992a, 'Congress games', in *Frontline*, August 14, 1992: 116.
Muralidharan, S., 1992b, 'Twisting history: with a skewed spade in Ayodhya', in *Frontline*, August 14, 1992: 119-120.
Muralidharan, S., 1992c, 'Prejudice as history: the great archeology scam', in *Frontline* September 11, 1992: 96-98.
Noorani, A.G., 1993, 'Legal aspects to the issue', in Gopal 1993b: 58-98.
Pande, S.K., 1991, 'Ayodhya dramatics: playing with temples and mosques', in *Frontline*, November 9-22, 1991: 12-16.
Pande, S.K., 1992, 'The RSS takeover', in *Frontline*, August 28, 1992: 108.
Panikkar, K.N., 1992, 'The secular way: to uphold democratic principles', in *Frontline*, 28 August 1992: 107, 109.
Panikkar, K.N., 1993, 'A historical overview', in Gopal 1993b: 22-37.
Ram, N., 1993, 'Appeasing *Hindutva*', in *Frontline*, January 29, 1993: 11.
Ramakrishnan, V., 1992a, 'Truce, for now: postponing the day of reckoning?', in *Frontline*, August 14, 1992: 13-15.

Ramakrishnan, V., 1992b, 'Throwing the gauntlet: Hindutva's combine next round', in *Frontline*, November 20, 1992: 18-19.
Ramakrishnan, V., 1992c, 'Flashpoint Ayodhya: despite a symbolic kar seva', in *Frontline*, December 18, 1992: 4-5, 9-10.
Ramakrishnan, V., 1992d, 'The BJP yatra', in *Frontline*, December 18, 1992: 9.
Ramakrishnan, V., 1993a, 'The wrecking crew: in Ayodhya, demolition and after', in *Frontline*, January 1, 1993: 10-12, 15.
Ramakrishnan, V., 1993b, 'The tragic sequence', in *Frontline*. January 1, 1993: 12-13.
Ramakrishnan, V., 1993c, 'Dateline Ayodhya', in *Frontline*, January 1, 1993: 9.
Ramakrishnan, V., 1993d, 'Looting the "mandir"', in *Frontline*, January 15, 1993: 22.
Rijk, M., de, 1994, 'Temple van tolerantie', in *NRC-Handelsblad*, 26 March 1994, Zaterdags Bijvoegsel: 3.
Roy, P.K., 1989a, 'Ayodhya again', in *Frontline*, August 5-18, 1989: 25-31.
Roy, P.K., 1989b, 'Eyes on Ayodhya', in *Frontline*, October 28-November 10, 1989: 4-7.
Roy, P.K., 1989c, 'Ayodhya epilogue', in *Frontline*, November 25-December 8, 1989: 26-32.
Rudolph, L.I., & S. Hoeber Rudolph, 1988, 'Confessional politics, secularism and centrism in India', in Björkman 1988: 75-87.
Saberwal, S., 1991, 'Elements of communalism', in Madan 1991a: 339-350.
Sankar, R.V., 1991, 'Rituals of confrontation', in *Frontline* October 26-November 8, 1991: 14-15.
Sarkar, S., 1993, 'The fascism of the Sangh Parivar', in *Economic and Political Weekly*, January 30, 1993: 163-167.
Shankar, R., 1993, 'The day of Ram's tigers', in *India Today*, December 31, 1992: 25.
Shridar, V., 1993, 'The RSS ban: from Godse to the kar sevak', in *Frontline*, January 18, 1993: 16-17.
Sidhu, W.P.S., & D. Awasthi 1992, 'Spineless spectators', in *India Today*, December 31, 1992: 18-19.
Snoek, J.A.M., 1987, *Initiations: a methodological approach to the application of classification and definition theory in the study of rituals*. Pijnacker: Dutch Efficiency Bureau.
Srivasthava, S., 1993, 'How the British saw the issue', in Gopal 1993b: 38-57.
Thakur, R., 1993, 'Ayodhya and the politics of India's secularism: a double standard discourse', in *Asian Survey; a Monthly Review of Contemporary Asian Affairs* 33, 7 (July 1993), 645-664.
Thapar, R., 1985, 'Syndicated moksha', in *Seminar* no. 313 (September 1985) 14-22.
Thapar, R., 1989, 'Imagined religious communities?; ancient history and the modern search for a Hindu identity', in *Modern Asian Studies* 23, 2: 209-231.
Thapar, R., 1993, 'A historical perspective on the story of Rama', in Gopal 1993: 141-163.
Veer, P. van der, 1982, 'Naakt geweld en zoete devotie: de veranderende

machtskansen van de Ramanandis in Noord-India', *Antropologische Verkenningen* 1, 2: 59-84.
Veer, P. van der, 1985, 'Brahmans: their purity and their poverty; on the changing values of brahman priests in Ayodhya', *Contributions to Indian Sociology* 19, 2, 301-321.
Veer, P. van der, 1987a, '"God must be liberated": a Hindu liberation movement in Ayodhya', *Modern Asian Studies* 21, 2, 283-301.
Veer, P. van der, 1987b, 'Taming the ascetic: devotionalism in a Hindu monastic order', *Man* 22, 680-695.
Veer, P. van der, 1988, *Gods on earth: the management of religious experience and identity in a North Indian pilgrimage centre*, London, etc., The Athlone Press.
Veer, P. van der, 1989, 'The power of detachment: disciplines of body and mind in the Ramanandi order', *American Ethnologist* 16, 3, 458-470.
Veer, P. van der, 1994, 'Hindu nationalism and the discourse of modernity: the Hindu Vishva Parishad', in Marty & Appleby 1994:653-668.
Vithal, B.P.R., 1993, 'Roots of Hindu fundamentalism', in *Economic and Political Weekly*, February 20-27, 1993: 335-338.
Vyas, N., 1991, 'Communal game: BJP, the central player', in *Frontline*, October 26-November 8, 1991: 12-13.
Wallace, P., 1988, 'The dilemma of Sikh revivalism: identity versus political power', in Björkman 1988: 57-74.
Yang, A.A., 1980, 'Sacred symbol and sacred space in rural India: community mobilization in the "Anti-cow Killing" riot of 1893', in *Comparative Studies in Society and History* 22: 576-596.
Yechuri, S., 1993, 'What is Hindu rashtra?: an exposé of Golwarkar's fascist ideology and the Saffron Brigade's practice', in *Frontline*, March 12, 1993: 11-20.

PART THREE
RESPONSES TO RELIGIOUS PLURALITY

RITUAL RESISTANCE AND SELF-ASSERTION

THE RECHABITES IN EARLY ISRAELITE RELIGION

Karel van der Toorn
(Leiden University)

Religious pluralism, though often regarded as a specifically modern phenomenon, was not unknown in antiquity. The romantic view of ancient cultures as corporate collectivities inhabited by a common religious ideology—a view found in the work of such scholars as Lucien Lévy-Bruhl (1857-1939)[1] and Gerardus van der Leeuw (1890-1950)[2]—owes more to a sense of nostalgia on the part of the researcher than to a dispassionate study of the facts. Perhaps the time-gap contributes to the distortion; viewed from a distance, cultures tend to take on a monolithic appearance. Yet there is little reason to believe that past societies were any more unified than our own. The fallacious use of name-tags—such as 'Mesopotamian civilization' or 'Israelite religion'—should not make us forget that these designations cover in fact a diversity of practices, groups, and opinions.

This contribution will be concerned with a specific instance of religious pluralism in antiquity. The geographical area upon which we shall focus is that of Central Palestine, and the culture which will be presented as an illustration of religious pluralism is that of early Israel—meaning Israel in the period between 1200-400 BCE. Instead of a panoramical view of the various currents and groups in early Israelite religion, I shall discuss one particular group, viz. the Rechabites. The Rechabites were considered an oddity by many of their contemporaries: they kept loyal to customs of the desert in a rural society. They refused to live in houses and to practise agriculture; nor did they drink wine.

The Rechabites present a suitable entry into the matter of religious pluralism. Whether they were a sect, a religious order, or a group of itinerant craftsmen—and all of these things have been said at one time or another—, they do attest to the cultural diversity

---

[1] See, e.g., Lévy-Bruhl 1910.

[2] Van der Leeuw 1937. Van der Leeuw makes no absolute distinction between 'primitive' and 'ancient' cultures. Thus, neither the primitives nor the Egyptians possessed the notion of contradiction (Van der Leeuw 1937: 40).

within early Israel. In fact, the diversity is more than merely cultural: it is the expression of a religious diversity. The reconstruction of the history of the Rechabites, tentative though it must be, can serve as a springboard for some broader conclusions about pluralism and identity in early Israel, and in antiquity in general.

The rule of the Rechabites

The principal source of information about the Rechabites is Jeremiah 35. This chapter contains the description of a meeting of the prophet with representatives of the Rechabites in the temple at Jerusalem, sometime around 600 BCE. Jeremiah brings the clan of the Rechabites ('Jaazaniah the son of Jeremiah, son of Habbaziniah, and his brothers, and all his sons, and the whole house of the Rechabites') to the temple and, having supplied them with cups and pitchers full of wine, invites them to drink. They refuse to do so, saying (Jer 35:6-10):

> We drink no wine, for Jehonadab ben Rechab our father gave us a rule: 'You shall drink no wine, neither you nor your sons, for ever. Nor shall you build houses, or sow seeds. Vineyards you shall neither plant nor possess. But you shall dwell in tents all your days, that your days may be many in the land in which you dwell as foreigners.' And we honour the wish of our father Jehonadab ben Rechab, in everything he commanded us: we never drink wine, neither we nor our wives, nor our sons and our daughters. Nor do we build houses as our dwelling place. And we possess neither vineyards, nor fields, nor sowing-land. But we live in tents, and observe and do everything Jehonadab our father commanded us.

The Rechabites would normally not be dwelling within a city, then. Indeed, the reason they find themselves in Jerusalem is the military pressure from the Babylonian king Nebuchadnezzar and his army (Jer 35:11).

Jeremiah admires their stubborn allegiance to ancestral custom. Thus instructed by the LORD, he sets the Rechabites as an example for the Judaeans and the inhabitants of Jerusalem (Jer 35:13-16):

> Will you not accept a correction, and listen to my words?—oracle of the LORD. The commandment which Jehonadab ben Rechab gave to his sons, to drink no wine, has been kept; to this very day they do not drink, because they listened to the commandment of their father. Now I have spoken to you without pause, but you did not listen to me. (...) Really, the sons of Jehonadab ben Rechab have kept the commandment of their father, which he gave them—but this people has not listened to me.

The point of the comparison is clear: if the Rechabites kept the commandment of their human father (i.e. ancestor), why could not the Judaeans and the inhabitants of Jerusalem keep the commandment of Yahweh whose word is far superior to that of any human father? Nothing is implied about the intrinsic value of Jehonadab's rule. Yet the end of the episode suggests that Jeremiah (or the author of this chapter) was in sympathy with the lifestyle of the Rechabites as well. In reward of their loyalty, the prophet announces that the Rechabites would always have a male descendant to 'stand before' Yahweh (*'ômēd lepânay*, Jer 35:19). The terminology refers to a lasting Rechabite presence in the temple ('before Yahweh'). Apparently, then, there was a religious side to the behaviour of the Rechabites, which here is valued positively.

Who were the Rechabites? In the scholarly literature on the subject, the characterization moves between two poles: they are understood either as a religious or as a mundane phenomenon. In the one case, authors describe them as a sect or a group of fanatics; in the other they emphasize that the Rechabites were a clan of semi-nomads or a guild of craftsmen. Of course, a clear-cut separation between the two realms is impossible. Yet there is a real difference between the characterization of the Rechabites as a religious order, and their characterization as a clan, a guild or an ethnic minority group: whereas the one implies religious pluralism, the other need not. A brief survey of opinions will illuminate the range of interpretative possibilities.

The interpretation of the Rechabites as a religious sect has been championed by Karl Budde. In an English article in the *New World*, published in 1895, Budde expressed the view that there were several groups in ancient Israel that cherished and propagated the 'nomadic ideal'.[3] The prime example of such groups were precisely the Rechabites. Were not the customs of the Rechabites typically those of the desert? It was during the journey through the wilderness that the people of Israel had dwelt in tents. According to Deuteronomy 29:6, the wandering Israelites had not eaten bread (which would imply the cultivation of grain), nor drunk wine or strong drink. By returning to this nomadic lifestyle, the Rechabites would have hoped to revive the religious purity of the desert. To them, the LORD was something of a nomad himself: he was a tent-dweller who spurned the settled life of the Canaanite farmers. Even in the days

[3] Budde 1895.

of Jeremiah, the Rechabites, being the descendants of the Kenites, a pure and noble desert people (1 Chr 2:55), continued to be the 'missionaries' (the term is Budde's) of a Yahwistic desert religion. Their 'nomadic ideal' was religious. This presentation of the Rechabites became a classic and exerted great influence on other studies.[4]

The interpretation of the Rechabites as a religious group also occurs in different guises. In a study published in 1979 it was argued that the Rechabites were a prophetic school rivalling the one headed by Elisha. Both the Rechabites and the Elisha prophets would have claimed succession to Elijah; the principal difference between the two guilds being that, in the eyes of the Rechabites, the Elisha group had lapsed from the prophetic ideal of poverty since they lived in houses. The Rechabites, on the other hand, remained steadfast in their obedience to the standards set by Elijah.[5] Another interpretation of the Rechabites as a religious group sees them as post-exilic priests. Jon D. Levenson notes the affinity between the priestly promise at Jer 33:18 ('and the Levitical priest shall never lack a man in my presence') and the promise to the Rechabites in Jer 35:19 ('Jonadab ben Rechab shall never lack a man to stand in my presence').[6] Another parallel between the Rechabites and the Levitical priests is their status as *gêrîm*, 'resident aliens': both the Levites (Deut 18:6) and the Rechabites (Jer 35:7) live as sojourners (the Hebrew root is *GWR*). If verses 18-19, which contain the promise to the Rechabites, are a post-exilic addition to the chapter, as many authors like to think, they could be considered a comment by which the editor turns the story into a defence of a priestly minority group: though they have some strange habits, they are nonetheless true servants of the LORD.[7]

The interpretation of the Rechabites as a mundane phenomenon also has its advocates. They, too, have come up with a variety of possibilities. A view that has won considerable support is that of Frank S. Frick.[8] Insisting that there is no explicitly religious motivation of their rule, Frick suggests that the Rechabite mode of life was an occupational pattern, not a religious vocation. He interprets the Rechabites as belonging to 'guild of metal-workers involved in the

[4] The views of Budde have found their way into a wealth of scholarly literature. See especially Meyer 1906: 136; Flight 1923: 167; Gautier 1927; Humbert 1921, 1925; Causse 1937: 69-70; Dietrich 1979: 72-73.

[5] Cummings 1979.

[6] Levenson 1976: 510-511.

[7] So especially McKane 1988: 119-121.

[8] Frick 1971; Frick 1977: 211-217.

making of chariots and other weaponry'[9], a suggestion based on the etymology of their name (compare the words *rôkêb*, 'charioteer', *rakkâb*, 'driver', and *markâbâ*, 'chariot'[10]) and their genealogical connections.[11] Metallurgists in antiquity were organized in guilds, a guild being similar to a clan; owing to the nature of their work they did not establish a permanent domicile; and their teetotalism might be explained as a precaution against the inadvertent divulgation of professional lore. Though Frick's guess that the Rechabites were chariot makers has elicited sceptical comments[12], his plea for a sociological interpretation of their lifestyle has found favour with a number of authors—though they do not necessarily deny the religious aspects of the Rechabite dissent.[13]

Another 'profane' solution to the riddle of the Rechabites has been offered by Karlheinz H. Keukens. In the latter's view, Jehonadab ben Rechab was a military man; more specifically, he was a commander in the Judahite army, and collaborated as such with Jehu in the extermination of the Omrides.[14] However, the 'sons of the house of the Rechabites'—the literal translation of the expression in Jer 35—are domestic servants, as a comparison with the terminology in Gen 15:2-3 and Eccl 2:7 would indicate. The prohibition to build houses, to practise agriculture, or to use alcohol has to be regarded as a measure preventing these slaves to emancipate themselves. There is nothing religious in Jehonadab's commandment at all. Jehonadab himself was perfectly free to build houses, to cultivate the land, and to drink wine. The thrust of the promise to the Rechabites, in Jer 35:18-19, is that they will be manumitted to enjoy all the rights of full citizens in the post-exilic temple-state of Judah.

This survey of opinions is by no means exhaustive; whatever the specifics of the particular interpretations, however, the latter may all of them be classified in two groups: the one seeing the Rechabites as a religious sect, the other as a social phenomenon. For the time being, a choice between these two options is best postponed. The only comment that should perhaps be made at this stage is that the one option need not exclude the other. This is

[9] Frick 1971: 285.
[10] Frick 1971: 282-283.
[11] Frick 1971: 286-287.
[12] See, e.g., Dietrich 1979: 72 note 6; Keukens 1983: 233. It should be noted that Frick, in his dissertation about the Israelite city (written in 1970, but published in 1977), argues for a link between the Rechabites and the ideology of the 'holy war', rather than to present them as metallurgists.
[13] E.g., Carroll 1977: 179.
[14] Keukens 1983: 234.

perhaps not a case of either/or: the elements of truth the one of them contains separately need to be brought into balance with those of the other. First, however, in order to obtain a more reliable picture, two further data need to be taken into account. The first concerns the genealogy of the Rechabites, and the second the historical place of Jehonadab ben Rechab.

The nomadic connections of the Rechabites

According to lists in the First Book of Chronicles, the Rechabites were related to the Calebites and the Kenites (1 Chr 2:55; 4:11.12 [read 'Caleb' for 'Celub', and Rechab for Rechah]). A crucial text is 1 Chr 2:55, which can be interpreted in two ways: the author refers to 'the Kenites who descended from Hammath the father of the Rechabites'[15], or 'the Kenites who descended from the in-laws of the father of the Rechabites'.[16] Whatever the solution one prefers, the text establishes a link between the Kenites and the Rechabites; they are related, either by a common ancestor or by connubial ties. Anthropological studies show that genealogies such as the ones found in the First Book of Chronicles reflect social realities in terms of descent and kinship.[17] Rechabites, Kenites, and Calebites need not have been kin-related in order to be presented as such; it suffices that they be perceived as sharing similar characteristics. One of those characteristics, for instance, is the fact that all three groups are connected with the area south-east of Palestine on the border of Judah with Edom.[18]

Another common trait that links the Rechabites with the Kenites and the Calebites is their nomadic background. From the Song of Deborah, it is clear that the Kenites used to dwell in tents and to keep cattle as a means of living (Judg 5:24-25). The ease with which one branch of the Kenite community moved from the South to the North (Judg 4:11) could be taken as a confirmation of their itinerant pastoralism. The Calebites were a Kenizzite clan (1 Chr 4:13-15) which existed as a distinct group in South Palestine.[19] The biblical genealogies suggest that the Kenizzites and the Calebites were

---

[15] So the majority of the modern Bible translations.
[16] Talmon 1958.
[17] Wilson 1977.
[18] For the Kenites see Josh 15:22.57; Judg 1:16; 4:11; 1 Sam 15:5-6. The Calebites are located around Hebron and Debir (Josh 14:6-15; 15:13.14-19; Judg 1:11-15) and in the Negeb (1 Sam 30:14).
[19] See Noth 1932; Beltz 1974: 64-70.

tribal groups that maintained close associations with their eastern Edomite neighbours. Like the other inhabitants of the Negeb, such as the Kenites and the Jerachmeelites, they practised a pastoral nomadism.[20] Most of these groups later lost their distinctness in the larger whole of Judah; only remnants of their nomadic past remained.

The nomadic antecedents which the Rechabites shared with the Kenites and the Calebites must be taken into account when the meaning of Jehonadab's rule is discussed. It has often been noticed that there is a striking similarity between the precepts honoured by the Rechabites and the customs which Diodorus Siculus ascribes to the early Nabataeans (XIX 94.2-3):

> They lead a life under the open skies, calling the uninhabited desert their homeland (. . .). It is their custom (*nomos*) to sow no grain and to plant no fruit-bearing trees; nor do they use wine or settle in houses. And whosoever among them is found doing such things is subject to the penalty of death.

The taboo on wine is confirmed by he votive inscription of a Nabataean horseman at Palmyra. This man dedicated his gift to Shay' al-Qaum, 'the good and bountiful god, who does not drink wine'.[21] It may be assumed that the characteristics of this Arab god reflect those, ideally, of his worshippers.[22] Viewed against this background, the rule laid down by Jehonadab was probably no innovation; the Rechabites traditionally followed these customs: it was part of their ancestral lore.

At this point it should be noted that the traditional lifestyle of the Rechabites had never been that of all Israel. Rather the contrary. Belonging to the 'Negebite' clans, the Rechabites have lived in a kind of symbiosis with the Judaeans before they eventually merged

---

[20] Knauf 1988: 112.

[21] *Corpus Inscriptionum Semiticarum* II/3: 156-157 no. 3973: 4-5; cf. Teixidor 1979: 85-86.

[22] It is true, of course, that the description of classical authors needs to be used with circumspection. Note, for instance, the rather different picture of the Nabataeans given by Strabo, *Geographica* XVI.i.21. Yet the votive inscription from Palmyra seems to confirm the observations of Diodorus Siculus. Compare also the reports about Amorite nomads in Mesopotamian texts: they dwell in tents, not in houses, eat uncooked food, and do not enjoy the blessings of city life, see Kramer 1990: 20, lines 129-139, cf. p. 27 commentary to line 133 [by Jacob Klein]. Note that the description of Enkidu in the OB version of the Gilgamesh Epic is modelled after the usual clichés about nomads: Enkidu knows nothing of eating bread, and of drinking beer. The attractions of a life outdoors are sung in the Erra Epic: 'City food, however fancy, cannot compare with what is cooked on the embers. Best beer, however sweet, cannot compare with water from a water-skin. A palace built on a platform cannot compare with the shelters of [a camp]' (tr. S. Dalley).

with the Judaean population. Like the Kenites, they were long considered non-Israelite. Their clinging to ancestral custom, therefore, should not be interpreted as an implicit call for a national revival of the Mosaic spirituality. Over against the proponents of the theory of the 'nomadic ideal' it has rightly been stressed that the overall picture of the Israelite journey through the desert is not very idyllic: the fertile soil of Canaan is the promised land, not the arid wilderness—the place of Israel's rebellion and murmuring. The prophetic ideal is that of the peasant sitting peacefully under his vine and his fig tree (1 Kgs 5:5[ET 4:25]; Mic 4:4).[23]

The Rechabite rule does not refer to a pan-Israelite past (whether fictive or real), but to the distinctive Rechabite origins. Also, it is erroneous to present the Rechabites as 'missionaries' of a nomadic lifestyle; on the contrary, they wanted to stress their identity. Had all Israelite adopted their customs, the Rechabites would no longer be recognized as a separate group.

The role of Jehonadab

If the lifestyle which Jehonadab made binding was not new, the very fact that he laid it down as a rule was itself an innovation. Until then, one assumes, the Rechabites had kept their customs as a matter of course. Some, perhaps, had adapted their behaviour to something better suited to their surroundings, or were tempted to do so. At any event, Jehonadab ben Rechab judged it necessary to formally demand that the old customs be honoured. In so doing, he changed their significance. In at least one respect, then, the role of Jehonadab has been crucial. In order to explain his place in the history of the Rechabites, the time in which he lived needs to be described first.

Jehonadab ben Rechab was active in North Israel in the latter days of the Omrides. He is mentioned as a contemporary of Jehu, a royal governor who carried out a military coup and killed all the members of Omri's house in 841 BCE. Jehonadab seems to have lived in the hill country of Manasseh, somewhere between Jezreel and Samaria (2 Kgs 10:12-17). In his lifetime, the State of Israel (to be distinguished from the State of Judah) had changed at a fast pace from a rather insignificant political entity into an important power.[24]

---

[23] For a critique of the thesis of the 'nomadic ideal', see esp. Talmon 1966.
[24] For a survey of the period of the Omrides, see Ahlström 1993: 569-606.

Under Omri (ca. 885-874) and Ahab (ca. 874-853) the Aramaean influence in Palestine was pushed back, and Transjordanian territories were incorporated into the kingdom (2 Kgs 3:4-5). Using diplomacy and alliances the Omrides developed good relations with the kingdoms of Tyre (the 'Sidonians', as they are called in the Bible) and Judah: the former were consolidated by the marriage of Ahab with Jezebel, the daughter of Ittobaal ('Ethbaal') of Tyre (Menander of Ephesus, as quoted by Josephus, *Antiquities* 8.13.2; see also 1 Kgs 16:31); the latter by the marriage of Ahab's daughter (or sister) Athaliah to Jehoram, then the Judaean crown prince (2 Kgs 8:18; 2 Chr 21:6).

The domestic politics of the Omrides bear out their ambition to lay the foundations of a powerful and efficient state. The division of the territory in districts was reorganized; each was placed under the supervision of a governor with a staff of 'servants' (1 Kgs 20:14-15.19). A decision that had also symbolical significance was the building of Samaria as the new capital. Until then, various places had served as centre of the administration. Samaria, however, was a city with no past. Around 880, Omri built it on virgin ground, having bought the land from the Shemer family (1 Kgs 16:24). Though the royal family also maintained a palace at Jezreeel (1 Kgs 18:46; 21:1; 2 Kgs 9:17), Samaria was the real capital. The kings ruled from Samaria (1 Kgs 16:29). Omri himself was buried in Samaria (1 Kgs 16:28); so were Ahab (1 Kgs 22:37) and Ahaziah (2 Kgs 1:17). The political role of Samaria is confirmed by the fact that, later on, 'Samaria' came to be the name of the Israelite state as a whole (e.g. 1 Kgs 13:32; 2 Kgs 17:24; 23:19). New, too, in the politics of the Omrides was the dynastic nature of their rule. So far, the Israelites had held fast to the ideal of a charismatic kingship; the transformation into a dynastic kingship was brought about by Omri.[25]

In an influential essay on the city of Samaria, Albrecht Alt has defended the view that the Omrides maintained two administrative centres in a deliberate attempt to satisfy both the Canaanite and the Israelite elements of the population.[26] Jezreel, in this view, was a traditionally Israelite town; Samaria, on the other hand, lay in Canaanite territory; also after the demise of the Omrides, it remained a Canaanite enclave. The suggestion is attractive but lacks sufficient proof. Its main weakness is the unwarranted supposition

---

[25] Alt 1951: 4-13.

[26] Alt 1954: esp. 4-13. The hypothesis was adopted and defended by quite a number of other authors. See, e.g., Donner 1977: 400-404.

that there was an opposition between Israelites and Canaanites. In fact, the archaeological research of these last years suggests that the greatest part of the Israelite population had come from a Canaanite background.[27] Yet if there can hardly be question of an ethnic opposition between Israelites and Canaanites, a coexistence, and perhaps conflict, of cultures—of religion as well as lifestyle—is quite conceivable. Though Yahweh had been the national god ever since the days of Saul, he was by no means the only deity worshipped in Israel.[28] Yahweh was the main, if not the only, god of the state religion, but outside the official cult he had a major rival in Baal. Baalism had long been popular with the early Israelites (or rather proto-Israelites) in the central hill country[29]; there is no reason to assume that the adoption of Yahweh as the national god led to a sudden reversal of religious loyalties among the population. In the Omride state, presumably, many citizens still honoured Baal as their god.

If the religious politics of the Omrides were not aimed at the pacification of two ethnic groups, then, they may nonetheless be interpreted as an attempt to give equal rights to the two largest religious communities in the Israelite State. In name Yahweh remained the national god, witness the inscription by the Moabite king Mesha.[30]

Yet contrary to the situation at Jezreel (1 Kgs 21:1-16), the temple which Omri built in Samaria was devoted to the cult of Baal (1 Kgs 16:32; 2 Kgs 10:18-29). No doubt Ahab's marriage with Jezebel stimulated the royal patronage of the cult of Baal: according to the Elijah legends, the cult personnel of Baal and Asherah, about 850 in numbers, ate at the table of Jezebel (1 Kgs 18:19). Yet Ahab's marriage was as much a result of, as an influence on, the Omride politics. Inevitably, the promotion of the cult of Baal went to the detriment of the official cult of Yahweh. The first to suffer from the development were the Yahwistic clergy; even if the reports about the execution of the 'prophets of Yahweh' are grossly exaggerated (1 Kgs 18:4.13), the cult personnel is bound to have experienced negative effects of the Omride politics. The Yahwistic ele-

---

[27] See Weippert 1979; Lemche 1985: 407-432; Callaway 1985: 43-46; Ahlström 1986: 25-36; Finkelstein 1988: 336-348; Finkelstein 1990: 682-685; Edelman 1991.

[28] Van der Toorn 1993.

[29] Mazar 1986: 48; Rosen 1988.

[30] Donner & Röllig 1962, no. 181: 14-18. For the interpretation of the text see Blau 1980; Lemaire 1987. An extensive bibliography up till 1987 can be found in Lemaire 1992: 561-568, esp. 564-565. The principal title to be added is Dearman 1989: 167-170.

ment of the population, too, must have been faced with a deterioration of position and influence.

It was to be expected that the Omride politics would meet with a mixed response. In the Bible we hear little to nothing about positive reactions—though presumably these were in the majority. The hostile reactions are better documented. The Omride politics elicited a strong counter-movement which eventually led to the revolt of Jehu. In 841 BCE Jehu seized the throne, killing Joram and all who remained from the house of the Omrides (2 Kgs 9-10). A military governor of the king, Jehu had been incited to disloyalty by 'one of the sons of the prophets'. Sent by Elisha, this anonymous prophet had secretly anointed Jehu king in the name of Yahweh 'the god of Israel' (2 Kgs 9:1-10). The ceremony was entirely in keeping with the Northern tradition of charismatic leadership; in like manner Saul had been appointed king by Samuel (1 Sam 10:1). The rebellion of Jehu, then, cannot be reduced to an act of wholly personal ambition; Jehu's revolt was also the expression of a widely-felt dissatisfaction with the Omride rule. Prophets such as those assembled around Elisha had made themselves the spokesmen of the popular discontent; with tyrants such as the Omrides the *vox populi* is almost forced to come in the trappings of the *vox dei.*[31]

As the Rechabites have been connected with these prophetic associations, the latter deserve to be discussed in some more detail.

The biblical picture of the prophetic 'guilds' or associations in the days of the Omrides is ambiguous. In some respects, they seem to have been religious orders comparable with monastic orders. Thus the prophets lived in a community where they had their meals in refectories (2 Kgs 4:38-41); they were led by a figure known as 'father' (*'âb*), the equivalent of the abbot (e.g. 2 Kgs 2:12; 6:21; the English term ultimately derives from Aramaic *'abbâ'*)[32]; they were recognizable by the tonsure (2 Kgs 2:23-24; cf. 1 Kgs 20:41). Judging by some of the stories about Elijah and Elisha, the prophets had taken a vow of poverty: the hairy mantle that was the proverbial dress of the prophet (2 Kgs 1:8; cf. Isa 20:2; Zech 13:4) is best interpreted as a symbol of soberness (cf. the contrast between John the Baptist who wore a garment of camel's hair [Matt 3:4] and those in kings' houses wearing soft raiment [Matt 11:8]). For these prophets it is not right 'to accept money and garments, olive orchards and vineyards, sheep and oxen, manservants and maidserv-

---

[31] For a study of the phenomenon of prophecy as the expression political opposition see Finet 1973: 136-137.

[32] For a study of the biblical term see Williams 1966.

ants' (2 Kgs 5:26). When they entered the order, prophets had to break with their former life and sacrifice their riches (1 Kgs 19:19-21).

This picture of the prophets as fervent religious men at the fringes of society needs to be counterbalanced by data showing their role as civil servants. The contrast in the Elijah stories between the prophets of Yahweh, on the one hand, and the prophets of Baal, on the other, is instructive in this respect. Since the latter are supported by the state to serve as religious functionaries at Baal temples (1 Kgs 18:19), the former presumably served in a civil capacity as well. It should be remembered that Yahweh remained the official god of Israel under the Omrides. The 'prophets' and the 'sons of the prophets', moreover, are not primarily men that give oracles and predictions: in the Northern Kingdom, they are the most important part of the cultic personnel of the sanctuaries.[33] Elijah officiates at the altar of Mount Carmel (1 Kgs 18); Elisha, too, has connections with the sanctuary on Mount Carmel (2 Kgs 4:25). There were Yahweh prophets at (or near) Gilgal (2 Kgs 4:38), Bethel (2 Kgs 2:3; cf. 1 Kgs 13:11), Jericho (2 Kgs 2:5.15), and Shiloh (1 Kgs 11:29)—all places which presumably had a temple.[34]

Among the tasks incumbent upon these prophets was the religious service on such holy days as New Moon and Sabbath (2 Kgs 4:23), and the collecting of taxes (2 Kgs 4:42). They were thus, in a sense, state officials.[35] Though they had probably joined the ranks of the prophets of their own free will (1 Kgs 19:19-21), or as oblates dedicated by their parents (cf. 1 Sam 1), their own decision had to be endorsed by a royal appointment (cf. 1 Kgs 13:33 'Jeroboam ... made priests for the "high places" from among all the people; any who so wished he consecrated to be priests of the "high places"'; cf. 1 Kgs 12:31).

The official position of the prophets is underscored by the close relations which someone like Elisha entertained with the court. Elisha is based in the capital, the city of Samaria, even though his ministry was largely itinerant (2 Kgs 2:24; 5:3; 6:19). As an advisor to the king (2 Ks 6:9.31), he has privileged access to the highest political and military leadership (2 Kgs 4:13; 8:4). In times of crisis,

---

[33] Johnson 1962: 25-29.

[34] There are scriptural references to a sanctuary at Gilgal (Amos 4:4; 5:5), Bethel (1Sam10:3; 1 Kgs 12:26-33; 2 Kgs 17:28; 23:17; Amos 3:14; 4:4; 5:5; 7:10-17), and Shiloh (1Sam1; Jer 7:12.14; 26:6.9; Ps78:60). On the strength of these references it may be assumed that there was a sanctuary near Jericho as well—perhaps the large altar by the Jordan mentioned in Josh 22:10.

[35] On priests as civil servants see Ahlström's thought-provoking observations in Ahlström 1982: 44-74.

the local leadership, known as the 'elders', also consults with Elisha (2 Kgs 6:32). As a royal supervisor, Elisha himself is not attached to any one sanctuary in particular. He makes a regular circuit of the various sanctuaries; when visiting, he is asked for advice by the local prophets (2 Kgs 2:21; 5:22). Was Elisha to report to the king about the various 'high places' in the land? The biblical text does not say so, yet makes it clear that Elisha acts as a kind of intermediary between the 'sons of the prophets' and the palace. The antagonism between the king and Elisha (e.g. 2 Kgs 6:13) is due to the circumstances; in fact, Elisha seems to have been a kind of minister of religious affairs more than anything else. Also, the king pays Elisha a formal visit when the latter lies on his death-bed (2 Kgs 13:14). In respect to the court, then, Elisha was as much an insider as an outsider.

The ambiguity in the relations between these prophets of Yahweh, led by Elisha, and the palace, results from the clash between the old order the prophets represented and the new order inaugurated by the Omrides. The Omride kings wanted to build a modern state based on the principles of a more or less 'neutral' religious politics, a realistic diplomacy, a liberal economy, and a dynastic kingship. Many citizens had difficulties adjusting to this new order. The conflict over Naboth's vineyard, described in 1 Kgs 21, illustrates the gap between royal politics and ancient customs: over against the prerogatives of the monarch, the landed gentry stuck to the notion of its patrimony being a divine inheritance.[36] The antagonism between Elijah and Elisha, on the one hand, and the Omride kings, on the other, can be seen as the manifestation of the conflict at its religious level. Elijah and Elisha held fast to the theocratic ideal: human rulers were to be chosen directly by God, quite like the religious leadership. To them, the far more 'secular' ideas on which the Omrides had founded their rule were a lapse from the divine order. Eventually, their religious conservatism led to the downfall of the Omrides and to a return, at least in appearance, of the old order. Yet the restoration proved to be in vain: it did not take long before it was clear that many of the changes that had occurred under the Omrides were irreversible.[37]

---

[36] Samuel's warning that a king would 'take the best of your fields and vineyards and olive orchards' (1 Sam 8:15) might be seen as a reflection of the Northern critique of the monarchy. For an analysis of Samuel's anti-monarchic speech, and an attempt to define its *Sitz im Leben*, see Crüsemann 1978: 66-73.

[37] Cf. Ahlström 1977: 47-69. Ahlström argues that Jehu's revolt was purely political in motivation, lacked popular support, and did not lead to the 'purification' of Israelite religion.

Since Jehonadab ben Rechab is associated with Jehu, who himself was supported by the prophets, the suggestion that the Rechabites were a prophetic guild, or at least comparable to one, cannot be dismissed without further discussion. Though the Rechabites are a clan and the prophets a guild, the actual structure of the two groups need not have been vastly different: clans include clients and servants; the prophetic guilds, on the other hand, lived in clan-like manner in one settlement under the authority of one paterfamilias. The self-imposed austerity of the prophets compares to some degree with the Rechabite rejection of agriculture and such luxuries as wine. Prophets, too, it has been suggested, did not use wine: is not the prophet mentioned in a synonymous parallelism with the Nazirite (*nâzîr*; Amos 2:12)? Since the latter had to abstain from wine, the former might well have been in the same position. The parallel between Rechabites and prophets would be even closer still if the hairy mantle of the latter derived its origin 'from a nomadic usage, well known among the inhabitants of the desert'.[38]

Many of the resemblances, however, are more apparent than real. To say that the prophet's mantle is the expression of a nomadic ideal is pure speculation; even if the garment had its origins in a nomadic context, it came to symbolize soberness and austerity in general. And was wine prohibited for prophets? There is no text that says so; only the giving of oracles for wine is condemned (Mic 2:11). Also, the prophets who regarded Elisha as their leader did live in houses—even if they were communal houses. It is begging the question to say that in this respect they deviated from the ideal which Elijah had propagated.[39] Where do we read that Elijah was against roofed dwelling and the building of houses? Nor is there, on the other hand, any indication to the effect that the Rechabites engaged in activities similar to those of the prophets. Jehonadab ben Rechab was a sympathetic observer of Jehu's zeal for the LORD (2 Kgs 10:16)—but that does not make him a prophet. From Jehonadab's endorsement of the revolt of Jehu it may be deduced that there must have been a mutual sympathy between the Rechabites and the prophets—not that they had the same role in Israelite society.[40]

Jehonadab was apparently at one with the prophets in their rejection of the religious pluralism promoted by the Omrides. His

---

[38] Lindblom 1962: 66.

[39] *Pace* Cummings 1979.

[40] Martin J. Mulder has argued that the Rechabites were exponents of a revolutionary religious current also represented by the 'Sons of the Prophets' and, later, Jeremiah (Mulder 1990: 29).

resistance cannot be reduced to mere social factors; it had a religious inspiration. From the personal names born by the Rechabites mentioned in Jer 35 (Jaazaniah, Jeremiah, and Habazziniah) it may be deduced that they worshipped Yahweh (whose name occurs as '-iah' in the anthroponyms) as their god. The impression is confirmed by the narrative about Jehonadab. When Jehu came upon Jehonadab, he invited him to come with him to see his 'zeal for the Lord' (2 Kgs 10:16). Jehonadab consented and became an accomplicc in the demolition of Baal's temple in Samaria and in the massacre of the god's worshippers (2 Kgs 10:18-27). The picture of Jehonadab, then, is that of an intransigent Yahwist. To him the religious politics pursued by the Omrides signified an erosion of the privileged position the cult of Yahweh had enjoyed in the Israelite state. He had a personal stake in the matter: apart from being the national god, Yahweh was also the god of his fathers. Official religion and clan religion coalesced in the case of the Rechabites; hence Jehonadab's strong reaction against the Omride policy.

Jehonadab's response to the Omride politics went beyond his support for Jehu's revolt. Jehonadab is allegedly the one who determined that the clan of the Rechabites were henceforth to strictly observe the habits of a nomadic lifestyle. It is a matter of speculation whether or not the Rechabites had maintained their customs up till the days of Jehonadab; there can be little doubt, though, that Jehonadab did not introduce new rules. Due to Jehonadab's promulgation of ancient custom as a binding rule, however, what used to be a natural lifestyle became, in a sense, artificial. These rules were originally designed to cope with a specific ecological situation. Transposed to a different context, they looked like an anachronism. Yet they were not meaningless; only their purpose had radically changed. In the time of the Omrides they were to serve as a ritual resistance to and, by the same token, a protest against the new culture of religious tolerance. The rules which the Rechabites chose to mark their distances from the contemporary society were not arbitrary; they followed from their nomadic past. In their original context these rules were practical; yet in their function as a symbolical protest they had become entirely ritual: what was once an economic strategy became a social strategy.

The religion of the Rechabites

A word needs to be said about the religion of the Rechabites, as it has been affirmed that they were not originally Israelites. How are we to explain, then, their persistent loyalty to Yahweh? Was theirs the zeal of converts?

This question leads us to one of the most intriguing aspects of Israelite religion. Though it cannot be doubted that, since the days of Saul, Yahweh was the official god of the Israelite state, he was not, so to speak, a native Israelite god. Outside Israel, Yahweh was not worshipped in the West-Semitic world—despite affirmations to the contrary.[41]

The stir caused by Pettinato who claimed having found the shortened form of the name Yahweh ('Ya') as divine element in theophoric names from Ebla (ca. 2400-2250 BCE) is unfounded[42]; the sign in question must be read as *il(um)* or *ilî* '(personal) god'.[43]

Yahweh was not known at Ugarit either; the singular name *Yw* (vocalisation unknown) in a damaged passage of the Baal Cycle (*KTU* 1.1 iv 14) cannot convincingly be interpreted as an abbreviation for 'Yahweh'.[44]

No more truth is there in the proposition that 'Yahweh was worshipped as a major god' in North Syria in the eighth century BCE.[45] The only North-West Semitic evidence that can be plausibly linked to the name 'Yahweh' are the Amorite theophoric anthroponyms containing the element *Yahwi-* or *Yawi-*. In view of their semantic equivalent in Akkadian *Ibassi-*, we are dealing with a finite form of the verb 'to be'. *Ya(h)wi-ila* thus means 'God is present'.[46] Such names do not, of course, attest to a cult of Yahweh among certain Amorites; they merely elucidate the etymology of his name.[47]

The absence of the name 'Yahweh' in West-Semitic epigraphy (excepting the Mesha Stela) agrees well with the biblical evidence on Yahweh's origins. A number of poetic—and presumably ar-

---

[41] Contra, e.g., Murtonen 1951; Garbini 1988: 52-65.

[42] Pettinato's principal contributions on the subject are 1980a and 1980b; Pettinato's proposals have been adopted by Dahood 1981.

[43] So Müller 1981. Müller regards the sign—NI, read—*yà* by Pettinato, as short for—NI-NI = *ì-lí*, 'my god'; see also Müller 1980. Others read the sign NI as il_x, 'god', so Archi 1979.

[44] *Pace* Cazelles 1967: 84; Garbini 1988: 56-57; De Moor 1990: 113-118 ['Ugaritic *Yw* as a deliberate caricature of YHWH'). For a critical discussion of the evidence assembled by De Moor, see Hess 1991. Cf. also Rowley 1963: 49.

[45] Contra Dalley 1990: 29. For a refutation see van der Toorn 1992: 88-90 (with lit.).

[46] Von Soden 1966: 78-88; Weippert 1980.

[47] The point needs to be made as Finet has argued, in two publications, that such names as Yahwi-ilum are to be translated as 'Ilum is Yahwi', thus obtaining Yahwi as a proper name (Finet 1964; Finet 1978). For a critique see von Soden 1966: 177-187.

chaic—texts have preserved the memory of a topographical link between Yahweh and the mountain area south of Edom. In these theophany texts Yahweh is said to come from Seir, from 'the field(s) of Edom' (Judg 5:4). According to the Blessing of Moses Yahweh comes from Sinai, 'dawns from' Seir, and 'shines forth' from Mount Paran (Deut 33:2). Elsewhere God is said to come from Teman and Mount Paran (Hab 3:3). The reference to 'Yahweh of Teman' in one of the Kuntillet 'Ajrud inscriptions is an extra-biblical confirmation of the topographical connection.[48]

All of these places—Seir, Mount Paran, Teman, and Sinai—are in or near Edom. 'Seir' is the biblical name for part of the country of Edom, and developed into a synonym for Edom.[49] 'Mount Paran' cannot be localized with certainty. If it was somewhere in the 'wilderness of Paran', it must be located West of Edom and South of Judah; the name survives as Jebel Fârân, a mountain area 80 km West of Petra.[50] 'Teman' seems to have designated the northern part of Edom and also, in biblical usage, Edom as a whole.[51] Mount Sinai, finally, often located in the Sinai peninsula, was actually in southern Edom or northern Midian.[52]

The biblical evidence on the topographical background of Yahweh is supported by the reference to 'the land of the Shasu-beduins of Yahu' (*t3 s3sw jhw3*) in two Egyptian texts[53], one from the reign of Amenophis III (first part of the 14th cent. BCE)[54] and one from the reign of Ramses II (13th cent. BCE)[55]. In the Ramses II list, the name occurs in a context which also mentions Seir (assuming that *s'rr* stands for *s'r*). It may be tentatively concluded that these 'Shasu-beduins of Yahu' were at home in the area of Edom and Midian.[56]

By the 14th century BCE, then, before the cult of Yahweh had reached Israel, groups of Edomite and Midianite nomads worshipped Yahweh as their god. Since attestations to an Edomite-Midianite cult of Yahweh precede the evidence of an Israelite cult of Yahweh, and in view of the fact that the biblical sources say that

---

[48] The text speaks of *[y]hwh[.]tymn.wl'srt[h]*, 'Yahweh of Teman and his Asherah'. For the interpretation see Emerton 1982: 13.
[49] Knauf 1992a.
[50] Baumgartner 1983: 860a; Hamilton 1992.
[51] Knauf 1992b.
[52] Cross 1988.
[53] Giveon 1971: nos. 6a, 16a.
[54] Herrmann 1967.
[55] Fairman 1939.
[56] *Pace* Weinfeld 1987: 304. For a fuller discussion of the evidence see Weippert 1974. For an alternative location see Astour 1979.

Yahweh came from the south, it must be supposed that Yahweh became a major god in Israel due to Edomite-Midianite influence.

There is reason to believe that the 'Edomite connection' was established in North Israel. It is not mere coincidence that the references to Yahweh's origins from the South occur predominantly in texts from the Northern Kingdom. Instructive in this respect is the comparison between the Song of Deborah and Psalm 68. The Psalm is a partial rewriting of the Song (or pieces of the Song) from a Judaean perspective, as the reference to the temple in Jerusalem shows (Ps 68:30[ET 29]). In verse 8[ET 7] of the Psalm, the mention of Seir and Edom (so in Judg 5:4) has been dropped and replaced by inoffensive phrases: 'When thou didst go forth from Seir' became 'When thou didst go forth before thy people'; 'When thou didst march from the Field of Edom' was changed into 'When thou didst march through the wilderness'. The 'tribe' of Judah is conspicuously missing in the Song of Deborah—which gives fuel to the assumption of its northern origin. Similar observations might be made about Deut 33:2-5 and Hab 3:2-15. Kuntillet 'Ajrud, where an inscription mentioning 'Yahweh of Teman' turned up, was an outpost of North Israel, too. Paradoxically, the belief that Yahweh came from the South was at home in the North.[57]

A combination of these data with the fact that the Rechabites and the Kenites were by origin from the area between Judah and Edom leads to the hypothesis that it was these non-Israelite groups that were instrumental in introducing the cult of Yahweh in Israel. The idea that the cult of the one who became the national god of Israel was originally propagated by non-Israelites may seem astonishing; it would be more astonishing still had the Israelites (or the proto-Israelites), most of whom were of Canaanite extraction, spontaneously begun to worship a god unknown in that area. Among the early Israelites in the central hill country there were enclaves of various other peoples: there were, amongst others, Gibeonites, Edomites, Kenites—and Rechabites. The origins of Israelite Yahwism is to be sought among one or more of such groups.

The explanation here offered is in fact a new version of the so-called 'Kenite' hypothesis. One of the first to advance this view on the origins of Yahweh was the Dutch historian of religion, Cornelis P. Tiele. In 1872 he characterized Yahweh historically as 'the god of the desert, worshipped by the Kenites and their close relatives

[57] Axelsson 1988.

before the Israelites'.[58] The idea was adopted and elaborated by Bernard Stade in his *Geschichte des Volkes Israels*, which appeared in 1887.[59] The theory has won considerable support, also among modern scholars.[60]

In its classical form the hypothesis assumes that the Israelites were acquainted with he cult of Yahweh through Moses. Moses' father-in-law Hobab, according to an old tradition (Judg 1:16; 4:11; cf. Num 10:29), was a Midianite priest (Exod 2:16; 3:1; 18:1) who worshipped Yahweh (see e.g. Exod 18:10-12). He belonged to the Kenites (Judg 1:16; 4:11), a branch of the Midianites.[61] By way of Hobab and Moses, then, the Kenites were the mediators of the cult of Yahweh.[62]

The strength of the Kenite hypothesis is the link it establishes between different but converging sets of data: The absence of Yahweh from West-Semitic epigraphy; Yahweh's topographical link with the area of Edom (which may be taken to include the territory of the Midianites); the 'Kenite' affiliation of Moses; and the positive evaluation of the Kenites in the Bible. Yet there are weaknesses, too: the main one being a disregard for the 'Canaanite' origins of Israel. The view that, under the influence of Moses, the Israelites became Yahwists during their journey through the desert, and then brought their newly acquired religion with them to the Palestinian soil, neglects the fact that the majority of the Israelites were firmly rooted in Palestine. The historical role of Moses, moreover, is highly problematic. It seems more prudent not to put

---

[58] 'Jahveh ... is de god der woestijn, door de Kenieten en hun naaste verwanten reeds vóór hen [=Israel] vereerd ...', (Tiele 1872: 559). Tiele's idea found its way to other scholars through the French translation of his work (Tiele 1882: 350-351). Tiele does not refer to F.W. Ghillany who in 1862, writing under the pseudonym 'Richard von der Alm', published his *Theologische Briefe an die Gebildeten der Deutschen Nation*, in which he defended the view that Yahweh the god of the Kenites was a sun-god, worshipped under the form of a metal image (Vol. 1: 216, 480). Cheyne (1903) observes that Ghillany may have been the first to advance the Kenite hypothesis, but that Tiele has earned the honour of being the first to present the hypothesis (independently from Ghillany, apparently) in an acceptable form.

[59] Stade 1887: 130-131. For a history of the hypothesis and its reception see Rowley 1950: 149-160; Rowley 1963: 50-58.

[60] See, e.g., Wensinck 1941; Eerdmans 1947: 15-19; Rowley 1950: 149-160; Gunneweg 1964; Schmidt 1983: 110-118; Mettinger 1990: 408-409; Weinfeld 1987.

[61] So Rowley 1950: 152-153; Dumbrell 1975.

[62] For presentations of the 'Kenite hypothesis' see e.g. De Vaux 1971: 313-321 [with a critique]; Albertz 1992: 82-84. A modified version of the hypothesis is formulated by Halpern 1992: 20-21. In support of some of his statements Halpern refers to an unpublished paper by Cross—now published, see Cross 1988.

too much weight on the figure of Moses. It is only in later tradition that he came to be the legendary ancestor of the Levitical priests and a symbol of the 'Yahweh-alone' movement; his real importance remains in the dark.

If the Kenite hypothesis is to be maintained, then, it is only in a modified form. Though it is highly plausible that the Kenites (and the Midianites and the Rechabites may be mentioned in the same breath) introduced Israel to the worship of Yahweh, it is unlikely that they would have done so outside the borders of Israel. Both Kenites and Rechabites are mentioned as dwelling in North Israel at an early stage; so are the Gibeonites, who are ethnically related to the Edomites.[63]

It must be supposed that these groups transmitted the cult of Yahweh to the Israelites after they had entered the Israelite territory. Owing to their association with the early political leadership (notably Saul) they even succeeded in raising Yahweh to the status of national deity.[64] Once the cult of Yahweh had attained such glory, it was bound to spread among other sections of the population.

If the above reconstruction can be accepted, the Rechabites were among the oldest strains in the Israelite population to have worshipped Yahweh. Yahweh was the god of their fathers, whom they had worshipped in the land of Edom, long before they came to Israel. In view of their religious background, then, it will not do to say that the Rechabites were simply attached to, or nostalgic for, their nomadic way of life by upholding the rule of Jehonadab. They associated that lifestyle with their religious identity; not because they took it as a reference to the Exodus or the Journey through the Desert, but as a reminder of their own distinctive past. It came to stand a symbol for their unswerving devotion to Yahweh—and to Yahweh alone.

---

[63] There is a remarkable overlap in the personal names attributed in 1 Chr 2:50-55 to the Gibeonites (including the inhabitants of Chephirah, Beeroth, and Kiriath-jearim—with Gibeon the constituents of the Gibeonite enclave, according to Josh 9:17) and those given in the Edomite genealogies in Gen 36. For the ethnic identity of the Gibeonites see also Blenkinsopp 1972: 14-27.

[64] Van der Toorn 1993.

The Rechabites after Jehonadab

After the mention of Jehonadab ben Rechab as the accomplice of Jehu (2 Kgs 10) the records remain silent about the Rechabites for about 250 years. It is not until the time of Jeremiah that the Rechabites surface again in our sources. Then we learn of the rule of Jehonadab—an information we used in the reconstruction of the Rechabite phenomenon under the Omrides. Owing to the data provided by Jer 35 it is possible to add a few pieces to the puzzle of the Rechabites.

It is necessary, first, to pause for a moment to ponder the significance of Jehonadab's rule for the Rechabite community in Jerusalem. Around 600 BCE, roughly the period in which the body of our text is to be situated ('in the days of Jehoiakim', i.e. between 609-598 BCE), the Rechabite customs were doubly out of place. Designed as a practical way of life to cope with the circumstances of desert nomadism, the lifestyle of the Rechabites acquired a new significance as Jehonadab turned it into a means of symbolical resistance against the religious pluralism promoted by the Omrides. In Jerusalem the Rechabites lived neither in the desert nor in the society created by the Omrides. Nevertheless they continued to live by Jehonadab's rule. Their customs, apparently, had acquired another dimension yet. This third layer in their meaning is related to their function as identity markers. Even under the dynasty of Jehu (which lasted for over a hundred years) the Rechabite rule had lost much of its significance as a rite of resistance. If it was nonetheless maintained, it was because it came to serve primarily as a means of group identification.

The culture against which Jehonadab had been reacting was that of pluralism. Pluralism itself was not new in Israel; it had existed as long as the Israelites themselves. Yet with the Omrides it had acquired what amounted to an official certificate. In an effort to lift the Israelite state above the level of a primitive theocracy, the Omrides supported the cults of both Yahweh and Baal. The administration tried to win the support of the various societal factions on a basis of equality. Though Jehu's coup promised a return to the old order in which Jahwistic groups were privileged above others, the expected changes failed to materialize. The effects of the Omride politics proved to be lasting. As a matter of consequence the Rechabites came to be perceived as one group among so many others. While their god had formerly been promoted as the principal god of Israel, he now had to share that position, in fact if not in theory, with Baal. At the same time the Rechabites seem to have lost the position of power and influence which Jehonadab possessed. In his days the Rechabites were a force to be reckoned with; hence Jehu's anxiety to win their support for his revolution (2 Kgs 10:15). In the days of Jeremiah, however, the Rechabites had dwindled to an insignificant group of people. Their contemporaries regarded them as a curiosity.

As the Rechabites became a minority with an almost negligible influence, the discipline imposed by Jehonadab slowly changed its meaning. Though it remained a silent protest against the dominant culture, its quality as an identity marker came increasingly to the fore. The change, of course, was gradual. Also in Jehonadab's time the Rechabite rule had been a means of self-assertion; 250 year later, the lifestyle still was a critical comment on the contemporary society. Yet the element of self-assertion and self-definition had come to dominate. The Rechabites had hardly the power to be looked upon as subversive; their concern now was not to lose their identity. In the transmission of Jehonadab's rule, religion and lifestyle combined to create and maintain the group identity. Group beliefs and group customs were closely interwoven. It was sheerly impossible to abolish one element without damaging the other.

The concern for a Rechabite identity was primarily a Rechabite concern—not of their surroundings. As a matter of consequence the audience to which the behaviour was to be displayed did not remain the same. As the customs became ritualized they acquired a demonstrative dimension. As long as resistance was their aim the rites were addressed to the out-group. Formally, the latter remained the audience when the Rechabite lifestyle subtly shifted from a ritual resistance into a ritual self-assertion. Yet they were not the real target. The ritualized self-assertion of the Rechabites was more a message to themselves than to the world about them: they were their own audience. The observation of Jehonadab's rule had become the visible sign of their loyalty to the faith of their fathers. Their lifestyle was in fact a demonstration of identity to the in-group.

The transformations in the function of the Rechabite lifestyle were not without consequences for the nature of the Rechabites as a group. Ancestral customs, designed to cope with a life in the desert, changed into a symbol of resistance, later to become an identity-marker: the lifestyle that was adopted as a means of physical survival came to be a means of social survival. As a matter of consequence, the identity of the group was no longer founded on common descent, but on the collective observation of a specific ritualized behaviour. Considering the small numbers of Rechabites in Jeremiah's days (if the indications in Jer 35 may be relied upon), there must have been people of Rechabite descent that did not belong to the Rechabite community. When Rechabite lifestyle came to determine Rechabite identity, those who rejected the lifestyle lost the identity. There may have been others, however, though not from a Rechabite lineage, that joined the group by submitting to its discipline. The relations between members of the community were still described in terms of kinship: the Rechabites were a 'house' with a 'father' (Jer 35). Yet the terminology cannot obscure the fact that the society of the Rechabites had taken on the characteristics of a religious community—or a 'religious sect', to use a much-abused term.[65]

To some degree the development of the Rechabite community mirrors the development in the use of the term 'Israel'. The nature of this development is captured in the title of a famous study by Antonin Causse, published in 1937: *Du group ethnique à la communauté religieuse.* Though neglected for a good many years, Causse's work is now increasingly being recognized as a major contribution to biblical scholarship.[66] It is one of the unmentioned sources of inspiration of Gösta W. Ahlström in his study of the significance of the name 'Israel'. Ahlström concludes that the name Israel was first a territorial name, then a political designation, and eventually a religious name.[67] In distinction from Causse, modern scholarship stresses the fact that Israel was not originally an ethnic designation. In that respect, the history of its use differs from that of the Rechabites. The *tertium comparationis,* of course, is the gradual metamorphosis of a group defined by common descent, habitat, or government, into one defined by common religion.

It is as a religious group that the Rechabites surface again in sources dealing with the Period of the Second Temple. The prime witness for this development is, once again, to be found in Jer 35. The promise to the Rechabites in Jer 35:18-19 is most likely post-exilic.[68] It refers to the religious prerogatives of the Rechabites in the post-exilic priestly state. The specific capacity in which they were active is in doubt: Abramsky regards them as sect similar to the later Essenes[69]; Kittel believes they were scribes[70]; and McKane

---

65 Thus, e.g., Montgomery & Gehman 1951: 411.
66 See Kimbrough 1978. Cf. the survey by Mayes 1989.
67 Ahlström 1986.
68 Abramsky 1971: 1611-1612; Abramsky 1967; Cornill 1905: 386-387; McKane 1988.
69 Abramsky 1967.
70 Kittel 1905: 482.

thinks they were a group of priests.[71] Targum Jonathan interprets the promise as a reference to sacerdotal service[72], and Jewish tradition has it that the Rechabites came to be connected with the temple by connubial ties with priestly families. The specific reference to the Rechabites in the Greek version of Ps 70 (LXX Ps 71) probably means that post-exilic tradition situated the Rechabites in circles of the Levite temple singers. Rechabite cult personnel are also referred to in Eusebius' *Ecclesiastical History* (II.23.17).[73]

Though the scattered data are not unanimous, they do suggest that the Rechabites survived as a religious community.[74]

Conclusions

The study of the Rechabites leads to a few specific, and some more general conclusions. Let me begin with the ones concerning the place of the Rechabites in the Israelite religion.

The history of Israelite religion is the history of the interaction of different religious groups and traditions in a culture that was neither politically nor cultically unified. The Rechabites were one of these groups. Linked with the political and religious establishment in North Israel, they were confronted with a severe decrease in position and influence under the Omride dynasty. The Omrides endeavoured to base their politics on the concept of a neutral state; the state continued to support religious institutions only on a basis of equality: Yahweh was no longer the only national deity, since that would imply a kind of favouritism. The latent pluralism of Israelite society was thus openly endorsed and propagated by the state. The Rechabites resisted. They began to emphatically observe their ancestral customs; not because this lifestyle was best suited to their occupational activities, but as a means of symbolical opposition. Their lifestyle was a message to their surroundings: a message of protest and resistance.

In the course of time the rule of the Rechabite changed from a symbolical means of resistance into an identity-marker. The religious side of that identity should not be played off against its social

[71] McKane 1988.

[72] Sperber 1962: 220 *l' ypswq gbr lywndb br rykb msmys qdmy kl ywmy'*.

[73] 'And while they were thus stoning him one of the priests of the sons of Rechab, the son of Rechabim, to whom Jeremiah the prophet bore witness, cried out ...' (tr. Kirsopp Lake; Loeb Classical Library 153).

[74] For a survey of late and post-biblical references see Abramsky 1967; Pope 1962: 16.

side. In antiquity—and also today, in many ways— religious identity cannot be easily separated from social identity. It would be equally wrong to reduce the Rechabites to a phenomenon of social resistance[75], as it would be to define them as an order of religious fanatics[76]. They were neither the one nor the other. In the time of Jeremiah, the Rechabites were a socially distinct minority group with religious convictions that are part of their identity. As a counter-culture they opposed both social and religious facets of the dominant culture. It is quite possible that they strongly disliked the urban character which the Israelite civilisation had developed—though even Jerusalem at the time would seem like a modest settlement to the modern observer. Yet to the Rechabites the rejection of the city was not just a social statement; it was also directed against the religious pluralism which in their eyes characterized urban life.

Parallels to the Rechabites are manifold. A few examples may be instructive, as they can retrospectively illuminate the social mechanisms behind the Rechabite behaviour. The survival of ancient customs in a new context is a frequent phenomenon. Having lost their original function they develop a new, often symbolic, one. Vestiary codes of different professional groups are a case in point. Why do practitioners of the law dress in mediaeval costume? Not because it is best suited to the atmospheric conditions in court, but to signal their identity as ministers of justice. Similar observations would hold good for other professional groups. The parallel with the Rechabites concerns the ritualization of originally instrumental forms of behaviour. Ways of life originally designed to cope with a life in the desert acquire ritual significance in an agricultural culture.

Subcultures such as certain youth groups furnish us with a parallel to the Rechabites in another respect. Sociological research among such groups shows that they too often practise rites of style that are meant to mark their distance from the dominant culture, as well as to signal their separate identity. Their behaviour, consisting of a code of dress, speech, and social manners, is a form of non-political—in fact: ritual—resistance.[77]

What links such youth cultures to the Rechabites, too, is their minority position. They act the way they do because they are not in a position of power. That is why the need for self-assertion is strong, and the chances to do so politically are small. In the case of

---

[75] *Pace* Frick *et alii*.
[76] *Pace* Budde and disciples.
[77] See Hall & Jefferson 1976: 47; Hebdige 1979: 17-19, 133.

such youth subcultures, too, the dissent is often social as well as ideological.

These comparisons could be multiplied and would serve only to confirm the central propositions made in this study. From the particular case of the Rechabites some general conclusions can be tentatively drawn. They are essentially two. What has become evident, on the one hand, is the mechanism of ritualization of traditional rules. The latter lose their original function, and acquire mainly demonstrative value. Ritual, indeed, requires an audience; so does ritual behaviour. The behavioral code of the Rechabites does not fulfil its purpose unless it be witnessed. If need be the actors can be their own audience, as happens in many rituals the world over. Yet in rituals designed to identify their actors over against other social groups, the presence of the latter—at least their virtual presence—is a precondition for the rites to be effective. Here it would be interesting—assuming such a thing would belong to the realm of practical possibility—to see what rites disappear in the absence of an audience, and what rites on the contrary do flourish in a situation of religious pluralism. In a pluralist situation rituals are performed by subcultures; in addition to their communicative value for the ritual actors themselves, they convey a message to the non-performers as well: they demonstrate the identity of the performing group. That is why such rites are often ostentatious: they are meant to be noticed.

The second aspect of the case of the Rechabites that may have a more general application is the role of ritual self-demarcation as a substitute of actual power. In the reconstruction here proposed, the ritual code of behaviour of the Rechabites was introduced (or emphatically reaffirmed) as the group lost its privileged position in Israelite society. Only when it became marginalized did it develop the need for symbolical self-assertion. Does this need vanish in a situation in which a minority group enjoys a prominent position? Is the willingness to adapt to new circumstances and surroundings proportional to the degree of security these surroundings offer? Such and similar questions are suggested by a study of the Rechabites. Comparative research, such as done in the context of this volume, must eventually provide the answers.

References

Abramsky, S., 1967, 'The House of Rechab', in *Eretz-Israel 8: E.L. Sukenik Memorial Volume* (Jerusalem): 255-264.76*.

Abramsky, S., 1971, 'Rechabites', in *Encyclopaedia Judaica* (Jerusalem) vol. 13: 1611-1612.

Ahlström, G.W., 1977, 'King Jehu—A prophet's mistake', in Merrill & Overholt 1977: 47-70.

Ahlström, G.W., 1982, *Royal administration and national religion in Ancient Palestine*. Leiden: Brill.

Ahlström, G.W., 1986, *Who were the Israelites?* Winona Lake: Eisenbrauns.

Ahlström, G.W., 1993, *The history of Ancient Palestine from the Palaeolithic period to Alexander's conquest*. Sheffield: Sheffield Academic Press (= JSOT Supplement Series, 146).

Albertz, R., 1992, *Religionsgeschichte Israels in alttestamentlicher Zeit; vol. 1.* Göttingen: Vandenhoeck & Ruprecht.

Alt, A., 1951, 'Das Königtum in den Reichen Israel und Juda', in *Vetus Testamentum* 1: 2-22 (= reprinted in Alt 1953: 116-134).

Alt, A., 1953, *Kleine Schriften, vol. 2.* München: C. H. Beck.

Alt, A., 1954, *Der Stadtstaat Samaria*. Berlin: Akademie-Verlag (= reprinted in Alt 1959).

Alt, A., 1959, *Kleine Schriften, vol. 3.* München: C. H. Beck.

Altman, A., (ed.) 1966, *Biblical motifs: origins and transformations*. Cambridge (Mass.).

Archi, A., 1979, 'The Epigraphic Evidence from Ebla and the Old Testament', in *Biblica* 60: 556-566.

Astour, M., 1979, 'Yahweh in Egyptian topographic lists', in Görg & Pusch 1979: 17-33.

Axelsson, L.E., 1988, 'God still dwells in the desert: a conception characteristic for North-Israelite Yahwism', in *'Wünschet Jerusalem Frieden': IOSOT Congress Jerusalem 1986* (Frankfurt: Peter Lang) 17-20.

Baumgartner, W., 1983, *Hebräisches und aramäisches Lexikon zum Alten Testament*, vol. 3. Leiden: Brill.

Beltz, W., 1974, *Die Kaleb-Traditionen im Alten Testament*. Stuttgart: Kohlhammer (= Beiträge zur Wissenschaft vom Alten und Neuen Testament, 5/18).

Blau, J., 1980, 'Short philological notes on the inscription of Mesa'', in *Maarav* 2: 143-157.

Blenkinsopp, J., 1972, *Gibeon and Israel*. Cambridge: Cambridge University Press.

Budde, K., 1895, 'The nomadic ideal in the Old Testament', in *The New World* 4: 726-745 (also published in German as 'Das nomadische Ideal im Alten Testament', in *Preussische Jahrbücher* 85 (1896) 57-79).

Callaway, J.A., 1985, 'A new perspective on the hill country settlement of Canaan in Iron Age I', in Tubb 1985: 31-49.

Carroll, R.P., 1977, 'Rebellion and dissent in Ancient Israelite society', in *Zeitschrift für die alttestamentliche Wissenschaft* 89: 176-204.

Causse, A., 1937, *Du groupe ethnique à la communautée religieuse: le problème sociologique de la religion d'Israël* Paris: Félix Alcan.

Cazelles, H., 1967, 'Mari et l'Ancien Testament', in *La civilisation de Mari; Compte-rendu de la 15ème Rencontre Assyriologique Internationale* (Liège) 82-86.

Cheyne, T.K. 1903, 'Kenites', in *Encyclopaedia Biblica* (New York: Macmillan), vol. 2: 2658.
Clements, R.E., (ed.) 1989, *The world of Ancient Israel: sociological, anthropological and political perspectives*. Cambridge: Cambridge University Press.
Cornill, C.H., 1905, *Das Buch Jeremia*. Leipzig.
Cross, F.M., 1988, 'Reuben, first-born of Jacob', in *Zeitschrift für die alttestamentliche Wissenschaft* 100, suppl.: 46-65.
Cross, M., (ed.) 1979, *Symposia Celebrating the Seventy-Fifth Anniversary of the Founding of the American Schools of Oriental Research (1900-1975)*. Cambridge (Mass.).
Crüsemann, F., 1978, *Der Widerstand gegen das Königtum*. Neukirchen: Neukirchener Verlag.
Cummings, J.T., 1979, 'The house of the sons of the prophets and the tents of the Rechabites', in Livingstone 1979: 119-126.
Dahood, M., 1981, 'The God Yaa at Ebla?', in *Journal of Biblical Literature* 100: 607-608.
Dalley, S., 1990, 'Yahweh in Hamath in the 8th century BC: cuneiform material and historical deductions', in *Vetus Testamentum* 40: 21-32.
Dearman, A., (ed.) 1989, *Studies in the Mesha inscription and Moab*. Atlanta: Scholars Press.
Dietrich, W., 1979, *Israel und Kanaan: vom Ringen zwei Gesellschaftssysteme*. Stuttgart: Katholisches Bibelwerk.
Donner, H., & W. Röllig 1962, *Kanaanäische und aramäische Inschriften*. Wiesbaden: Harrassowitz.
Donner, H., 1977, 'The separate states of Israel and Judah', in Hayes & Miller 1977: 381-434.
Dumbrell, W., 1975, 'Midian—a land or a league?', in *Vetus Testamentum* 25: 323-337.
Edelman, D., (ed.) 1991, *Toward a consensus on the emergence of Israel in Canaan: papers read at the SBL/ASOR Hebrew Bible, History and Archaeology section, AAR/SBL Annual Meeting, New Orleans 18th November 1990*. Aarhus.
Eerdmans, B.D., 1947, *Religion of Israel*. Leiden: Universitaire pers.
Emerton, J.A., 1982, 'New light on Israelite religion: the implications of the inscriptions from Kuntillet `Ajrud', in *Zeitschrift für die alttestamentliche Wissenschaft* 94: 2-20.
Fairman, H.W., 1939, 'Preliminary report on the excavations at `Amarah West, Anglo-Egyptian Sudan, 1938-9', in *Journal of Egyptian Archaeology* 25: 139-144.
Finet, A., 1964, 'Iawi-Ilâ, roi de Talhhayûm', in *Syria* 41: 117-122.
Finet, A., 1973, *La voix de l'opposition en Mésopotamie*. Bruxelles: Institut des Hautes Etudes Belges.
Finet, A., 1978, 'Réflexions sur l'onomastique de Mari et le dieu des Hébreux', in *Mélanges A. Abel* (Leiden: Brill), vol. 3: 64-78.
Finkelstein, I., 1988, *Archaeology of the Israelite settlement*. Jerusalem.
Finkelstein, I., 1990, 'The emergence of Early Israel: anthropology, environment and archaeology', in *Journal of the American Oriental Society* 110: 677-686.
Flight, J.W., 1923, 'The nomadic ideal in the Old Testament', in *Journal of Biblical Literature* 42: 158-226.
Frick, F.S., 1971, 'The Rechabites reconsidered', in *Journal of Biblical Literature* 90: 279-287.

Frick, F.S., 1977, *The city in Ancient Israel.* Missoula: Scholars Press.
Garbini, G. 1988, *History & ideology in Ancient Israel.* New York: Crossroad.
Gautier, L., 1927, *A propos des Récabites: un chapitre de l'histoire religieuse d'Israel avant l'exil.* Lausanne.
Giveon, R., 1971, *Les bédouins Shosu des documents égyptiens.* Leiden: Brill.
Görg, M., & E. Pusch (eds.) 1979, *Festschrift Elmer Edel: 12. März 1979.* Bamberg.
Gunneweg, A.H.J., 1964, 'Mose in Midian', in *Zeitschrift für Theologie und Kirche* 60: 1-9.
Hall, S., & T. Jefferson 1976, *Resistance through rituals: youth subcultures in Post-war Britain.* London: Hutchinson.
Halpern, B., 1992, 'Kenites', in *Anchor Bible Dictionary* (New York: Macmillan), vol. 4: 17-22.
Hamilton, J.M., 1992, 'Paran', in *Anchor Bible Dictionary* (New York: Macmillan), vol. 5: 162.
Hayes, J.H., & J.M. Miller (eds.) 1977, *Israelite & Judaean History.* London, etc.: SCM Press/Trinity Press.
Hebdige, D., 1979, *Subculture: the meaning of style.* London: Methuen.
Herrmann, S., 1967, 'Der Name Jhw in den Inschriften von Soleb', in *Fourth World Congress of Jewish Studies* (Jerusalem), vol. 1: 213-216.
Hess, R.S., 1991, 'The divine name Yahweh in Late Bronze Age sources?', in *Ugarit-Forschungen* 23 [1992]: 181-188.
Humbert, P., 1921, 'Osée, le prophète bedouin', in *Revue d'histoire et de philosophie religieuses* 1: 97-118.
Humbert, P., 1925, 'La logique de la perspective nomade chez Osée et l'unité d'Osée II 4-22', in *Festschrift Karl Marti.* Berlin (= BZAW, 41): 158-166.
Johnson, A.R., 1962², *The cultic prophet in Ancient Israel.* Cardiff: University of Wales Press.
Keel, O., (ed.) 1980, *Monotheismus im Alten Israel und seiner Umwelt.* Fribourg: Schweizerisches Katholisches Bibelwerk.
Keukens, K-H.H., 1983, 'Die rekabitischen Haussklaven in Jeremia 35', in *Biblische Zeitschrift* N.F. 27: 228-235, esp. 233.
Kimbrough, S.T., 1978, *Israelite religion in sociological perspective: the work of Antonin Causse.* Wiesbaden: Otto Harrassowitz.
Kittel, R., 1905, 'Rechabiter', in *Realencyklopädie für protestantische Theologie und Kirche* (Leipzig: J.C. Hinrichs), vol. 16: 480-482.
Klein, J., & A. Skaist (eds.) 1990, *Bar-Ilan studies in Assyriology dedicated to Pinhas Artzi.* Ramat Gan: Bar-Ilan University Press.
Knauf, E.A., 1988, *Midian: Untersuchungen zur Geschichte Palästinas und Nordarabiens am Ende des 2. Jahrtausends v.Chr..* Wiesbaden: Harrassowitz.
Knauf, E.A., 1992a, 'Seir', in *Anchor Bible Dictionary* (New York: Macmillan), vol. 5: 1072-1073.
Knauf, E.A., 1992b, 'Teman', in *Anchor Bible Dictionary* (New York: Macmillan), vol. 6: 347-348.
Kramer, S.N., 1990, 'The marriage of Martu', in Klein & Skaist 1990: 11-27.
Leeuw, G. van der, 1937, *De primitieve mensch en de religie.* Groningen, etc.: J. B. Wolters.
Lemaire, A., 1987, 'Notes d'épigraphie nord-ouest sémitique (la stèle de Mésha: épigraphie et histoire)', in *Syria* 64: 205-214.
Lemaire, A., 1992, 'Transjordanian epigraphy', in *Anchor Bible Dictionary* (New York: Doubleday), vol. 2: 561-568.

Lemche, N.P., 1985, *Early Israel*. Leiden: Brill (= Supplements to Vetus Testamentum, 37).
Levenson, J.D., 1976, 'On the promise to the Rechabites', in *Catholic Biblical Quarterly* 38: 508-514.
Lévy-Bruhl, L., 1910, *Les fonctions mentales dans les sociétés inférieures*. Paris: Félix Alcan (= English translation: Lévy-Bruhl 1966)
Lévy-Bruhl, L., 1966, *How natives think*. New York: Washington Square Press.
Lindblom, J., 1962, *Prophecy in Ancient Israel*. Oxford: Blackwell.
Livingstone, E.A., (ed,) 1979, *Studia Biblica 1978, I: papers on Old Testament and related themes*. Sheffield: JSOT Press (= JSOT Supplement Series, 11).
Mayes, A.D.H.,1989, 'Sociology and the Old Testament', in Clements 1989: 39-63.
Mazar, B., 1986, 'The early Israelite settlement in the hill country', in S. Ahituv & B.E. Levine (eds.), *The Early Biblical Period*. Jerusalem: Israel Exploration Society, 1986: 35-48.
McKane, W., 1988, 'Jeremiah and the Rechabites', in *Zeitschrift für die alttestamentliche Wissenschaft* 100, suppl.: 119-121.
Merrill, A.L. & T.W. Overholt (eds.) 1977, *Scripture in history and theology: essays in honor of J. C. Rylaarsdam*. Pittsburg: The Pickwick Press.
Mettinger, T.N.D., 1990, 'The elusive essence: YHWH, El and Baal and the distinctiveness of Israelite faith', in *Die hebräische Bibel und ihre zweifache Nachgeschichte: Festschrift Rolf Rendtorff* 393-417.
Meyer, E., 1906, *Die Israeliten und ihre Nachbarstämme*. Halle an der Saale.
Miller, P.D., *et alii* (eds.) 1987, *Ancient Israelite religion; Festschrift Cross*. Philadelphia: Fortess Press.
Montgomery, J.A., & H.S. Gehman 1951, *The Books of Kings*. Edinburgh: T. & T. Clark.
Moor, J.C. de, 1990, *The rise of Yahwism: the roots of Israelite monotheism*. Leuven: Peeters.
Müller, H.-P., 1980, 'Die Texte aus Ebla', in *Biblische Zeitschrift* N.F. 24: 161-179.
Müller, H.-P., 1981, 'Gab es in Ebla einen Gottesnamen Ja?', in *Zeitschrift für Assyriologie* 70: 70-92.
Mulder, M.J., 1990, *De Rekabieten in Jeremia 35: fictie, secte of stroming?* Kampen: Kok.
Murtonen, A., 1951, *The appearance of the name YHWH outside Israel*. Helsinki.
Noth, M., 1932, 'Eine siedlunsgeographische Liste in 1. Chr. 2 und 4', in *Zeitschrift des Deutschen Palästina Vereins* 55: 97-124.
Pettinato, G., 1980, 'Polytheismus und Henotheismus in der Religion von Ebla', in Keel 1980: 31-48.
Pettinato, G., 1980, 'Ebla and the Bible', in *Biblical Archaeologist* 43: 203-216.
Pope, M.H. 1962, 'Rechab', in *The Interpreter's Dictionary of the Bible* (Nashville: Abingdon Press), vol. 4: 14-16.
Rosen, B., 1988, 'Early Israelite cult centres in the hill country', in *Vetus Testamentum* 38: 114-117.
Rowley, H.H., 1950, *From Joseph to Joshua: Biblical traditions in the light of archaeology; the Schweich Lectures of the British Academy 1948*. London: Oxford University Press.

Rowley, H.H., 1963, 'Moses and monotheism', *From Moses to Qumran: Studies in the Old Testament.* London: Lutterworth, 35-63 (earlier published in German in *Zeitschrift für die alttestamentische Wissenschaft* 69 (1957) 1-21).
Schmidt, W.H., 1983, *Exodus, Sinai, Wüste.* Darmstadt: Wissenschaftliche Buchgesellschaft.
Soden, W. von, 1966, 'Jahwe "Er ist, Er erweist sich"', in *Welt des Orients* 3 (= repr. in von Soden 1985).
Soden, W. von, 1985, *Bibel und Alter Orient.* Berlin: W. de Gruyter.
Sperber, A., 1962, *The Bible in Aramaic.* Leiden: Brill, vol. 3.
Stade, B., 1887, *Geschichte des Volkes Israels.* Berlin, vol. 1.
Talmon, S., 1958, 'hmh hgynym hb'ym mhmt aby byt rkb', in *Eretz-Israel 5; Festschrift Benjamin Mazar.* Jerusalem: Israel Exploration Society/Hebrew University, 31-63, 111-113.
Talmon, S., 1966, 'The "desert motif" in the Bible and in Qumran literature', in Altman 1966.
Teixidor, J., 1979, *The pantheon of Palmyra.* Leiden: Brill.
Tiele, C.P., 1872, *Vergelijkende geschiedenis van de Egyptische en Mesopotamische godsdiensten.* Amsterdam: P.N. van Kampen.
Tiele, C.P., 1882, *Histoire comparée des anciennes religions de l'Egypte et des peuples sémitiques.* Paris: G. Fischbacher.
Toorn, K. van der, 1992, 'Anat-Yahu, some other deities, and the Jews of Elephantine', in *Numen* 39: 80-101.
Toorn, K. van der, 1993, 'Saul and the rise of Israelite state religion', in *Vetus Testamentum* 43: 519-542.
Tubb, J.N., (ed.) 1985, *Palestine in the Bronze and Iron Ages: papers in honour of Olga Tufnell.* London.
Vaux, R. de, 1971, *Histoire ancienne d'Israël.* Paris: Gabalda.
Weinfeld, M., 1987, 'The tribal league at Sinai', in Miller 1987: 303-314.
Weippert, M., 1974, 'Semitische Nomaden des zweiten Jahrtausends: Über die *s3jsw* der ägyptischen Quellen', in *Biblica* 55: 265-280, 427-433.
Weippert, M., 1979, 'The Israelite "conquest" and the evidence from Transjordan', in Cross 1979: 15-34.
Weippert, M., 1980, 'Jahwe', in *Reallexikon der Assyriologie* (Berlin: W. de Gruyter), vol. 5: 246-254, esp. 251-252.
Wensinck, A.J., 1941, 'De oorsprongen van het Jahwisme', in *Semietische Studiën uit de nalatenschap van Prof.Dr. A.J. Wensinck* . Leiden: A.W. Sijthoff, 23-50.
Williams, J.G., 1966, 'The prophetic "father"', in *Journal of Biblical Literature* 85: 344-348.
Wilson, R.R., 1977, *Genealogy and history in the Biblical world.* New Haven: Yale University Press.

ISLAMIC PURITY AT ODDS WITH JAVANESE IDENTITY

THE MUHAMMADIYAH AND THE CELEBRATION OF THE GAREBEG MAULUD RITUAL IN YOGYAKARTA

Herman Beck
(Theologische Faculteit Tilburg)

The *Muhammadiyah* was founded in 1912 in Yogyakarta. Ahmad Dahlan (1868-1923), its founder, endorsed the principles of Islamic modernism, which had spread from Egypt all over the Islamic world. One of the main themes in Islamic modernism was the conviction that the backwardness of the Islamic world, compared with the Western world, had been caused by the deviation of Muslims from pristine Islam. In particular, Islam had become distorted by the admission of all kinds of innovations (Ar., *bid'a*) and all sorts of superstitions (Ar., *khurafa*). Purifying the essential elements of Islam, therefore, was the first step towards the elevation of the Muslim peoples. By founding the *Muhammadiyah* movement, Ahmad Dahlan hoped to contribute to the struggle for the restoration of Islam to its original state, which had supposedly existed during the time of the prophet Muhammad and the first four Caliphs.

As for Ahmad Dahlan himself, his aim was to purify Islam by openly opposing various manifestations of innovation and superstition which had crept in, such as the ritual community meals (Jav./In., *slametan* or *kenduren*), the visits to graves and the veneration of saints, the belief in amulets (Jav./In., *jimat*) and heirlooms (Jav./In., *pusaka*) as possessing magical power and sacred energy, and religious relics dating from the Hindu and Buddhist periods in Indonesia.[1] He considered these religious phenomena, often referred to as expressions of *adat*, as *shirk* or polytheism, to be the worst sin possible, in flat contradiction to the most important Islamic doctrine of *tawhid*, the profession of the unity of God. Surprisingly, however, neither Ahmad Dahlan nor any other representative member of the *Muhammadiyah* has, to my knowledge, ever made an official statement condemning the celebration of the *Garebeg Maulud* ritual[2] by the Sultan of Yogyakarta as innovation or superstition. This *Garebeg*

---

[1] Arifin 1987: 105 ff.

[2] I use the definitions of ritual and rite as proposed and agreed by the Research Group on Religious Pluralism (Faculty of Theology, Leiden University): 'ritual is a sequence of customary symbolic actions', and 'rite is a customary symbolic action'.

Maulud ritual is, nonetheless, impregnated with concepts, rites and symbols, which are generally renounced by the *Muhammadiyah*.

In order to trace the motive(s) which held the *Muhammadiyah* back from officially condemning the *Garebeg Maulud* ritual, I will first sketch its celebration in broad outlines, and then try to ascertain, by tracing the origin and the historical development of the *Garebeg Maulud* ritual, which of its features should be considered as integral and indispensable parts of the ritual. Thirdly, I will dwell on some interpretations of, and comments on, the *Garebeg Maulud* ritual and its various parts, made by both *Muhammadiyah* members and others. In section four I will discuss the social environment in which the *Muhammadiyah* developed in early 20th century Yogyakarta. Finally, in the concluding section, I will demonstrate that it is the social environment of the movement which is responsible for its historical and current attitude towards the *Garebeg Maulud* ritual.

Description of the Garebeg Maulud ritual

Traditionally, three Islamic festivals are celebrated each year as grand ceremonies, commonly known as *garebeg*, at the Javanese *kratons*, or 'royal courts', of Yogyakarta, Surakarta and Cirebon. Although the *Mawlid al-nabi*, or 'Muhammad's birthday festival', is not, according to the *shariʿa*, an official Islamic feast, its celebration at the Javanese *kratons*, as indeed elsewhere in Indonesia, seems to surpass in importance, liveliness and splendour, the two official Islamic festivals of *ʿid al-fitr*, or 'festival of the breaking of the fast', and *ʿid al-adha*, or 'sacrificial feast'.[3] In Java these festivals are called respectively *Garebeg Maulud*, *Garebeg Puasa* and *Garebeg Besar*. This present article concentrates on the *Garebeg Maulud* ritual, not only because it is more elaborate than the *Garebeg Puasa* and the *Garebeg Besar*, but more particularly because it is the only one of the three *Garebegs* during which the Sultan and his entourage visit the Grand Mosque of the Yogyakarta *kraton*.[4] A third reason for focusing on the *Garebeg Maulud* ritual is its close, almost inseparable, connection with the *Sekaten*, a festival commemorating the birthday of the prophet Muhammad. The decision to study the *Garebeg Maulud* ritual of the Yogyakarta *kraton* was prompted by the fact that the *Muhammadiyah* movement started in this city.

---

[3] Cf. Hoëvell 1857: 309; Snouck Hurgronje 1893-1894, I: 220ff.
[4] Soelarto 1979-1980: 32-34.

Both Javanese and non-Javanese authors have left us accounts of the *Sekaten* and *Garebeg Maulud* rituals, the most important being Groneman (1895), Soedjono Tirtokoesoemo (1931), Bonneff (1974), Soelarto (1979-1980), Parmin (1991), and Soepanto (1991-1992), all of them providing extensive supplementary information. These reports are summarized here without, however, concentrating on all their minor differences, which are due partly to the fact that the manner in which the *Garebeg Maulud* ritual is celebrated underwent occasional variations. On the basis of these reports and other accounts,[5] the following phases of the *Sekaten* and the *Garebeg Maulud* rituals can be distinguished.

1. Nowadays, the *Sekaten* is preceded by a *Pasar Malam*, or 'fair', which lasts about a month. This novelty has formed a part of the *Sekaten* since the early 1980s and takes place on the northern *alun-alun*, a broad grassy area about the size of four soccer fields.[6] In 1992, the *Pasar Malam Sekaten* was opened by Paku Alam VIII, the governor of Yogyakarta's special territory. At the opening ceremony, a sacred dance, called *Beringharjo*, was performed symbolizing the meeting of the first Sultan of Yogyakarta with the goddess Rara Kidul, the Queen of the South Sea.[7]

Although the *Sekaten* fair has not (yet) been given an obligatory structure, it is characterized by all kinds of economical activities; agricultural products, as well as domestic and light industry products are on sale to the visitors at the *Sekaten* fair. Apart from this commercial aspect, the *Pasar Malam Sekaten* is there primarily to provide various forms of entertainment. In addition to a fairground, many youngsters and adults are attracted to the *Pasar Malam Sekaten* because of the *dangdut disco*, a mixture of popular music, performed by groups of male musicians and female lead singers dressed erotically and provocatively.[8]

2. The *Sekaten* begins officially when the first tones of the gamelan *Kyai Sekati* have been sounded after the *salat al-'isha'*, the 'evening prayer', on the eve of the 6th of *Rabi' I*, which in Indonesia is

---

[5] Abuseri Dimyati dan Aburisman 1984: 16ff; Van Beek 1990: 78ff; Groneman 1896; Miyazaki 1988: 119-129, 185ff; Muhkijab dan Hary Daryanto 1992; Pigeaud 1932; Simuh 1983-1984: 66-72; Soedjono Tirtakoesoema 1932b; Soeratman 1989; Soeroto 1951-1952; Woodward 1989: 205-214; Woodward 1991.

[6] Susanto 1992: 202.

[7] Muhkijab dan Hary Daryanto 1992: 11.

[8] Susanto 1992: 209.

usually known as the *Mulud* month. *Kyai Sekati* is considered to be one of the most sacred heirlooms of the Yogyakarta *kraton*;[9] the *Sekaten* owes its name to this *gamelan* and is one of the rare occasions on which the *Kyai Sekati* is played. The *gamelan Kyai Sekati* consists of two sets of *gamelan*, one called *Kyai Gunturmadu* and the other *Kyai Nagawilaga*. In order to play the sounds with which the *Sekaten* is opened, the *Kyai Gunturmadu* is placed in a building, called *Srimanganti*, to the right of the northern gate of the *Kraton*, while the *Kyai Nagawilaga* is placed in a building, called *Trajumas*, to the left of the same gate. At this stage of the *Sekaten*, *udhik-udhik* or coins are distributed by, or on behalf of, the Sultan.

3. At around midnight, the *gamelan Kyai Sekati* is transferred, via a set route, to the forecourt of the Grand Mosque. The Grand Mosque is located on the west side of the northern *alun-alun*. Again, the *gamelan Kyai Sekati* is divided, the *Kyai Gunturmadu* being placed in a building on the southern part of the yard and the *Kyai Nagawilaga* in a building to the north of the Mosque forecourt. After its transfer, the *gamelan Kyai Sekati* is sounded every day for the next six days, from after the *salat al-'isha'* until midnight, and following the *salat al-subh*, or 'morning prayer', except for the period from Thursday evening until Friday afternoon.

4. The high point of the *Sekaten* is probably the arrival of the Sultan and his entourage at the Grand Mosque, for the reading of the biography of the prophet Muhammad on the eve of the 12th *Rabi' I*. This ritual is called *pasowanan* or *tebiran maulud*, the '*Maulud* prayer-meeting'. At approximately 8 p.m., after the *salat al-'isha'*, the Sultan and his party proceed from the *Kraton* to the Grand Mosque. Having entered the forecourt of the Grand Mosque, the Sultan protected by his golden *songsong* or 'umbrella', goes to both the *gamelan* sets, where he distributes *udhik-udhik* and then continues his way to the Grand Mosque. At the threshold of the *surambi* or 'veranda', which is not actually part of the Mosque, the Sultan is welcomed by the *pangulu*, the highest religious official of the *Kraton*. According to the older reports,[10] the *pangulu* kisses the hands of the Sultan, whereas the most recent account states that he shakes hands with His Majesty.[11] Interesting is Groneman's comment that the

---

[9] Groneman 1895: 5ff; Soedjono Tirtokoesoemo 1931: 18ff; Soepanto 1991-1992: 39ff.

[10] E.g. Groneman 1895: 12.

[11] Soepanto 1991-1992: 51.

Sultan and his suite, unlike the ordinary believers, do not have to wade through the water, which is meant to purify their feet.[12]

When this greeting ceremony is completed, the Sultan enters the Grand Mosque and takes up his position at the place where the *imam* usually stands facing westward, when conducting the Friday service. On this occasion, however, the Sultan and the *pangulu* stand facing eastward, whilst the members of his retinue are seated on the floor of the Mosque. A servant hands a plate of *udhik-udhik* to the Sultan, who then throws some of the coins around the four central pillars of the Grand Mosque; he then makes his way to the *surambi*, where once again he throws some *udhik-udhik* among his servants seated there. Subsequently, the Sultan sits down, his legs crossed and his face turned to the East, in the centre of the western part of the *surambi*. The *pangulu* and the other *'ulama'* sit down in front of the Sultan, their faces turned to the West. The princes, servants and visitors sitting to the right of the Sultan, face northwards, while those sitting to his left face southwards. On the occasion of the celebration of the so-called *Garebeg Maulud Dal*, which occurs every eighth year of the Javanese calendar, however, the Sultan is seated in the centre of the southern part of the *surambi*, his face turned to the North, with his attendants adjusting their positions accordingly. In this case, for example, the *pangulu* faces South.[13]

The Sultan then signals the *pangulu* to start his reading of the *al-Barzandji* version [1690-1765] of the biography of the prophet Muhammad. Before starting, however, the *pangulu* informs the attendants that the biography of the Prophet will be recited at the Sultan's command, so that this reading will have a salutary influence on His Majesty's health, on the magnificence of his reign, on the constancy of his dignity, on his longevity, on law and order in his realm, on his loyalty to Islam and, finally, on his consort and relatives. Then the *al-Fatiha* is said and the reading of the Prophet's biography is commenced.[14] After some time, the Sultan, together with the heir-apparent and the adult princes, leaves the *surambi* for the Grand Mosque where they remain until the Sultan is informed that the reading of the passage of the actual birth of the Prophet, called the *asrakal* or *srokal* after its beginning,[15] is about to be read. The Sultan and his sons return to their places, while everybody

---

[12] Groneman 1895: 12.
[13] Groneman 1895: 53; Soedjana Tirtakoesoema 1932b: 288. Cf. also Bonneff 1974: 142; Soelarto 1979/1980: 93; Parmin 1991: 37.
[14] Soedjono Tirtokoesoemo 1931: 107.
[15] Zoetmulder 1965: 290.

stands in honour of the memory of Muhammad's birth—this is the so-called *Berdiri Mawlid* rite.[16] The reading of the biography of the Prophet ends with the *selawatan Maulud* or 'benedictions for the Prophet'. Finally, the *pangulu* offers flowers (magnolia or jasmine) to the Sultan, who then places them behind his ears, the other attendants following his example.[17] This 'flower rite' is called the *sahos sekar sumping*, literally 'the offering of flowers as decoration of the ear'. At about 11.30 p.m. the Sultan and his suite leave the *surambi* for the *Kraton*.

5. The *Sekaten* ends somewhere around midnight, when the *gamelan Sekati* is brought back to the *Kraton*, once again via a set route.

6. The actual celebration of the *Garebeg Maulud* ritual takes place the following morning, the 12th of *Rabi^c I*. The main elements of the *Garebeg Maulud* ritual are the Sultan's mustering of the *Kraton*-troops and his offering of the *gunungans*, or 'rice-mounds', to his people. However, in order to ensure that the celebration of the *Garebeg Maulud* ritual proceeds smoothly, several rites have to be performed, namely, the *Gladhi Resik* and the *Numplak Wajik*. The *Gladhi Resik* rite is a kind of final rehearsal by the Sultan, whereby he can check whether all the *Kraton*-troops are fully prepared for the *Garebeg Maulud* ritual dress parade. This inspection takes place in the southern *alun-alun*, on the 10th of *Rabi^c I*. The *Numplak Wajik* rite, on the 8th *Rabi^c I*, is carried out as a signal to start the official preparation of the *gunungans*, which are offered by the Sultan to his people during the *Garebeg Maulud* ritual.

7. At 10.00 a.m. approximately, the Sultan and his entourage make their way in solemn procession, via a fixed route, to the *Siti Hinggil*, the 'High Ground'. Here the Sultan will be seated for the duration of the parade of his troops, a symbol of pomp and circumstance to his people. On this occasion, in marked contrast to the *Sekaten* procession (4.), the Sultan is accompanied not only by his spouse(s) and the princesses but, more particularly, by his female servants whose task it is to carry the *upacara* or 'greater regalia' and *ampilan* or 'lesser regalia'.[18] The heavy *pusaka*, however, are carried by male

---

[16] Soelarto 1979-1980: 93.

[17] Soelarto 1979-1980: 93ff.; Soepanto states that a flower is put only behind the right ear.

[18] A description of the regalia and the servants is given by Soedjono Tirtokoesoemo 1931: 74ff.

servants. These sacred heirlooms of the *Kraton* constitute all kinds of pre-Islamic symbolism. On the occasion of the *Garebeg Maulud Dal* celebration even the most sacred heirlooms are carried in procession.

When the Sultan and his suite have taken their seats, the Sultan gives a sign to start the playing of the *gamelan* and the muster begins. Each brigade, in their full regimental colours, has its own distinctive features, as is evident from the different uniforms, standards and weapons. As the troops march past the *Siti Hinggil*, the Sultan remains motionless on his golden throne, his eyes fixed on the *tugu*, an obelisk shaped monument, some two and a half kilometres to the North of the *Kraton*.[19]

8. The military ceremony is followed, after the *gamelan* tune has switched to the *kodok ngorèk*, or 'the frog's croak' melody [20] by the procession of the *gunungan*s. At a normal *Garebeg Maulud* ritual, five types of rice mounds of different shapes, colours and ingredients are prepared and paraded, whilst the *Garebeg Maulud Dal* ritual includes a sixth variety, representing a volcano. When all the *gunungan*s have arrived on the northern *alun-alun*, the troops, in line, fire a treble volley of gunfire. At the same time, the male peasants among the attending crowds crack the whips they have just bought, while the females follow the procession holding small rice knifes, which they have also just purchased.[21]

Without speaking a word, the Sultan, signifies that the *gunungan*s must now be taken to the Grand Mosque, where the *pangulu* will pronounce the benediction. The *pangulu* says the prayer for His Majesty's health, the magnificence of his reign, the constancy of his dignity, long life, and law and order in his realm. The *gunungan*s are then divided among the important personages as well as the ordinary people. After the Sultan has been informed that his command has been executed, he leaves the *Siti Hinggil* for the *Kraton* where he will have a *slametan* with his court.[22] The *slametan*, on the occasion of the *Garebeg Maulud Dal* ritual, is held in the *surambi* of the Grand Mosque.[23]

---

[19] Groneman 1895: 30; Soedjono Tirtokoesoemo 1931: 105f.
[20] Soedjono Tirtokoesoemo 1931: 87.
[21] Simuh 1983-1984: 70.
[22] Groneman 1895: 34ff.; Soedjono Tirtokoesoemo 1931: 90.
[23] Soedjono Tirtokoesoemo 1932b: 287ff.

Origin and historical development of the Garebeg Maulud ritual

In all probability, it is Sultan Agung [1613-1646] who must be held responsible for the way in which the *Sekaten* and *Garebeg Maulud* rituals are celebrated today.[24] It is well known that the Mataram dynasty, which culminated in the reign of Sultan Agung and his successor Mangku Rat I [1646-1677], was of humble, farming descent. This meant that Islam, with its doctrine of egalitarianism, was of far greater advantage to the Mataram rulers in establishing their power, than Hinduism which at that time was the prevailing religion in the region and would have worked against them, because of its adherence to the caste system. Once in power, however, the Islamic Mataram kings left no stone unturned in their endeavours to strengthen their positions by separating themselves from the common people. They created a social gap by introducing both a new style of culture with a special etiquette and a language with different speech levels.[25]

Sultan Agung turned out to be a great innovator, making use of old pre-Islamic religious traditions to establish new palace traditions in honour of the Mataram dynasty in general, and his own reign in particular.[26] Sultan Agung also ordered the composition of the *Babad Tanah Jawi*, the court chronicle of the Mataram dynasty[27], which stated that the Mataram dynasty possessed supernatural power, thanks to the sacred marriage of Senopati, the first Mataram king, and Sultan Agung with the goddess Rara Kidul, the Queen of the South Sea.[28] Today, the Sultan of Yogyakarta, heir to the Mataram dynasty, still makes yearly offerings to the Queen of the South Sea, with whom he is thought to be related in a mystical union, in the *Labuhan* ritual.[29] The *Beringharjo* dance, which symbolizes the meeting of the first ruler of Mataram with the goddess Rara Kidul, is still performed as a court ritual. This relation with the goddess, therefore, confirms for all to see that the Mataram kings and their heirs, the Sultans of Yogyakarta, are no ordinary mortals.

Sultan Agung also added some Islamic titles to the traditional Javanese royal titles, such as sultan, Abdurrahman, *sayidin* (*panatagama*), and *khalifatullah*, which are still incorporated in the

---

[24] For this paragraph on Sultan Agung I heavily lean on Moedjanto 1990.
[25] Moedjanto 1990: 125, 135.
[26] Moedjanto 1990: 98.
[27] Moedjanto 1990: 98; cf. also Ras 1985: 7.
[28] *Babad Tanah Djawi* 1987: 81ff, 145.
[29] Simuh 1983-1984: 72ff.; Abuseri Dimyati dan Aburisman 1984: 12ff.

official name of Hamengkubuwana X, the present sultan of Yogyakarta.[30] By adding these Islamic titles, Sultan Agung sought not only the favour of his Islamic subjects, but he also wanted to demonstrate that the right was invested in him to take the final decisions in all matters of a religious nature.

As an Islamic ruler, Sultan Agung faithfully observed the festivals of this religion. By combining them, however, with the traditional *Sekaten* and *Garebeg* festivals, and by incorporating the *gamelan Sekati* into them, he knew how to exploit these festivals for his own glory and prestige, the so-called *keagungbinataraan*, one of the cornerstones of Javanese kingship.[31] It was the celebration of the *Mawlid al-nabi*, or 'Muhammad's birthday festival', an unofficial Islamic feast, in particular, which offered the greatest possibilities. On the one hand, the *Mawlid* festival, which at that time was already widely celebrated, and with great pomp, throughout the Islamic world, could now serve to legitimize and consolidate the dynasty which had organized it.[32] Rulers generally regarded the celebration of the *Mawlid* as an attractive means of testing the loyalty of their subjects and of making propaganda for themselves.[33] The celebration of the *Mawlid* together with the *Garebeg Puasa* were also used later by the Javanese rulers for the twice-yearly tax collection. In my view, however, the most important aspect of the celebration of the *Garebeg Maulud* ritual for rulers such as Sultan Agung and his successors, was the possibility of merging into one ritual the concept of Muhammad as Perfect Man and the ruler as semi-divine and, thus, a Perfect Being. Sultan Agung, on the other hand, tried to bridge the gap which he had created between his Mataram house and his subjects, by introducing the *Garebegs* celebration and, more especially, the *Garebeg Maulud* ritual. These celebrations provided the unifying force between king, nobility and the common people and radiated out to the whole of Javanese society. The strongest bond possible was, and is still, created by the *Garebeg Maulud* ritual, in which the division of food is regarded as a royal *slametan*; it fosters a sense of *manunggiling kawula lan gusti*, or 'the unity of subject and king' or, 'the unity of man and God', necessary for the maintenance of the state.[34]

---

30 Moedjanto 1990: 22, 128.
31 Moedjanto 1990: *passim*.
32 Beck 1989: *passim*; Kaptein 1993a.
33 Beck 1989: 113, 116, 124.
34 Selosoemardjan 1962: 29ff.; Moedjanto 1990: 127.

The rulers of the Mataram dynasty who followed Sultan Agung, continued to celebrate the *Garebegs*, and after the division of the Mataram realm into the two kingdoms of Surakarta and Yogyakarta (c. 1755), both royal courts carried on the tradition of celebrating the *Garebegs* with due pomp and circumstance. If we look at the *Kraton* of Yogyakarta during the colonial rule, we will see that the Dutch dignitaries were also allotted a role in the celebration of the *Garebeg Maulud* ritual. The Dutch governor of Yogyakarta, for example, attended the muster and the procession of the *gunungans*, sitting on the *Siti Hinggil* to the left of the Sultan. Following the division of the *gunungans*, it was customary for the governor to offer a toast to the *Garebeg Maulud*, to the Sultan, the heir-apparent and the Queen.[35]

During the Japanese occupation, the struggle for independence and the subsequent period of national reconstruction, the *Garebeg Maulud* ritual was restricted to such an extent, that it was felt that the *garebegs* had lost much of their splendour and significance.[36] It was even said that 'the elaborate *garebeg* state ceremonies were abolished'.[37] On closer investigation, however, it transpires that it was only a question of cutting-back on certain elements of the *Garebeg Maulud* ritual. During the years 1941-1970, the *Kraton* troop parade was suspended and the size of the rice mounds was reduced. As far as the *Garebeg Maulud* ritual was concerned, the procession and division of the *gunungans* were apparently considered of greater importance than the muster.

In the early 1970s, the *Sekaten* and *Garebeg Maulud* ritual were revived, the late Sultan Hamengkubuwana IX, the inspirator behind the revival, being motivated both by religio-political and tourism-based economic factors.[38] Thanks to Sultan Hamengkubuwana-IX's attitude towards the Dutch during the colonial period and the struggle for independence, Yogyakarta and its surrounding areas was acknowledged as a *Daerah Istimewa*, namely a special territory with considerable administrative autonomy, under the Sultan's rule. Although Sultan Hamengkubuwana IX, by virtue of his position in the national government, almost always resided in Jakarta, he never failed to attend the celebration of the royal ceremonies and rituals in Yogyakarta.[39]

---

[35] Groneman 1895: 35; Soedjono Tirtokoesoemo 1931: 93.
[36] Zoetmulder 1965: 292.
[37] Koentjaraningrat 1985: 369.
[38] Bonneff 1974: 145; Koentjaraningrat 1985: 369.
[39] Kleden 1989: 25.

Sultan Hamengkubuwana IX stressed, from the very beginning of his rule, that he was first and foremost a Javanese and that, as such, he felt obliged to re-establish and safeguard the Javanese features of his *kraton*, of which he was the heart.[40] It was the *Garebeg Maulud* ritual, pre-eminently, which confirmed his *keagungbinataraan*, the glory, greatness and power of his Sultan-ship, demonstrating unequivocally his central position in Javanese culture. The *Garebeg Maulud* ritual consolidated the 'unity between subject and king', essential to the survival of the state. Because Sultan Hamengkubuwana IX had proved his ability to bridge and link tradition and modernity, he also wanted to emphasize the fact that the person of the ruler guaranteed both the preservation of the state and its future prosperity. By safeguarding their Javanese identity, for which loyalty to the Sultan and the court rituals were a prerequisite, the Sultan's subjects could face the future with confidence.

Sultan Hamengkubuwana IX also earned himself the reputation of being a dynamic and progressive statesman, determined to reform and modernize society, thereby awakening the hopes of orthodox and reformist Muslims alike, that the *Garebeg Maulud* ritual could be channelled in the direction of scriptural Islam. Sultan Hamengkubuwana IX and his successor Sultan Hamengkubuwana X seem to have been prepared, at least in part, to meet the wishes of the orthodox and reformist Muslims. In the late 1980s and the early 1990s, they were able to propagate their perception of scriptural Islam by arranging the sale of Islamic books and public recitations of the Qur'an, and by developing missionary activities on the northern *alun-alun* during the *Pasar Malam Sekaten*.[41] It is worth noting at this point, however, that the *Garebeg Maulud* ritual itself has not, as yet, been touched or changed by these reformist ideals.

Interpretations and comments

Clearly, the *Sekaten* and *Garebeg Maulud* ritual form a rich and highly complicated whole, full of religio-political, polysemic symbols.[42] In this section I will discuss some interpretations of the *Sekaten* and *Garebeg Maulud* ritual, without claiming to give an exhaustive analysis of all the possible meanings of the ritual and its various parts. The interpretations are presented in the order of the phases of the *Sekaten* and the *Garebeg Maulud* ritual.

---

40 Soelarto 1979-1980: 11; Kleden 1989: 26.
41 Cf. Woodward 1991: 127.
42 Cf. Geertz 1980: 105.

1. The *Pasar Malam Sekaten* is both a novelty and the subject of severe criticism, the *dangdut disco* in particular. One critic, born in East Java, refers to the Pasar Malam Sekaten as an example of moral collapse, contrary to God's law, and totally irrelevant to the celebration of Muhammad's birthday. He classifies it as a *bid'a haram*, a 'forbidden, objectionable innovation'.[43] The former president of the *Muhammadiyah*, A.R. Fakhruddin, commented more kindly when I interviewed him about the *Garebeg Maulud* ritual.[44] His view, in fact, came close to that of the secretary of the *Majelis Ulama Indonesia DI Yogyakarta*, who stated that he did not object to the *dangdut disco*, as long as *dangdut* groups' behaviour and dress contributed to creating a sense of humility in the minds and attitudes of their audiences.[45]

This difference of opinion between the two Yogyakarta residents and the East Java critic is striking and I think it can only be understood in the light of the fact that most inhabitants of Yogyakarta consider the *Pasar Malam Sekaten* to be an extension of the *Sekaten* and *Garebeg Maulud* ritual, instituted by the Sultan himself. The post-Independence generation of Yogyakarta natives lives in a period of transition from an agricultural to an industrial age. It is no longer attracted by the old-fashioned *gamelan* and *wayang*, which used to give the *Sekaten* and *Garebeg Maulud* ritual its appeal; it is a generation in search of a new identity compatible with the dynamic, modern world of its time.

The *Pasar Malam Sekaten* with its sale of industrial products, its modern entertainment and its *dangdut disco*, offers youngsters what they want.[46] The *dangdut disco* represents corporality, spontaneity and emotion[47], all characteristics of the dynamic and modern world. By adding the *Pasar Malam Sekaten* to the existing *Sekaten* and *Garebeg Maulud* ritual, the Sultan has made it attractive again to a new generation. And at the same time, the Sultan has made the *Pasar Malam Sekaten* part of the *adat*, in the sense of 'the entire framework of social action embracing man, Sultan and God'[48], of the *kraton* of Yogyakarta. The *Pasar Malam Sekaten* is meant to be that part of the *Garebeg Maulud* ritual which symbolizes the perfect compatibility of the Sultan's order with the dynamic, modern world, and none of the native citizens of Yogyakarta would dare to

---

43 Alhamid Alhusaini 1983: 61, 63, 65, 155.
44 Interview of 16.06.1993.
45 Susanto 1992: 212.
46 Cf. Soeratman 1989: 4, 11.
47 Cf. Susanto 1992: 220.
48 Freely rendered from Geertz 1980: 51.

reject this conception. It should also be noted in this context, therefore, that no comments against the *Beringharjo* dance, instituted on the Sultan's instructions, have been heard.

2. (Ad 2) The *gamelan Kyai Sekati* plays a very important role in the *Sekaten* and it is believed that it was Sultan Agung who incorporated it into the *Sekaten* and *Garebeg Maulud* ritual, the *Sekaten* itself dating from pre-Islamic times. Some of its elements resemble the Hindu *Rajawada* ritual, or 'royal sacrifice; offering of food'[49], and the Hindu *Asmawada*, a ritual with lauds, dances, music and prayers in honour of the ancestral spirits.[50] The *gamelan Kyai Sekati* is a *pusaka*, a sacred heirloom, and is only played during *Sekaten*. Playing the *gamelan* and listening to it, is a controversial point in modernist Islam, especially when accompanied by a female singer. The attempts of the attendants of the *Sekaten* to touch the *gamelan Kyai Sekati* during its transfer to and from the Grand Mosque, in the belief that it possesses sacred energy (Jav., *kasekten*; In., *kesaktian*), rewarding the toucher with a long life[51], are considered highly improper in orthodox, modernist Islam. The belief that the playing of the *gamelan Kyai Sekati* invites the ancestral spirits to attend the ritual, or that evil spirits are kept away by it, is rejected completely by orthodox, modernist Muslims of the *Muhammadiyah* movement.

In *Muhammadiyah* circles, the playing of the *gamelan Kyai Sekati* is thought to have been instituted by Sunan Kali Jaga, one of the nine saints considered to have brought Islam to Java. Sunan Kali Jaga knew the strong attachment of the Javanese to *gamelan* music and he declared, therefore, that the *gamelan* should be used as an instrument to propagate Islam, and he knew that the Javanese people would be easily attracted to places where *gamelan* music was played. Islamic missionaries would be in attendance to inform them about the teachings of Islam, inviting their listeners to pronounce the *syahadatain*, or 'Two Words', the Islamic creed. According to *Muhammadiyah* members, *Sekaten* is related to *syahadatain*, of which it is considered to be a derivative.[52] It is not surprising, therefore, that members of this movement deliver lectures during the *Sekaten* about Islam, in the courtyard of the Grand Mosque.[53]

---

[49] Soedjono Tirtokoesoemo 1931: 1; Bonneff 1974: 121; Soelarto 1979-1980: 14.
[50] Parmin 1991: 22.
[51] Soedjono Tirtokoesoemo 1931: 19.
[52] Simuh 1983-1984: 64ff.; Fakhruddin 1990: 89 ff.
[53] Soedjono Tirtokoesoemo 1931: 21.

As for the *udhik-udhik*, these coins are believed to possess magic power bringing good luck[54], but according to the *Muhammadiyah*, they are the *sadaqa*, or the Sultan's 'alms giving', intended primarily for the Islamic missionaries. And this means that the Sultan is, in fact, stimulating Islamic propaganda.[55]

4. (Ad 4) The role of the Sultan on the eve of 12th *Rabiʿ I* is problematical although all the rites and symbols seem to stress his high and central position. The golden *songsong*, which only the Sultan may carry, is a symbol of his status at the pinnacle of the Javanese social hierarchy, and the positions taken by the attendants at the *surambi*, indicate His Majesty's centrality. Whereas, according to Islam, the *qibla* is the required direction for the *salat* and the recommended one for the *duʿa'*, or 'personal prayer', the Sultan always determines the direction in which all the attendants face during the *duʿa'* and the reading of Muhammad's biography. The *duʿa'* of the *pangulu* before he starts to read the Prophet's biography is striking. Muhammad is not mentioned in this prayer, revolving completely, as it does, around the Sultan and his well-being.

Especially interesting, but difficult to explain, is why the Sultan, the heir-apparent and the adult princes remain in the Grand Mosque during the reading of a certain part of Muhammad's biography, later returning to their places, at which point everybody rises. It may be an expression of the belief that the perfection of the Sultan and his house is comparable to that of the Prophet. Although the rite of *berdiri Mawlid*, or 'the rising in honour of Muhammad's birth', is rejected as innovative by modernist Muslims elsewhere in Indonesia[56], the *Muhammadiyah* of Yogyakarta offers no comment on the matter of the Sultan remaining in the Grand Mosque, nor on the *berdiri Mawlid* rite. According to *Muhammadiyah* members, the attendance of the Sultan at the reading of the Prophet's biography symbolizes the inextricable link between the *kraton* and Islam.[57]

Finally, the 'flower rite' is a typical Javanese rite expressing the purity and holiness of its bearer.[58] The *Muhammadiyah*, on the other hand, tries to focus attention on the life of the Prophet, as an example to be followed by all who listen to the reading of his biography.

---

54 Simuh 1983-1984: 66.
55 Parmin 1991: 67.
56 Kaptein 1993b.
57 Parmin 1991: 68.
58 Soelarto 1979-1980: 93.

5. The 'unity of subject and king' is seen both by *Muhammadiyah* members[59] and others[60], as the principal goal of the *Garebeg Maulud*. Like the *Sekaten*, several elements of the *Garebeg Maulud* ritual also date from the pre-Islamic period of Java. The *Paregreg agung*, or 'high feast of the Buddhist king', for instance, is purported to offer an explanation for its origin.[61] Whatever the case may be, the word *garebeg* in this context means something like 'escorting someone important' or 'the thunderous tramping of many feet'.[62] It reflects the show element of the *Garebeg Maulud* ritual, which is intended to demonstrate the glory, greatness and power of the Sultan to his subjects.[63]

6. (Ad 7) The stipulated route followed by the Sultan and his retinue from the *kraton* to the *Siti Hinggil*, is interpreted as 'a model of the introspective formulation of the mystical path'. All stages and buildings along the route have a special significance.[64] The *upacara*, *ampilan* and other *pusaka* carried in procession, are of great importance and believed to possess sacred energy. I have, as yet, found only one commentary indicating the *Muhammadiyah*'s viewpoint on these sacred heirlooms of the Sultan. It concerns the most holy banner *Tunggul Wulung*, which is only carried in procession during the *Garebeg Maulud Dal* ritual and actual catastrophes. When Yogyakarta was in the grip of an epidemic in 1932, the *Tunggul Wulung* banner was paraded in order to exorcise the evil spirit which had caused the disaster, and again the *pangulu* played a very important role in this ritual. Some modernists opposed this tradition at the time, however, recommending instead the use of modern medical treatment.[65]

The motionless sitting of the Sultan on his golden throne, his eyes fixed on the *tugu*, is considered to be a reminder of an old *yoga* technique on the *linga* of Shiva, proving the existence of 'some traces of *Shiva-linga* worship' in the *Garebeg* ceremony.[66]

7. (Ad 8) The 'frog's croak' melody, the treble gun volley, the cracking of the whips and the use of small rice knifes are all relics of a pre-Islamic fertility cult, which has now become part of a royal

---

59 E.g. Arifin 1987: 51.
60 Selosoemardjan 1962: 30; Bonneff 1974: 126; Moedjanto 1990: 127.
61 Berg 1962: 111ff.
62 Simuh 1983-1984: 68; Miyazaki 1988: 119.
63 Miyazaki 1988: 185.
64 Woodward 1989: 205ff.
65 Soedjono Tirtakoesoema 1932a: 42ff.
66 Hooykaas 1964: 145ff.

ritual. The *gunungans*, however, are the most interesting phenomenon of the *Garebeg Maulud* ritual and its most important element. At a 'normal' *Garebeg Maulud* ritual, there are five types of *gunungan*, of which the cone-shaped 'male' rice mound symbolizes a *linga*, or phallus, while the 'female' rice mound symbolizes a *yoni*, or 'female genital organ'.[67]

The concept of there being a link between a *Garebeg* ritual and the *slametan*, and that the *Garebeg* is in fact an elaborate *slametan*, deserves special consideration here.[68] The idea corresponds, in fact, to Maurice Bloch's theory that '..., at least in Madagascar, the grand royal ceremonials were themselves developments and extensions of ordinary, widespread, commonplace rituals, and it was this which gave royal display its compelling force'.[69] What separates a *Garebeg* from a *slametan*, however, is the fact that the Sultan is the sole host of the *Garebegs*, whereas in the *slametan* the roles of host and guest are interchangeable.[70] The absence of a principle of reciprocity and any form of equality between the Sultan and his subjects, highlights once again the extra-ordinarily high and central position he holds.

If, then, the *Garebeg Maulud* ritual is a huge, royal *slametan*, as implied in the term *hajat dalem*, which is another name for the offering of the *gunungans* to the people by the Sultan, it is even more interesting to realize that the Sultan does not, in fact, offer 'ordinary' food to his subjects, but that he offers both himself and his 'house' as sustenance. This concept is obviously expressed in the symbolism of the five types of *gunungans*; the *gunungan lanang*, or male rice mound, is symbolic of His Majesty as a person; the *gunungan wadon*, or female rice mound, his spouse and consorts; the *gunungan dharat*, or 'earth' rice mound, his sons; the *gunungan gepak* his daughters; and finally, the *gunungan pawuhan* his grandchildren.[71] The 'consuming' of the Sultan and his 'house' reflects the 'unity of subject and king' in its supreme sense. The Sultan as 'sustenance' also explains why his subjects are so eager to acquire a piece of the *gunungans*; the Sultan is, after all, the core of the universe and thus the best guarantee of a prosperous and fertile land.

The only comment made by the *Muhammadiyah* on the *gunungans* is that they are the *sadaqa* of the Sultan to his people. Even the

---

67 Bonneff 1974: 133ff; Miyazaki 1988: 120f. However, cf. also Soelarto 1979/1980: 43ff; Rassers 1982: 294, n. 11; Woodward 1991: 115.
68 Miyazaki 1988: 186ff; Woodward 1988: 66.
69 Maurice Bloch as rendered by Cannadine 1987: 11.
70 Miyazaki 1988: 190.
71 Soepanto 1990-1991: 97f.

governor and Sultan's customary offering of a toast, with the raised glass of wine during the Dutch colonial period, did not provoke the *Muhammadiyah* to make any formal reference to the dictates of Islamic Law.

The cradle of the Muhammadiyah

The description of the *Garebeg Maulud* ritual, its origin and historical development, the interpretations of the ritual both in its entirety and in its various parts, all place the Sultan at its heart. For example, apart from the reading of Mohammad's biography, the Prophet is never actually mentioned by name during the *Garebeg Maulud* ritual. Instead, the glorification reserved for the Sultan alone, and expressed in the concepts of *keagungbinataraan* and *manunggiling kawula lan gusti*, verges almost on *shirk* or polytheism. The *gamelan Sekati*, the *udhik-udhik*, the *pusaka*, the *upacara*, the *ampilan*, the *gunungan* and the eating of the *gunungan* as a *slametan*, can all be regarded as *khurafa*. The *Garebeg Maulud* ritual itself can also be referred to as a *bid'a*, characterized further by all kinds of other *bid'a*'s, such as the *Berdiri Mawlid* rite. We are thus faced with the question of why neither Ahmad Dahlan nor the board of the *Muhammadiyah* ever made any official or public condemnation of the celebration of the *Garebeg Maulud* ritual at the Sultan's *kraton* in Yogyakarta. After all, it was Ahmad Dahlan and the *Muhammadiyah* who wanted to purify Islam by abolishing *shirk*, *bid'a*, and *khurafa*; in 1927, the *Muhammadiyah* even set up a special department, the *Majlis Tarjih*, to achieve it. The answer to the question has to be sought in the social and cultural environment which cradled the *Muhammadiyah* movement in Yogyakarta.

Ahmad Dahlan belonged to the *kauman* milieu of Yogyakarta; the *kauman* can generally be defined as that part of an Indonesian town close to the main mosque and inhabited by devoted, orthodox Muslims. A feature of the Yogyakarta *kauman* is its strong link with the Sultan's *kraton*.[72] Indeed, at that time most residents of the *kauman* had a master-servant relationship with the Sultan, expressed in their title of *abdidalem*, meaning 'court servant' or 'court official'. Ahmad Dahlan's father, for example, was one of the *ketib*s (Ar., *khatib* or 'preacher') of the Grand Mosque, while his mother was a daughter of *pangulu* Ibrohim Kamaluddiningrat and a sister of *pangulu* Fadhil Rakhmaningrat. Ahmad Dahlan himself married a

---

[72] For the *kauman* of Yogyakarta, cf. Bonneff: 1985.

first cousin, the daughter of *pangulu* Fadhil Rakhmaniningrat[73] and in 1890 he was appointed *ketib* by Sultan Hamengkubuwana VII, in succession to his recently deceased father, a function which obliged him to deliver a *khutba*, or 'sermon' in the Grand Mosque once a month. He was also a member of the *Raad Agama Islam Hukum Kraton*, the 'Religious Council of the Kraton in the field of Islamic Law'.[74]

Ahmad Dahlan showed his interest in Islamic orthodoxy very early on in his career, as is evident from the well-documented conflict which surrounded the *qibla*, or 'direction to which Muslims turn in praying', in the Grand Mosque, around the year 1896.[75] Ahmad Dahlan discovered that the *qibla* of this mosque was not facing exactly towards Mekka and he tried to correct it by indicating the proper direction by means of lines drawn on the floor of the Grand Mosque. This initiative, however, was not well received by *pangulu* H. Cholil, the highest servant of the Sultan in religious affairs. It ultimately came to a clash, culminating in the demolition of Ahmad Dahlan's private prayer house on the orders of the *pangulu*. Ahmad Dahlan was finally reconciled to his fate with the help of his brother-in-law, Muhammad Kamaluddiningrat. H. Cholil, on the other hand, was a well-known traditionalist, which was one of the reasons why Sultan Hamengkubuwana VII appointed him *pangulu* around 1880 to replace *pangulu* Fadhil Rakhmaningrat. This Fadhil Rakhmaningrat was Ahmad Dahlan's uncle and had been dismissed as *pangulu* because of his disagreements with the Sultan on certain matters.[76] Both the *qibla* affair and the dismissal of a *pangulu* illustrate only too clearly that the Sultan's subjects and servants were not expected to defy his orders.

In order to bring his ideals to fruition, Ahmad Dahlan founded the *Muhammadiyah* on 18th November 1912, and in the first decade of its existence, the *kraton* circle's opposition to its modernistic principles was strong indeed. The death of *pangulu* H. Cholil in 1914 heralded the first signs of any softening in this approach; the old *pangulu* was succeeded by Muhammad Kamaluddiningrat, Ahmad Dahlan's brother-in-law and kindred spirit. Another turning point came with the abdication of Sultan Hamengkubuwana VII, a staunch *Muhammadiyah* opponent, in favour of his son Sultan

---

73 Bonneff 1985: 182, esp. n. 27.
74 Arifin 1987: 82.
75 E.g., Bonneff 1985: 183; Arifin 1987: 86ff; Alfian 1989: 146f.
76 Bonneff 1985: 185.

Hamengkubuwana VIII [1921-1939], who sympathised with the movement.[77]

It is worth noting here that most of the members of the *Muhammadiyah*'s first central board were *kauman* residents and servants of the Sultan.[78] This tendency to appoint such people to the central board, or indeed to other important and influential positions within the *Muhammadiyah*, continued through the years. Some examples are: the second chairman of the *Muhammadiyah*, K.H. Ibrohim, was a son of *pangulu* Fadhil Rakhmaningrat and thus one of Ahmad Dahlan's cousins.[79] *Pangulu* Muhammad Wardan Dipaningrat—son of *pangulu* Muhammad Kamaluddiningrat, who held this function from 1914 until 1940—was a distinguished member of the highly influential *Majlis Tarjih* of the *Muhammadiyah*.[80] At the same time, in his function as *pangulu* from 1956 onwards, Wardan Dipaningrat was also responsible for the smooth running of the celebration of the *Garebeg Maulud* ritual, witness the description of the 1981 celebration.[81] Finally, AR Fakhruddin, chairman from 1968 until 1990, was the son of Fakhruddin, a *kauman* resident considered to be the spiritual son of Ahmad Dahlan, as well as serving for a long time as secretary of the movement.[82]

Conclusion: Islamic purity at odds with Javanese identity

It is obvious that from its very beginning, the interests of the *Muhammadiyah* movement were, and are, closely bound-up with the interests of the Sultan and his *kraton*, on the basis of family ties, the master-servant relationship and *kauman* residence. This explains why the *Muhammadiyah* did not condemn the *Garebeg Maulud* ritual—history had shown already that resistance to the Sultan and his institutions would have ill effects. The *Muhammadiyah* leaders resident in the *kauman* wanted neither to lose the prestige they enjoyed as *abdidalem*, nor to damage the reputation of relatives holding similar positions.

The spiritual motive behind the decision not to subject the *Garebeg Maulud* ritual to public censure, has its roots in Javanese identity. From the time of the first Mataram kings, the Sultans of

---

77 Bonneff 1985: 185.
78 Bonneff 1985: 186.
79 Bonneff 1985: 186.
80 Bonneff 1985: 199 n. 10.
81 Soelarto 1979-1980 (!): 92.
82 Bonneff 1985: 187.

Central Java have claimed to be both the centre of the Javanese world and the Javanese culture. They had reason enough to adhere to Islam, but it was a religion which could work as a centrifugal force, with all its harmful consequences. To counteract this, therefore, they created with the *Garebeg Maulud* ritual a centripetal force. This ritual was a public demonstration to the Javanese subjects that their ruler was a Muslim, emphasizing at the same time that he was also the centre of their universe.

The celebration of the *Garebeg Maulud* ritual as practised since the 1970s, seems to prove that both Sultan Hamengkubuwana IX and his successor Sultan HamengkubuwanaX have maintained this principle. Although they accepted some scriptural innovations, they simultaneously applied themselves to consolidating their central and prominent positions. If Sultan Hamengkubuwana IX had really wanted Islamic modernism to triumph, he could easily have abandoned the *Garebeg Maulud* ritual, but decided instead to revive and extend it.

The *Muhammadiyah* leaders, with their Yogyakarta *kauman* background, knew that if they openly expressed their disapproval of the *Garebeg Maulud* ritual, on the grounds that it 'soiled' their ideal of a purified Islam, their statement would be tantamount to renouncing their origins. It would place them outside the Javanese *adat*, in the sense of 'the entire framework of social action embracing man, Sultan and God'.[83] It is only by stressing that the *Garebeg Maulud* ritual is a commemoration of Muhammad's birthday, and by reinterpreting some of its parts and neglecting others, that the *Muhammadiyah* can endure the manner in which it is celebrated in the Yogyakarta *kraton*.

When asked how they could reconcile their ideal of purifying Islam with the *Garebeg Maulud* ritual, the *Muhammadiyah* members I spoke to (residents of the *kauman* and the special territory of Yogyakarta), all responded in a fairly standard way : 'It is not our business, but it is part of *Kraton* life'. This answer is diametrically at odds with the opinion expressed by *Muhammadiyah* members, originating e.g. from the Minangkabau or the city of Pekalongan, who when replying to the same question[84] referred to a statement once voiced by Mohammed Hatta [1902-1980]. This former Vice President and Prime Minister of Indonesia, a native of the

---

[83] Freely rendered from Geertz 1980: 51.

[84] I interviewed some members of the *Muhammadiyah* movement, both from Yogyakarta and the Minangkabau and Pekalongan, during my stay in Yogyakarta in June—July 1993.

Minangkabau, is believed to have made the following comment, or something to the effect, on the *Muhammadiyah* movement: 'The Muhammadiyah movement never will be able to realize its ideal of purifying the faith if it does not free itself from its Yogyakarta *kauman* roots'. With this reference to a saying attributed to Hatta, the *Muhammadiyah* members I spoke to from the Minangkabau and Pekalongan, made it clear that they reject the policy of the *Muhammadiyah* leadership of Yogyakarta, which tries to adopt a middle course between Javanese conformism and the exclusivism of Islamic modernism.[85]

As long as the board of the *Muhammadiyah* movement is appointed predominantly from the *kauman* of Yogyakarta, and as long as it clings to its cultural and social environment, Javanese identity will remain at odds with Islamic purity.

References

Abuseri Dimyati dan Aburisman, 1984, *Islam di Kraton Yogyakarta; Laporan Penelitian.* Yogyakarta: Lembaga Research dan Survey Institut Agama Islam Negeri Sunan Kalijaga.

Alfian, 1989, *Muhammadiyah: the political behavior of a Muslim modernist organization under Dutch colonialism.* Yogyakarta: Gadjah Mada University Press.

Alhamid Alhusaini, H.M.H., 1983, *Sekitar Maulid Nabi Muhammad s.a.w. dan Dasar Hukum Syari'atnya.* Semarang: C.V. Toha Putera.

Arifin, M.T., 1987, *Gagasan pembaharuan Muhammadiyah dalam pendidikan.* Jakarta: Pustaka Jaya.

Babad Tanah Djawi, 1987, *Javaanse rijkskroniek; W.L. Olthofs vertaling van de prozaversie van J.J. Meinsma lopende tot het jaar 1721; tweede herziene druk verzorgd en ingeleid door J.J. Ras.* Dordrecht, etc.: Foris Publications.

Beck, H.L., 1989, *L'image d'Idris II, ses descendants de Fas et la politique sharifienne des sultans marinides (656-869/1258-1465).* Leiden, etc.: E.J. Brill.

Beek, A. van, 1990, *Life in the Javanese Kraton.* Singapore, etc.: Oxford University Press.

Berg, C.C., 1962, *Het rijk van de vijfvoudige Buddha.* Amsterdam: N.V. Noord-Hollandsche Uitgevers Maatschappij.

Bonneff, M., 1974, 'Le renouveau d'un rituel royal: les Garebeg à Yogyakarta', in *Archipel* 8: 119-146.

Bonneff, M., 1985, 'Le *kauman* de Yogyakarta: des fonctionnaires religieux convertis au réformisme et à l'esprit d'entreprise', in *Archipel* 30: 174-205.

Cannadine, D., 1987, 'Introduction: divine rites of kings', in Cannadine & Price 1987: 1-19.

---

[85] Arifin 1987: 138.

Cannadine, D., & S. Price (eds.) 1987, *Rituals of royalty: power and ceremonial in traditional societies*. Cambridge, etc.: Cambridge University Press.
Fakhruddin, A.R., 1990, *Soal-Jawab yang Ringan-Ringan*. Yogyakarta: P.D. Hidayat.
Geertz, C., 1980, *Negara: the theatre state in nineteenth-century Bali*. Princeton (N.J.): Princeton University Press.
Groneman, J., 1895, *De Gar_b_g's te Ngajogyåkartå*. 's-Gravenhage: Martinus Nijhoff.
Groneman, J., 1896, 'De Gar_b_g's te Ngajogyåkartå; naschrift', in *Bijdragen tot de Taal-, Land, en Volkenkunde van Nederlandsch-Indië*, 6, 2: 149-152.
Hoëvell, W.R. van, 1857, 'Djokdjokarta: Garebek Moeloed (fragment uit een Reisverhaal)', in *Tijdschrift voor Nederlandsch Indië* 19: 301-328.
Hooykaas, C., 1964, *Agama tirtha: five studies in Hindu-Balinese religion*. Amsterdam: N.V. Noord-Hollandsche Uitgevers Maatschappij.
Kaptein, N.J.G., 1993a, *Muhammad's Birthday Festival: early history in the Central Muslim lands and development in the Muslim West until the 10th/16th Century*. Leiden, etc.: E.J. Brill.
Kaptein, N.J.G., 1993b, 'The *Berdiri Mawlid* issue among Indonesian Muslims in the Period from circa 1875 to 1930', in *Bijdragen tot de Taal-, Land- en Volkenkunde* 149: 124-153.
Kleden, I., 1989, 'The changing political leadership of Java: the significance of Sultan Hamengku Buwono IX', in *Prisma* 46: 21-31.
Koentjaraningrat 1985, *Javanese culture*. Singapore, etc.: Oxford University Press.
Miyazaki, K., 1988, *The King and the people: the conceptual structure of a Javanese kingdom* (Leiden University: unpublished Ph.D. thesis).
Moedjanto, G., 1990, *The concept of power in Javanese culture*. Yogyakarta: Gadjah Mada University Press.
Moedjanto, G., B. Rahmanto, & J. Sudarminta (eds.) 1992, *Tantangan Kemanusiaan Universal: Antologi Filsafat, Budaya, Sejarah-Politik dan Sastra; Kenangan 70 Tahun Dick Hartoko*. Yogyakarta: Kanisius.
Muhkijab dan Hary Daryanto 1992, 'Merayakan Maulud Nabi Lewat Sekaten', in *Pelita*, September 13th: 11.
Parmin 1991, *Simbolisme dalam Upacara Muludan di Kasultanan Yogyakarta* (Yogyakarta: unpublished SI thesis Fakultas Ushuluddin, IAIN Sunan Kalijaga).
Pigeaud, Th., 1932, Vorstenlandsche Garebeg's', in *Djawa* 12, 1: 24-31.
Ras, J.J., 1985, *Het ontstaan van de Babad Tanah Jawi: herkomst en functie van de Javaanse rijkskroniek*. Leiden: Rijksuniversiteit Leiden (= Inaugurale rede).
Rassers, W.H., 1982, *Pañji, the culture hero: a structural study of religion in Java; second edition with an introduction by P.E. de Josselin de Jong*. The Hague: Martinus Nijhoff.
Selosoemardjan 1962, *Social changes in Jogjakarta*. Ithaca (N.Y.): Cornell University Press.
Simuh 1983-1984, *Sejarah interaksi sosial Budaya dan Agama pada Keraton Yogyakarta*. Jakarta: Proyek Penelitian Keagamaan Departemen Agama R.I.
Snouck Hurgronje, C., 1893-1894, *De Atjèhers*. Batavia: Landsdrukkerij—Leiden: E.J. Brill, 2 vols.

Soedjono Tirtokoesoemo 1931, *De Garebegs in het Sultanaat Jogjakarta.* Jogjakarta: Drukkerij en Uitgeversfirma v.h. H. Buning.
Soedjono Tirtakoesoema 1932a, 'De ommegang met den Kangdjeng Kjahi Toenggoel Woeloeng te Jogjakarta, donderdag—vrijdag 21/22 januari 1932 (Djoemoeah-Kliwon 13 Pasa, Djé 1862)', in *Djawa* 12: 41-49.
Soedjono Tirtakoesoema 1932b, 'De viering van de garebeg Moeloed Dal in 1863 in Jogjakarta (18 juli 1932)', in *Djawa* 12: 276-291.
Soelarto, B., 1979-1980, *Garebeg di Kesultanan Yogyakarta.* Jakarta: Proyek Sasana Budaya, Direktorat Jenderal Kebudayaan, Departemen Pendidikan dan Kebudayaan.
Soepanto, S., & B. Sularto 1991-1992, *Upacara tradisional Sekaten Daerah Istimewa Yogyakarta.* N.Pl.: Departemen Pendidikan dan Kebudayaan.
Soeratman, D., 1989, 'Perayaan Sekaten di Yogyakarta: Lampau dan Kini', in *Kedaulatan Rakyat,* October 14th: 4, 11.
Soeroto, 1951-1952, 'Wat is Sekatèn?', in *Indonesië* 5: 244-250.
Stöhr, W., & P. Zoetmulder 1965, *Die Religionen Indonesiens.* Stuttgart, etc.: W. Kohlhammer.
Susanto, B., 1992, 'Dangdut Sekaten: Penguasa, "Agama", dan Musik Rakyat di Yogyakarta', in Moedjanto e.a. 1992: 195-224.
Woodward, M.R., 1988, 'The *Slametan*: textual knowledge and ritual performance in Central Javanese Islam', in *History of Religions* 28: 54-89.
Woodward, M.R., 1989, *Islam in Java: normative piety and mysticism in the Sultanate of Yogyakarta.* Tucson: The University of Arizona Press.
Woodward, M.R., 1991, 'The *Garebeg Malud* in Yogyakarta: veneration of the Prophet as imperial ritual', in *Journal of Ritual Studies* 5 (1): 109-132.
Zoetmulder, P., 1965, 'Die Hochreligionen Indonesiens', in Stöhr & Zoetmulder 1965: 223-254.

CIRCUMCISION IN INDONESIA

MUSLIM OR NOT?

Nico Kaptein
(INIS, Leiden University)

The principal aim of this paper[1] is to elaborate on the background of the gradual disappearance of an indigenous Indonesian circumcision technique. The period I will deal with starts at the end of the 19th century and continues up to the present-day.

'Circumcision' is a collective term which denotes various types of operations on the human genitals, male as well as female. Here I will only deal with circumcision as it is practised on males, because I do not have any original data on female circumcision, which means I am not able to add anything new to the existing studies on the subject.[2] But even in the sense of male circumcision the term is in need of further limitation and specification.

Forms of male circumcision

In his rather unstructured, yet informative study on the subject, entitled *Die Beschneidung bei Mann und Weib*, which appeared in 1931, the ethnographer Felix Bryk gathered all kinds of examples of 'circumcision' from many related and unrelated cultures from all over the globe. Bryk mentions at least 18 different forms of male circumcision, among which he also included, for instance, the *amputatio penis*, the *castratio*, the *extirpatio testiculi sinistri*, the *perforatio glandis*, in which a pin or a bar is pierced crosswise through the penis, and the *implantatio*, in which bells, balls, or all kinds of other objects were inserted under the skin of the glans or the shaft of the penis by operative means.[3] Although most of the data known on these two latter operations refer to the past[4], the piercing of the penis is also recorded in recent times, for instance in Redmond O'Hanlon's

---

[1] My thanks are due to R. Robson McKillop B.A. (Hons.) for the accurate way in which she improved my English.

[2] See e.g. Hicks 1993.

[3] Bryk 1931: 100-101

[4] See also Brown, Edwards and Moore 1988.

bestseller based on his 1983 trip to West Kalimantan *Into the heart of Borneo*[5], while it is also known that in a Dutch hospital in 1985 a jade bead was implanted in the penis of a Malaysian man.[6]

The operation on the foreskin is the form of circumcision with which Westerners are most familiar through references made to it in the Bible, through the presence of Jews who perform it on religious grounds and, especially in Western Europe in recent decades, through the arrival of Muslim immigrants. In fact, this operation can also take various forms, but for the proper understanding of this paper only three have to be mentioned here. In the first place there is the actual circumcision, in which the entire foreskin is removed from the penis, which is called *circumcisio totalis*. This operation is usually carried out by clipping the foreskin in a pincer, after which it is cut off with a knife. The second operation relevant here is the *circumcisio partialis* to use Bryk's terminology, in which only a part of the foreskin is cut off. This operation is also performed with the help of a pincer, albeit only a triangular part of the upper side of the foreskin is clenched and removed; this technique was and still is practised in various parts of the Indonesian Archipelago, and is also known as *excisio*[7] or *praecisio*.[8] Finally, I should mention here the operation in which the upper side of the foreskin is cloven, leaving the glans exposed, although nothing is actually cut off from the foreskin; this is what Bryk calls the *incisio praeputii*. In modern medical terms this is called the dorsal slit. In a traditional setting this operation is usually performed by inserting a piece of wood between the upper side of the glans and the foreskin, which is subsequently cut open lengthwise along the shaft of the penis, using the inserted piece of wood as a basis.[9] In the rest of this paper I will make use of the term circumcision to denote one of these three operations, so also as a collective term, although in a far more restricted sense than Bryk.

Circumcision in Islamic Law

Circumcision (Arabic *khitân*) does not play an important role in the Islamic legal handbooks and its status within the Law differs; some-

---

[5] O'Hanlon 1989[5]: 104.
[6] Nicolai 1991.
[7] Schrieke 1921: 384.
[8] Rumidjah 1979-1980: 24.
[9] See for the various instruments used in Indonesia at the beginning of this century, Schrieke 1921; 1922.

times (e.g. according to Mâlik) it is regarded as recommended (*sunna*), while at other times (e.g. according to al-Shâfi'î) it is regarded as obligatory (*wâjib*). Concerning the nature of the operation it is relevant to quote the opinion of the 13th century Shâfi'ite jurist Abû Zakaryâ' Yahyâ al-Nawawî (631/1233—676/1277), who has always been counted among the highest authorities in Indonesian Islam.[10] This scholar stated that 'as regards males it is obligatory to cut off the whole skin which covers the glans, so that this latter is wholly denuded'.[11] If an adult male converts to Islam, it is not necessary for him to be circumcised if he is afraid of undergoing the operation.[12]

Despite this marginal position in the legal handbooks, circumcision, together with the abstention from pork, can be regarded as one of the most important identity markers of a Muslim.

Circumcision in Indonesia

In 1885, the Dutch ethnologist G.A. Wilken (1847-1891) published an article in which he dealt with circumcision in the Netherlands East-Indies. After having presented many ethnographic data from throughout the entire Archipelago, Wilken concluded that circumcision was an original cultural feature in the Indonesian region, which was already being practised before the advent of Islam to this part of the world. To support this view, he pointed to the existence of the practice of incision among a number of Muslim peoples from the Archipelago, in particular the Javanese and the Gorontalese; because this practice was not an Islamic custom, this could not have been adopted from Islam. Furthermore, he adduced the argument that circumcision was also practised by non-Muslim peoples in the Archipelago and by peoples who had never had any contacts with Islam.[13]

Wilken's thesis was later confirmed by B.J.O. Schrieke (1890-1945) who, supplementing the arguments of Wilken, indicated a pre-Islamic artefact from Middle Java kept in the Batavia Museum representing a phallus which was circumcised. Furthermore, he drew attention to the circumstance that all kinds of practices in connection with the circumcision ceremony were of pre-Islamic ori-

[10] *The Encyclopaedia of Islam²*, vii: 1041-1042.
[11] *The Encyclopaedia of Islam²*, v: 20.
[12] Ibn Qudâma 1401/1981, I: 86.
[13] Wilken 1885: 181-182.

gin. As an example Schrieke mentioned the so-called *kobongan*, the temporary building in which the operation was performed, which he regarded as a survival of the ancient-Javanese house-temple.[14]

From the beginning of the 19th century onwards Christian missionaries in Java were also confronted with circumcision, because the Javanese who had been converted to Christianity continued to circumcise their children. This shows that the Javanese did not regard circumcision as an initiation to Islam, but primarily as a custom which formed part of their original culture. The continuation of this practice evoked different reactions on the part of the missionaries. In the first place, there were missionaries who strictly forbade circumcision, because it was a non-Christian practice. The German layman Johannes Emde (1774-1859) who was active in Middle Java in the first half of the 19th century could be mentioned as an example of this.[15]

Another view was adopted by those missionaries who presented the Christian message by means of the so-called 'assimilation' method. This method aimed to establish Christianity through seeking alliance with all kinds of indigenous concepts and through presenting Christianity as being in harmony with traditional culture[16]. It is understandable that missionaries who thus allowed room for indigenous culture took a more liberal stance in answering the question about whether or not a Christian might be circumcised. Many persons from these circles allowed circumcision as a traditional custom. For instance, this view was voiced in 1933 by the Dutch missionary H. Kraemer (1888-1965), who when discussing the position of Sundanese Christians stated that, among the Sundanese, circumcision did not have a religious significance, and that every Christian Sundanese was free to perform the operation, both on himself and on his children; the operation had, however, to be carried out by a medical doctor and without any accompanying ceremony[17].

A further step was taken by the Sundanese minister of religion, Wesley Mintardja Rikin (b. 1928), who wrote a dissertation on circumcision among the Sundanese, which he defended at Leiden University in 1973. This minister of the *Geredja Kristen Pasundan* ('Christian Sundanese Church') had noticed that from time to time members of his parish in Bogor had their children circumcised. For

---

[14] Schrieke 1921: 383.
[15] Guillot 1981: 57-63.
[16] Rikin 1973: 144; Guillot 1981: 309-321.
[17] Rikin 1973: 155-156; cf. also Schrieke 1921: 442.

this reason, at the end of his dissertation, he pleads for the incorporation of circumcision within his church, with a formally accepted ritual modelled upon the Christian wedding ceremony.[18]

If we return now to the end of the 19th century, we see that at that time three different operations could be carried out on the male genitals among Muslims in the Archipelago: full circumcision, partial circumcision, and incision. From a number of publications it is clear that in Aceh and in Java incision gradually fell into abeyance.[19] In the next sections we will see how this came about.

Meccan fatwas on Indonesian incision from the latter part of the 19th century

Mecca has always attracted large numbers of persons from the Malayo-Indonesian Archipelago, who initially came to there to perform the pilgrimage and many of whom stayed in the Holy City for devotional purposes or study, sometimes for a very limited period, sometimes for the rest of their lives without ever returning to their country of origin. As a group these persons formed the so-called Jâwah colony. We are well-informed about this community at the end of the 19th century, because the Dutch orientalist C. Snouck Hurgronje (1857-1936) devoted a detailed chapter to it in his book on Mecca[20].

As a result of this stay in the Holy City, doubt was cast on all kinds of indigenous Indonesian practises, and one of these was circumcision. The precise nature of the difficulties related to circumcision becomes clear from a number of *fatwas* which have been preserved in a *fatwa* collection from the Jâwah colony in Mecca, called *Muhimmât al-nafâ'is fî bayân as'ilat al-hâdith*, 'The precious gems dealing with the explanation of questions about current topics'. This work is a bilingual collection of *fatwas*, which was published in a lithograph edition in Mecca in 1310/1892. This compilation of religious *responsa* was made by a certain 'Abd al-Salâm al-Âshî (= the Acehnese).[21] It contains some 130 *fatwas* and, in most cases, has the following form: the *fatwa* begins with a question in Arabic, whereupon this question is rendered into Malay (in Arabic script). Next, the answer is given in Arabic, followed by a rendering in

---

18 Rikin 1973: 158-166.
19 Snouck Hurgronje 1893: 440.
20 Snouck Hurgronje [1889] 1970: 215-292.
21 *Muhimmât al-nafâ'is* 1892: 108.

Malay. For the most part, the *fatwas* are signed by the *mufti* who issued them. In many cases this is Ahmad ibn Zaynî Dahlân, who was the *mufti* of the Shâfi'ites from 1871 until shortly before his death in Medina in 1886, and who received questions from Shâfi'ite Muslims from all over the world.[22] Apart from Ahmad Dahlân, other *muftis* also feature in the collection. From the form of the *fatwas*, as well as from their contents, it is clear that these opinions were asked by persons who were indigenous to the Netherlands East-Indies. In short, one might say that the *Muhimmât al-nafâ'is* reflects all kinds of difficulties certain members of the Jâwah colony in Mecca at the end of the 19th century experienced in the religious domain and about which they consulted the Meccan religious authorities.

In 10 out of the around 130 *fatwas* of the entire collection the topic of male circumcision is dealt with, mostly in connection with other matters. I will first go into the contents of the relevant *fatwas*, in the order in which they appear in the collection.

The first *fatwa* treats the question of whether or not an uncircumcised man (Arabic *rajul lam yakhtun*; Malay *seorang laki laki yang tiada berkhatan*) could function as a legal guardian in marital affairs (*walî*[23]). If this is not the case, should this task then be carried out by a more distant relative (*walî al-ab'ad*) or by a representative of the government (*hâkim*)?[24] In his answer the aforementioned Ahmad Dahlân states that anyone who omits circumcision without a valid excuse, is a sinner (*fâsiq*[25]), and that as a result of this could not function as a *walî*. As long as he remains in this condition, the guardianship should be transferred to a distant relative (*ab'ad*). If this sinner lets himself be circumcised, he automatically becomes able to participate in the conclusion of a valid marriage. It is interesting to note that the *fatwa* ends with the remark that Ahmad Dahlân himself ordered this *fatwa* to be noted down, which shows the importance which he attached to it.[26]

The next *fatwa* deals with the question of whether or not a person who is uncircumcised (Arabic *aqlaf*; Malay *yang berqulpah*), but who is able to remove the dirt from under his foreskin during the

---

[22] Snouck Hurgronje [1887] 1923: 67-68.

[23] If between brackets only one term is given, this means that the Malay rendering uses the same word as the Arabic original.

[24] Cf. Juynboll 1930[4]: 178.

[25] This is a person who has committed a major transgression of the Law or who habitually commits minor transgressions (Juynboll 1930: 176).

[26] *Muhimmât al-nafâ'is* 1892: 4-5.

ritual washing of his genitals (Arabic *'inda istinjâ'*[27]; Malay *pada waktu dia bersuci*), is allowed to give his daughter in marriage. It is asked whether or not this marriage is valid, given the fact that his continued refusal to become circumcised makes this man a *fâsiq*. In the answer to these questions, in which the *mufti* is not mentioned by name, it is stated that the omission of circumcision (*khitân*) after having reached maturity (*bulûgh*) is a great sin (Arabic *kabîra min kabâ'ir al-dhunûb*; Malay *dosa besar*) which renders one a *fâsiq*. Because this person persists in avoiding circumcision, he cannot give his daughter in a valid marriage.[28]

The following *fatwa* again comes from Ahmad Dahlân and deals with a rather bizarre case. It is stated that the lower half of a corpse (from the navel to the feet) was found, and that this part of the body was not circumcised (*aqlaf*) as a result of which the water could not be introduced under the foreskin. The question is whether or not the *tayammum*[29] should be performed. If the answer is negative, should then the burial service for the dead (*salât* sc. *al-jinâza*[30]) be carried out for this deceased person or not? According to Ahmad Dahlân this corpse should be buried without *salat*, because the obligatory great ritual washing (*ghusl*) could never be carried out completely, if this excludes what is under the foreskin. Furthermore, it is impossible to bring about purity through the *tayammum*, because the limbs for performing this are absent.[31]

The next *fatwa* is less bizarre and brings us back to the reality of daily life. A certain man wished to marry, and the legal guardian (*walî*) of the bride had asked him to show him his penis in order to establish whether or not this intended bridegroom is circumcised (Arabic *mutahhir*; Malay *bersuci*; 'pure'). The marriage candidate agreed to this and, after the *walî* had approved of the penis, he gave his daughter in marriage to the man. Some time later, the son-in-law asked his father-in-law for an expiatory gift (*kaffâra*) for having seen his shame (*'awra*), for this was mentioned 'in his book' and threatened him that should his father-in-law not pay him, his faith would be nullified. Because of this threat yet another person called

---

27 This legal term means the washing or wiping of the anus and the penis to obtain ritual purity, which is for instance needed to perform the *salat* (Nawawî al-Jâwî no year: 18-20).

28 *Muhimmât al-nafâ'is* 1892: 7-8.

29 In certain cases it is allowed to obtain ritual purity by rubbing the face, the hands and the forearms with sand. This is called *tayammum*. This may, for instance, take place when wounds make the normal purification with water impossible (Juynboll 1930[4]: 58; cf. also *The Encyclopedia of Islam*[2], ii: 1104, s.v. *ghusl*).

30 Juynboll 1930[4]: 162.

31 *Muhimmât al-nafâ'is* 1892: 16.

the son-in-law an apostate (*murtadd*), and on the basis of this statement the spouse and his wife have been isolated from each other and they are both waiting for the response to the following questions: is this threat to the *walî* grounds for apostasy and should the wife therefore be divorced? In his answer Ahmad Dahlân states that this remark as such is not to be regarded as apostasy. This man, however, needed instruction, but his wife should not be divorced. If after this instruction he stills demands a expiatory gift from his father-in-law, then he should be given a suitable penalty for this.[32]

Yet another *fatwa* does not deal with marriage law, but with the performing of the ritual prayer. The question is whether the ritual prayer of a person holding a still uncircumcised small boy (Malay adds: or holding his *kain*, 'clothes') is valid. In his answer Ahmad Dahlân states that if there is no dirt (*najâsa*) around and if his foreskin (*qulfa*) is not dirty, the *salat* of the person who holds this boy is valid.

The next relevant textual fragment from the *Muhimmât al-nafâ'is* is not a *fatwa*, but consists of two lines of Arabic poetry by Ibn 'Imâd. In translation these lines run as follows:

> *An uncircumcised man whom the judge had allowed a vulva strove for pious conduct (*'ibâda*) despite the urine from [under] his foreskin;
> *and he said: 'Our example (*qudwa*) is repugnant (*kariha*) for what it retains', as a result of the urine from [under] his foreskin, as has been laid down in the text of the *Rawda*.

These Arabic verses are followed by an explication in Malay which mentions as an example of *'ibâda* the ritual prayer (*sembahyang*) and adds that the *Rawda* was written by Imam Nawawî.[33] This work should be identified as the *Rawdat al-tâlibin* by the Shâfi'ite jurist Abû Zakaryâ' Yahyâ al-Nawawî who was mentioned above.[34] The Ibn 'Imâd mentioned is probably the Hanbalite scholar from Damascus (1032/1622—1089/1679), who wrote a 'Poem on Impurities'.[35]

The next relevant passage again consists of a *fatwa* which is given in Malay only. A woman wishes to get married, but her *walî mujbir*[36] is still a child. Must the guardianship be transferred to the sultan or

---

32 *Muhimmât al-nafâ'is* 1892: 16.
33 *Muhimmât al-nafâ'is* 1892: 82.
34 Brockelmann 1943-1947, I: 424; Suppl. II: 682.
35 Brockelmann 1943-1947, Suppl. II: 403.
36 In certain cases the (grand)father is able to give his (grand)daughter away in marriage without her consent (Juynboll 1930:175). If he does so, he is called a *walî mujbir*, a 'compelling' *walî*. It is not clear to me what category of *walî mujbir* is meant here.

to a distant relative (*ab'ad*)? When this *walî* has become an adult, but is still uncircumcised without a valid excuse, should this guardianship then be transferred to a government official (*hâkim*) or to a distant relative? The question adds, by way of explanation, that in his *Kitâb al-nikâh Ibn Hajar* has said that in a situation of general distress it is possible to let a sinner (*fâsiq*) function as a *walî*. Does this, however, also apply to an uncircumcised person? Ibn Hajar al-Haytamî (909/1504—974/1567) is the famous Shâfi'ite scholar who spent most of his life in Mecca.[37] The *Kitâb al-nikâh* is a chapter of his *fiqh* work, the *Kitâb tuhfa*, which was one of the two legal handbooks *par excellence* in Shâfi'ite Islam at the end of the 19th century.[38] The answer states that should the *walî* still be too young, the guardianship should be transferred to a more distant relative and not to a government official; an adult who is not circumcised is a sinner, who is not able to function as guardian in marital affairs (*walî nikâh*). The lack of obedience in not being circumcised does not fall under the dispensation mentioned by Ibn Hajar.[39]

The next *fatwa*—a brief one—makes precisely clear what was at stake. In this *fatwa*, like the previous one also only in Malay, the name of the *mufti* is likewise absent. In translation it runs as follows:

Question. Is it sufficient if a person has been circumcised (*berkhatan*) by the cleaving of the skin of his penis (*dibelah kulit dhakarnya*), so that it lays open to his glans (*hashafa*)? Is it right that this person acts as *walî* at the marriage of his child and could he act as a witness (*shaksi*[40]) at a wedding or not?

The answer thereof. The cleaving is not sufficient. Bajîramî[41] and others say that it is compulsory to remove the foreskin which covers the glans of a male (*wajib dikerut akan kulit yang menutupi hashafa pada laki-laki*). Whosoever does not do so, commits a sin (*berdosa*) and may even be considered a *fâsiq*, who is not allowed to become a *walî nikâh*, or a witness. And God knows best.[42]

The next question on circumcision in the collection is very similar to a previous one[43] and tackles the question to whom the guardian-

[37] *The Encyclopaedia of Islam*[2] iii: 778—779.
[38] Snouck Hurgronje [1894] 1924: 290.
[39] *Muhimmât al-nafâ'is* 1892: 88.
[40] The marriage contract should be concluded in the presence of at least two witnesses (Juynboll 1930[4]: 191). Although the normal spelling is *saksi*, throughout the entire *Muhimmât al-nafâ'is* the spelling *shaksi* is used.
[41] Died 1007/1783; Brockelmann 1943-1947, II: 324.
[42] *Muhimmât al-nafâ'is* 1892: 90.
[43] *Muhimmât al-nafâ'is* 1892: 88; cf. supra.

ship in marital affairs should be transferred in the event that the *walî mujbir* of a woman is still underage. The second part of the question addresses the case in which the *walî mujbir* is an adult, but uncircumcised. Is such a person allowed to act as a *walî*, or should this role be assumed by the *hâkim* or by a more distant relative? The answer is given by the Shâfi'ite *mufti* Muhammad Sa'îd [Bâbasîl] (d. 1330/1912), who was one of the best known pupils of Ahmad Dahlân for whom he issued *fatwas* during the latter part of his teacher's life.[44] It runs as follows: if a relative of a woman is not an adult, insane, or a *fâsiq* because of his continuous refusal to be circumcised without a valid excuse, she should be represented at her wedding by another relative, and not by a government official.[45]

The final *fatwa* on circumcision in the *Muhimmât al-nafâ'is* was also asked of Muhammad Sa'îd and shows a somewhat different view from the one he expressed in the previous *fatwa*. Because this *fatwa* includes most of the issues at stake with regard to the topic of this paper, I will translate it in its entirety. The text reads as follows:

Question. What is your opinion—may your excellence endure—about the foreskin of an uncircumcised (Arabic *qulfat al-aqlaf*; Malay *kulit qulub orang berqulub*)? Should it be cut off or not? If you say that it should, what then is your opinion about a person who has only cloven the skin on the upper side of the glans, by means of which it has been exposed? Is this cleaving sufficient or not? If you say that it is not sufficient, but the cutting off is necessary, what then do you say about a person who has not cut off his foreskin? As a result of this, does he become a sinner to whom it is forbidden to act as a legal guardian in marital affairs or not? If you answer: 'Yes, he becomes a *fâsiq* as a result of that', what do you say then about the indigenous people (Arabic *ahl al-balad*; Malay *orang ahl negeri*) who are accustomed to do so? Are they excused or not? Please, give us a *fatwa* on this, because the question is of current interest.

[The answer thereof.] O, God, [give us] guidance to what is right. Circumcision (*khitân*) is indeed compulsory in order to obtain the rights of an adult (*bâligh*). The cleaving of the skin is not sufficient for this, even if it does expose the glans. As a result of what has been mentioned, a man does not become a sinner to whom the guardianship in marital affairs is forbidden, because whosoever states that the uncircumcised is a sinner motivates this by saying

---

[44] Snouck Hurgronje [1887] 1923: 68; 'Abd al-Jabbâr 1385/1965: 277.
[45] *Muhimmât al-nafâ'is* 1892: 93.

that he is persistently committing sinful acts, to wit the non-validity of the *istinjâ'* and the non-validity of the *salat*, and that all this is nonexistent in a person whose glans has been uncovered by the cleaving mentioned. The legal judgement (*hukm*), however, might take a different turn despite the motivation. But God knows best. Shaykh Muhammad Sa'îd, *mufti* of the Shâfi'ites in the protected city of Mecca.[46]

The following picture emerges from all of the *fatwas* just summarized. In Mecca, Muslims originating from the Netherlands-East Indies were present who had been circumcised at home through the cleaving of the foreskin. Apparently these Muslims did not regard this as being in contradiction with Islam, otherwise they would not have entered Mecca. Because many of the *fatwas* deal with circumcision in connection with marriage, it is perhaps through intermarriages between members from the Jâwah colony and autochthonous inhabitants of Mecca that this incision technique became known in the Holy City.[47] Whatever the case may be, from the fact that ten out of 130 *fatwas* in the *Muhimmât al-nafâ'is* deal with circumcision, it is clear that this topic must have been frequently discussed in the Jâwah colony. Undoubtedly the fact that this deviant incision technique resulted in a physical and clearly visible difference will also have stimulated the debate. Since we do not hear of any objection against the partial removal of the foreskin, we may conclude that this did not constitute a problem.

In Mecca, the cleaving of the foreskin was regarded as improper and tantamount to the complete absence of circumcision. An uncircumcised man was regarded as a *fâsiq*. The reasons given for this differ: from one point of view a person could be regarded as such because, as a result of the continued presence of the foreskin, the *istinjâ'* could not be properly performed. From another point of view an uncircumcised person could be judged a *fâsiq*, not because he was not able to reach ritual purity—in principle this was possible—, but because the avoidance of circumcision after having reached maturity was viewed as a great sin, and on these grounds he became a *fâsiq*.

Abstention from circumcision had a number of consequences: an uncircumcised man was not able to marry, to represent a woman at her marriage as her legal guardian (*walî*), or to function as a witness at a marriage and, in general, was not entitled to the rights of an

---

[46] *Muhimmât al-nafâ'is* 1892: 99-100.
[47] Snouck Hurgronje [1889] 1970: 88, 284.

adult. Furthermore, he was not able to carry out the five compulsory daily prayers and other devotional acts in a valid manner. A final consequence may be gathered from the bizarre *fatwa* concerning the uncircumcised corpse we met earlier in this paper. Because Ahmad Dahlân deemed it unnecessary in this *fatwa* to perform the prayer service for the dead in this case, this text perhaps aimed at making clear to the uncircumcised that after their death there would be no prayer service held for them, as a result of which their corpses would not undergo the necessary preparations for the Last Judgement. This *fatwa*, therefore, should perhaps be understood as a warning or a threat. In short, we can say that abstention from circumcision had grave social and ritual consequences and possibly even affected the position of the deceased in the afterlife.

A number of solutions to the issue of circumcision are also discussed. In the first place, on the basis of a statement by Ibn Hajar, there seems to have been attempts to get dispensation for not being properly circumcised, but this was not granted. In one single *fatwa*, Muhammad Sa'îd underlines the necessity of a full circumcision, but nevertheless allows a person whose foreskin is only cloven to act as a *walî nikâh*. This is quite strange, because in another *fatwa* the same Muhammad Sa'îd takes the opposite view. Whatever the reason for these two contradictory opinions might be, they show that these *fatwas* deal with concrete cases. Another solution is contained in the advice of Ahmad Dahlân, that the man concerned should undergo full circumcision, and thereby save himself from being a *fâsiq*. In real terms, for an Indonesian Muslim who had been operated by means of the cleaving of the foreskin, this meant that he had to submit himself to a second operation on the penis, in which the entire foreskin was removed.

From a number of publications it is clear that there were indeed Indonesians in Mecca who followed this advice and who were circumcised for a second time to satisfy the opinion of the Meccan religious establishment.[48] The former *hoofdpanghulu* of Bandung, Haji Hasan Moestapa (d. 1930) also reported that in 1880 many Javanese men in Mecca were circumcised once again (Moestapa 1946:53).

[48] Snouck Hurgronje [1889] 1970: 228.

The influence of Mecca in Indonesia

Once the indigenous Indonesian method of cleaving had been pushed back among the Muslims from the Dutch East Indies in Mecca, this change also made itself felt in Indonesia. There was an intensive traffic between Mecca and the Netherlands East-Indian Archipelago, from where each year thousands of pilgrims visited the Holy Land.[49]

Haji Hasan Moestapa, mentioned above, reported that from approximately 1885 incision disappeared among the Sundanese in favour of circumcision, as the result of an improved knowledge of Muslim Law and the arrival of an operator who had learned the skill in Mecca and who was used to removing the entire foreskin from the penis.[50] Other reports on other parts of the Archipelago, which reflect the situation of about 1920, further substantiate this claim. These reports were written in connection with an exhibition on all kinds of circumcision instruments and accoutrements, which was held in Batavia in August 1921. On the occasion of this exhibition, many persons like civil servants, medical doctors, and school teachers from throughout the entire Archipelago were invited to submit a 'fieldwork' report on circumcision in their place of residence. This resulted in some 60 reports which the Dutch scholar B.J.O. Schrieke collected and published in 1921 and 1922. From these reports it appears that in the 1920s, incision still existed in various parts of the Archipelago[51], but that this was becoming more and more unusual. A number of reports mentions that incision was still carried out at the end of the 19th century[52], but that the practice had been replaced by circumcision by the time the reports were written. One report explicitly mentions that this change occurred under Meccan influence.[53] According to some reports, both incision and circumcision existed alongside each other.[54] This was, for instance, the case in Surakarta. According to the reporter from this region, a 'dokter-djawa' by the name of Wirjodipoero, incision was performed on boys with a short foreskin, while the (partial) circumcision was practised on boys with a long foreskin; he adds that the

[49] See Vredenbregt 1962.
[50] Moestapa 1946: 51-52.
[51] See e.g. Schrieke 1921: 452, 479, 523.
[52] Schrieke 1921: 409 on Ciamis; 1922: 84 on North Celebes.
[53] Schrieke 1921: 414 on West Java.
[54] See e.g. Schrieke 1921: 452, 469, 523.

'ulama' preferred the latter method, because they thought that incision did not result in effective purity.[55]

If by way of conclusion we try to reconstruct the way in which circumcision in Indonesia developed from the end of the 19th century onwards, we can give the following picture. In Indonesia at the end of the 19th century, apart from (partial and full) circumcision, incision was also practised. This technique was an indigenous cultural feature and had its origins in pre-Islamic times. With the arrival of Islam in the Archipelago, incision continued to be carried out and was incorporated into Islam. When Indonesian Muslims, who had undergone incision, came into close contact with Muslims with a thorough knowledge of scripturalist Islam, this operative technique must have become a matter of debate. Although it seems likely that these debates must have already begun prior to the end of the 19th century, the first evidence of them consists of a number of Meccan *fatwas* dating from this period. These legal opinions, given by a number of leading Meccan *muftis*, show that the latter did not approve of incision from a Muslim legal point of view and that, in their opinion, the consequences for a person who was not circumcised but 'incised' were grave in the social, ritual, and eschatological domain. These *fatwas* must have impressed the Indonesians in question, because it is known that many of them had themselves operated on for the second time to have the entire foreskin removed. The idea of rejecting incision spread to Indonesia from Mecca and in the Archipelago also resulted in the disappearance of this operative technique in a number of places.

Recent developments in Indonesia

I know of no comprehensive research with regard to circumcision in present-day Indonesia. For this reason, I have asked the assistance of the seven Indonesian scholars who come from different parts of the Archipelago, currently studying at Leiden University within the framework of the *Indonesian-Netherlands Co-operation in Islamic Studies* (INIS). In personal conversations and through answering a questionnaire they have been extremely kind in supplying me with data about their own circumcision, that of their children, if they have them, and on the subject in general. From these data, among other things, it can be learned that in present-day Indonesia incision seems to have disappeared completely.

---

[55] Schrieke 1921: 461-463.

For the disappearance of incision I have the following tentative explanation. In the first place, we may expect an ongoing influence from the scripturalist views on circumcision, which the Meccan *muftis* advocated. As we have seen above, this influence made itself felt in Indonesia from at least the end of the 19th century onwards, and it will have increased, when Muslim reformist ideas from the Middle East started to spread in South-East Asia from the beginning of the 20th century. As is well-known, amongst other goals, the aim of this movement was to eradicate local customs from Islam.

In the second place, it appears that circumcision has been subject to an ever increasing medicalization, both as far as the operation itself is concerned—which less frequently takes place in a traditional setting, but increasingly in a medical atmosphere—and also with regard to the meaning of circumcision, which is more and more being regarded as a form of prophylactic surgery.[56] Concerning this last point it is interesting to mention that in North America around 1987, 85% of the newborn American males were circumcised for reasons of hygiene to prevent diseases.[57] As a result of this medicalization, we may expect that the government will increasingly intervene in this matter. In his classic book, *The Religion of Java*, based on fieldwork in 'Modjokuto' in east Central Java at the end of the 1950s, Clifford Geertz mentions that the persons who used to perform circumcision were all registered at the local office of the Ministry of Religious Affairs, while government health regulations required the use of antiseptics, which were supplied by the Ministry of Health.[58] Despite these observations by Geertz, no one among my informants is aware of any government regulation with regard to circumcision. Whatever the involvement of the government might be, it might be expected that through this medicalization, which sees circumcision primarily as a hygienic measure, incision was no longer practised.

Finally, a third factor seems likely to have contributed to the disappearance of incision, to wit an ongoing process of centralization of circumcision, which seems to have increased the influence of the two previous factors mentioned. Collective circumcisions have already been recorded in traditional settings. This occurred, for instance, in 1916 in Perbaungan, East Sumatra, when approximately 30 boys were circumcised simultaneously with the son of the sultan. On such occasions, all expenses for the festivities, the new

---

[56] Rumidjah 1979-1980: 69-70.
[57] Beidelman 1987: 512.
[58] Geertz (1960) 1976: 52.

clothes for the boys, the remuneration for the operator, and the like were borne by the sultan.[59] In this way the sultan added lustre to the circumcision of his son and at the same time reconfirmed his ties with his subjects. Since the 1970s, all kinds of social and religious organizations, like Darmawanita and the modernist Muhammadiyah movement, have organized collective circumcisions, called *khitanan masal*, on Muslim festivals or public holidays[60]. These organizations regard these events as a form of internal mission and, at the same time it is an attractive proposition for the people to participate because the operator is being paid by the organization, while sometimes even the required medicines are distributed free of charge.

Another factor which has contributed to the centralization of circumcision lies in the fact that people tend increasingly to take their children to clinics which specialize in circumcision. The most famous of these is probably Bong Supit Bogem, located between Yogyakarta and Surakarta, which receives clients from the entire region of Central Java, but also from more distant parts of Indonesia. The founder of this clinic, Mbah Noto (d. 1992) has even circumcised the sons of President Soeharto. On normal days in this clinic, now supervised by three sons of the founder, some 20 boys arrive for circumcision, but in school holidays this number can rise to four or five hundred a day. It is interesting to note that non-Muslims clients are also circumcised in this clinic.[61] This increasing centralization of circumcision will have resulted in a more and more effective spread of scripturalist Islamic and modern medical views on circumcision, and therefore in a further repudiation of the traditional incision.

To substantiate this preliminary explanation for the disappearance of incision in Indonesia—ongoing influence of scripturalist Islam, medicalization of circumcision, and its centralization—it is necessary to carry out fieldwork, which I hope to embark on in the near future.

---

[59] Louwerier 1917: 1453.

[60] Rikin (1973: 24) wonders whether this emerged as a reaction against Christian mass baptisms.

[61] Saksono 1993; I would like to thank Drs. Moh. Hisyam (LIPI) for this reference.

References

'Abd al-Jabbâr, 1385/1965, *Siyar wa-tarâjim ba'd 'ulamâ'inâ fî l-qarn al-râbi' 'ashar li-l-hijra.* Makka: mu'assasat Makka li-l-tabâ'a wa-l-i'lâm.
Beidelman, T.O., 1987, 'Circumcision', in: Eliade 1987, vol. 3: 511-514.
Brockelmann, C., 1943-1947, *Geschichte der arabische Litteratur: zweite den Supplementbänden angepasste Auflage.* Leiden: Brill. 2 vols. and 3 supplementary vols.
Brown, D.E., J.W. Edwards, & R.P. Moore 1988, *The penis inserts of Southeast Asia; an annotated bibliography with an overview and comparative perspectives.* Berkeley: University of California.
Bryk, F., 1931, *Die Beschneidung bei Mann und Weib: ihre Geschichte, Psychologie und Ethnologie.* Neubrandenburg: Verlag Gustav Feller.
Eliade, M. (ed.), 1987, *The Encyclopedia of Religion.* New York: MacMillan, 16 vols.
Encyclopaedia of Islam, The; new edition prepared by a number of leading orientalists, 1960—. Leiden: Brill.
Geertz, C., 1976, *The Religion of Java.* Chicago, etc.: University of Chicago Press 1960[1].
Guillot, C., 1981, *L'affaire Sadrach: un essai de christianisation à Java au XIXe siècle.* Paris: Editions de la Maison des Sciences de l'Homme (= Études insulindiennes/Archipel, 4).
Hicks, E.K., 1993, *Infibulation; Female mutilation in Islamic Northeastern Africa.* New Brunswick, etc.: Transaction Publishers.
Ibn Qudâma, 1401/1981, *Al-mughnî; ed. Ri'âsat idârat al-buhûth al-'ilmiyya.* al-Riyâd: Maktabat al-Riyâd al-hadîtha (9 vols.).
Juynboll, Th.W., 1930[4], *Handleiding tot de kennis van de Mohammedaansche wet volgens de leer der Sjâfi'itische school.* Leiden: Brill.
Louwerier, J., 1917, 'Een besnijdenis in Sumatra', *De Indische Gids* 39, 2: 1452-1455.
Moestapa, Hadji Hasan, 1946, *Over de gewoonten en gebruiken der Soendanezen; uitgegeven en vertaald door R.A. Kern.* 's-Gravenhage: Nijhof (= KITLV, Verhandelingen, 5; Dutch translation of the 1913 Sundanese original).
Muhimmât al-nafâ'is fî bayân as'ilat al-hâdith pada menyatakan beberapa masalah jang dihimpunkan segala jawabnya daripada ... Ahmad Dahlân dan lain-lain. Makka: Matba'at fath al-karîm al-islâmiyya. [Arabic and Malay in Jawi script.]
Nawawî al-Jâwî, M., no year, *Al-thamâr al-yâni'a fî l-riyâd al-badî'a.* Semarang: Usaha keluarga.
Nicolai, J.-P.A., 1991, 'Een peniele jade-implantatie in Nederland', in *Bijdragen tot de Taal-, Land- en Volkenkunde* 147, 1: 139.
O'Hanlon, R., 1989[5], *Naar het hart van Borneo.* Amsterdam: De Arbeiderspers.
Rikin, W. Mintardja, 1973, *Ngabersihan als knoop in de Tali Paranti; bijdrage tot het verstaan van de besnijdenis der Sundanezen.* Meppel: Racmo [Ph.D. thesis Leiden University].
Rumidjah, Jumeiri Siti, 1979-1980, *Adat sunatan di Daerah Istimewa Yogyakarta dan Jawa Tengah.* Yogyakarta: Balai penelitian sejarah dan budaya.
Saksono, Bani, 1993, 'R.Ng. Noto Pandoyo: Bong Supit Kesayangan Pak Harto', in *Republika* 29 Agustus, hal. 8.

Schrieke, B., 1921, 'Allerlei over de besnijdenis in den Indischen Archipel', *Tijdschrift voor de Indische Taal-, Land- en Volkenkunde* 60: 373-578.
Schrieke, B., 1922, 'Allerlei over de besnijdenis in den Indischen Archipel', *Tijdschrift voor de Indische Taal-, Land- en Volkenkunde* 61:1-94.
Snouck Hurgronje, C., [1887] 1923, 'Een rector der Mekkaansche universiteit', in Snouck Hurgronje 1923-1927, vol. 3: 65-122 [originally published in *Bijdragen tot de Taal-, Land- en Volkenkunde* 5, 2 (1887) 344-404].
Snouck Hurgronje, C., [1889] 1970, *Mekka in the latter part of the 19th century; daily life, customs and learning; the Muslims of the East-Indian Archipelago, transl. by J.H. Monahan.* Leiden: Brill [reprint of the 1931 English translation of the second volume of the 1888-1889 German original].
Snouck Hurgronje, C., 1893, *De Atjèhers; deel I.* Batavia/Leiden: Landsdrukkerij/Brill.
Snouck Hurgronje, C., [1894] 1924, 'Sajjid Oethman's gids voor de priesterraden', in Snouck Hurgronje 1923-1927, vol. 4/1: 285-303 [originally published in *Indisch Tijdschrift van het Recht* 63 (1894):722-744].
Snouck Hurgronje, C., 1923-1927, *Verspreide Geschriften.* Bonn, etc.: Kurt Schröder; Leiden: Brill, 6 vols.
Vredenbregt, J., 1962, 'The haddj; some of its features and functions in Indonesia', in *Bijdragen tot de Taal-, Land- en Volkenkunde* 118: 91-154.
Wilken, G.A., 1885, 'De besnijdenis bij de volken van den Indischen Archipel', in *Bijdragen tot de Taal-, Land- en Volkenkunde* 34: 165-206.

LANGUAGE AND IDENTITY

PLURALISM AND THE USE OF NON-ARABIC LANGUAGES IN THE MUSLIM WEST[1]

Gerard Wiegers
Leiden University

The translation [of the Qur'ân] is to be compared to the symbolic ritual purification (*tayammum*)... (Muhammad al-Hajawî 1936: 198).

Introduction: the classical doctrine

It is a well-known fact that the Arabic language occupies an important place in Muslim worship. It is nearly always the language in which the Qur'ân is recited, not only during prayer, but also on other occasions. From early times however some use has also been made of non-Arabic languages. To those unable to recite it in Arabic some *ᶜulamâ'*, in classical times and in modern times particularly those of the Hanafite *madhhab*, allowed recitation of the Qur'ân in a non-Arabic language.[2] During the *hajj* one is allowed to say the *talbiya* in any language, even though the Arabic wording of the Prophet's *talbiya* is related in the Tradition.[3] Another form of worship in which a believer may use non-Arabic is the invocation or *duᶜâ'*. *Duᶜâ's*, in the sense of their being forms of individual prayers, were, even if said during the salât, allowed unconditionally to be said in non-Arabic languages.[4] Preachers (*khutabâ'*) are allowed to render parts of the *khutbas* (sermons) in vernacular languages after they have been delivered in Arabic.[5] The basis for the relationship

---

1 The research of G.A. Wiegers has been made possible by a fellowship of the Royal Netherlands Academy of Arts and Sciences. Acknowledgements: I thank Professor P.S. van Koningsveld (Leiden) for drawing my attention to several sources discussed in this paper, and Professor L.P. Harvey (London) for his critical reading of the draft version and his valuable comments.

2 See the article '*al-Kur'ân*' in *The Encyclopedia of Islam, 2nd edition*, § 9: 'translation of the Kur'ân'; Graf 1974: 116-119.

3 Kister 1980: 46, and the sources referred to there. The *talbiya*, it will be recalled, is the formula which the pilgrims will be saying continuously in a loud voice after the *irâm* is assumed until almost the end of the pilgrimage.

4 Khalîl ibn Ishâq al-Jundî 1318/1900: 19, and see also below.

5 Ibrahim n.y.: 42-44; Al-Sinânî 1383/1963: 77-78.

between liturgical usage of Arabic and non-Arabic was laid by Al-Shâfi'î (d.829/204), the founder of the science of the *usûl al-fiqh*. He states in his *Risâla*:

> It is obligatory upon every Muslim to learn the Arab tongue to the utmost of his power in order [to be able] to profess through it that 'there is no God at all but God and Muhammad is His servant and Apostle', and to recite in it [i.e. the Arabic tongue] the Book of God, and to utter in mentioning what is incumbent upon him, the *takbîr*, the *tasbîh*, the *tashahhud* and others. Whatever learning he gains of the language which God made to be the language of him [Muhammad], by whom He sealed His prophethood and by whom He revealed the last of His Books, is for his [man's] welfare, just as it is his [duty] to learn [how] to pray and recite the *dhikr* in it, to visit the [Sacred] House and perform its duties, and to be a follower [in the performance] of the duties imposed upon him or recommended to him, [rather] than to be followed.... Calling the attention of the public to the fact that the Qur'ân was revealed in the Arab tongue in particular is [a sincere piece] of advice to [all] Muslims.[6]

This illustrates very clearly that al-Shâfi'î was aware of the existence of non-Arabic speaking Muslims. The term 'follow' is apparently to be interpreted as each believer's duty to learn as much Arabic as is needed to be able to perform his/her religious obligations in a proper manner. This discussion, therefore, left the position of the Arabic language in Muslim culture reasonably well defined. Being the language of the Qur'ân, which is the first source of Muslim theology, law and ethics, and the vehicle of the fulfilment of the ritual obligations, Arabic has occupied a fundamental place in Muslim religious life right up to the present day. Later, under the influence of theological developments, particularly the doctrine of the inimitability, or *i'jâz*, of the Qur'ân, the place of Arabic in worship became even stronger.[7]

With the expansion of Islam many non-Arabophone Muslims were included in the abode of Islam, *dâr al-islâm*. In addition, Islam spread in non-Muslim territories, where large established non-Arabic speaking Muslim minorities came into being. It is estimated that nowadays thirty percent of the Muslims are living as minorities. In classical Islamic political thought, as we will see shortly, the keyword in the relationship between *dâr al-islâm* and the abode of war (*dâr al-harb*) was struggle. In addition, Islamic law was supposed to be in force in Muslim territory only, for here the Muslim authorities offered protection to their subjects, both Muslims and non-Mus-

---

6 Al-Shâfi'î 1359: 48-50, translation M. Khadduri (1961: 92-94).

7 Art. *i'jâz* in EI² (art. G.E. von Grunebaum).

lims.[8] The boundaries between the abodes of Islam and War were marked by restrictions with respect to the way the Qur'ân was to be handled. Tradition has it that it was not allowed to travel with a copy of the Qur'ân (a *mushaf*) to *dâr al-harb*, lest it might fall in the hands of the Unbelievers.[9] Rules of purity forbad Unbelievers (and other ritually unclean people) from touching the Holy Book.[10] The same restrictions marked to some extent the boundaries between different religious groups within Islamic territories. Several Malikite sources mention, for example, that it was forbidden for Muslims to teach the Qur'ân to Jewish and Christian children.[11] One might summarize the classical paradigm as follows: the spread of Islam and the propagation of the faith was to be stimulated by the extending Muslim territory rather than by the use of propaganda and persuasion.[12] Thus, in the classical period the spread of the faith was not in the first place carried out by explanation of the Faith and the Holy Books, but by military struggle, i.e. by the expansion of territory. The classical doctrine foresaw the eventual disappearance of the abode of war, caused by the final victory of Islam.

It is against this background that the many problems arising from situations of Muslim constituting a minority in the West, should be viewed. Many Maghribi jurists voiced suspicions about the status of established minorities in Christian territories, raising doubts about their properties, the status of judgements passed upon them by their qadis (who were not appointed by Muslim authorities), and their religious beliefs in general.

Language also played a role in assessing the qualities of those beliefs. Shortly after the fall of Marbella in the 1480s the famous Tilimsân-born *muftî* al-Wansharîshî (d. 1508) was asked to give his considered opinion about a man who wished to remain in Marbella after the conquest of his native town by the Christians, this in order to find his brother, lost during the hostilities, and in order to assist the *dhimmî* ('protected') Muslims, i.e. Muslims who had stayed behind under Christian rule. The *muftî*'s answer was negative, arguing that it was impossible to practise Islam among the Polytheists. It

---

[8] Johansen 1986: 17.
[9] Al-Wanshârîshî 1401/1981, II: 114-115.
[10] Juynboll 1930: 168.
[11] Muhammad b. ᶜUmar al-Lubâba, in Al-Wansharîsî 1401/1981, XI: 96. The schools of law probably expressed different opinions about the problem. According to the Shâfiᶜite scholar al-Nawawî it was allowed to teach the Qur'ân to an Unbeliever if there was hope that he might convert, and to let him hear the recitation of the Qur'ân; cf. al-Nawawî 1934/1353: 35, see also Moreno 1925: 540.
[12] Sadan 1980: 103; cf. Peters 1979: 117-121.

was well known, he argued, that the religion of these minorities is endangered in a number of ways, among which also by way of their language. This is shown by the fact that the people of 'Abulla' and other places have lost the Arabic language entirely, and 'where the Arabic language is entirely lost, "its" devotions (*muta*ᶜ*abbudâtuhu*) die out as well'.[13] This view reflects very much that of al-Shâfiᶜî, who stated that in order to be a good Muslim some knowledge of Arabic was necessary, and, according to al-Wansharîshî, the Muslims of Abulla, identified by most scholars as the town of Ávila in Castile, no longer had any mastery over it.[14] Though the *muftî* does not say so, Romance must have replaced Arabic in 'Abulla'.

It follows from what has been stated above, that both inter- and intra-religious pluralism played a role in the discussions on the place of Non-Arabic languages; the interreligious aspect being Muslim/non-Muslim relations, the intra-religious aspect being the relationship between Muslims who spoke Arabic and those who did not. The interplay of these two aspects is the subject of the present contribution.

Non-Arabic languages in the Maghrib

Four ᶜ*ajamâ*, i.e. non-Arabic languages[15], have played a role in the Maghrib, namely Berber, Turkish, Spanish and French. The first two languages were mainly languages spoken by Muslims. Spanish and French were mainly spoken by the 'extra-communities'.[16] *Berber* was the spoken language of the Berbers even before the rise of Islam. Many religious texts circulating in Sunni circles from a later date survive[17]. *Turkish* was the spoken and literary language of the Ottomans who established themselves in the Maghrib in the second half of the 16th century. Their presence led to some adaptations with respect to ritual, for example through the introduction of Hanafite prayer rites in some of the mosques.[18] From that time onwards, Turkish was used in education and administration as

[13] Al-Wansharîsî 1401/1981, II: 141.
[14] Harvey 1990: 58.
[15] See: EI², articles ᶜadjam [F. Gabrieli], aljamía [E. Lévi-Provençal/L.P. Harvey].
[16] The term is coined in Sadan 1980.
[17] Basset 1920 (on early written texts, see 60ff., where the heterodox Berber 'Qur'âns' of the Barghawâta and that the Berber prophet Hâ-Mâm in the tenth/third century are also discussed); Grandguillaume 1983; Merad 1967: 356ff; van den Boogert & Stroomer 1993.
[18] Abdesselem 1973: 28.

well.[19] *Spanish* became a spoken and written language of the Muslim minorities in Christian Spain between the 13th and 16th centuries[20]. In the 16th century the use of Arabic in speech and writing[21] was prohibited, thus forcing the crypto-Muslim minority to pass it on to subsequent generations in secret, with the inevitable consequence that Arabic fluency became rare and Spanish subsequently became both the spoken and written language. After their expulsion from Spain in 1609 these communities continued to use Spanish in their new North African countries of refuge. *French*, finally, penetrated the Maghrib with the arrival of the French colonial powers in the 19th century. It became the official language in Algiers in 1830, in 1881 in Tunisia and in Morocco in 1912.[22] The present study will deal mainly with the two non-Arabic languages in the Maghrib which were identified with extra-communal forces, Spanish and French.

Islamic texts in Spanish before the expulsion of the Moriscos

Elsewhere I have argued that the earliest Islamic texts in Spanish date from the early 14th century[23], but that we may assume that even before that time, Spanish translations of some doctrinal Berber texts of the Almohad *mahdî* Ibn Tûmart circulated, which should probably be dated to the 12th century. This means that the earliest Romance religious texts were probably written when Islam was still the dominant religion in Spain, and that it is possible that such texts were even in circulation in Muslim territory itself. Some scholars argue that there may have been some sort of oral phase in the history of Islamic religious writings in Romance.

That this may indeed be the case is suggested by a *fatwâ* given by the Malikite scholar Ibn Rushd al-Jadd (450/1059-520/1126) dealing with accusations about a man who had allegedly said: 'I [can] recite *sûrat Yûsuf* in Romance'. One witness also testified that he had said: 'May God curse the Arabic language, and him, who produced it'.[24] These are statements, which, although they could also be interpreted as mere boasting of this man that he was able to recite this

[19] Abdesselem 1973: 28, 29n.
[20] It was the language of many Jews as well (see EI², art. Maghrib [G.S. Colin]). They will not be dealt with.
[21] Except in profane, scientific works; see Ladero Quesada 1969: 318.
[22] Grandguillaume 1983: 12-13.
[23] See Wiegers 1994: 62ff.
[24] Ibn Rushd 1987: 545.

sûra in Romance, seem to indicate that there must have been people in early 12th-century Muslim Spain who in fact 'recited' religious texts in Romance. Moreover, the rejection of Arabic coupled with the preference for Romance indicates that some Andalusian Muslims held opinions which bear a strong resemblance to the Linguistic Shu^cûbiyya of the Middle East during the same period.[25]

In 1455 the Segovian *faqîh* (religious scholar) Yça 'Gidelli' made a translation into Spanish of the Qur'ân at the request of a Christian theologian, Juan de Segovia.[26] Although it is a literal translation (Sp. *de pe a pa*) and therefore, in itself, a very interesting initiative, there are no indications that it was ever used for recitation[27]. In the introduction to his *Breviario Sunní*, a compendium of Muslim law preceded by a 13 article creed and a short chapter about the signs heralding the end of the world, written in Spanish some seven years later (i.e. 1462), the same author reflects upon his earlier undertaking and states that he made it on the demand of

> that Lofty authority that commands us and tells us that someone who knows the Law ought, if possible, to teach it to all the creatures in the world in such a language that they may understand it, and so to avoid the insults which were brought against it [sc. the Qur'ân], it pleased the Divine piety to grant me that with his help while I had the commentary [*tafsîr*] open before me I might render it into Romance...

thereby indicating that he had had important reasons, both apologetic and missionary, to undertake his work of translation.[28]. This same treatise contains several *du^câ*'s in Spanish, which were obviously meant to be said in Spanish as well.

At the end of the 15th century the socio-religious situation of the Muslim minorities changed. After the fall of Granada in 1492 firstly the Jews were expelled from Spain. The Muslims of Granada were forced to convert between 1499 and 1501. Then in 1502 those living in Castile had to convert, followed by the Muslims in all other parts of Spain in 1526. They became known as Moriscos, a word closely related to the word 'Moros', the common term for Muslims in Medieval Spain. No longer allowed to adhere to Islam, the overwhelming majority of the Moriscos nevertheless kept practising Islam secretly. In 1566, however, the authorities wished to

---

[25] Richter Bernburg 1974.
[26] Wiegers 1994.
[27] See Wiegers 1994: passim.
[28] 'Suma de los mandamientos y devedamientos de la santa ley y sunna' (= *Breviario Sunni*, edited by P. de Gayangos), in *Memorial Histórico Español* 5 (1853) 247-417.

prohibit all Moriscos usages they connected with Islam, including the oral and written use of the Arabic language. In a Memorial, dated 1567, and directed to Pedro de Deza, President of the Audiencia of Granada, Don Fernando Núñez Muley, himself of Morisco extraction, protested on behalf of the Granadan Muslim community, using two arguments mainly: a) that the Moriscos customs and traditions the authorities were seeking to annihilate were of a purely regional nature and not incompatible with Christian doctrine, and b) that the measures were likely to have disastrous consequences, which indeed appeared to be true.[29] According to the said spokesman, the first archbishop of Granada, Hernando de Talavera, had been known to have used Arabic during mass in 1502, saying, for example, *Ybara Figun* (i.e. *baraka 'llâhu fikum*) instead of *Dominus Bobispon* [sic]. Moreover, Hernando de Talavera had encouraged Moriscos to pray for rain in their traditional way, i.e. in Arabic.[30]. Fernando Núñez Muley also drew the attention of the authorities to the existence of the Arabic-speaking Christians in Palestine who use Arabic even in their liturgy.

Indeed, it was the Pragmática of 1566 which led to the Morisco uprising in the Kingdom of Granada (1568), which continued through to 1570. Perhaps it was the strongly repressive anti-Islamic policy of the Spanish authorities in the 1580s which led to a reconsideration of the religious use of Spanish on the part of the Moriscos themselves, as is evident from comments on the use of that language in Moriscos writings. On the one hand we read the following remark in a Qur'ân translation with interpolated commentaries, written in 1606[31]:

> It [the MS] is written in the letters of the Christians[32] [...], the writer begs that on account of being in those letters it not be belittled, but rather respected; because, being set down in this way, it can be seen by those Muslims who know how to read Christian, but not Muslim, letters. *For it is true that the Prophet Muhammad, s'm, said that the best language was the one that could be understood* (my italics, G.W.).

---

[29] Garrad 1954.

[30] 'Como los solían pedir en arabigo'. This had taken place in 1506-7. Apparently he had encouraged the Moriscos to pray the *salât al-istisqâ'*.

[31] MS T 235 of the Biblioteca Pública in Toledo, f. 81v-82r: 'esta eskrito en letra de los kristyanos [...] y suplica que por estar en dicha letra no lo tengan en menos de lo kes antes en mucho porque pues esta asi declarado esta mas a vista de los muçlimes que saben leer el cristiano y no la letra de los muçlimes porque es çierto que dixo el annabî Muammad, alla Allahu wa-sallam, ke la mejor lengwa era la ke se entendia ...', in López-Morillas 1983: 499.

[32] In contradistinction to many other Morisco MSS, it is written in Arabic characters, i.e. in Aljamiado; see Hegyi 1984 and 1990.

On the other hand, we also see a tendency to identify Spanish with the oppressive majority and it is no wonder then that in the preface of an Islamic work of instruction, we read:

> God having been pleased to permit that the Moors of this country should be afflicted and oppressed with so many persecutions, allowed in his infinite wisdom that the affairs of our religion should be brought to such extremity, that it is not practised either in public or in private. Prayer is laid aside and forgotten, and the few who still perform it do it secretly, and consequently with fear, and without the necessary devotion: the fast is not observed, or if so, far from the manner in which it ought to be; the customary alms abolished; the annual festivals and their tithes sunk in oblivion; the invocation of Allah and his beloved messenger never heard; or, *if they invoke them, they do not call them by their proper names in our language* [my italics, G.W.]. All this is owing, first of all, to the circumstances which have placed the Moors for so many years far from any spiritual advice; and secondly, to the tyranny of the Christians, who have caused them to be all forcibly baptized through fear and terror. Their books are all lost, and scarcely any remembrance remains of them; the doctors of the law are no more, some are dead, others lie in prison; the Inquisition displays against us its utmost fury and oppression, so that few parts of the kingdom are free from fire and faggot; the newly-baptized Moors are everywhere seized and punished with gallies, rack and fire, and other chastisements best known to God, the master of all secrets. These intolerable torments and other calamities we have endured till the present day, for a space of seventy-six years, with greater fury and vigour than at the first beginning. Now, I ask you what knowledge can we have of religion and its dogmas, how can we serve God, if we are continually disturbed and perplexed? and therefore how can it be wondered that some of the holy mysteries of our religion are become strange and inhabitual to us, especially when we consider that we are surrounded by many inveterate and implacable enemies, among which is the world, that, with its temptations and snares, is continually inciting us to forget our supreme welfare, and barring the way to salvation? Some people among us do not know what prayer is, nor by whom it was instituted; if you ask them when our lord and prophet, Mohammed, was born, they will not answer you; and if you happen to mention in their presence Mecca, that mother of cities and cradle of our religion, they will stare in your face, and shrug up their shoulders. Therefore I, who profess to be a good Mussulman, although the number and depth of my sins God only knows, have undertaken the meritorious task of writing this *Guide to Salvation*, and have composed it in Spanish: may God forgive me for using any other language than that in which the sublime Korán was revealed.[33]

This is a fragment from the *Guía de la Salvación*, written apparently in 1603 by ʿAbd al-Karim Juan del Rincón from Huesca in the kingdom of Aragon. We read that the author excuses himself for

---

[33] Gayangos 1839: 79-80.

using Spanish instead of Arabic, and that he adduces many reasons to justify this[34]. In another work the following statement is found:

> Not one of our fellow-believers knows Arabic, the language in which our Holy Quran was revealed, nor does he understand the Truths of our religion and its purified excellence, if these are not aptly explained in a foreign language, which is that of the Christian dogs, our tyrants and oppressors, may God confound them. And thus, may He forgive me, who can read what is written in the hearts and who knows that my intention is only to open the way of salvation to the Muslim believers, even though it is by such a vile and despicable medium.[35]

This last source, probably dating from the end of the 16th century or beginning of the 17th century, explicitly qualifies Spanish as the language of the Christian oppressors and as a vile and despicable medium. A slightly different thought is expressed by another Morisco, Ahmad b. Qâsim al-Hajarî, writing at the beginning of the 17th century, who states that according to a Morisco maxim there was no Arabic without God, and no *ᶜajamî* without the Devil, for they perceived that Christians mentioned him often in their *ᶜajamî* speech.[36]

This would indeed seem to suggest that remarks about the religious status of the Romance vernacular cannot be evaluated without taking the 'Sitz im Leben' of a text into account. Derogatory remarks about the (ritual) use of Spanish mainly date from the end of the 16th and the early 17th century when Spanish began to be perceived as the language of the oppressive majority, which indeed the Spanish Christians turned out to be. The relationship between the Muslim minority and the extra-community appears to be a major influence on the Muslim attitude towards to the use of Spanish.

---

[34] The introduction to Abdelkarim Juan del Rincón's work was put into verse by Muhammad Rabadan; see Rabadan's *Discurso de la luz*, in *Journal of the Royal Asiatic Society* 3 (1868) 386.

[35] 'Ni uno solo de nuestros correligionarios sabe algarabía en que fué revelado nuestro santo alcorán, ni comprende las verdades del adin ni alcanza su excelencia apurada, como no le sean convenientemente declaradas en una lengua extraña, cual es la de estos perros cristianos, nuestros tiranos y opresores ¡confúndalos Alá! Así, pues séame perdonado por aquel que lee lo que hay escrito en los corazones, y sabe que mi intencion no es otra que abrir á los fieles muslimes el camino de la salvacion, aunque sea por tal vil y despreciable medio' (quoted in Saavedra y Moragas 1889: 144-5). The MS itself is no longer extant.

[36] Al-Hajarî 1987: 108.

The use of Spanish after the expulsion

The expulsion of almost the entire Morisco population from Spain between 1609 and 1614 did not bring to end the use of the Spanish language among them. In North Africa the exiled Moriscos had to build up a new life in their respective countries of refuge, where their new Tunisian neighbours mistrusted them and had doubts about their status as Muslims. Their Spanish speech and writing only served to reinforce such doubts, as is reflected in a Morisco text written after the expulsion in Tunis.[37] In it the author tells us of the help he and other Moriscos had received from ᶜUthmân, the Dey of Tunis, who exempted them from paying certain taxes and assisted them to settle in the country.[38] The famous mystic Sidi Abu' l-Ghayth al-Qashshâsh[39] took care of their well-being and made sure that the neediest among them could live for some time in the *zâwiyas*. The children of these poor Moriscos defiled the *zâwiya* of 'Çiti el Zulaychi' and when some of the inhabitants of Tunis complained about this, the saint sided with the exiles and branded those who complained as *munâfiqûn*, 'hypocrites'. Moreover he acknowledged the need to instruct the expelled Moriscos in the faith anew, and that 'it was needed to show these exiled people how to perform the ritual ablutions, in particular to those who did not master Arabic'. Thereupon a Morisco said to al-Qashshâsh: 'Sir, should one not write for them in Castilian what they are to believe and do?' He (al-Qashshâsh) showed great satisfaction and pleasure, saying that it would be a pious work, most meritorious, and that he who would write it, would have the approval and a *fatwâ* of such a great saint.[40] This passage confirms the picture presented to us by the aforesaid *Guide to Salvation*, written shortly before the expulsion: the majority of the Moriscos had become quite ignorant of their religion, and had to be instructed anew. Due to their ignorance of Arabic, this had to be done in Castilian.

---

[37] MS S 2 of the Real Academia de la Historia in Madrid, recently discussed by López Baralt in a study published under the entirely misleading title *Una Kâma Sûtra espanol* (López Baralt 1992).

[38] S 2, apud López Baralt 1992: 79.

[39] Abdesselem 1973: 25.

[40] 'Y que a la jente espelida demostrase como abian de tomar guado y les adbiertiese lo que habian de haçer particular a los que no sabian la lengua arabiga. Entonçes le dixo: 'pues señor, si a los tales se les escribiese en castellano lo que se deue creer y saber es cosa que se puede haçer' y respondio mostrando grande gusto y contento que seria obra muy açepta y de mucho premio y que el que la hiçiera lo ganaria muy cumplido y con fatwa dada por tan grande santo' (S 2 f. 8r-v, apud López Baralt 1992: 81).

This state of affairs also explains the fairly large number of works of instruction written in Castilian to have come down to us. One of the most interesting is a work which unfortunately lacks part of the very important first folio: MS 9653 of the National Library in Madrid. In the introduction the author explains that he is writing for those Muslims who had left the land of the Christian heretics, in order to discover the Truth, but who had as yet been unable to master the Arabic language[41], which is the perfect one, and therefore needed the Castilian vulgar tongue, with which God allowed them to grow up, without any possibility to learn the other language.[42] He goes on to explain that for this reason it was necessary (*fuerça*) to compile this treatise for them so that they might learn the necessary attributes of their Creator. The author had been severely criticized by some on account of his previous works and activities. These things had confused him for some time, but then he remembered the reward God promises to anyone instructing others on their religion (*abeça alguien alguna cossa en su ley*). The author knows several Traditions which confirm his points of view, but in view of the necessity to put them in Arabic he omits them.[43] Yet he goes on to paraphrase several Traditions which tell us about the merits of knowledge. He had already composed some short works of religious instruction and these have been of some use for beginners sadly lacking in religious knowledge and awareness of the ways to serve God, because they did not master the language and had lost their hopes of learning it because of their advanced age, particularly his Aragonese brothers, to whom he had always been devoted.[44]. In the present work he has chosen to comment upon a religious work in verse, so that his readers would have some pleasure in reading the things they needed to know. He goes on to argue that when teach-

---

[41] MS 9653 f. 1r.

[42] See also MS 9534 of the National Library in Madrid, in which it is said that man should be concerned about his soul, and should resist the worldly temptations, and that for this reason the book will deal with religious matters, basing it on the opinions of some Malikite authors. The author hopes it will be of some use 'a quien por la poca dispussiçion y maestros y lenguaje no puede en el aravigo saver lo que agora en este Bulgar con que no quedara escusa a quien por pereza la tenia' (the same text in MS 9067 of the said library, f. 15r).

[43] 'por neçeçidad de ponerlos en arabigo no los pongo en esta lugar'.

[44] '... que en el discursso de mis estudios e hecho algunos otros tratados cortos porque no me daba mas lugar lo que ssabia por entonçes... y questos an sido de algun probecho para prinçipiantes que todo punto estaban resmotos y apartados de ssaber lo que les conbenia en su creyençia y modos del serbiçio e dios por falta de entender la lengua y perdidas las esperanças de adquirilla porque la hedad no da lugar a ello sigun costumbre y particularmente los hermanos aragonesses a quien e ssido siempre afiçionado por sus buenas yntençiones y desseos de saber' (MS 9653 f. 5v).

ing people about the twenty attributes of God, what difference does it make to say '*quidam*' (Ar. *qidam*), i.e. timelessness, one of the attributes of God, rather than '*eternidad*'?[45] They have exactly the same meaning! By avoiding the use of a language that is understood, much damage is caused.[46] He tells us all this because he has heard that some have opposed him and scorned him because of certain things he had written. Those who had reproached him, however, themselves only write commentaries (his term is *sarxes*, from Ar. *sharh*) and supercommentaries (his term is *hassias* from Ar. *hâshiya*) with the sole intent of showing their vanity and arrogance. Therefore he has written this Spanish work, of which he hopes that it may be useful for those who do not master Arabic. He reminds his readers that the *sharî*ᶜ*a* permits a believer during the *salât* (which is in Arabic) to utter a *du*ᶜ*â'* (an ejaculatory prayer) in Spanish, or in any other language, and this even when he knows Arabic, and it is noteworthy that Khalîl [i.e. Khalîl ibn Ishâq al-Jundî[47]] qualified it only as *makrûh* (reprehensible) and not as forbidden. The author has witnessed people who knew Arabic being taught in Turkish. Many other arguments could be adduced, he argues, such as the fact that the Prophet spoke every language, to show that writing in Spanish was not a reprehensible innovation (*bid*ᶜ*a*) but rather was to be seen as an aspect of the collective duty (*fard kifâya*) to translate [religious] works which was incumbent on anyone with a knowledge of the two languages.[48]

---

[45] For the doctrine of the Divine attributes, see Stieglecker 1962: 23-96.

[46] 'que todo biene a sser una sustançia y assi para deçille a uno que le es fuerça a dios beyente atributos y dellos la eternidad que diferençia tiene deçir el quidam o la eternidad siendo un mesmo sentido y que lo uno y lo otro es no tener prinçipio y de no deçirselo en lenguaxe que entienda quedarrse sin sabello y de no ssaberlo proçederle tanto daño luego de estorbar esto se le sigara mayor a quien fuere causa dello' (MS 9653 f 6r-6v).

[47] The well-known Malikite author of the *Mukhtasar fi 'l-fiqh* (d. 767/1365).

[48] 'y de probecho para quien fue serbido de dalles cortedad en la lengua y limitarssela en que fuesse esta bulgar castellana. Y permitio en su santa sarea que en el çuchut de la çala hiçiesse el doa con ella o con semejante, no pudiendo alcançar la arabiga y aunque la sepa le sera su çala çierta y solo le es macruh (...), y assimesmo perdono al que tubiesse perturbaçion la lengua por ocassion de ser tartamuda o ᶜachami aunque perturbe las letras y no las diga como ellas son, y esto en el reçado de la çala ora haga solo o ssea mamum cymam (...), demas de que no haçemos ynobaçion en esta traduction pues yo e bisto a quien sabe la lengua turquesca y arabiga dar liction en la turquesca a quien sabe las dos. Y muy usada cossa es en el mundo la traduçir por que a no sser assi ¿como se entenderian unos contra otros y como los que no saben mas de una lengua entenderan en la otra si no ubiera quien lo declarara? Y nuestro profeta (...) hablo todas las lenguas que a abido en el mundo y a todos los que ssabian la suya les mostro con ella lo que les conbino y otras muchas cosas y raçones pudiera traer para dar a entender ques fard cafaya el aber traduction en castellano a quien en castellano de liction, porque de no abello se sigue quel que no ssabe otra lengua se quede sin saber lo que le ynporta y lo ssera sobre el que entendiere las dos lenguas ...' (MS 9653 f. 7r-v)

According to the author some of his opponents said that it is not permissible to translate the Divine attributes (*sifât*) into non-Arabic[49], but he flatly denies the validity of that statement, arguing that this is a futile problem compared to everyday reality, in which people are completely ignorant of even the most basic notions of their religion and badly need instruction.

Those who oppose the author seem to be certain local *ᶜulamâ'*, as can be seen from the fact that he pictures them as being occupied with writing commentaries and supercommentaries. Clearly, these *ᶜulamâ'* had questioned the orthodoxy of his previous works. They did not only doubt the orthodoxy of translating the *sifât*, they apparently also opposed translating *Hadîth*.[50] The use of Turkish in education is something the author has witnessed himself in Tunis; the Ottomans, it will be recalled, dominated Tunis from the middle of the sixteenth century onwards. It is clear that the author tries to demonstrate that the Moriscos form part of the Muslim community and that they are not be dealt with as non-Muslims, even though their customs and language seem to indicate otherwise.

In yet another Spanish Morisco manuscript, written after the expulsion, we find a short note about four languages of revelation which also seems to deal with the problem of the use of an *ᶜajamî* language, though in a very indirect way.[51] It simply mentions the languages used in different revealed books. The languages mentioned here are Hebrew (scil. the language of the *tawra Musa*), Syriac (*Çurriani*) (scil. the *zabûr* of Dâwud [*azabor Dau*]), *chamia* (scil. the Gospel [Sp. *inchil eza*]), and Arabic (scil. the *Alcoran Muhammad*). Chamia is undoubtedly Ar. *ᶜajamîyya*, non-Arabic. The purpose of these remarks can easily be seen if compared with some of the arguments as found, for example, in the work of Ibn Hazm (384/994-456/1064).[52] The problem discussed by Ibn Hazm (and also implicitly by our Morisco author) is whether the Arabic language has a special religious place. Ibn Hazm formulates the problem as follows: Did speech come into being through Divine teaching or is its source human convention? The answer is as follows. Revelation and human reason both demonstrate that language must have a divine origin and proof comes from the Qur'ân, cf. Q.2: 31/29

[49] Cf. Sayyid ᶜUthmân 1327/1909: 7, quoting al-Ghazzâlî.

[50] The question whether one is allowed to translate religious texts of Divine origin such as Traditions was also discussed in Al-Andalus, for example in an 11th-century polemic between Ibn Hazm and Al-Bâjî (1021/402-1081/471), cf. al-Turkî 1975: 121. I am grateful to Prof. L.P. Harvey for drawing my attention to this study.

[51] Biblioteca Nacional Madrid, MS 9067 f. 135v.

[52] *Al-ihkâm fi uûl al-akâm*, translated in Gräf 1974: 101-107.

'God taught Adam all names ...'. It is inconceivable that speech came into being when man was not yet fully able to express himself, since it is impossible that man in that stage would be able to reach agreement upon it. Hence it cannot be of human origin. From this it also follows that a Creator taught man to speak. After one language was taught to mankind, i.e. to Adam, by human convention several languages came into being. It is unknown which language was taught to Adam, but some say that it was Syriac, others that it was Hebrew, others again that it was Arabic. According to many traditions the first to speak Arabic was Ismâ^cîl, and Ishâq the first to speak Hebrew. Ibrâhîm undoubtedly spoke Syriac. There is no preferred language: all languages are equal, as is shown by Qur'ân 14:4: 'We have sent no messenger save with the tongue of his people, that he might make all clear to them ...'.[53] By stating that the Gospel had been revealed in the *ᶜajamî* language (which implies that the Prophet ᶜÎsâ spoke *ᶜajamî*), the Morisco author implicitly confirms that the use of that language did have an authoritative precedent.

The use of Spanish among Andalusians was still evident in Tunis at the beginning of the 18th century, when the English diplomat Morgan wrote that a well-known Spanish poem, Muhammad Rabadan's *Discurso de la Luz* was still being sung: 'At the Town of *Tessatore*, in the Kingdom of *Tunis*, I heard some of the Inhabitants, of both Sexes, sing, in Concert, whole Chapters out of this work, to the Sound of Lutes and Guitars'[54], adding that 'The Name and Memory of this Author are still held in no small Veneration among the Off-spring of the *Moriscoes*, especially in the Kingdom of *Tunis*, where is the most compact Body of those People; and they still retain the Dialect of their Forefathers.'

Modern developments

As we have seen already, the boundaries between the Muslims and non-Muslims were in the classical period well defined, both in everyday reality and in the context of religious and political theory. With the advent of modern times and particularly under the influence of colonial rule, however, the classical doctrines began to change. Movements such as the Ahmadiyya, which arose in India when it was under British domination, began to question the classi-

---

53 Translation by Arberry (1983).
54 Morgan 1723-1725, I: xxi, note.

cal paradigm by refuting the 'expansionist' doctrine of *jihâd*, the distinction *dâr al-islâm—dâr al-harb* and by looking anew at traditional views on purity.[55]. More than perhaps any other modern Islamic movement the Ahmadiyya directed its missionary efforts at non-Muslims by means of religious literature, and particularly by translating Islamic books, and above all the Qur'ân, into foreign languages. Since the 1930s the distinction *dâr al-harb—dâr al-islâm* has become obsolete; the basic notion ruling the relations between Muslims and Non-Muslims now becoming *da^cwa*, i.e. peace.[56] This implies that the nature of the theoretical and practical relations between the *umma* and the non-Muslims underwent very important changes. The transition from the classical paradigm to modern ones was marked by fierce debates, such the discussions about the abolition of the caliphate, and also the closely related ones about the lawfulness of translating the Qur'ân and whether it was permissible to recite translations of the Qur'ân. Among several factors tending to encourage debates[57] about translating the Qur'ân we may note: (1) the installation of a Turkish Committee setting up a Turkish translation (closely connected to the revolution of the Young Turks and Turkish nationalism, in this connection we may also not proposals to replace Arabic by Turkish in some liturgical elements such as the call to prayer), and (2) the coming into being of translations of the Qur'ân made by Muslims in general[58], but in particular the seizure of a copy of an English translation of the Qur'ân made by Muhammad ^cAli, an important member of the Ahmadiyya, by the Egyptian authorities.[59] This seizure led to a discussion at *Dâr al-^cUlûm*, during which al-Jîzâwî, *shaykh al-Azhar* from 1917 until 1928[60], quoted the aforementioned Tradition that it was not allowed to travel with a copy of the Qur'ân to *dâr al-harb*, lest it might fall into the hands of the Unbelievers.[61] By translating the Qur'ân into their languages, he argued, one enables them to touch the *Mushaf*. Hence it is forbidden to do so. From Egypt, the debate spread into other parts of the Muslim world, including the Ma-

---

[55] Muhammad ^cAli 1950: 400 n. 1; Friedmann 1989: 165-180; Peters 1979: 121-135.
[56] Peters 1979: 131-150; Sadan 1980: 103-104; van Koningsveld 1993: 84-88, 104-108, 128-130.
[57] The general background is complex; see Rashîd Ridâ 1926/1344 passim.
[58] Cf. Rashîd Ridâ 1926/1344: 12.
[59] Moreno 1925; Rashîd Ridâ 1926/1344: 24 (justifying the seizure of the Ahmadiyya translation).
[60] See Schulze 1990: 75.
[61] Moreno 1925: 533, 539.

ghrib[62], and because it has been amply discussed elsewhere[63], I will confine myself to some of its inter/intra-religious aspects in the Maghrib.

The sources discussed below would seem to indicate that one of the chief issues underlying the debate was the future relationship between non-Muslims and the *umma* (a notion which was itself undergoing important changes with the rise of the nation-states).

Moroccan Salafist positions: inter-religious aspects

Muhammad b. al-Hasan al-Hajawî, the Moroccan Minister of Education, well-known for his Salafist views[64], stressed the *interreligious* aspect.[65] According to him, it was allowed for someone to translate the Qur'ân, so long as he had mastered both Arabic and the 'target' language. Authoritative sources such as the Qur'ân and the Sunna showed that the focus of the Prophet's activities had been on universal *tablâgh* (preaching) and *da*ᶜ*wa* (mission) and not on the expansion of Islam by means of an arms struggle. During his *hajj* of Farewell the Prophet had said: 'Let those of you present here preach to the absent.' This means that the Arabs have to preach to the other peoples, which implies the use of translations, as the Prophet himself had done.[66] Al-Hajawî based this view on a number of sources. In this connection, Al-Hajawî and indeed all those who advocated the translation of the Qur'ân frequently cited the 14th century Andalusian scholar al-Shâtibî.[67]. In his *al-Muwafâqât*[68], al-Shâtibî had convincingly argued (according to al-Hajawâ and others[69]) that a translation of the absolute meanings (*ma*ᶜ*ânîn mutlaqa*) of the Qur'ân was *possible* on the basis of the fact that it was allowed to explain the Qur'ân to the common people (ᶜ*âmma*) and to comment upon it. Al-Hajawî reached the conclusion that it was even a collective duty (*fard kifâya*) to translate the Qur'ân into all the world's languages.[70] Al-Hajawî, therefore, strongly advocated for the establishment of committees of ᶜ*ulamâ'* which should devote their efforts to preparing translations of the Qur'ân in every

[62] See, for example, Sayyid ᶜUthmân 1327/1909.
[63] Ahmad 1963: 32-44, and the sources referred to there; Tibawi 1962.
[64] See his al-Hajawî 1977/1397.
[65] Al-Hajawî 1936: 191.
[66] Al-Hajawî 1936: 190.
[67] See al-Marâghî 1936: 76ff; Ahmad 1963: 39; Tibawi 1962: 15.
[68] Al-Shâtibî n.y., I: 44-46.
[69] But see al-Shâtir 1355/1936: 142ff.
[70] Al-Hajawî 1936/1355: 190.

language of the world and to examine existing translations (a task nowadays indeed carried out by the Muslim World League (*Râbitat al-ᶜâlam al-islâmî*).[71] The opponents of this view, such as Shaykh Muhammad al-Shâkir and al-Shâtir[72], argued that the correct way of spreading Islam did not lie in making translations of the Qur'ân, but, as the former put it, in the ways 'the Holy Book had shown and which had been used by peoples and nations, in spite of the variety of languages'. He argued further that the spread of Islam was not dependent upon translations, as the defenders argue: 'Oh, people, do you wish Muslims to approach God reciting a translation [...]?'[73] Here we note a transition to the intra-religious aspects, to be discussed below, namely the alleged dangers of translations of the Qur'ân for the unity of the Muslim community, political, spiritual and ritual. Al-Hajawî believed that since ancient times recitation and memorisation of the Qur'ân had been made easier for Berbers in his home country, Morocco, by explaining and paraphrasing the text in the vernacular.[74]

> Upon my life, how does he, who states that it is forbidden to translate [the Qur'ân], imagine the existence of Islam in India, China, Turkey, among the Khazar, the Syrians, the Greek, the Berbers, Africans and other non-Arabic speaking people, who still cling to their own language. How did Islam enter into the depth of their hearts? Did these peoples understand its meanings, principles and excellent qualities or not? We for our part do not doubt that they understood them [...], as far as possible after translation of the Qur'ân. Therefore a Muslim should be convinced that the Faith spread by [furnishing] proof and by persuasion and not by the sword and by violence. And the greatest proof of all is the Qur'ân, its excellent qualities and its marvels. *God most high said: '[so obey not the Unbelievers,] but struggle with them*[75] *thereby*[76] *mightily'* (Q.25:52; my italics, G.W.).[77]

These last lines clearly refer to the distinction between the military *jihâd* and the 'spiritual' *jihâd*, which is often qualified as the great *jihâd*, i.e., the most important form of *jihâd*. 'Thereby' in the quoted verse refers to the Qur'ân. According to al-Hajawî the spread of Islam was first and foremost a spiritual movement. Teaching the Qur'ân in the vernaculars occupied a central position in this proc-

---

[71] See Schulze 1990: 333-336.
[72] In his *Al-Qawl al-Fasl fî tarjamat al-Qur'ân ilâ lughât al-aᶜjamiyya*, Cairo 1925/1343; cf. Shakir 1926. The Arabic original was inaccessible to me.
[73] Quoted in Ahmad 1963: 33.
[74] Al-Hajawî 1936: 192.
[75] I.e., the Unbelievers [G.W.].
[76] I.e., with the Qur'ân [G.W.].
[77] Al-Hajawî 1936: 192 (translation Arberry 1983).

ess. The ritual restrictions on taking the *mushaf* to *dâr al-harb* are implicitly dealt with, though he does not go into these matters openly. He stresses that a translation of the Qur'ân ceases to be the Qur'ân and is therefore to be judged as *tafsîr*. He maintains that such written translations are therefore not subjected to restrictions of purity.[78] Translations of the Qur'ân may be used at all sorts of occasions: sermons (*khutbas* and *wa*ᶜ*z*), the propagation of the faith (*da*ᶜ*wa*), etc, with the exception of recitation. In conclusion al-Hajawâ states that the translation [of the Qur'ân] is to be compared to the symbolic ritual purification (*tayammum*), i.e. a recourse available to believers when compliance with the normal requirements of the law was not possible.

Moroccan Salafist positions: intra-religious aspects

The intra-religious aspect of the debate is stressed in works such as those of Rashîd Ridâ and Al-Shâtir and then also took the form of educational, cultural and political discussions to the Maghrib. Rashîd Ridâ had argued that the Qur'ân should not be translated from the 1900s onwards in publications of the Salafist press, in *al-Manâr* itself, in the *Tafsîr al-Manâr*, and in separate publications.[79] His main argument was the risk that might ensue for Muslim unity, religious and political. Rashîd Ridâ's arguments were later supported by Muhammad Mustaphâ al-Shâtir[80], who stated that the Qur'ânic message aims at religious and political unity, also with respect to language. It is well known that the Prophet was not only sent to the Arabs, but also to the ᶜ*ajam* i.e. his was a universal message, but it clearly appears that all Muslims have to recite the Qur'ân in Arabic and learn it by heart. According to al-Shâtir the connection between the Arabic language and Islam is such that the ᶜ*ulamâ'* agree that all Muslims, for the sake of the Unity to which God calls them, need to master Arabic and that to speak another language than Arabic is reprehensible![81] We find such views in a radicalized anti-Western (i.e. anti-colonial) form in the early Muslim Brotherhood. Hasan al-Bannâ', the founder of the Brotherhood, urged that the use of Arabic in Egypt should be made com-

[78] I.e., polluted persons are allowed to touch it (Hajawî 1936: 198). The Malikite and anafite *madhhab* (to which al-Hajawî belonged) do not share his opinion in this matter: Hanafites extend purity restrictions to *tafsâr* as well.
[79] See Ahmad 1963: 32; Rashîd Ridâ 1926/1344.
[80] *Al-Qawl al-sadâd fi ukm tarjamat al-Qur'ân al-majîd.* Cairo 1355/1936.
[81] Al-Shâtir 1936: 6-9.

pulsory, and wanted the use of European languages on signs, in newspapers, etc. to be prohibited.[82]. Such a view had important consequences in terms of education and culture.

According to Tibawi, Muhammad ᶜAbduh had argued that Muslim children preferably should not attend the colonial educational institutions, because he 'deprecated in the products of such schools the use of foreign speech and conversation and the blind imitation of European manners'.[83] But in the Maghrib, Muhammad al-ᶜAlamî (d. 1954/1373)[84] in 1908/1326 gave a *fatwâ* about the problem of the religious status of *speaking* other languages than Arabic, arguing that this is a matter to be left at the discretion of every individual. He dedicated the *fatwâ* to Sultan ᶜAbd al-Hafîz (r. 1908-1911). According to Abun-Nasr ᶜAbd al-Hafîz had been won over to the ideas of the *Salafiyya* by Abu Shuᶜaib al-Dukkâlî (1878-1937).[85] As is the case in other parts of the Muslim world, one can detect two main stages in the Moroccan *Salafiyya*, i.e. the primarily religious *Salafiyya* until World War I and the Neo-*Salafiyya*, with a strong nationalistic basis, in the post-World War II period.[86] In the first phase, there is little to suggest that *Salafiyya* doctrine on the use of other languages than Arabic contained any anti-colonial sentiments. In the second phase, however, the emphasis on the use of Arabic was a clear reflection of the growing pressure for cultural and political independence.[87] In Algeria the *Salafiyya* stressed that Arabic should be used and taught in private schools taking care of the religious formation of the Muslims, contrary to the public schools controlled by the French, in which French was spoken and in which the curriculum was primarily secular.[88] In 1930 the Salafists expressed the idea that these private schools would not only serve to revive the Arabic language (the language of the community) but also the diffusion of the French language, the language

---

82 According to Heyworth-Dunne 1950: 62ff; but see Al-Bannâ' 1975: 129, and 1977: 92, on his thought in about 1936.

83 Tibawi 1979: 71-72; cf. al-Nabhânî 1322/1904.

84 *Kitâb al-Iᶜlân bi-hurriyyat al-insân fî takallum bi-ayyi lisân bi-dalâ'il al-sunna wa 'l-qur'ân.* MS in private ownership, copied in Rabîᶜ 1330/March 1912; cf. al-Manûnî 1989/1410, II: 266 (no. 1486).

85 Abun-Nasr 1963: 97-98.

86 Abun-Nasr 1963: 99.

87 Abun-Nasr (1963: 100): 'The Arabic language should become the common language of all the Muslim countries; through it the Muslim mentality would be unified, and all its diverse elements brought together ... But all this, he [ᶜAllâl al-Fasî], concludes, cannot be achieved if foreign domination is not brought to an end.' On the views of ᶜAllâl al-Fâsî on Arabisation, see Grandguillaume 1983: 88-9.

88 See Merad 1967.

of the natural sciences and humanities.[89] Clearly Salafists such as Ibn Bâdîs identified Western languages to some extent with the secular sciences and with 'instrumental learning'.[90] Though their slogan 'Arabic is my Language, ... my Fatherland, and Islam my Religion' clearly did not imply the exclusive use of Arabic, in spite of this the Salafist movement seems to have had a negative attitude towards many aspects of Berber culture.[91]

In modern times the discussion about the place of the Arabic language in Muslim life still goes on, particularly in the context of the linguistic and educational politics in the independent Maghrib states.[92] After independence these states used Arabisation as a means of stimulating national and religious identity and national unity. According to the Moroccan *muftî* ᶜAbd al-Salâm al-Samîj (d. 1396/1976)[93], for example, it is reprehensible for someone who knows Arabic to speak another language when staying in a non-Arabic environment. He draws attention to the existence of a Tradition according to which the Prophet had given the advice to Arabic-speaking Muslims on their way to Persia not to speak Persian there. This advice, according to ᶜAbd al-Salâm al-Samîj, was based on the view that speaking other languages has negative consequences for a person's ability to speak and read Arabic. In fact, according to a commentary upon this Tradition, the Arabic language will be burdensome to such a person until the moment he [again] emigrates to Arab territory. Since it is well known that knowledge of Arabic is indispensable for knowledge of the Word of God and the Prophet: both the Qur'ân and the Sunna are written in the language of the Arabs. It is very difficult not be reminded here of the situation of the Moroccan migrants living in Western Europe.

In conclusion: from struggle to peace

The process of modernization which has characterized the Muslim world since the end of the 19th century, led to a revision of the spiritual and political relations between the *umma* and the non-Muslims. If relations between Muslims and non-Muslims were no

---

89 Merad 1967: 342.
90 Cf. Rahman 1984: 67.
91 See Haleber 1992: 274 ff.
92 Grandguillaume 1983; Yacine 1993 (I am grateful to Dr. L. Buskens for procuring a copy of this work for me); Micaud 1974.
93 Al-Samîj 1411/1991: 62.

longer to be characterized by struggle, what then should be the guiding principle? The answer was: *da^cwa* or *tablîgh*. The *Salafiyya* and the modernists (with the exception of some individuals, such as ^cAlî ^cAbd al-Râziq[94]) tried to show that these notions had indeed been the guiding principles of the expanding *umma* since the birth of Islam. According to them, the expansion of Islam was not brought about by force but had been peaceful. The foremost means by which the expansion was achieved was by expounding the Holy Sources in the vernaculars; 'translating' the Qur'ân had in fact been a practice of the Pious forefathers (*al-salaf al-sâlih*). Their opponents denied this. They qualified a translation of the Qur'ân as a *bid^ca*, a reprehensible innovation. Translations of the meanings of the Qur'ân, *made by or furnished with the approval of ^culamâ'*, would endanger Muslim unity, for they would eventually take the place of the Divine revelation. They would be used as the source of Muslim law instead of the Arabic text and eventually even used to recite during prayer. Nationalism, with its stress on national languages was an ideology which, according to the Neo-Salafist Rashîd Ridâ, had been forced upon the Muslims by the colonial powers and would lead to an everlasting division of the Muslim world.[95]. The early unified *umma* had been characterized by unity of language, scil. the Arabic language. Subsequently the division of the *umma*, brought about by bad rulers, had led to the unfortunate situation of linguistic diversity. In the colonial situation, the European powers stimulated this national division of the Muslim world, for it would facilitate their rule over the Muslims. Thus some of the Neo-Salafists, such as Al-Bannâ', began to put more stress on the use of Arabic in writing and speech as Muslim 'identity markers'. The Salafists had a more 'harmonious' view of the relations between the Muslim world and the West.[96] Al-Hajawî, for example, maintained that in the modern situation, characterized by the existence of international treaties between Europe and the Muslim world, Europe can no longer be classified as *dâr al-harb*.[97] In the article discussed above, his view upon the duty to translate the Qur'ân is clearly connected with the conceptions which, in his view, should guide the relations between Muslims and the Non-Muslims.

---

94 See Rosenthal 1965: 94.

95 Rashîd Ridâ 1926/1344: 13. See on Al-Afghânî, Keddie 1983: 56; cf. Bashshâr ^cAwwâd 1405: 64.

96 Cf. Schulze 1990: 87-92.

97 Al-Hajawî 1977/1397, II: 316.

References

Abdesselem, A., 1973, *Les historiens Tunisiens des XVIIe, XVIIIe et XIXe siècles; essay d'histoire culturelle.* Paris: Klincksieck.

Abun-Nasr, J., 1963, 'The Salafiyya Movement in Morocco', in *Middle Eastern Affairs* 16: 90-105.

Ahmad, ᶜAbdelhamîd Muhammad, 1963, *Die Auseinandersetzung zwischen Al-Azhar und der modernistischen Bewegung in Ägypten von Muammad Abduh bis zur Gegenwart.* (Unpublished Ph.D. thesis, University of Hamburg).

al-ᶜAlamî, Muhammad, *Kitâb al-Iᶜlân bi-hurriyyat al-insân fî takallum bi-ayyi lisân bi-dalâ'il al-sunna wa 'l-qur'ân.* MS in private possession.

ᶜAli, Muhammad, 1950, *The Religion of Islam.* Lahore: The Ahmadiyya anjuman ishâᶜat islâm (reprint of the 2nd edition, 1935).

Anonymous, Biblioteca Nacional, Madrid: MSS 9534, 9067, 9653.

Anonymous, Real Academia de la Historia, Madrid: MS S 2.

Anonymous (ed.) 1990, *Conversion and continuity: indigenous Christian communities in Islamic lands, eighth to eighteenth centuries.* Toronto: Pontifical Institute of Medieval Studies.

Arberry, A.J., 1983, *The Koran interpreted.* Oxford: Oxford University Press.

ᶜAwwâd, Bashshâr, 1405/1984, 'Al-ᶜarabiyya shiᶜâr al-islâm wa ahlihâ', in *Al-Durûs al-Hasaniyya.* No place of publication: Wizârat al-awqâf wa'l-shu'ûn al-islâmiyya, 59-70.

al-Bannâ', Hasan, 1977/1407, 'Nahwa'l-nûr', in *Majmûᶜâ rasâ'il al-imâm al-shahîd Hasan al-Bannâ'.* Alexandria: Dar al-daᶜwa.

al-Bannâ', Hasan, 1975, *Five tracts of asan al-Bannâ'; translated by C. Wendell.* Los Angeles: University of California Press.

Basset, H., 1920, *Essay sur la littérature des Berbères.* Alger: Ancienne Maison Bastide-Jordan Jules Carbonel.

Boogert, N. van den, & H. Stroomer 1993, 'De Berberse literaire en orale traditie van de Sous (Zuid Marokko)', in *Sharqiyyât* 5: 55-77.

Friedmann, Y., 1989, *Prophecy continuous: aspects of Amadî religious thought and its Medieval background.* Berkeley, etc.: University of California Press.

Garrad, K., 1954, 'The original memorial of Don Francisco Núñez Muley', in *Atlante* 2, 4: 199-226.

Gayangos, P. de, 1839, 'Language and literature of the Moriscos', in *British and Foreign Review* 8: 63-95.

Graf, E., 1974, 'Recht und Sprache im Islam', in *Zeitschrift für vergleichende Rechtswissenschaft* 74: 116-119.

Grandguillaume, G., 1983, *Arabisation et politique linguistique au Maghreb.* Paris: Maisonneuve & Larose.

al-Hajarî, Ahmad b. Qâsim, 1987/1407, *Nâsir al-dân ᶜalâ 'l-qawm al-kâfirin; edited by M. Razuq.* Casablanca: Kulliyat al-âdâb wa'l-ᶜulâm al-insaniyya.

al-Hajawî, Muhammad, 1936/1355, 'Tarjamat al-Qur'ân al-Karîm', in *Majallat al-Azhar* 7: 190-197.

al-Hajawî, Muhammad, 1977/1397, *Al-fiqr al-sâmi fi ta'rîkh al-fiqh al-islâmî.* Medina: no publisher (= 4 parts in 2 vols.; first edition, Fes 1345/1926).

Haleber, R., met medewerking van P.S. van Koningsveld, 1992, *Islam en humanisme: de wereld van Mohammed Arkoun.* Amsterdam: VU-Uitgeverij.

Harvey, L.P., 1990, *Islamic Spain 1250 to 1500*: Chicago: University of Chicago Press.

Hegyi, O., 1984, 'Language between Christianity and Islam: the case of aljamiado literature', in *Scripta Mediterranea* 5: 29-38.
Hegyi, O., 1990, 'Tradition and linguistic assimilation among the Spanish Moriscos during the sixteenth century', in Anonymous 1990: 381-388.
Heyworth-Dunne, J., 1950, *Religious and political trends in Modern Egypt.* Washington: The author.
Ibn Rushd 1987, *Fatâwâ; edited by M. al-Talîlî.* Beirut: Dâr al-gharb al-islâmî.
Ibrahim, Mustapha, no year, *Guidance to prayers.* Riyad: King Saud University Press.
Joffé, G., (ed.), *North Africa: nation, state and region.* London, etc.: Routledge.
Johansen, B., 1986. 'Staat, Recht und Religion im sunnitischen Islam: können Muslime einen religionsneutralen Staat akzeptieren?', in *Essener Gespräche zum Thema Staat und Kirche* (Münster: Aschendorf) 20.
Juynboll, Th.W., 1930, *Handleiding tot de kennis van de Mohammedaansche wet volgens de leer der Sjâfi*[c]*itische school.* Leiden: Brill.
Keddie, N., 1983, *An Islamic response to imperialism: political and religious writings of Sayyid Jamâl ad-Dîn 'al-Afghânî'.* Berkeley, etc.: University of California Press.
Kister, M.J., 1980, 'Labbayka Allâhumma, labbayka ...; on a monotheistic aspect of a Jâhiliyya practice', in *Jerusalem Studies in Arabic and Islam* 2: 33-57.
Khadduri, M., 1961, *Islamic jurisprudence: Shâfi*[c]*î's Risâla.* Baltimore: The John Hopkins Press.
Khalîl ibn Ishâq al-Jundî 1318/1900, *Mukhtasar al-shaykh Khalâl b. Ishâq fâ l-fiqh* [c]*alâ madhhab al-imâm Mâlik b. Anas.* Paris: matba[c]at al-dawla al-jumhuriyya.
Koningsveld, P.S. van, 1993, *Sprekend over de islam en de moderne tijd.* Amsterdam: Prometheus.
Ladero Quesada, M.A., 1969, *Los Mudéjares de Castilla en tiempos de Isabel I.* Valladolid: Instituto 'Isabel la Católica' de historia eclesiástica.
López-Baralt, L., 1992, *Una Kâma Sûtra español.* Madrid: Siruela.
López-Morillas, C. 1983, '"Trilingual" marginal notes (Arabic, Aljamiado and Spanish) in a Morisco manuscript from Toledo', in *Journal of the American Oriental Society* 103, 3: 495-504.
Al-Manûnî, M., 1989/1410, *Al-masâdir al-*[c]*arabiyya li-ta'rîkh al-maghrib*, II, *Al-fatra al-mu*[c]*âsira* (1790-1930). Rabat: Jâmi[c]a Muhammad al-khâmis, Manshûrât kulliyat al-âdâb wa'l-[c]ulûm al-insâniyya. Silsilat al-dirâsât al-bibliyûghrâfiyya. 2 vols.
Al-Marâghî, M.M., 1936/1355, 'Bahth fi tarjamat al-Qur'ân', in *Majallat al-Azhar* 7: 77-112.
Merad, A., 1967, *Le réformisme musulman en Algérie de 1925 à 1940; essay d'histoire religieuse et sociale.* Paris, etc.: Mouton.
Micaud, C.A., 1974, 'Bilingualism in North Africa: cultural and socio-political implications', in *The Western Political Quarterly* 27, 1: 92-103.
Moreno, M.M., 1925, 'È lecito ai Musulmani tradurre il Corano', in *Oriente Moderno* 5: 532-543.
Morgan J., 1723-1725, *Mohametism fully explained.* London: no publisher, 2 vols.
al-Nabhânî, Yûsuf b. Ismâ[c]îl, 1322/1904, *Kitâb irshâd al-hayârâ fî tahdhîr al-muslimîn min madâris al-nasârâ.* Cairo: no publisher.
al-Nawawî, Abu Zakariyâ b. Yahyâ b. Sharf al-dîn, 1934/1353, *Al-Tibyân*

fi âdâb hamalat al-Qur'ân. Cairo: Matba[c]at Mustaphâ al-Bâbî al-Halabî.
Peters, R., 1979, *Islam and colonialism: the doctrine of jihad in modern history*. The Hague: Mouton.
Rahman, Fazlur, 1984, *Islam and modernity: transformation of an intellectual tradition*. Chicago, etc.: University of Chicago Press.
Rashîd Ridâ, Muhammad, 1926/1344, *Tarjamat al-Qur'ân wa-mâ fîhâ min mafâsid wa-munâfât al-islâm*. Cairo: Matba[c]at al-Manâr.
Richter Bernburg, L., 1974, 'Linguistic Shu[c]âbîya and early neo-Persian prose', in *Journal of the American Oriental Society* 94: 55-64.
Rosenthal, E.I.J., 1965, *Islam in the modern national state*. Cambridge: Cambridge University Press.
Saavedra y Moragas, E., 1889, 'Discurso que el Ecsmo. Sr. D. Eduardo Saavedra leyó en Junta Públíca de la Real Academia Española, el dia 29 de diciembre de 1878, al tomar posesión de su plaza de Académico de número', in *Memorias de la Real Academia Española* (Madrid) 6, apendice I: Indice general de la literatura aljamiada.
Sadan, J., 1980, '"Community" and "extra-community" as a legal and literary problem', in *Israel Oriental Studies* 10: 102-115.
al-Samîj, [c]Abd al-Salâm, 1411/1991, *Al-fawâ'id al-jâmi[c]a fi [c]iddat masâ'il nâfi[c]a*. Rabat: Wizârat al-awqâf wa'l-shu'ûn al-islâmiyya lil-mamlaka al-maghribiyya.
Schulze, R., 1990, *Islamischer Internationalismus im 20. Jahrhundert; Untersuchungen zur Geschichte der islamischen Weltliga*. Leiden. etc.: Brill.
al-Shâfi[c]î, 1357/1938, *Al-Risâla; edited by A.M. Shâkir*. Cairo: no publisher.
Shakir, M., 1926, 'Translations of the Koran', in *The Moslem World* 16: 161-165.
Shaltût, Mahmûd, 1936/1355, 'Tarjamat al-Qur'ân wa nusüs al-[c]ulamâ' fâhâ', in *Majallat al-Azhar* 7: 123-34.
al-Shâtibî, no year, *Al-Muwâfâqât fi usûl al-fiqh*. No place of publication: dâr al-fikr, 2 vols.
al-Shâtir, Muhammad Mustaphâ, 1355/1936, *Al-Qawl al-sadîd fi hukm tarjamat al-Qur'an al-majîd*. Cairo: matba[c]at hijâzî.
al-Sinânî, Muhammad al-Radî, 1383/1963, *Al-Shadharât wa'ltiqât al-fawâ'id wa ghurar al-[c]awâ'id*. Casablanca: matba[c]at al-najâh, 2 vols.
Stieglecker, H., 1962, *Glaubenslehren des Islam*. Paderborn, etc.: Ferdinand Schöningh.
Tibawi, A.L., 1962, 'Is the Qur'ân translatable?', in *The Muslim World* 52: 4-16.
Tibawi, A.L., 1979[2], *Islamic Education*. London: Luzac & Company.
al-Turki, [c]Abd al-Magid, 1975 (?), *Polémiques entre Ibn Hazm et al-Bâgî sur les principes de la loi musulmane*. Algiers: no publisher.
[c]Uthmân, Sayyid ([c]Uthmân b. [c]Abd Allâh b. [c]Aqîl b. Yayâ), 1327/1909, *Hukm al-rahmân bi'l-nahy [c]an tarjamat al-Qur'ân*. No place of publication: no publisher.
al-Wansharîsî, Ahmad b. Yahyâ, 1401/1981, *Al-Mi[c]yâr al-mu[c]rib wa 'l-djâmi[c] al-mughrib [c]an fatâwâ ahl Ifrîqiya wa 'l-Andalus wa 'l-Maghrib; edited by Muhammad Hajjâ and others*. Rabat: Wizârat al-awqâf wa'l-shu'ûn al-islâmiyya lil-mamlaka al-maghribiyya, 12 Vols.
Wiegers, G.A., 1994, *Islamic literature in Spanish and Aljamiado: Yça of Segovia (fl. 1450), his antecedents and successors*. Leiden etc.: Brill.
Yacine, R., 1993, 'The impact of the French colonial heritage on language politics in independent North Africa', in Joffé 1993: 221-232.

BETWEEN COMMUNALISM AND SECULARISM

MODERN SUNNITE DISCUSSIONS ON MALE HEAD-GEAR AND COIFFURE

Sjoerd van Koningsveld
(Leiden University)

The presence of non-Muslim religious groups has been a characteristic aspect of most Muslim societies, through all periods of their history until this very day. Traditionally, the sociopolitical and juridical space available for each individual, Muslim and non-Muslim, was primarily defined on the basis of his or her religious denomination. Thus, in pre-modern Islamic history, religious pluralism was first and foremost communalism: several non-Muslim religious communities lived side by side with the Muslim majorities in the various Muslim polities enjoying a high degree of internal autonomy. At the same time, the Islamic ethical and juridical code had developed a detailed set of behavioral norms and rules governing the daily contacts between Muslims and non-Muslims, especially in the public sphere. An important principle underlying the traditional Islamic etiquette regarding the contacts with non-Muslims was the injunction ascribed to the Prophet to act differently from the ways of Jews, Christians, etc. Specifically Islamic, Christian, Jewish and other ways of dressing and coiffure, served as important markers for expressing and strengthening the identity of Muslims and other religious groups. Within these pluralistic societies based on the system of communalism, the religious affiliation of individuals could be quickly determined from their outer appearance.

However, during the late 19th and the 20th centuries, fundamental changes took place in the socio-juridical position of Muslim and non-Muslim groups in all these societies. In the two most important reform prescripts, of 1839 and 1856, all Ottoman citizens, Muslims as well as non-Muslims, were declared equal before the law. A long struggle to effectuate this theoretical equality was still ahead, but eventually this reform led to the complete collapse of the old order[1]. During the colonial period and especially through the creation of nation-states, the prevailing systems of communalism were replaced by systems based on citizenship and nationality, without regard to religious affiliation in most Muslim countries.

[1] Sharabi 1962, 17.

The degree of secularization of these systems varies in the different countries, but in most of them some elements of communalism have survived, especially in the sphere of family law. Moreover, Islam, as the religion of the majority, has usually (though not always) been given a privileged position in the contemporary constitutional law of Muslim countries. Nevertheless, citizenship and nationality in countries like Jordania and Egypt (where both Muslim and Christian family law continue to be applied), are based, as a matter of principle, not on religious affiliation, but on residence and descent. The segmentation of society along strictly religious lines, as it prevailed in pre-modern times, has been abolished. This important event has, so to speak, 'outdated' many aspects of traditional Islamic etiquette, especially in as far as they were directed towards strengthening the basic principles of communalism. Among the most conspicuous changes of the Islamic etiquette are those related to dressing and coiffure.

A general survey of the changes in the dressing habits in the Near East in the past century has been given by Stillman.[2] According to this author, traditional, loose-flowing garments were gradually abandoned in this period in favour of clothes tailored after Western fashion. The transition was slow at first and did not take place at the same time in every place and among all groups. The first to begin to abandon traditional attire in large numbers were the westernized Christians and Jews. Most Christian and Jewish women abandoned the veil a full generation or more before their Muslim counterparts. By the end of the 19th century, the question: 'to veil or not to veil', had become one of the burning issues for modernist reformers and for the small but growing Egyptian feminist movement.

Muslim men abandoned traditional attire more rapidly than women. The first Muslim men to adopt the European mode of dress were members of the bureaucracy and the upper-class who were in direct contact with westerners and had often visited Europe. They remained a small minority throughout the 19th century. However, change became rapid after the First World War. One aspect of the male wardrobe that has resisted change even in places where the transition to Western attire has been more or less complete is the headgear. It is still common to see men dressed in a Western suit wear a *taqiyya*, a *tarbûsh*, or a *kâfiyya*. This is due to the importance that is traditionally attached to the covering of the head and to the fact that the headgear concerned (originally the turban)

---

[2] Stillman 1986.

served as a badge of Islam. The traditional turban is now worn almost exclusively by the religious scholars.[3]

The changes discussed sofar have provoked many discussions among the religious scholars of Islam. They were not only about female dress, but also about male head-gear and coiffure, particularly of the beard and the moustache. The present contribution attempts to survey the arguments put forward in the discussions about the habits of gentlemen and to analyze the main issues underlying them. For this purpose, I have selected a number of sources which reflect the main trends in these debates. These sources in fact represent two major trends. The first one of these I have termed 'Liberalism and reformism'. It tends to be rather pragmatic: it looks for practical solutions of the problems posed by new socio-cultural circumstances. The second I label 'Conservatism and traditionalism'. It is interested primarily in maintaining the fundamental religious principles, including the differentiation between Muslims and non-Muslims, and between men and women. The two trends espouse views about certain central issues, such as the status of the *Sunna* of the Prophet and the desirability of secularization and modernization of society, which are diametrically opposed. Whereas the protagonists of 'Liberalism and reformism' are found mainly among the great and officially recognized scholars of Sunnite Islam with an international standing, the defenders of 'Traditionalism and conservatism' occupy a more marginal or polemical position and can be shown to wield an influence that is restricted to specific regions in the first place.

Liberalism and reformism

The earliest discussions which I know of took place in Paris, during the sixties of the 19th century among Muslim students from the Near East and North Africa who were reading medicine or taking courses in the natural or military sciences in the French capital. These students were confronted with some practical problems connected with daily life in Western Europe: was it permissible for Muslims to eat the meat of French butchers; could one exchange the traditional Islamic headgear for the French hat?

---

[3] So far my summary of Stillman. See also the literature mentioned in Stillman 1986. I cannot, however, support Stillman's view that the turban is still commonly worn in the Maghrib, and in particular Morocco, even by men who have adopted Western dress.

Sulaymân ibn ᶜAlî al-Harâ'irî, a scholar of Tunisian descent who was teaching Arabic in the *Ecole des Langues Orientales Vivantes* in Paris[4] defended a liberal point of view in several *fatwâs* which he published in printed editions in Paris. Though Al-Harâ'irî himself was not a religious scholar in the strict sense, his *fatwâs* formed the starting-point of a long discussion in Islam which accompanied the acceptation of some Western dressing habits.

His *fatwâ* concerning the French hat of 1862 was entitled 'Answers to the perplexed ones concerning the statute of the hat of the Christians'.[5] It is stated in its preface that the more than 300 Muslim students in Paris had various practical reasons for discussing the permissibility of wearing the French hat. In the streets and during the lectures Frenchmen were gazing at them full of astonishment because of their strange appearance. They pointed out that the wearing of the French hat had some clear advantages, as France was a very cold country and the brim of the French hat gave extra protection to the eyes. However, some of the students had stressed that by wearing this hat one in fact committed apostasy with all its consequences. Wives in the countries of origin would be divorced automatically, and after returning to the Islamic world one would have to convert to Islam again, and to remarry officially with one's own spouse. The author, on the other hand, saw no objection whatsoever to the wearing of the 'hat of the Christians', because this practice did not imply any form of assimilation in strictly religious

---

[4] He had been appointed *ra'îs al-kuttâb* (approximately secretary-general) of Tunisia by the Bey of Tunis in 1840. He was a specialist in the natural sciences, medicine and mathematics. In 1857 he was 'notaire et secrétaire arabe au Consulat général de France à Tunis, membre de plusieurs Sociétés savantes de Paris, auteur de plusieurs ouvrages arabes, de traductions du français en arabe, etc.' (cf. al-Harâ'irî 1857: title-page). In the preface to this work, the translator defends, among other points, the legitimacy of social relations with Christians and Jews, including the participation in meals, if they do not wage war against the Muslims for the purpose of making them abandon their religion (al-Harâ'irî 1857: XV). He defends cooperation with the French and praises their wise and just administration and their promotion of culture and science (al-Harâ'irî 1857: XV). He lists the various kinds of French scientific books which he translated into Arabic (al-Harâ'irî 1857: XXV). He is proud of being the first to translate a French grammar into Arabic. In Paris, he edited also the journal entitled *Birjîs Barîs* [The 'Jupiter of Paris'], published by Rushaid Dahdâh, a Lebanese-Christian scholar. This form of interreligious cooperation was characteristic of the budding Arabic nationalism of this period. Apart from these activities, Al-Harâ'irî published several literary texts. He was, however, not a religious scholar. (Some biographical data may be found in Al-Ziriklî's encyclopedia *Al-Aᶜlâm*, vol. 3: 131).

[5] The only copy known to me so far is preserved in the Bibliothèque Nationale in Paris. I should like to thank my friend Prof. Dr. J. Sadan for having drawn my attention to this valuable source.

matters. It was only that form of assimilation which was forbidden by Islam.

The problem of the Christian hat reappears in a *fatwâ* by the founder of modern Sunnite Reformism, Muhammad ᶜAbduh (d. 1905). In his quality of *Mufti* of Egypt he answered a few questions which a Muslim from South Africa by the name of Mustafâ al-Tiransfâlî had submitted to him.[6] The Muslim minority in Transvaal faced problems similar to those of the Muslim students in Paris. The petitioner explained that some Muslims in their daily life in Transvaal were wearing *burnaytas*. He also stressed that the method of slaughtering applied in Transvaal differed in many aspects from the Islamic rules. Cows were struck down with an axe and were slaughtered without God's name having been invoked first. Sheep were also slaughtered straightaway, without God's name having been invoked. A last problem put before ᶜAbduh concerned the fact that some Muslims of the Shafi'ite law school were accustomed to perform their prayers (also during the two annual Feasts) while standing behind followers of the Hanafite law school thereby imitating them; moreover, attention was drawn to a few other (minor) differences between the prayer rituals of the two schools. The petitioner asked whether all these deviations from Islam were permitted?

Concerning the problem of the head-gear, ᶜAbduh defended precisely the same opinion as Al-Harâ'irî, though he did not refer to him. He explained that the intention of these Muslims in South Africa were of decisive importance as were the circumstances under which they were wearing the Christian hat. As long as their wearing the *burnayta* was not an expression of their intention to apostatize from Islam and to enter into another religion, they should not be branded as unbelievers for the mere fact of wearing it. Moreover, if there were some need to wear it, such as seeking protection against the heat of the sun, then the wearing of the Christian hat was not even to be deemed rejectable. Under these circumstances, no assimilation to another religion, as the result of an inner inclination and a rapprochement to Christianity, occurred, which was what Islam truly forbade. Muhammad ᶜAbduh also permitted the consumption of the meat of animals slaughtered in the manner mentioned above, for which he appealed to the rule of the Qoran that Muslims could eat the food of the People of the Book. At the same time he also referred to the opinion of the 12th century scholar Abû Bakr ibn al-ᶜArabî, who had also permitted Muslims to eat from the

---

[6] The text of this *fatwâ* is found in ᶜAmâra 1972-4, vol. 6: 255-256.

animals which had been slaughtered by the People of the Book.[7] He also sanctioned the practices current in Transvaal of performing the prayer ritual after the rules of a law school other than one's own. Islam was one religion, not many. No sensible man could object to this in a country in which Muslims were a tiny minority.

Problems such as these were initially formulated by the small groups of Muslims living as minorities in a non-Muslim environment. They began to play an important role in the Muslim world itself in the first half of the 20th century, when the European political and cultural influence induced growing numbers of people to exchange their traditional costume for some form of European dress, and to adopt Western customs and habits in many other sectors of social life.

The line of Al-Harâ'irî and ᶜAbduh was further developed by the *mufti* of Egypt of great repute and rector of Al-Azhar, Shaykh Mahmûd Shaltût, who published a selection of his *fatwâs* under the significant title: *A study of the problems of the contemporary Muslim in his daily and general life*.[8] This collection has been published numerous times and circulates in the Muslim world in several translations, e.g., in Indonesian and Urdu. It has played a prominent role in the reconciliation of religious norms with the demands of modern times, and continues to do so. Shaltout states plainly that Islam does not order men to perform *salât* with their heads covered. A Muslim may pray with his head uncovered or with any traditional or modern head-gear, as long as it does not prevent him from touching the ground during the prescribed prosternation. A specifically Islamic head-gear does not exist. Islam leaves it to the 'custom' *(ᶜurf)* which the people in any given place and time observe to determine how one should dress and whether one should cover one's head. The idea that the hat *(qubbâᶜa)* is a typically non-Islamic dress is wrong. Muslims and others are completely equal in this respect. The wearing of hats by Muslims does not imply that they intend to assimilate to others in the particularities of their religion. They only wear hats to protect themselves against the heat of the sun or the cold of the winter, or because local custom demands it.[9]

According to Shaltout, the shaving of the beard is a matter of dispute among the religious scholars. Some consider it forbidden,

---

[7] This opinion caused a long string of debates because it disassociated itself from a long tradition of complicated discussions. For the classical viewpoints about this problem see e.g. Ibn Qayyim al-Jawziyya, 1961, vol. 1: 244-269: 'Section concerning the rules about the slaughter cattle'.

[8] Shaltût 1980[10].

[9] Shaltût 1980[10]: 88.

others classify it among the deeds which are to be sharply disapproved. The Prophet did indeed allow his beard to grow, but he did attend to it by trimming it and washing it with water. Among the numerous traditions about the natural disposition *(fitra)* of mankind, several state that the Prophet summoned men to let their beard grow. The concept of *fitra* directs the attention of the believers towards all those matters which enhance the nature of men in its most beautiful form. Apart from the growing of a beard, several practices fall within the scope of the *fitra*, such as the use of a toothbrush, the trimming of the moustache, the clipping of the nails, the washing of one's phalanges, the sniffing of water in order to clean the nose, the removal of hair from arm-pits and pubis, as well as circumcision. Some scholars considered these practices merely recommendable, or deemed omitting them as only rejectable. Certain traditions indeed order Muslims to grow a beard for the sake of distinguishing themselves from the Magians and the polytheists.

However, the duty imposed by these traditions should not be understood as a strict command but rather as a rule for 'the best form of behaviour' *(al-afdal)*. Assimilation to adherents of a different faith is forbidden only in as far as specific aspects of their religion are concerned. There is no harm in matters which pertain to 'general customs'. When Abû Yûsuf, the companion of the famous scholar Abû Hanîfa, was reproached for wearing sandals which had been repaired with nails—a practice which could be observed also in the sandals of Christian monks, he retorted that the Prophet himself had been wearing leather sandals with hair, a custom which monks had followed as well. If one would have to regard as forbidden everything by which Muslims resembled Christians, one would have to forbid even the growing of the beard, because that custom was observed also by monks in every country. One would then have to forbid also the wearing of the hat, 'after time has turned over its page and these matters have taken their place as general customs which have no relation to religiosity, moral corruption, belief or unbelief. Dress and personal externals, including the shaving of the beard, are in fact matters in which men should conform to the society in which they live.' The same principle must be applied to the problem of painting one's hair.[10]

All this does not mean, however, that Shaltout did not see the wisdom of the Prophet's admonition to Muslims that they should distinguish themselves from others. It exhorted them to preserve

---

[10] Shaltût 1980[10]: 227-229.

their inner Islamic identity. Assimilation of externals might lead easily and unconsciously to adaptation in internal, spiritual matters. One may find that Muslims who frequently associate with foreigners pay less attention to religious matters than those who do not. Moreover, one may also notice that a similar outer appearance creates a certain affection and love, for instance between two men hailing from the same country who meet abroad, or between men who wear the same type of dress or head-gear. All Easterners who stick to their Eastern dress share this experience whenever they meet in a Western country. For that reason the Prophet ordered his Companions to distinguish themselves in externals from the others in several ways, such as dress, coiffure, the position of the *imam* in the *mihrâb*, etc., during the first phase of the development of his community in Medina. This is the meaning of the Prophet's injunction: 'Distinguish yourselves from them!'

Certain recent discussions concerning the position of Muslims in a non-Muslim environment reflect a similar attitude. Doi, a Professor of Shari^{c}ah at the International Islamic University at Kuala Lumpur, Malaysia, took a position in the issue in an article on the 'Duties and responsibilities of Muslims in non-Muslim states'.[11] He stressed that

> 'there is no definite Islamic dress as such. Any dress that covers the *satr*[12] either for men or women is quite sufficient as an Islamic dress. (...) In non-Muslim countries if Muslims have to wear European dress or Hindu dress or wrappers like Buddhist monks according to the tradition of that land, there is absolutely no harm even if prayers *(salat)* are offered in that dress. *Salat* will be accepted in these attires. It is however essential that these dresses cover a Muslim's *satr*. Supposing there prevails complete freedom to wear any dress in a non-Muslim country and Muslims choose to wear dresses which resemble other Muslims in other parts of that country or outside, it is advisable to do so, in order that people can recognize from a distance that they are Muslims. To put on dresses like the majority of [the] non-Muslim community in order just to please them without any need for it will come under the category of "imitating the non-Muslims": "*Whosoever imitates a community [of non-Muslims], he is amongst them*" (Al-Qur'an).'[13]

Also the leader of the Tunisian Islamist party *Al-Nahda* ('Renaissance'), Râshid Al-Ghanoushî, commented upon the Islamic view

---

[11] Doi 1992. I would like to thank my colleague Dr. J.G. Platvoet for drawing my attention to this publication, which would not have come to my notice otherwise.

[12] The author uses this word as a synonym for *'awra*, the part of the body which should be covered according to the Sharî^{c}a, especially during the performance of prayer.

[13] Doi 1992: 131-132; his italics.

of dress in a similar way, in a collection of interviews published in 1992.[14] Al-Ghanoushî holds that Islam did not bring a certain type of clothing.

> 'Islam is not a tailor. (...) Islam is a source of values, a source of ethical guidance. It calls upon us to cover ourselves, but it does not define the type of dress. It has laid down general principles of covering, but it did not say: "You have to cover yourselves with Pakistani cloths or with Egyptian, French or American cloths. This belongs to the sphere of earthly life. The thing which matters in Islam is that we adorn ourselves with uprightness and, at the external level, with the value of dignity".'

Conservatism and traditionalism

Quite a different attitude is reflected, however, in the writings which aimed to preserve unadulterated the traditional norms of Islam. Al-Harâ'irî's *fatwâ* of 1862 was apparently sent to the Near East soon after its publication and brought to the attention of the orthodox Malikite scholar of Al-Azhar, Muhammad ᶜIllaysh[15]. In contrast to Al-Harâ'irî, Muhammad ᶜIllaysh defended an outspokenly anti-Western political point of view. He took part in the anti-British Urabi-revolt and died in prison in 1882. His opinion about the permissibility of the Christian hat crystallized in an unpublished *fatwâ* entitled: 'Refutation of the Epistle "Answers to the Perplexed concerning the statute of the Hat of the Christians".'[16] It is preserved in a manuscript in the Tetouan General Library which was copied from the copy the author had written author's own copy 1279 ((1862 or 1863).

The author first contests that Al-Harâ'irî is qualified to give a learned opinion about religious matters in the form of a *fatwâ*. He disagrees with Al-Harâ'irî's use of the word *qalansuwwa* for denoting the Christian hat. The *qalansuwwa* is used in Arabic, says the author, exclusively for a piece of head-gear worn by Muslims. That of the Christians is called *al-burnayta*. This piece of head-gear is forbidden for a Muslim for various reasons. First of all, one cannot per-

---

[14] Cf. al-Darwîsh 1992: 150-157 ('The Islamists and the West').

[15] The family of Muhammad ibn Ahmad ibn Muhammad ᶜIllaysh (1802-1882) was of Moroccan origin. See on him de Jong 1985.

[16] *al-Radd ʿalâ Risâlat ajwibat al-hayârâ ʿan hukm qalansuwwat al-nasârâ*, manuscript nr. 236 in the General Library of Tetouan (Morocco), 26 pp. I thank the authorities of the library for their permission to use this manuscript and for the photocopy of it. This text does not appear in the collection of *fatwâs* of ᶜIllaysh in ᶜIllaysh 1901-1903.

form the *salât* while wearing it, because its brim hinders the worshipper to touch the ground with his forehead during the prosternation. Furthermore, as outer apparel it indicates the low position proper to Christians but not fitting for Muslims. Thirdly, it is unnecessary that Muslim students study outside their own countries, because the only sciences which are obligatory from a religious point of view are the religious disciplines. As these cannot be studied outside the Muslim world, students should return to their countries of origin as quickly as possible: they must perform the 'emigration' (*hijra*) to the 'territory of Islam' (*Dâr al-Islâm*) and no longer commit the offence of assimilation to the Infidels.[17]

A substantial contribution to the corroboration of the conservative standpoint was provided by the Moroccan scholar Al-Kattânî in his book *A support for the knowledge of the rules concerning the [religiously sanctioned] custom of the turban.*[18] One reads the following slogans on the cover of the book: 'Turbans are the crowns of the Arabs', and: 'Turbans mark the distinction between belief and unbelief'. These slogans indicate clearly the tenor of the book. Despite its outspokenly conservative viewpoint, it contains a remarkable historical essay about the wearing of turbans in Islamic history. The author reveals his personal commitment in a few passages by the choice of his subject and the manner in which he treats it. 'In many Eastern countries[19]', he says, 'we have remarked, when we entered them, that both the young and many adults have completely aban-

---

[17] The broader context of this view are undoubtedly the numerous discussions at that time about the problem whether Muslims who had been subjected by the armies of Christians (Europeans), were allowed to continue to live under Christian rule, or ought to follow the example of the Prophet and perform the 'emigration to the territory of Islam'. These discussions reflected vital political interests of the Muslim peoples during the period of expansion of colonial rule. They were provoked by the French intervention in Algeria, by the Dutch war against Acheh, etc. ʿIllaysh himself also wrote an extensive treatise about this problem, in which he, among others, referred to certain early 16th century *fatwâs* about the position of Muslims who had remained in (Christian) Spain after the fall of Granada (cf. ʿIllaysh 1901-1903 [1319-1321 H.], vol. 1: 313-334).

[18] al-Kattânî 1923-1924 (1342 H.). The author was born in Fès in 1275 (1858-9), performed the pilgrimage in 1905 and 1907 and left his homeland in protest against the French rule in 1910. He settled in Medina, whence he was banished by the Turks. He was teaching in Damascus in 1922. He returned to his home town in 1926 and died there in 1927. He was a gifted historian who wrote many important works about the history of Fès. Cf. Lévi-Provençal 1922: 379-385.

[19] The author refers to the countries of the Mashriq (the East) in contradistinction to the countries of the Maghrib (the West). The changes of dressing habits took place in the Near East first. The countries of the Maghrib followed suit only some decades later. This explains, to some extent, the amazement and indignation of the author.

doned this venerable custom, viz. the custom of wearing the respected turban'.[20] They feel ashamed to wear it when they go to the market and other public places, let alone to parties and gatherings. Those who do wear it may even be ridiculed and mocked by their own people. The author adds:

> 'It has been reported to me that certain wives will not accept the turban under any circumstance, and cannot bring themselves to look at their husband when he is wearing it. This goes even so far that some of them, by way of exaggeration say: 'The daffa is better than the laffa!', by which they mean that they prefer to see their husbands being carried into [their houses] on the bier (daffa) for washing by them prior to their burial, than to see him wear a turban (the laffa) [in his lifetime]. To that extent they hate this custom.'

The author holds that the way in which these wives reject well-founded *sunnas* does not in itself necessarily result from unbelief but rather from a low natural inclination and of a lack of readiness to submit to the Law and the religion of the almighty God. Husbands should therefore correct their wives and tell them:

> 'How can you reject something which has been approved by the Lord of the Universe, by whom the heavens and earth have been created? This is a shame upon him who wears it, an infringement upon religion and a stain on its honour!'

However, if this attitude would be caused by an explicit intention to reject and to hold in contempt the prophetical *Sunna*, then one is dealing with apostasy and unbelief, as has been correctly explained by some earlier authorities. How could this happen to a Muslim? The author is aware that some Muslims would claim that they do not reject this *sunna* as a matter of principle, but would only consider it an infringement upon one's sense of honour because of the different customs of the country in which they live. The author's reply to them is that the turban, as an emblem of Islam indicates the distinction between Islam and unbelief, and can therefore never infringe upon anyone's sense of honour whether or not the custom prevailing in a given country stimulates the wearing of the turban. It is, on the contrary, to be rejected that this custom is abandoned completely, because this would result in the destruction of a prophetical *sunna* and the adoption of a non-Muslim custom, even during prayers, religious feasts, the visiting of the mosque and the festive gatherings of the believers. The author therefore pleads that this *sunna* be revived, in support of which he duly refers to the

[20] 'Tark hâdhihi 'l-sunna al-mukarrama allatî hiya sunnat al-ʿimâma al-muhtarama tarkan battan' (al-Kattânî 1923-1924 [1342 H.]: 17).

reward the Prophet promised to those who revive an abandoned *sunna*.[21]

The author also draws attention to the fact that discarding the turban is accompanied often by two other 'outrageous matters', viz. the shaving of the beard and the growing of the moustache, and the latter to such an extent that it covers the greater part of the mouth or even covers it completely. He stresses that the religious scholars have pointed out that the shaving of the beard originally belonged to the customs of the Persians and was sanctioned by their religion.[22] The prophetical order not to shave the beard was therefore given to distinguish the Muslims by their outer appearance from the Persians. The same holds true for cutting the moustache. Today, however, many Jews and despicable Muslims join the Europeans in shaving their beards and letting their moustaches grow. Together with the use of different cloths and modern cosmetics, these new habits have induced many youngsters to behave in a most ignominious manner towards those who are still attached to the old, respectable ways. They are frequenting doubtful and obscene places where people drink wine, play instruments, dance and indulge in various kinds of abominable amusement. Those who do not want to follow these 'rules' are not accepted and are ridiculed. The only solution the author sees is religious admonition by which those committing these offenses should be induced to repent and to attend again scholarly meetings which are above reproach.[23]

The author had begun his study of the turban at the time when he still lived in Morocco. Originally, it had a literary and historical character. However, having entered the countries of the Near East, he decided to complete it by taking into account the decay of this prophetical custom which he was now witnessing daily. Al-Kattânî admitted that he did not know the precise prescriptions of Tradition and Law about the age for boys to start wearing the turban. Was this to start during the 7th or 10th year of their life, like the duty of the *salât*, or on the moment of their becoming an adult[24], or from the time their beards began to grow, which coincided with the moment their manliness began to develop and they began to mix with people? The actual customs of people were different in this respect, as he had observed himself. The inhabitants of Mecca and Medina followed the first option, especially on Fridays and festivals. Those of the Maghrib rather followed the third. The opinions of

[21] al-Kattânî 1923-1924 (1342 H.): 19.
[22] al-Kattânî 1923-1924 (1342 H.): 21.
[23] al-Kattânî 1923-1924 (1342 H.): 28-29.
[24] This stage is reached at the moment of sexual maturity, viz., in the case of a boy, when he starts producing sperm. He is then *mukallaf*, responsible for the fulfilment of all the prescriptions of Islam.

Mâlik ibn Anas seem to point to the first or the second of these choices. However, it is the author's view that people should follow the custom of their country in this matter, and the same holds true, he says, for the size and the outer appearance of the turban.

Al-Kattânî's point of view was followed in a sharply radicalised form in the outspokenly traditionalist circles defending the undiminished authority of the prophetical *Sunna* as a major source of Islamic norms and values in the matter of the social customs of dress and hygiene. One of the exponents of this strictly orthodox trend is the Moroccan scholar Muhammad al-Zamzamî ibn al-Siddîq (d. 1988).[25] In order to assess the impact of his views correctly, one has to take into account his position within the landscape of contemporary Moroccan Islam. First of all, he was known for a specific doctrine in matters related to the hermeneutical science of the Sources (the *ᶜilm al-usûl*). The import of this doctrine is that one must follow the rules of Islam which the texts (of Qoran and Tradition) explicitly provide. These rules may neither be subjected to the independent research by the great scholars *(ijtihâd)*, nor, per consequence, to the imitation of their religious leaders by the ordinary believers *(taqlîd)*. They must merely be 'followed' *(ittibâᶜ)*. This stern point of view had, of course, many implications for the application of rules which may be derived from the *Sunna*.

Al-Zamzamî was a preacher, first in the *Zâwiya Siddîqiyya* in Tangier, then in the Friday Mosque of the Banî Makkâda in the same town, and finally in the Mosque of the Guidance of the Prophet *(Jâmiᶜ Hudâ al-Rasûl)* founded by his own supporters who had organized themselves into the *Ansâr al-Sunna* ('The Supporters of the *Sunna*'), in the same city. Al-Zamzamî served the Ministry of Religious Affairs as a preacher for a number of years by giving lectures in the Great Mosque of Tangier. His views, however, brought him into conflict with the authorities, presumably in the early seventies[26]. Therefore, one may say that Al-Zamzamî was a religious

[25] See on him: Ibn al-Hâjj al-Sulamî 1992: 121-123.

[26] He refers to these difficulties in al-Zamzamî 1974/1394, a booklet of 108 pages, the publication of which was financed by the 'Community of the Supporters of the Muhammadan *Sunna*'. He informs the reader about his success as a preacher in the Great Mosque of Tangiers, which caused a great deal of opposition and animosity in many circles. The author defends his views against the accusations of crypto-Wahhabism, etcetera, which had been launched against his group. He reminds his readers that the Prophet had warned against hypocritical scholars. In our lifetime, they can be recognized by certain characteristics. They are: scholars who are raving about Westernization, scholars who follow a certain law school, scholars who have been appointed by the government, and, finally, scholars who are attached to mystical societies. Though I do not possess the proper evidence to prove this, I conclude tentatively that the author had been dismissed from his official post during the early seventies. The silence of Ibn al-Hâjj about this aspect of Al-Zamzamî's life should, I suppose, be attributed to the political climate prevailing in Morocco.

personality of primarily local and regional importance. This is confirmed by the nature of his numerous publications, many of which were published in limited editions by small publishers, or even privately. His views can be assessed as more or less representative of the ideas prevailing in traditionalist centres and surviving up till the present time in the Muslim world. These views attempt to resist various forms of change which their proponents consider to cause much damage to the true tenets of their religion.

Al-Zamzamî published various smaller pamphlets in which he opposed modernist views about dress and coiffure. One is the booklet entitled *Clear evidence that he who shaves his beard is cursed and that his prayers are of no value.*[27] The author fulminates against 'assimilation to the Infidels' which he observes everywhere around him, especially by the adoption of Western customs. This phenomenon contradicts the Prophet's injunction *Lâ tashabbahû bi-'l-kuffâr!* ('Do not assimilate to the Infidels!'). He contradicts the *mufti* of Radio Rabat who stated that it was permitted to shave. The prayers of the shaver are nil and void, let alone that such a man could act as an *imam*! Similar viewpoints are defended by many other traditionalist authors, though at times in a milder form[28].

In his booklet *Islam and Westernization*, al-Zamzamî presents his views in the broader perspective of the corruption of Islamic norms and values under the nefarious influence of Europe and the West in general[29]. According to this booklet, Westernization *(tafarnuj)* is one of the greatest disasters befalling the Islamic world. Islam itself is wiped out by it. Al-Zamzamî attributes the beginning of Westernization to the government of the Ottoman Sultan Mahmoud II in the early 19th century, who, under the influence of his French

---

[27] Al-Zamzamî 1967a/1387. This pamphlet provoked a refutation by a preacher of the Hamdûshiyya Zâwiya; cf. al-Maghribî 1966/1386. The author is mentioned on the title-page of this pamphlet sarcastically as 'one of the scholars of the Sunna and one of those who support its adherents'. The preface, comment and corrections were written by Muhammad ibn Muhammad al-Baqqâlî according to the same title-page. Al-Zamzamî, in his turn, produced a frontal counter-attack in Al-Zamzamî 1968/1387. He opens it by quoting a tradition according to which the Prophet has said: 'At the end of time there will be panic among my community. The people will turn to their scholars, but what will be the case? These (scholars) will have been transformed into pigs and monkeys!' Another refutation of Al-Zamzamî 1967a/1387 was published by ᶜAbd al-ᶜAzîz Ibn ᶜAbdallâh, professor at the Qarawiyyîn University (Dâr al-Hadîth al-Hasaniyya) and the University of Muhammad V, both in Rabat. His attack was entitled *Tahâfut al-Zamzamî wa-'stihtârihi bi-'l-sharîᶜa al-islâmiyya* ('The collapse and derision of Al-Zamzamî by the Islamic Law'); see Ibn ᶜAbd Allâh, n.y.: 33-75, esp. 51-53.

[28] Cf. e.g. al-Ashqar 1991^4, esp. 33-48; ᶜAbd al-Hamîd 1984^3: 17-32; ᶜAmr' 1985^2: 412-421; al-Kândahlawî 1987/1403^3: 71-72.

[29] Al-Zamzamî 1967b/1387.

mother, had ordered to replace the Islamic dress of the army by European uniforms. Quran and *Sunna* forbid such an assimilation. Nowadays there are people who claim that this prohibition concerns/respects strictly religious matters only. That is an incorrect view which stems from the opinions of the orientalists and is contradicted by the unanimous opinion of the true scholars of Islam. Those who commit the offence of assimilation have become unbelievers themselves.

The author tries to refute in an elaborate manner the sophism which states that Westernization is necessary for the cultural development and progress of the Muslims. According to him, it is a denial of Islam and its great past. On the contrary, many depravities have their origin in Westernization. Among these turpitudes are, e.g.: (1) expressing doubt of religious beliefs and even of the Quran, which is looked upon by people in the way Christians view the Bible; (2) publicly defaming and criticizing religion in schools, newspapers and radio broadcasts; (3) unlimitedly admiring Reason and putting it above the authoritative religious sources, as a result of which the laws created by human reason *(al-qânûn)* are followed rather than the divine Law. One should keep in mind that countries which do not respect the divine Law cannot be classified as Muslim countries in the true sense, but must regarded as (a part of the) 'Territory of War'; (4) granting freedom of religions and morals, which leads to serious forms of corruption, among others by the admission of Christian and Bahai missionaries; (5) scorning religion, also in schools where European culture occupies a central place in the curriculum, but hardly any attention is paid to the teaching of the Quran. Moreover, (6) Muslim states have become like European states: state officials have no opportunity to perform their prayers during their work, not even to attend the Friday prayers. Friday is an ordinary working-day, whereas Saturday and Sundays are official days of rest. In the market-places wine, pig meat and carrion are sold openly. Prostitution is public and official. (7) Under Christian influence, religion tends to be looked at as a purely spiritual matter. (8) Religions are held to be equal. (9) The miracles performed by the Prophet are denied. (10) The authenticity of prophetical traditions is denied, under the influence of the orientalists who therein follow the Muᶜtazilites. (11) Islamic penal law is eliminated. (12) Under Western influence, even in the schools, the Prophet is degraded to the rank of a great, highly gifted man who received the Quran from the People of the Book, etc. (13) Boys and girls are mixed in the schools which affects the honour of women and opens the door for many depravities, such as the loss of virginity. (14) Girls and women walk on the streets almost naked. Their hair is visible, their faces uncovered, their ornaments shine through their transparent cloths. (15) Men and women mix during wedding parties, even in the presence of preachers, judges and scholars. (16) Wine is drunk publicly during parties, as if it were tea. (17) Photographers are admitted for taking pictures of women, in festive attire or even uncovered. This is an infringement upon the honour of their husbands. (18) Mixed swimming in the sea and mixed sunbathing is practised. Men are looking at the privy parts of their daughters, brothers at those of their sisters, etcetera, like wild animals in the woods. (19) Women have begun to behave and dress like men. They smoke, ride a bicycle and drive a car. (20) Men are becoming effeminate: they shave their beards and depilate the little hairs on their cheeks, against the injunction of the Prophet. (21) Muslims following the old ways of Islam are mocked at. Even religious people wear European cloths underneath their *jallâba's*, under the influence of this cultural climate. Their exterior is blessed, but their interior is cursed! The turbans have been abandoned, forever. The same pattern may be observed among veiled women, who, e.g., are using make-up by which it becomes impossible for them to perform the ablutions prescribed by Islam. (22) Modern men are indifferent to everything religious, including the performance of prayers and fasting. (23) The religious sciences are abhorred, and the popularity of literature and poetry is low. (24) Several political parties have sprung up and have divided the community. (25) Corrupt philosophies like communism and existentialism have spread and gained much influence, even though they combat religion.

The main issues and the emerging compromise

The most fundamental issue dividing the conflicting opinions of the two trends seems to boil down to a different evaluation of the status of the Prophetical *Sunna* as an authoritative source of Islamic norms and values. On the surface, the pragmatic approach of the liberal and reformist line is substantiated by various reinterpretations of the 'real' meaning of certain prophetical traditions, e.g. by restricting the prohibition of assimilation to certain intentions of those who assimilate, or by claiming that certain prophetical injunctions did not have the character of a general command, but were meant to show the 'best' way of behaviour only. All the spokesmen of the liberal and reformist line avoid to discuss explicitly the fundamental issue of the status of the *Sunna*. Nevertheless, their reinterpretations seem to have a rather arbitrary nature and thus tend to destroy much of the historical authority of the *Sunna*. The 'fundamentalist' traditionalists fight for the very maintenance and survival of the Prophetical Tradition as a main fundament of Islam, second in importance to the Qoran only. So far, we are dealing with an unresolved crisis which can be observed in many other areas of conflict within contemporary Islam.

A second issue underlying the debates is that of secularization. Part of the approach of the liberal and reformist line is the claim that matters like dress and coiffure are not specifically 'religious' issues but belong to 'life in general'. They can be regulated quite adequately by human customs that may vary according to place and time, as long as certain general religious principles are taken into account. This view implies a radical departure from the way in which the Islamic rules of dressing and coiffure functioned traditionally for distinguishing and socially separating the various religious groups. This position is, however, fully compatible with modern ideas of citizenship and of the nation-state. As such it is part of a modernizing process which leads towards a clearer distinction between public life and religion. And in this respect it clearly conflicts with the traditionalist approach which fights for the restoration (or 'revival') of an undiminished influence of Islam in many sectors of society, including those which are now recognized by the reformist approach to be of a 'general' nature. The fight is, therefore, also a political one, as it is about the structuring of society in relation to Islam. The enormous changes in everyday social and economic life which have come about in most Muslim countries during the last century lie, of course, at the very basis of all these debates. These changes are an indisputable fact and religion will have to accommodate them. The constant complaint of the traditionalists that those who want to adhere to the old and respectful ways are mocked at or held in contempt, is in itself a clear indication of the increasing marginality of their position. An Islamist politician like Rashid Al-Ghanoushi shows much more sense of reality than the exponents of the traditionalist views which indeed seem to belong to the past.

Notwithstanding the ongoing debates between these two diametrically opposed views, it seems to be an emerging compromise which will set the trend for the future development of Islamic etiquette. Persons who lead religious services, the *imâms*, and religious functionaries and scholars in general should, under all circumstances, strictly observe the *Sunna* of the Prophet with regard to dress and coiffure. By giving the right example, they should also exhort the Muslims in general to obey these rules, even though the actual reality shows a high degree of neglect on their part. No prayer performed behind an *imam* who disobeys these rules can be regarded as valid in the religious sense. Such an *imam* should be replaced by one showing correct behaviour, unless this would cause such disorder as would damage the general interest of the community concerned[30]. This kind of accommodation tends to accept tacitly the widespread changes of etiquette as a fact of life, especially among laymen, without sanctioning them officially. In fact, this compromise adds to the secularization and desacralization of Muslim societies by (indirectly) legitimizing the ever growing distinction between religious specialists and laymen.

References

ᶜAbd al-Hamîd, ᶜA.H. ᶜAlî, 1984³, *Hukm al-dîn fî 'l-lihya wa-'l-tadkhîn* ('The rule of religion on the beard and on smoking'). ᶜAmmân: Al-Maktaba al-Islâmiyya.

ᶜAmâra, M., (ed.), 1972-1974, *Al-Aᶜmâl al-kâmila li-'l'imâm Muhammad ᶜAbduh* ('The complete works of Imam Muhammad ᶜAbduh'). Bayrout: Al-Mu'assasa al-ᶜarabiyya li-'l-dirâsa wa-'l-nashr, 6 vols.

ᶜAmr', M.ᶜA., 1985², *Al-Libâs wa-'l-zîna fî 'l-sharîᶜa al-islâmiyya* ('Dress and attire in Islamic Law'). Beyrouth: Mu'assasat al-Risâla, Dâr al-Furqân.

Ashqar, ᶜU.S. al-, 1991⁴, *Thalâth shaᶜâ'ir: al-ᶜaqîqa, al-adhiya, al-lihya* ('Three rites: ᶜaqîqa, sacrifices and the beard'). ᶜAmmân etc.: Dâr al-Nafâ'is, Maktabat al-Falâh.

Darwîsh, Qusayy Sâlih al-, 1992, *Hiwârât: Râshid al-Ghanûshî* ('Dialogues: Râshid al-Ghannûshî'). London: Khalil Media Service.

Doi, A.R., 1992, 'Duties and responsibilities of Muslims in non-Muslim states: a point of view', in *Al-ᶜIlm, Journal of the Centre for Research in Islamic Studies* (University of Durban-Westville, South Africa) 12: 117-46.

Hâmid, M. al-, no year⁷, *Hukm al-lihya fî 'l-islâm* ('The Islamic rule regarding the beard'). Cairo: Dâr al-Jihâd.

[Harâ'irî, Sulaymân ibn ᶜAli al-,] 1857, *Grammaire française de Lhomond traduite en arabe [...] par M. Soliman al-Harairi.* Paris: Benjamin Duprat.

Harâ'irî, Sulaymân ibn ᶜAli al-, 1862 (?), *Ajwibat al-hayârâ ᶜan hukm qalansuwwat al-nasârâ* ('Answers to the perplexed about the religious rule concerning the hat of the Christians'). Paris: H. Carrion, 11 pp. in 8⁰.

Ibn ᶜAbdallâh, ᶜAbd al-ᶜAzîz , no year, *Turrahât al-Zamzamî* ('The humbug of Al-Zamzamî'). [Tetouan].

Ibn al-Hâjj al-Sulamî, Muhammad ibn al-Fâtimî, 1992, *Isᶜâf al-ikhwân al-râghibîn bi-tarâjim thulla min ᶜulamâ' al-Maghrib al-muᶜâsirîn.* Casablanca: Matbaᶜat al-Najâh al-Jadîda.

Ibn Ismâᶜîl, Muhammad ibn Ahmad, 1988¹⁴(1409 H), *Adillat tahrîm halq al-lihya* ('The arguments to prohibit the shaving of the beard'). Cairo: Dâr al-Safwa.

[30] Fatwa of Ibn Bâzz, *mufti* of Saudi Arabia, dated 7/8/1397, in: al-Kândahlawî 1987/1403³: 71-72.

Ibn Qayyim al-Jawziyya, 1961(1381), *Ahkâm ahl al-dhimma* ('The rules concerning the People of the Protection'), edited by S. Sâlih. Damascus: Matba^cat Jâmi^cat Dimashq, 2 vols.

^cIllaysh, Muhammad, 1862-3, *Al-Radd ʿalâ Risâlat ajwibat al-hayârâ ʿan hukm qalansuwat al-nasârâ* ('Refutation of the Epistle entitled "Answers to the perplexed about the religious rule concerning the hat of the Christians"'). Manuscript Nr. 236 of the General Library in Tetouan (Morocco). (The text was written by the author in Cairo, ca. 1862-1863.)

^cIllaysh, M., 1901-1903 (1319-1321 H.), *Fath al-ʿalî al-mâlik fî 'l-fatwâ ʿalâ madhhab al-imâm Mâlik.* Cairo: Matba^cat al-taqaddum al-^cilmiyya, 2 vols.

Jong, F. de, 1982, '^cIllaysh', in *Encyclopedia of Islam; second edition.* Leiden: Brill, Suppl. fasc. 5/6: 411.

Kândahlawî, M.Z. al-, 1987(1403 H.)[3], *Wujûb iʿfâ' al-lihya* ('The obligatory character of growing a beard'). Ed. F.A. al-Hindâwî. Cairo: Maktabat al-Sunna.

Kattânî, Muhammad ibn Ja^cfar al-, 1923-1924 (1342 H.), *al-Diʿâma li-maʿrifat ahkâm sunnat al-ʿimâma* ('The pillar to know the [religious] rules regarding the custom of the turban'). Damascus: Matba^cat al-Fayhâ', 124 pp.

Lévi-Provençal, E., 1922, *Les historiens des Chorfa. Essai sur la littérature historique et biographique au Maroc du XVIe au XXe siècle.* Paris: Larose.

Maghribî, ^cAbd Allâh ibn ^cAbd al-Rahmân al-, 1966(1386), *Al-Hujja al-dâmigha ʿalâ butlân daʿwâ man zaʿama anna hâliq al-lihya malʿûn wa-salâtuhu bâtila* ('The stigmatizing evidence of the futility of the claim of him who stated that the man who shaves his beard is cursed and that his prayers are nil and void'). Tetouan: Al-Matba^ca al-Mahdiyya, 57 pp.

Shaltût, M., 1980[10], *al-Fatâwâ: Dirâsa li-mushkilât al-muslim al-muʿâsir fî hayâtihi al-yawmiyya wa-'l-ʿâmma* ('Fatwas: a study of the problems of the contemporary Muslim in his common daily life'). Cairo: Dâr al-Shurûq.

Sharabi, H.B., 1962, *Governments and politics of the Middle East in the 20th century.* Princeton: Van Nostrand.

Stillman, Y.K., 1986, 'Libâs': The Ottoman period (to early modern times), in *Encyclopedia of Islam; second edition.* Leiden: Brill, 739-740.

Zamzamî ibn al-Siddîq, Muhammad al-, 1967a (1387 H.)[2], *Al-Hujja al-wâdiha ʿalâ anna hâliq al-lihya malʿûn wa-salâtuhu bâtila.* Tetouan: Al-Matba^ca al-Mahdiyya, 36 pp., small 8°; first edition 1966/1386 H.

Zamzamî ibn al-Siddîq, Muhammad al-, 1967b (1387 H.), *Al-Islâm wa-'l-tafarnuj* ('Islam and Westernization'). Tetouan: Al-Matba^ca al-Mahdiyya, 63 pp.

Zamzamî ibn al-Siddîq, Muhammad al-, 1968 (1387 H.), *Al-Qunbula al-dhurriyya ʿalâ 'l-khatîb alladhî ya'muru 'l-nâs bi-halq al-lihya* ('The atom-bomb against the preacher who orders the people to shave their beard'). Tetouan: Al-Matba^ca al-Mahdiyya, 80 pp., small 8°.

Zamzamî ibn al-Siddîq, Muhammad al-, 1974 (1394 H.), *Mawqif Ansâr al-Sunna min al-mukhâlifîn l-'l-sunna* ('The standpoint of the Supporters of the *Sunna* towards the Opponents of the *Sunna*'). Tetouan: Al-Matba^ca al-Mahdiyya (Printed at the expenses of the union called 'Ansâr al-Sunna'), 108 pp.

EPILOGUE

PLURALISM AND IDENTITY

AN EPILOGUE

Jan Platvoet & Karel van der Toorn
(Leiden University)

The contributors to this volume were asked to write about a subject of their own choice under the rubric of 'pluralism and identity'. The result is a richly variegated collection of studies covering widely different geographical areas—from Australia to Brazil, and a good deal in between—, times—from the Iron Age to the late twentieth century—, themes—from beards and foreskins to mass rallies and controversies about the language of scripture—, and religions—from folk and missionary to public and esoteric. As editors, we have arranged the contributions into a certain order, thus imposing a unity upon this diversity and highlighting the ways in which some may be shown to form particular groups, such as those contributing to theoretical development; those dealing with the ritualization of the encounter of religions; and those treating responses of religions to internal and external religious plurality—, and why all of them may be collected into this one volume: they all deal with the ritual response to religious plurality. In this concluding essay, we will reflect on the title under which these studies are presented by delineating the role of ritual in creating identities in situations of plurality.

The social nature of plurality

'Pluralism' is a popular but imprecise term. In its most current usage, it refers to the co-existence, within one society, of a diversity of ideologies, faiths and world views. As such it is better termed 'plurality', as we argued in the introduction, the term 'pluralism' being reserved for an ideological attitude of receptivity which may, or may not, be present in situations of plurality. Pluralism, and in particular religious pluralism, conceived of as 'plurality', was, however, uppermost in the minds of most of the contributors to this volume when they wrote their essays. Focused on religion, this concept of pluralism has another disadvantage: it is too narrow for it risks losing sight of the more fundamental fact of social plurality. What is at stake is not merely the co-existence of different ideologies, but of different social, or cultural, groups living alongside each other, each professing a different faith, philosophy or ideology. Ideological pluralism, or its opposite, the ideologies of separation, are, therefore, adventitious to social plurality. In many contemporary societies Humanism, Christianity, Judaism, Islam, Hinduism and several other faiths exist side by side, each 'incarnated', so to speak, and made visible by its own culturally and socially distinct community of adherents. Ethnicity is often as important, or more important, a factor in the constitution of such a social group, but so are other factors such as education, profession, income, social skill, and others.

The social nature of plurality, and pluralism, needs to be emphasized, if only to bring out the inequalities inherent in situations of plurality. Between the different social groups present in one and the same society, relations are, as a rule, asymmetrical. For the modern liberal philosopher, with a pluralist frame of mind, religions and ideologies may all be equally good, or equally bad. But this is certainly not so for the many present-day believers of doctrinal religions espousing in the traditional manner the claim to the exclusive validity of their salvific doctrines. As claims to truth tend to be confused with rights to power, plurality of religions is often not a segmentation of society into groups of equal rank and status, but its stratification through relations of dominance and subordination, one group wielding power over others. As minorities, the Yeminite Jews, the Moriscos in Spain, and the Rechabites in Israel were socially underprivileged, and they represented not merely a different religious orientation, but a group of people at the wrong end of the hierarchy.

The majority group need not be seen in numerical terms; colonial societies are a case in point, although certainly not the only one. The various social groups that make up a plural society are cultural groups; and the small groups, of 'high birth', upper-caste, or some other elite origin, were often successful in claiming cultural superiority. In order to have that claim recognized by others, it is, however, essential to be in a position of power; political power usually, but other kinds of power may be just as effective: wealth, fame, or the privileged access to some other type of social capital, such as education, or a combination of all of them.

If plurality is not so much the cohabitation of different beliefs and ideologies, but the co-existence of cultural groups differing in rank and power, the utility of the distinction between external and internal plurality becomes questionable. Until quite recently, the notion of religious plurality was understood predominantly as interreligious plurality, i.e. as the existence of two or more religions within one nation. There is an increasing awareness, nowadays, of the stratified nature of separate religions as well. Within virtually every religion there is some kind of plurality: the religion of the common folk in the country is often far removed from the state religion practised in the capital. The one plurality may be termed external, and the other internal, but these qualifications have limited value. In both cases the distinction is above all one of different social groups. Who is able to determine with precision what it is that distinguishes religions from religious currents? It is largely a matter of nomenclature, of our imposition of categories, just as the distinction between cultures and subcultures.

Each society is a constellation of cultural groups, and each group is a society to itself. The fragmentation of society into separate societies is, in theory, a never-ending process. Seen from a distance, modern Western societies seem divided into a restricted number of cultural groups. At closer inspection, however, each social group proves to be a universe in itself that is divided into various subgroups, and this is true no matter which criteria are used to define their boundaries. When religion is the criterion, there may, at first sight, seem to be groups of atheists, Christians, Jews, and Muslims—to mention some of the more conspicuous ones. But a closer look will reveal that each of these groups is internally divided, on the basis of different interpretations and customs, in numerous smaller groups.

The point of these potentially discouraging subtleties is that pluralism cannot be studied in abstraction from issues of power and dominance. Among the various factions of society—and their number is theoretically legion—there is always competition to gain access to the limited resources available—however varied in nature. Such competition occurs at all levels, i.e. between the different groups themselves, as well as between factions within those groups. To discuss pluralism purely in terms of religious conflict or consensus is to misrecognize the issues at stake. Jan Snoek is right in invoking the notion of group dynamics. In practice, pluralism is indeed a form of social interaction and is subject to its laws.

The social nature of identity

Identity, under these circumstances, may be defined as membership of a cultural group. This means that it is always a particular identity. The individual man or woman cannot lose his or her identity altogether. One may lose a particular identity, by losing membership of a particular group, but complete loss of identity is rare indeed. After all, even outcasts belong to some group or other, however marginal it may be. It would be wiser to avoid the use of the term identity as if it were something absolute and wholly transcendental. The premium set upon identity as an ultimate concept and concern is based on the—modern—fallacy that there is such a thing as a true and authentic identity. This notion is apparently connected with the very similar belief in the existence of a real person behind or under one's own successive social personae. This true self, however, is Utopian. Humans do not exist in pure and unalloyed state, as if they were entities separable from their historical situation. Their identity derives from the group to which they belong; membership of a different group gives them a different identity.

Identity is, thus, by definition social identity; and the combination of the two terms a pleonasm. One's self-image need not coincide with one's social identity, because it is the social identity as perceived or pursued by the individual. Yet the difference is due to defective vision, rather than to an alternative means of assessment. Without other human beings around us, i.e. divorced from society, the individual is no one. Identity is something acquired; it must, so to speak, be achieved. This is not to say that each human being has to forge his own identity, although this is also true. Yet we do not start with nothing to identify us; we are all born with a particular identity which we inherit, along with other products of human culture, such as speech and table manners. Such things are learned; they need not be invented anew.

The fact that one's identity is determined by the group to which one belongs means in practice that an individual has a multiple identity. Or, to use Jan Snoek's more colloquial phrase, 'we all wear different hats'. The identity of an Indonesian Muslim in Mecca is multiple: he is a Muslim, an Indonesian, and, as a *hadji*, a member of a religious elite. One of these identities may clash with another; as an Indonesian, for instance, he has undergone a ritual incision, but as a *hadji* he wishes to fulfil the strict demands of his faith and submit to ritual circumcision. The example, taken from Nico Kaptein's contribution, incidentally shows that a custom adopted by the elite may eventually percolate down to the entire population. But tension between different identities will often subsist, because the multiplicity we have discussed is usually infinitely more complex; in fact, conflicting identities are more the rule than the exception. The professional, religious, and family man, and woman, come together in one person, and the only way to deal with it is to change hats, and faces, as the scenery changes. Identity is chameleonic by nature.

Given the reality of multiple identity, people may find it to their advantage to accumulate identities, or to change them. The available resources being unevenly distributed, cultural groups are hardly ever equal. Since identity coincides with membership of a group, subgroup, or sub-subgroup, some identities are more honorific than others. Upward mobility may be realized by the accumulation of highly valued identities, just as one accumulates capital. Few can resist the temptation of exchanging a humble identity for one more honourable, even if this means abandoning one group for another. This point needs to be made in order to combat the idea that people will generally maintain their identity at all costs. In everyday life, pragmatism reigns almost unopposed. In the case of conflicting identities, most people gladly sacrifice the lesser for the better—the better being that which allows easier access to the limited resources as wealth, social esteem and power. The sentimental clinging to past identities is hardly more than the nostalgia for the 'good old days' that are gone forever.

The ritual expression of identity

If the individual acquires identity through membership, the group bestows it by admitting its members to its rituals. Its rites, performed collectively though not necessarily simultaneously, are often exclusive and create distinction, in the full sense of the term. Let us take academic society as an example. One of the distinctive marks of membership, and in some universities of full membership, is the wearing of gown and cap. It is a vestiary code that distinguishes those entitled to wear it from the rest; lower ranking university staff would transgress a boundary if they adopted these vestments, unless for the purpose of mockery. The lone professor wearing his gown and cap still conforms to a collective ritual, even if no colleague is present, and by performing the prescribed rite, he proclaims his identity as a member of Academia. His performance, modest though it may be, creates that identity each time anew.

The example is but one among many. It may be appropriate to refer here to the case of the Hindu marches for national integration in modern India studied by Jan Platvoet. Contrary to the vestiary code of academics, these marches did not have the overt purpose to delineate the boundaries of a group. They were presented as marches for a cause—the liberation of Rama from his Muslim prison in Ayodhya—and, beyond that, the unification of all India under the banner of Hinduism. What they achieved, however, was something different: they created the Hindu identity—a more precisely: a new version of it. Those who joined the marches, or publicly sympathized with the cause, acquired this identity as their own, in varying degrees, and for some time at least. In particular, these marches had an element of contest in them which greatly contributed to the creation of a Hindu identity: by emphasizing the boundaries, the in-group was separated from the out-group. This ritual was divisive, but the division it realized was aimed to highlight the exclusivity that is essential to collective identity.

The illustrations could easily be multiplied, but they would all show, among other things, that virtually every object, every action, and every event can be used for ritual purposes. The objects, actions, and events are not exceptional in themselves: they are taken from ordinary life, and owe their ritual quality to the exceptional context in which they are placed. They have—to use Catherine Bell's[1] fashionable term—been 'ritualized', and this ritualization often consists in alienating them from their primary, or original, purpose. Let us remain for the moment with our two examples. The gown and cap are originally simply clothes; clothes of remarkable quality, perhaps, but clothes nonetheless, and designed to do nothing more than protect their owners against the inclemencies of the climate. But now that they have become a form of ritual dress, they are, so to speak, denatured. In their secondary, ritual use, they are often worn over a daily outfit. Theirs has become a symbolic function: they signal the membership of a group. Something similar holds good for the Ayodhya marches. A march's primary purpose is to move from A to B, but the ritual march is not merely locomotion; it is a demonstration, a manifestation of identity. The instrumental role has, secondarily, given way to a symbolic role. Ritual thus dispossesses its raw material of its erstwhile function, and even when it has completely lost its former use, it may be retained because it has come to serve a symbolic function.

As said before: nearly everything goes. There are few things that are not grist to the mill of ritualization. A small catalogue based on the contributions to this volume include: languages—the 'dialect of the tribe' being not merely a means to render thoughts into sounds, but an identity marker as well—; script—Latin characters do not have the same symbolic value as Arabic letters—; garments; hairstyles; dietary habits; a nomadic mode of life; subscription to the correct journals; exorcism; the washing of feet, and a number of

[1] Cf. Bell 1992: 7-8, 73-74, 140-141, *passim*.

other things. By ritualization, all of them have acquired a significance well beyond their original purpose. They may still serve that purpose in varying degrees, but their primary function has shifted to a symbolic one. They serve to mark membership of a distinctive group. After all, even unopened, the correct journal conspicuously displayed distinguishes its subscriber as the member of a select group.

A comparison between ritual behaviour and the observance of a code of etiquette may help to further clarify matters. Etiquette, like ritual, has an emphatic character. It is demonstrative behaviour, artificial and unnatural, and when taken out of context slightly ridiculous. Yet, when used with a finely attuned sense of propriety, a feeling for what ought and ought not to be done, etiquette confers distinction on those who observe it. Ritual has the same effect. What the two have in common as well is their seeming lack of utility. Ritual acts, like proper behaviour, are not utilitarian in a narrow sense; they serve a 'higher' purpose. Both etiquette and ritual can be viewed as performance. They are, in a way, performance arts to be learned by example and imitation. Some have more talent for it than others, thus providing room for ritual specialists with a more highly developed sense of ritual than others, and who know how to improvise when the circumstances demand it. But they are not solipsists: the fact that their ritual talents, or sense of etiquette and ceremonial, are acknowledged by the community, indicates that it is based on a culturally shared and transmitted capacity for ritual and etiquette.

Ritual assertion of identities in plural societies

Because identity is not, of itself, an ultimate concern to be cherished more than anything else, the need to define and proclaim it is not universal. Some groups have reason to hide their identities. And because identities may be negative and humble in stead of positive and honorific, some may wish to escape from them and live unobtrusively in the shadows. Identities are a valuation of one's social position, and it is in the interest of the cultural majority, therefore, to protect its position and privileged status by defining unequivocally who is 'in' and who is 'out'. It achieves this by means of ritual: the Muslim authorities forced their Jewish minorities to manifest their identity by certain visible signs of dress and apparel. To stress their social inferiority, cultural minorities may even be submitted to symbolic forms of humiliation. Cleaning the latrines is simply dirty work that must be done by somebody, but by imposing it on the Jews as a task exclusively for them, the Yeminite authorities added a symbolic value to the collection of excrements. That the majority group was aware of this added significance—actually more degrading than the unpleasantness of the job itself—, is shown in the debate among Yeminite Muslim scholars discussed by Joseph Sadan.

Asserting identity is useful only as long as it does not run counter to the interests of the group concerned. Herman Beck's analysis of the attitude of the Indonesian *Muhammadiyah vis-à-vis* the traditional celebration of the Prophet's birthday offers a good illustration. The Yogyakarta leadership of the *Muhammadiyah* movement served its own best interests by accepting the celebration of the *Garebeg Maulud* and contenting itself with merely reinterpreting the various rites in such a way as to make them palatable for a reformist Islamic faith. The logic of their theological position would normally have led them to condemn the festivities as reprehensible innovation; such at least was the conclusion of various representatives of the movement, who were not from Java. The Yogyakarta aristocracy, however, faced with a conflict of interests, was influenced, not unnaturally, by considerations of prestige rather than piety. If identity assertion is at detrimental to social prestige, then it is generally avoided. Power and prestige are usually valued more highly than an unambiguous identity.

One may object that counter examples abound. Is not the case of the Rechabites one where the—ritual—assertion of identity amounts to a form of insubordination that can hardly have served the social interests of the members of the group? On second thought, however, it is not as simple as that. Because the underprivileged are by definition more numerous than the happy few, and they will always be—privileges being as protean as the times are prone to change—, minority groups will often not even try to penetrate into the higher milieus, preferring instead to create their own societies. Society as a whole is made up of cultural groups, and each—as we said above—is a society to and in itself. This means that rank and hierarchy are as much a reality in these miniature societies as they in society at large. For most people, social prestige and self-esteem reside in memberships of these particular societies. Take an Egyptological society, for instance: its fifty or so members take more pride in their affiliation with this antiquarian brotherhood than in any other social identity. They are celebrities in their own right, even if their fame extends no further than the confines of their fellow Egyptologist circle. And even in so small a society, the seeds of discord often flourish, producing rival factions and cold-war combat groups.

These last remarks bring us to the paradox noted by Jan Snoek, viz. that the desire for distinction increases at about the rate in which the actual differences between groups decrease. The rivalry between regular and irregular Freemasonry Lodges, and the repeated divisions of Pentecostal churches are well-chosen illustrations. There is no need to mark the difference between worlds that are already wide apart; the chasm is simply too deep. Competition occurs between groups that are in the same league; they vie for the highest nomination on their common Official List. In the Parisian high society of Marcel Proust's time, the competition was not between the aristocracy and the proletariat, but between the different factions of the aristocracy. The various coteries which an outsider would all put in one box, were to those directly involved ever so many distinct societies, which together represented a hierarchy of values. Each circle had its ritual code; admittance was for members only, and new members had to submit to forbidding rites of initiation. Departure from the collective code led to excommunication, and the uncrowned leaders of the group kept an unwritten record of those who were in and those who were out: the former were invited, whereas the latter had to find a safe haven in lower-ranking coteries.

The thirst for distinction seems often insatiable. When people think they have reached the highest peak of Olympus, where all are impeccably dressed and respect the most formal manners, they will usually find that there are still higher peaks to be conquered, where people distinguish themselves from those slightly below by purposely dressing shabbily and behaving informally. Such insouciance about distinction is deceptive: the very suggestion that they have no need for formal etiquette is, in itself, a mark of superiority. Paradoxically, they create distinction by parading a specially cultivated kind of indifference. Such is the liberty of those in positions of unassailed power and prestige. Where Muslims are a cultural majority, with the promise of remaining so for a long time to come, they can easily tolerate the use of non-Arabic tongues for religious purposes. But when they are oppressed, the survival of their identity may rest on the overriding necessity to insist on linguistic purity; the language of their oppressors is then so fraught with negative associations that it must be eschewed as repugnant to God. Gerard Wiegers' study of the ritual role of Arabic, offers some remarkable historical insights.

The rituals of distinction

The search for identity by means of ritual assertion is never-ending, because people always tend to strive for the highest distinctions—in their class. There is always an identity more noble than the one they now have. The pursuit of identity, then, is in reality the pursuit of power, honour, and prestige. They constitute what Bourdieu calls 'symbolic capital'[2]; the more of this capital one accumulates, the more benefits one enjoys. The adjective 'symbolic' underlines the fact that the advantages are not necessarily crudely material. They are, as André Droogers observes, not personal possessions, but largely the outcome of ritual negotiation.

A fundamental mechanism in ritual behaviour as an assertion of identity, emphasized by both Bourdieu and Bell, is that it causes the 'misrecognition' of its purpose. To say that those who are addressed misrecognize its nature, means that the participants, be they performers or audience, are usually unaware of what a ritual really does.[3] People cannot bear too much reality; they prefer to deceive themselves and each other into thinking that what is at stake is the orthodoxy of their doctrine, the propriety of their conduct, and the purity of their community. They invoke higher powers whose desires they claim to obey, and they may even get trapped in the 'logic' of constructions of their own making. The figments of their imagination may lead them to sacrifice their dearest possessions as an act of devotion. What was once as a ritual means to confer distinction can derail and become a source of unhappiness, until the believers—and belief is the foundation of distinction—are undeceived. No one ever is, totally; without a minimum of belief (whether in the infallibility of the Pope, the final authority of the Supreme Court, or the value of the banknotes) the world does not turn.

---

[2] Cf. Bourdieu 1992: 112-121; 1993: 171-183. In Bourdieu & Wacquant (1992: 119), four types of capital are distinguished: economic, cultural, social, and symbolic. The first three Bourdieu terms the 'three fundamental species' of capital. They are different from symbolic capital, which he defines as 'the form which one or another of these [three] species takes when it is grasped through categories of perception that *recognize* its specific logic, or, if you prefer, misrecognize the arbitrariness of its possession and accumulation' (Bourdieu's italics). Symbolic capital operates at the cognitive level; it is the instrument—by means of the recognition and misrecognition which it evokes in the minds of those addressed—through which the other three capitals become instruments of power.

[3] Bourdieu and Bell both discuss ritual in Durkheimian fashion as standardized performance in culturally homogeneous societies and as serving hidden strategic ends. Platvoet, in his contributions to this volume, shows that ritual may also serve manifest political intentions, and that the Durkheimian paradigm should be widened in other respects also.

Religion and ritual create distinction and difference. Yet there is also the moment in and out of time at which they may forge a *communitas* beyond the usual divisions. During the betwixt and between of the intersection time, rituals may afford relief from the unremitting pursuit of social prestige. This is what seems to happen at the pilgrimage to the Bodhi-tree in Bodhgaya, studied by Albertina Nugteren. Though her florid description makes it clear that not all distinctions disappear at Bodhgaya, the rites around the Bodhi-tree are conducive to a mood in which they are largely irrelevant. Pilgrimages can be compared, in this respect, to modern holidays—or rather holidays to pilgrimages. As long as the 'holy days' last, social differences diminish and barriers are taken more easily: people of different rank and standing find themselves as neighbours on the same camping ground. All of a sudden they are wearing a more or less similar outfit, and having to adapt to similar conditions.

Gerrie ter Haar's study of the African-led churches in South-East Amsterdam should be seen in this context too. The liminality of these churches does not follow from their place in time, but from the situation of their members. They are themselves in between two states, in more than one sense of the term; they are in transit. As long as they belong to neither the European nor the African society, they will seek a safe haven: a community of equals beneath an underground parking lot can offer them a specific identity. It is in the nature of things, however, that a phase of liminality cannot endure. Pilgrimages come to a term, holidays end, and exile does not last for ever. At some point people are reinserted into the 'real' world. And then, after the appropriate rites of aggregation, the search for distinction begins anew. New identities beckon, and yielding to their calling people engage again in an interminable *cursus honorum*. In this respect, a plural society does not differ from any other society—if, in truth, there are societies that are not plural. Each identity, established by participation in the rituals of a group, is a springboard to a more prestigious identity. You never know who you are or who you will end up becoming—that is ultimately for others to determine.

In conclusion

Looking back, from this last page, to the diversity of essays that have been presented in this volume, what advances—we may ask—have been made in this book in the notoriously complex, yet highly important field of the study of ritual, in particular religious ritual, and identity in plural and pluralist societies? Without being unduly immodest, we feel that they are seven. (1) An instrument for the analysis of ritual in situations of (religious) plurality is developed in Jan Platvoet's two essays. (2) A sophisticated model for analyzing the interplay of the factors that determine a religious group's identity in a situation of religious plurality is set out in the contribution by André Droogers. (3) A second model is presented in Jan Snoek's article, which explains when similarity is likely to lead to competition, identity demarcation and boundary maintenance, and when to integration with other groups. (4) Wouter Belier presents a study of an important negative case. It proves that religion is not used universally for demarcation; or, to put it more strongly but just as accurately, that it does not serve that function in the greater number of mankind's religions, nor in the greater part of its religious history. (5) Gerrie ter Haar's study demonstrates that the classical theory of rites of passage may be usefully applied to the situation of religious and ethnic communities in the diaspora. (6) Three competent descriptions of the ritualization of particular encounters of religions, of the accommodative as well as of the contesting kind, are presented in the essays of Albertina Nugteren, Joseph Sadan, and Jan Platvoet. (7) The volume is concluded by five scholarly essays in which Karel van der Toorn, Herman Beck, Nico Kaptein, Gerard Wiegers and Sjoerd van Koningsveld discuss specific instances of religions coping with internal as well as external religious plurality.

References

Bell, C., 1992, *Ritual theory, ritual practice*. New York, etc.: Oxford Un.Pr.

Bourdieu, P., 1992[2], *The logic of practice*. Cambridge: Polity Press (1990[1]).

Bourdieu, P., 1993[10], *Outline of a theory of practice*. Cambridge: Cambridge Un.Pr. (1977[1]).

Bourdieu, P., & L.J.D. Wacquant 1992, *An invitation to reflexive sociology*. Cambridge: Polity Press.

INDICES

INDEX OF AUTHORS

SUBJECT INDEX

STUDIES IN THE HISTORY OF RELIGIONS
NUMEN BOOK SERIES

Recent publications:

52 J. G. Griffiths. *The Divine Verdict.* A Study of Divine Judgement in the Ancient Religions. 1991. ISBN 90 04 09231 5
53 K. Rudolph. *Geschichte und Probleme der Religionswissenschaft.* 1992. ISBN 90 04 09503 9
54 A. N. Balslev & J. N. Mohanty (eds.). *Religion and Time.* 1993. ISBN 90 04 09583 7
55 E. Jacobson. *The Deer Goddess of Ancient Siberia.* A Study in the Ecology of Belief. 1993. ISBN 90 04 09628 0
56 B. Saler. *Conceptualizing Religion.* Immanent Anthropologists, Transcendent Natives, and Unbounded Categories. 1993. ISBN 90 04 09585 3
57 C. Knox. *Changing Christian Paradigms.* And their Implications for Modern Thought. 1993. ISBN 90 04 09670 1
58 J. Cohen. *The Origins and Evolution of the Moses Nativity Story.* 1993. ISBN 90 04 09652 3
59 S. Benko. *The Virgin Goddess.* Studies in the Pagan and Christian Roots of Mariology. 1993. ISBN 90 04 09747 3
60 Z. P. Thundy. *Buddha and Christ.* Nativity Stories and Indian Traditions. 1993. ISBN 90 04 09741 4
61 S. Hjelde. *Die Religionswissenschaft und das Christentum.* Eine historische Untersuchung über das Verhältnis von Religionswissenschaft und Theologie. 1994. ISBN 90 04 09922 0
62 Th. A. Idinopulos & E. A. Yonan (eds.). *Religion and Reductionism.* Essays on Eliade, Segal, and the Challenge of the Social Sciences for the Study of Religion. 1994. ISBN 90 04 09870 4
63 S. Khalil Samir & J. S. Nielsen (eds.). *Christian Arabic Apologetics during the Abbasid Period (750-1258).* 1994. ISBN 90 04 09568 3
64 S. N. Balagangadhara. *'The Heathen in His Blindness...'* Asia, the West and the Dynamic of Religion. 1994. ISBN 90 04 09943 3
65 H. G. Kippenberg & G. G. Stroumsa (eds.). *Secrecy and Concealment.* Studies in the History of Mediterranean and Near Eastern Religions. 1995. ISBN 90 04 10235 3
66 R. Kloppenborg & W. J. Hanegraaff (eds.). *Female Stereotypes in Religious Traditions.* 1995. ISBN 90 04 10290 6
67 J. Platvoet & K. van der Toorn (eds.). *Pluralism and Identity.* Studies on Ritual Behaviour. 1995. ISBN 90 04 10373 2

ISSN 0169-8834